International Journal on Advances in Intelligent Systems

2017 vol. 10 nr. 1&2

Printed from e-media with permission by:

Curran Associates, Inc.
57 Morehouse Lane
Red Hook, NY 12571

CURRAN ASSOCIATES INC. proceedings.com

Some format issues inherent in the e-media version may also appear in this print version.

Printed by Curran Associates, Inc. (2018)

International Academy, Research, and Industry Association (IARIA)
412 Derby Way
Wilmington, DE 19810

Phone: (408) 893-6407
Fax: (408) 527-6351

petre@iaria.org

Additional copies of this publication are available from:

Curran Associates, Inc.
57 Morehouse Lane
Red Hook, NY 12571 USA
Phone: 845-758-0400
Fax: 845-758-2633
Email: curran@proceedings.com
Web: www.proceedings.com

The *International Journal on Advances in Intelligent Systems* is Published by IARIA.
ISSN: 1942-2679
journals site: http://www.iariajournals.org
contact: petre@iaria.org

Sponsored by IARIA
www.iaria.org

International Journal on Advances in Intelligent Systems
Volume 10, Number 1 & 2, 2017

Freimut Bodendorf, Universität Erlangen-Nürnberg, Germany
Karsten Böhm, FH Kufstein Tirol - University of Applied Sciences, Austria
Pierre Borne, Ecole Centrale de Lille, France
Christos Bouras, University of Patras, Greece
Anne Boyer, LORIA - Nancy Université / KIWI Research team, France
Stainam Brandao, COPPE/Federal University of Rio de Janeiro, Brazil
Stefano Bromuri, University of Applied Sciences Western Switzerland, Switzerland
Vít Bršlica, University of Defence - Brno, Czech Republic
Dumitru Burdescu, University of Craiova, Romania
Diletta Romana Cacciagrano, University of Camerino, Italy
Kenneth P. Camilleri, University of Malta - Msida, Malta
Paolo Campegiani, University of Rome Tor Vergata , Italy
Marcelino Campos Oliveira Silva, Chemtech - A Siemens Business / Federal University of Rio de Janeiro, Brazil
Ozgu Can, Ege University, Turkey
José Manuel Cantera Fonseca, Telefónica Investigación y Desarrollo (R&D), Spain
Juan-Vicente Capella-Hernández, Universitat Politècnica de València, Spain
Miriam A. M. Capretz, The University of Western Ontario, Canada
Massimiliano Caramia, University of Rome "Tor Vergata", Italy
Davide Carboni, CRS4 Research Center - Sardinia, Italy
Luis Carriço, University of Lisbon, Portugal
Rafael Casado Gonzalez, Universidad de Castilla - La Mancha, Spain
Michelangelo Ceci, University of Bari, Italy
Fernando Cerdan, Polytechnic University of Cartagena, Spain
Alexandra Suzana Cernian, University "Politehnica" of Bucharest, Romania
Sukalpa Chanda, Gjøvik University College, Norway
David Chen, University Bordeaux 1, France
Po-Hsun Cheng, National Kaohsiung Normal University, Taiwan
Dickson Chiu, Dickson Computer Systems, Hong Kong
Sunil Choenni, Research & Documentation Centre, Ministry of Security and Justice / Rotterdam University of Applied Sciences, The Netherlands
Ryszard S. Choras, University of Technology & Life Sciences, Poland
Smitashree Choudhury, Knowledge Media Institute, The UK Open University, UK
William Cheng-Chung Chu, Tunghai University, Taiwan
Christophe Claramunt, Naval Academy Research Institute, France
Cesar A. Collazos, Universidad del Cauca, Colombia
Phan Cong-Vinh, NTT University, Vietnam
Christophe Cruz, University of Bourgogne, France
Beata Czarnacka-Chrobot, Warsaw School of Economics, Department of Business Informatics, Poland
Claudia d'Amato, University of Bari, Italy
Mirela Danubianu, "Stefan cel Mare" University of Suceava, Romania
Antonio De Nicola, ENEA, Italy
Claudio de Castro Monteiro, Federal Institute of Education, Science and Technology of Tocantins, Brazil
Noel De Palma, Joseph Fourier University, France
Zhi-Hong Deng, Peking University, China
Stojan Denic, Toshiba Research Europe Limited, UK
Vivek S. Deshpande, MIT College of Engineering - Pune, India
Sotirios Ch. Diamantas, Pusan National University, South Korea
Leandro Dias da Silva, Universidade Federal de Alagoas, Brazil
Jerome Dinet, Univeristé Paul Verlaine - Metz, France
Jianguo Ding, University of Luxembourg, Luxembourg
Yulin Ding, Defence Science & Technology Organisation Edinburgh, Australia
Mihaela Dinsoreanu, Technical University of Cluj-Napoca, Romania
Ioanna Dionysiou, University of Nicosia, Cyprus

Vitaveska Lanfranchi, Research Fellow, OAK Group, University of Sheffield, UK
Mikel Larrea, University of the Basque Country UPV/EHU, Spain
Philippe Le Parc, University of Brest, France
Gyu Myoung Lee, Liverpool John Moores University, UK
Kyu-Chul Lee, Chungnam National University, South Korea
Tracey Kah Mein Lee, Singapore Polytechnic, Republic of Singapore
Daniel Lemire, LICEF Research Center, Canada
Haim Levkowitz, University of Massachusetts Lowell, USA
Kuan-Ching Li, Providence University, Taiwan
Tsai-Yen Li, National Chengchi University, Taiwan
Yangmin Li, University of Macau, Macao SAR
Jian Liang, Nimbus Centre, Cork Institute of Technology, Ireland
Haibin Liu, China Aerospace Science and Technology Corporation, China
Lu Liu, University of Derby, UK
Qing Liu, The Commonwealth Scientific and Industrial Research Organisation (CSIRO), Australia
Shih-Hsi "Alex" Liu, California State University - Fresno, USA
Xiaoqing (Frank) Liu, Missouri University of Science and Technology, USA
David Lizcano, Universidad a Distancia de Madrid, Spain
Henrique Lopes Cardoso, LIACC / Faculty of Engineering, University of Porto, Portugal
Sandra Lovrencic, University of Zagreb, Croatia
Jun Luo, Shenzhen Institutes of Advanced Technology, Chinese Academy of Sciences, China
Prabhat K. Mahanti, University of New Brunswick, Canada
Jacek Mandziuk, Warsaw University of Technology, Poland
Herwig Mannaert, University of Antwerp, Belgium
Yannis Manolopoulos, Aristotle University of Thessaloniki, Greece
Antonio Maria Rinaldi, Università di Napoli Federico II, Italy
Ali Masoudi-Nejad, University of Tehran, Iran
Constandinos Mavromoustakis, University of Nicosia, Cyprus
Zulfiqar Ali Memon, Sukkur Institute of Business Administration, Pakistan
Andreas Merentitis, AGT Group (R&D) GmbH, Germany
Jose Merseguer, Universidad de Zaragoza, Spain
Frederic Migeon, IRIT/Toulouse University, France
Harald Milchrahm, Technical University Graz, Institute for Software Technology, Austria
Les Miller, Iowa State University, USA
Marius Minea, University POLITEHNICA of Bucharest, Romania
Yasser F. O. Mohammad, Assiut University, Egypt
Shahab Mokarizadeh, Royal Institute of Technology (KTH) - Stockholm, Sweden
Martin Molhanec, Czech Technical University in Prague, Czech Republic
Charalampos Moschopoulos, KU Leuven, Belgium
Mary Luz Mouronte López, Ericsson S.A., Spain
Henning Müller, University of Applied Sciences Western Switzerland - Sierre (HES SO), Switzerland
Susana Munoz Hernández, Universidad Politécnica de Madrid, Spain
Bela Mutschler, Hochschule Ravensburg-Weingarten, Germany
Deok Hee Nam, Wilberforce University, USA
Fazel Naghdy, University of Wollongong, Australia
Joan Navarro, Research Group in Distributed Systems (La Salle - Ramon Llull University), Spain
Rui Neves Madeira, Instituto Politécnico de Setúbal / Universidade Nova de Lisboa, Portugal
Andrzej Niesler, Institute of Business Informatics, Wroclaw University of Economics, Poland
Kouzou Ohara, Aoyama Gakuin University, Japan
Jonice Oliveira, Universidade Federal do Rio de Janeiro, Brazil
Ian Oliver, Nokia Location & Commerce, Finland / University of Brighton, UK
Michael Adeyeye Oluwasegun, University of Cape Town, South Africa
Sascha Opletal, University of Stuttgart, Germany

Fakri Othman, Cardiff Metropolitan University, UK
Enn Õunapuu, Tallinn University of Technology, Estonia
Jeffrey Junfeng Pan, Facebook Inc., USA
Hervé Panetto, University of Lorraine, France
Malgorzata Pankowska, University of Economics, Poland
Harris Papadopoulos, Frederick University, Cyprus
Laura Papaleo, ICT Department - Province of Genoa & University of Genoa, Italy
Agis Papantoniou, National Technical University of Athens, Greece
Thanasis G. Papaioannou, École Polytechnique Fédérale de Lausanne (EPFL), Switzerland
Andreas Papasalouros, University of the Aegean, Greece
Eric Paquet, National Research Council / University of Ottawa, Canada
Kunal Patel, Ingenuity Systems, USA
Carlos Pedrinaci, Knowledge Media Institute, The Open University, UK
Yoseba Penya, University of Deusto - DeustoTech (Basque Country), Spain
Cathryn Peoples, Queen Mary University of London, UK
Asier Perallos, University of Deusto, Spain
Christian Percebois, Université Paul Sabatier - IRIT, France
Andrea Perego, European Commission, Joint Research Centre, Italy
Mark Perry, University of Western Ontario/Faculty of Law/ Faculty of Science - London, Canada
Willy Picard, Poznań University of Economics, Poland
Agostino Poggi, Università degli Studi di Parma, Italy
R. Ponnusamy, Madha Engineering College-Anna University, India
Wendy Powley, Queen's University, Canada
Jerzy Prekurat, Canadian Bank Note Co. Ltd., Canada
Didier Puzenat, Université des Antilles et de la Guyane, France
Sita Ramakrishnan, Monash University, Australia
Elmano Ramalho Cavalcanti, Federal University of Campina Grande, Brazil
Juwel Rana, Luleå University of Technology, Sweden
Martin Randles, School of Computing and Mathematical Sciences, Liverpool John Moores University, UK
Christoph Rasche, University of Paderborn, Germany
Ann Reddipogu, ManyWorlds UK Ltd, UK
Ramana Reddy, West Virginia University, USA
René Reiners, Fraunhofer FIT - Sankt Augustin, Germany
Paolo Remagnino, Kingston University - Surrey, UK
Sebastian Rieger, University of Applied Sciences Fulda, Germany
Andreas Riener, Johannes Kepler University Linz, Austria
Ivan Rodero, NSF Center for Autonomic Computing, Rutgers University - Piscataway, USA
Alejandro Rodríguez González, University Carlos III of Madrid, Spain
Paolo Romano, INESC-ID Lisbon, Portugal
Agostinho Rosa, Instituto de Sistemas e Robótica, Portugal
José Rouillard, University of Lille, France
Paweł Różycki, University of Information Technology and Management (UITM) in Rzeszów, Poland
Igor Ruiz-Agundez, DeustoTech, University of Deusto, Spain
Michele Ruta, Politecnico di Bari, Italy
Melike Sah, Trinity College Dublin, Ireland
Francesc Saigi Rubió, Universitat Oberta de Catalunya, Spain
Abdel-Badeeh M. Salem, Ain Shams University, Egypt
Yacine Sam, Université François-Rabelais Tours, France
Ismael Sanz, Universitat Jaume I, Spain
Ricardo Sanz, Universidad Politecnica de Madrid, Spain
Marcello Sarini, Università degli Studi Milano-Bicocca - Milano, Italy
Munehiko Sasajima, I.S.I.R., Osaka University, Japan
Minoru Sasaki, Ibaraki University, Japan

Hiroyuki Sato, University of Tokyo, Japan
Jürgen Sauer, Universität Oldenburg, Germany
Patrick Sayd, CEA List, France
Dominique Scapin, INRIA - Le Chesnay, France
Kenneth Scerri, University of Malta, Malta
Rainer Schmidt, Austrian Institute of Technology, Austria
Bruno Schulze, National Laboratory for Scientific Computing - LNCC, Brazil
Ingo Schwab, University of Applied Sciences Karlsruhe, Germany
Wieland Schwinger, Johannes Kepler University Linz, Austria
Hans-Werner Sehring, Namics AG, Germany
Paulo Jorge Sequeira Gonçalves, Polytechnic Institute of Castelo Branco, Portugal
Kewei Sha, Oklahoma City University, USA
Roman Y. Shtykh, Rakuten, Inc., Japan
Robin JS Sloan, University of Abertay Dundee, UK
Vasco N. G. J. Soares, Instituto de Telecomunicações / University of Beira Interior / Polytechnic Institute of Castelo Branco, Portugal
Don Sofge, Naval Research Laboratory, USA
Christoph Sondermann-Woelke, Universitaet Paderborn, Germany
George Spanoudakis, City University London, UK
Vladimir Stantchev, SRH University Berlin, Germany
Cristian Stanciu, University Politehnica of Bucharest, Romania
Claudius Stern, University of Paderborn, Germany
Mari Carmen Suárez-Figueroa, Universidad Politécnica de Madrid (UPM), Spain
Kåre Synnes, Luleå University of Technology, Sweden
Ryszard Tadeusiewicz, AGH University of Science and Technology, Poland
Yehia Taher, ERISS - Tilburg University, The Netherlands
Yutaka Takahashi, Senshu University, Japan
Dan Tamir, Texas State University, USA
Jinhui Tang, Nanjing University of Science and Technology, P.R. China
Yi Tang, Chinese Academy of Sciences, China
John Terzakis, Intel, USA
Sotirios Terzis, University of Strathclyde, UK
Vagan Terziyan, University of Jyvaskyla, Finland
Lucio Tommaso De Paolis, Department of Innovation Engineering - University of Salento, Italy
Davide Tosi, Università degli Studi dell'Insubria, Italy
Raquel Trillo Lado, University of Zaragoza, Spain
Tuan Anh Trinh, Budapest University of Technology and Economics, Hungary
Simon Tsang, Applied Communication Sciences, USA
Theodore Tsiligiridis, Agricultural University of Athens, Greece
Antonios Tsourdos, Cranfield University, UK
José Valente de Oliveira, University of Algarve, Portugal
Eugen Volk, University of Stuttgart, Germany
Mihaela Vranić, University of Zagreb, Croatia
Chieh-Yih Wan, Intel Labs, Intel Corporation, USA
Jue Wang, Washington University in St. Louis, USA
Shenghui Wang, OCLC Leiden, The Netherlands
Zhonglei Wang, Karlsruhe Institute of Technology (KIT), Germany
Laurent Wendling, University Descartes (Paris 5), France
Maarten Weyn, University of Antwerp, Belgium
Nancy Wiegand, University of Wisconsin-Madison, USA
Alexander Wijesinha, Towson University, USA
Eric B. Wolf, US Geological Survey, Center for Excellence in GIScience, USA
Ouri Wolfson, University of Illinois at Chicago, USA

Yingcai Xiao, The University of Akron, USA
Reuven Yagel, The Jerusalem College of Engineering, Israel
Fan Yang, Nuance Communications, Inc., USA
Zhenzhen Ye, Systems & Technology Group, IBM, US A
Jong P. Yoon, MATH/CIS Dept, Mercy College, USA
Shigang Yue, School of Computer Science, University of Lincoln, UK
Claudia Zapata, Pontificia Universidad Católica del Perú, Peru
Marek Zaremba, University of Quebec, Canada
Filip Zavoral, Charles University Prague, Czech Republic
Yuting Zhao, University of Aberdeen, UK
Hai-Tao Zheng, Graduate School at Shenzhen, Tsinghua University, China
Zibin (Ben) Zheng, Shenzhen Research Institute, The Chinese University of Hong Kong, Hong Kong
Bin Zhou, University of Maryland, Baltimore County, USA
Alfred Zimmermann, Reutlingen University - Faculty of Informatics, Germany
Wolf Zimmermann, Martin-Luther-University Halle-Wittenberg, Germany

International Journal on Advances in Intelligent Systems
Volume 10, Numbers 1 & 2, 2017

CONTENTS

International Journal on Advances in Intelligent Systems, vol 10 no 1 & 2, year 2017, http://www.iariajournals.org/intelligent_systems/

Spreading Activation Simulation with Semantic Network Skeletons

Kerstin Hartig
Technische Universität Berlin, Germany
Email: kerstin.hartig@tu-berlin.de

Thomas Karbe
aklamio GmbH, Berlin, Germany
Email: thomas.karbe@aklamio.com

Abstract—**Spreading activation algorithms are a well-known tool to determine the mutual relevance of nodes in a semantic network. Although often used, the configuration of a spreading activation algorithm is usually problem-specific and experience-driven. However, an excessive exploration of spreading behavior is often not applicable due to the size of most semantic networks. A semantic network skeleton provides a comprised summary of a semantic network for better understanding the network's structural characteristics. In this article, we present an approach for spreading activation simulation of semantic networks utilizing their semantic network skeletons. We show how expected spreading activation behavior can be estimated and how the results allow for further effect detection. The appropriateness of the simulation results as well as time-related advantages are demonstrated in a case study.**

Keywords–Spreading Activation; Simulation; Semantic Network; Semantic Network Skeleton; Information Retrieval.

I. INTRODUCTION

Semantic networks are a well-established technique for representing knowledge by nodes and connected edges. Widely used in many areas, their utilization is object of scientific research itself such as creating, transforming, and searching these networks. Such networks often tend to be large in order to profit from the semantic expressiveness of detailed contained knowledge. Despite their graphic structure, increasing network size might hinder their comprehensibility, and their usage might become cumbersome and time-consuming.

Semantic network skeletons are a tool designed for better understanding a semantic network's structural properties [1]. A skeleton summarizes basic characteristics of a semantic network and, thus, focuses on a few essential pieces of information. Its abstracted and comprised character enables various analyses.

One essential operation when using semantic networks is retrieving information, e.g., with semantic search algorithms such as spreading activation. Spreading activation algorithms are a long-known tool to determine relevance of nodes in a semantic network. Originally from psychology, they have been used in many other application areas, such as databases, artificial intelligence, biology, and information retrieval [2].

All spreading activation algorithms follow a basic pattern: chunks of activation are spread gradually from nodes to neighboring nodes, which marks receiving nodes as being relevant to a certain degree. However, practically, each known implementation differs in many details, such as the amount and distribution of activation. Whether a specific configuration for such an algorithm leads to useful results depends largely on two factors: the problem to be solved by spreading and the structure of the underlying semantic network. Although there are many working examples of such algorithms, until now there are almost no guidelines on how to achieve a good configuration. Knowledge about effects and their causes facilitates pre-configuration analyses in order to optimize the settings to retrieve the desired effects. Since semantic networks tend to be very large, an excessive examination of spreading behavior with a multitude of configuration settings can be a time-consuming task.

Therefore, we propose to utilize the comprised structural summary of a semantic network skeleton for spreading activation simulation. In this article, we aim to gain insights on the spreading activation behavior on a semantic network by simulating spreading activation on its network's skeleton. We present a framework for spreading activation simulation that supports detailed observations of two basic properties. First, we observe the activation strength, i.e., the pulsewise development of activation values within a network. Second, we track the spreading strength, i.e., the number of nodes that are activated, which is a measure for activation saturation in the semantic network. The simulation results can reveal desired and undesired effects and allow for further pre-configuration analyses such as sink detection.

In Section II, we will give a short summary about semantic networks and spreading activation. In Section III, we provide a formal framework for spreading activation in semantic networks, and introduce an extension that we refer to as spreading modes. Section IV is dedicated to semantic network skeletons formally and visually. In Section V, we introduce our spreading simulation approach formally, and provide examples for the simulation steps. Section VI is dedicated to the evaluation of the presented simulation approach. We will show that simulation results match their corresponding spreading results at an appropriate average, and we present time-related advantages. We finish the article with conclusions and an outlook on future research potentials regarding spreading activation simulation and semantic network skeletons.

This article is an extension of a previous paper [1], where we introduced the concept of semantic network skeletons. In this article, we extend this approach by showing how skeletons can be used for simulating spreading activation. We furthermore show that the simulation results are predictors for the actual spreading activation on the original network.

II. BASICS AND RELATED WORK

We simulate spreading activation as semantic search technique on semantic networks. Therefore, we shed some light on the underlying concepts.

A. Semantic Network

Historically, the term semantic network had its origin in the fields of psychology and psycholinguistics. Here, a semantic network was defined as an explanatory model of human knowledge representation [3][4]. In such a network, concepts are represented by nodes and the associations between concepts as links. Generally, a semantic network is a graphic notation for representing knowledge with nodes and arcs [5][6]. Notations range from purely graphical to definitions in formal logic.

Technically, among others semantic networks can be described by the Resource Description Framework (RDF) and RDF Schema (RDFS). The RDF data model [6] is defined to be a set of RDF triples whereas each triple consists of a subject, a predicate and an object. The elements can be Internationalized Resource Identifiers (IRI), blank nodes, or datatyped literals. Each triple can be read as a statement representing the underlying knowledge. A set of triples forms an RDF Graph, which can be visualized as directed graph, where the nodes represent subject and object and a directed edge represents the predicate [6].

B. *Spreading Activation*

Spreading activation, like semantic networks, has a historical psychology and psycholinguistic background. It was used as a theoretical model to explain semantic memory search and semantic preparation or priming [3][4][7].

Over the years, spreading activation evolved into a highly configurable semantic search algorithm and found its application in different fields. In a comprehensive survey, Crestani examined different approaches to the use and application of spreading activation techniques, especially in associative information retrieval [2]. Spreading activation is capable of both identifying and ranking the relevant environment in a semantic network.

1) Processing: The processing of spreading activation is usually defined as a sequence of one or more iterations, so-called pulses. Each node in a network has an activation value that describes its current relevance in the search. In each pulse, activated nodes spread their activation over the network towards associated concepts, and thus mark semantically related nodes [2]. If a termination condition is met, the algorithm will stop. Each pulse consists of different phases in which the activation values are computed by individually configured activation functions. Additional constraints control the activation and influence the outcome considerably. Moreover, constraint-free spreading activation leads to query-independent results [8]. Fan-out constraints limit the spreading of highly connected nodes because a broad semantic meaning may weaken the results. Path constraints privilege certain paths or parts of them. Distance constraints reduce activation of distant nodes because distant nodes are considered to be less associated to each other. There are many other configuration details such as decays, thresholds, and spreading directions.

2) Application Areas: Álvarez et al. introduced the OntoSpread Framework for the application and configuration of spreading activation over RDF Graphs and ontologies [9]. They use their framework for retrieving recommendations, e.g., in the medical domain [10]. Grad-Gyenge et al. use spreading activation to retrieve knowledge graph based recommendations for email remarketing [11]. Crestani et al. applied constrained spreading activation techniques for searching the World Wide Web [12]. An approach for Semantic Web trust management utilizes spreading activation for trust propagation [13]. Another area of application is the semantic desktop, which aims at transferring semantic web technologies to the users desktop. Schumacher et al. apply spreading activation in semantic desktop information retrieval [14].

3) Configuration: A challenge mentioned in spreading activation related research is the tuning of the parameters, e.g., values associated with the different constraints as well as weighting or activation functions. For evaluation of the prototype WebSCSA (Web Search by Constrained Spreading Activation) in [12], values and spreading activation settings are identified experimentally, empirically, or partly manually according to the experiments requirements. Álvarez et al. state that a deep knowledge of the domain and the semantic network is necessary and domain-specific customization configuration is needed [9]. In a case study from the medical systems domain, they emphasize the need for automatic support for proper configuration selection, e.g., by applying learning algorithms [10]. It is a known fact that spreading activation configuration has a huge impact on the quality of the spreading results. Currently, there exists no systematic approach for the determination of proper configuration settings. Moreover, not even guidelines for the appropriate configuration are available to potential users. There is a lack of systematic analyses of the impact and interaction of different settings and parameters. The simulation approach presented in this article aims at facilitating such analyses in order to gain helpful insights and support appropriate configurations.

C. *Simulation*

The common idea of simulation is to imitate the operation of real-world processes or systems over time [15]. Simulation is applied in different domains, such as traffic, climate, medical science, or engineering [16]. Usually, simulation is performed on a model, which is an approximation of the item to be simulated, because real world is often too complex [16]. Simulation on this model facilitates repeated observation of specific events, which can be utilized for analyses in order to draw conclusions.

In this article, we aim at simulating the behavior of an algorithm under different configurations on a specific data structure, i.e., very large semantic networks. Here, the simulation model is the semantic network skeleton, which is used to approximate the behavior of the spreading algorithm on the underlying semantic network. Another approach uses simulation of algorithms, for example, in the context of signal processing [17]. Here, simulation was performed on a MATLAB model in order to optimize parameters such as sampling rates or filter designs before implementing the algorithm in hardware. In [18], the authors describe the necessity of tuning coordination algorithms for robots and agents as well as the challenge of finding proper configurations due to a large configuration space. They use simulation to collect data to train neural networks in order to optimize performance data.

Our approach also aims at tuning configuration parameters. However, our simulation method does not target direct configuration optimization, but indirectly targets approximated results to better understand the beforementioned interdependence.

III. SPREADING ACTIVATION IN SEMANTIC NETWORKS

Spreading activation based algorithms follow a common principle but may vary in detail. Therefore, we present a framework that we will use as foundation for the simulation approach introduced in Section V. We focus on the basic pure spreading approach and describe three well-established constraints. Additionally, we introduce an extension that we refer to as spreading modes.

A. Semantic Networks

Let L be a set of labels. The semantic network G (here also source network) is a directed labelled multigraph and defined by

$$G = (N, E, s, t, l, \omega)$$

where

- N is a non-empty set of nodes,
- E is a set of edges,
- $s : E \to N$ is the edge source mapping,
- $t : E \to N$ is the edge target mapping,
- $l : N \cup E \to L$ is the labelling,
- $\omega : E \to \mathbb{R}$ is the edge weight mapping.

B. Basic Spreading Activation Functions

The principle of spreading activation is a combination of pulse-wise computations of the three spreading activation functions. For $n \in N$, $e \in E$, and spreading pulse $p \geq 0$:

- the output function $out : N \times E \times \mathbb{R} \to \mathbb{R}$ determines the state of output activation $o_n^{(p)}$ for node n at pulse p,
- the input function $in : N \times E \times \mathbb{R} \to \mathbb{R}$ determines the state of input activation $i_{n,e}^{(p)}$ for node n via edge e at pulse p,
- the input function $in : N \times \mathbb{N} \to \mathbb{R}$ determines the state of input activation $i_n^{(p)}$ for node n at pulse p, and
- the activation function $act : \mathbb{R} \times \mathbb{R} \to \mathbb{R}$ determines the activation level $a_n^{(p)}$ for node n at pulse p.

These functions are computed in each spreading pulse $p \geq 0$, where $p = 0$ denotes the initial state and, therefore, the starting point of the algorithm. The computations in each pulse follow a specified order. A new pulse starts with calculating the output activation utilizing the latest activation level from the previous pulse. Subsequently, the input activation of all nodes are determined from the output activation, which is finally used for calculating the new activation level.

A node is defined to be activated as soon as it received any activation value in a spreading activation step. In subsequent steps, the strength of a node's activation may increase, but a node can not be deactivated.

On Spreading Directions: Spreading activation can consider or ignore the direction of edges. Neglecting edge directions is more intuitive since the direction solely reflects the reading direction of an edge's property. Redirecting an edge does not change the semantic meaningfulness between the connected nodes, e.g., *x hasMalfunction y* can be read as *y isMalfunctionOf x*. Spreading activation based algorithms utilize semantic relatedness within semantic networks symbolized by their structure. Therefore, we present spreading activation functions that ignore edge directions and spread activation over all edges connected to a node, referred to as *undirected spreading* in the remainder of this article. However, the presented algorithms can easily be adapted to adhere to the assigned edge property directions.

Output activation function: The state of output activation $o_n^{(p)}$ for node $n \in N$, $e \in E$ at each pulse $p > 0$ is determined by the output function:

$$o_n^{(p)} = out(n, e, a_n^{(p-1)}), \tag{1}$$

where in pure undirected spreading

$$out(n, e, a) := \begin{cases} a & \text{if } s(e) = n \vee t(e) = n, \\ 0 & \text{else.} \end{cases} \tag{2}$$

Input activation function: The input activation $i_{n,e}^{(p)}$ for nodes $n, m \in N$ via edge $e \in E$ at each pulse $p > 0$ is determined by the input function:

$$i_{n,e}^{(p)} = in(n, e, o_m^{(p)}), \tag{3}$$

where in pure undirected spreading

$$in(n, e, o) := \begin{cases} o_{s(e)} \cdot \omega(e) & \text{if } t(e) = n, \\ o_{t(e)} \cdot \omega(e) & \text{if } s(e) = n, \\ 0 & \text{else.} \end{cases} \tag{4}$$

The consolidated input activation of a node n received via all edges can be combined:

$$i_n^{(p)} = in(n, p), \tag{5}$$

where

$$in(n, p) := \sum_{e \in E} i_{n,e}^{(p)}. \tag{6}$$

Activation function: The activation level $a_n^{(p)}$ for node $n \in N$ describes the current assigned activation value at each pulse $p \geq 0$, where $a_n^{(0)}$ denotes the initial activation level of n. For $p > 0$, the activation level is determined by the activation function:

$$a_n^{(p)} = act(i_n^{(p)}, a_n^{(p-1)}), \tag{7}$$

where in pure spreading the input activation is added directly to the latest activation level of node n:

$$act(i, a) := i + a. \tag{8}$$

The definition of spreading activation functions can be versatile. Additional computations can be applied such as normalization functions. Here, only basic spreading activation functions are presented. However, we apply some well-known constraints and several newly defined spreading modes that will be integrated in the output activation function.

Constraints: There are various known spreading configuration parameters, also called constraints, applied in several applications and presented in information retrieval research work [2]. Constraints allow for additional control of the three kinds of activation functions. In this article, we chose three known constraints, and show how we include them into our spreading approach. Other parameters are known and can be applied in the same manner.

First, the *activation threshold* controls whether or not nodes with only very low activation values under a specified threshold are excluded from spreading their activation in the specific pulse. Since the activation value is a measure for the relevance of a node, it impedes semantically non-relevant nodes to contribute in the spreading process. Here, the activation threshold is controlled by $\tau : N \to \mathbb{R}$. If no activation threshold is applied, $\tau = 0$.

Second, the *fan-out* constraint provokes the splitting of outgoing activation due to the assumption that highly connected nodes have a broad semantic meaning and, therefore, may weaken the informative value of the spreading result. This punishes highly connected nodes by reducing the activation value to be passed, mostly by splitting the activation equally to those nodes. Whether or not the fan-out constraint is applied is controlled by the boolean parameter $fanout$.

Third, the *pulse decay* decreases the transported activation over the amount of activation steps, i.e., pulses. On the one hand, this punishes distant nodes. On the other hand, it curbs the overall activation distribution over the iterations. The pulse decay is controlled by the decay factor d. If the pulse decay constraint is not applied, $d = 1$.

The three presented constraints affect the level of output activation and must be considered in the output activation function. The constraints-aware output functions are defined as follows:

The output function with a pulse decay and a decay factor d is defined by:

$$out(n, e, a) := \begin{cases} d \cdot a & \text{if } s(e) = n \vee t(e) = n, \\ 0 & \text{else.} \end{cases} \tag{9}$$

The output function with an activation threshold τ:

$$out(n, e, a) := \begin{cases} a & \text{if } s(e) = n \vee t(e) = n, a \geq \tau, \\ 0 & \text{else.} \end{cases} \tag{10}$$

The output function with a fan-out constraint that equally divides the available activation by the outgoing edges:

$$out(n, e, a) := \begin{cases} \frac{a}{deg(n)} & \text{if } s(e) = n \vee t(e) = n, \\ 0 & \text{else,} \end{cases} \tag{11}$$

with the degree of a node $n \in N$ when ignoring edge directions:

$$deg(n) := |\{e \in E | s(e) = n \vee t(e) = n\}|. \tag{12}$$

Constraints can be combined in the output function, e.g., choosing all three presented constraints results in the output activation:

$$out(n, e, a) := \begin{cases} d \cdot a & \text{if } s(e) = n \vee t(e) = n, \\ & a \geq \tau, \neg fanout, \\ \frac{d \cdot a}{deg(n)} & \text{if } s(e) = n \vee t(e) = n, \\ & a \geq \tau, fanout, \\ 0 & \text{else.} \end{cases} \tag{13}$$

C. Extension - Spreading Activation Modes

The processing of spreading activation based algorithms in information retrieval applications can follow manifold conceptions of how the activation is supposed to spread over networks. Mostly, the processing of spreading activation is based on the assumption that in each pulse every activated node of the network is allowed to spread its activation (or part of it) to neighbor nodes. In that case, whether or not a node indeed provides output activation only depends on restrictions coming from additional constraints such as an activation threshold.

However, we see potential in an extended and more distinguished treatment of nodes by deciding whether a node gets permission to spread (and receive) activation. Therefore, we distinguish between various so-called spreading modes. Such modes define spreading rules and, therefore, control the paths taken during the activation process. Moreover, we can distinguish between the edges that transport activation, e.g., a node does not necessarily have to be allowed to spread via each of its connected edges. Formally, each spreading mode affects the output activation by the spread permission function φ. The spread permission function can be applied to any output activation function. Here, we introduce three intuitive modes. The mode- and constraint-aware output activation function is defined by

$$out(n, e, a, \varphi) := \varphi \cdot out(n, e, a). \tag{14}$$

The presented modes ignore edge directions since output functions carry this information already before mode-aware extension. We distinguish between the following spreading modes.

1) ***Basic Mode:*** As mentioned before, the *basic spreading mode* allows each node to spread activation to all neighbors in each pulse, regardless of the edge's directions. Of course, only activated nodes with activation values greater than zero can generate an amount of output activation for spreading. However, this is controlled by the output function. The permission function is defined as:

$$\varphi(n, e) := 1. \tag{15}$$

This means that each node is theoretically allowed to spread via all edges. Practically, a node is usually not connected with all edges. Note, that for a non-connected edge e of node n, the spreading permission is repealed by the non-existing output activation $o_{n,e}$.

2) ***Recent Receiver Mode:*** Another mode solely allows nodes that were receivers of activation in the last pulse to spread activation to their neighbor nodes. The permission function is defined as:

$$\varphi(n, e, p) := \begin{cases} 1 & \text{if } p = 0, \\ 1 & \text{if } i_n^{(p-1)} > 0, p > 0, \\ 0 & \text{else.} \end{cases} \tag{16}$$

3) ***Forward Path Mode:*** Another mode evolves when nodes may not directly spread back to the nodes they just received activation from. The permission function is defined as:

$$\varphi(n, e, p) := \begin{cases} 1 & \text{if } p = 0, \\ 1 & \text{if } i_{n,e}^{(p-1)} = 0, p > 0 \\ 0 & \text{else.} \end{cases} \tag{17}$$

In Figure 1, the spreading paths of the three presented modes are depicted. Not each activated node must necessarily be permitted to spread to neighbor nodes. While in basic mode each activated node is permitted to spread over all connected edges, the figure reveals that in recent receiver mode the spreading permission of node A and D will pulse-wise alternate. In forward path mode, we observe that spreading back is only permitted on circular paths, e.g., A-B-C-A, but not

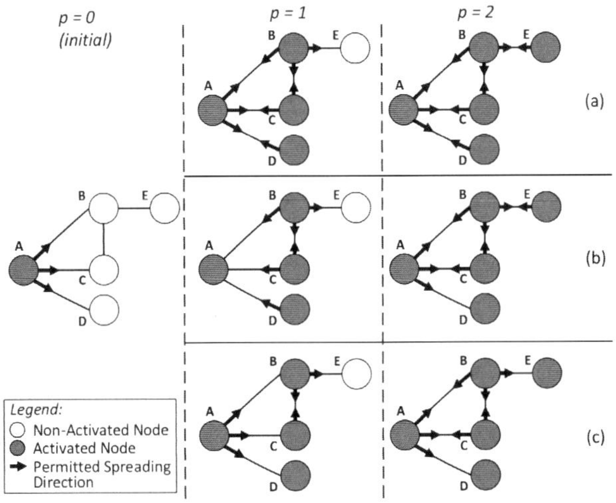

Figure 1. Mode-Aware Permitted Spreading Behavior in three Activation Pulses in a) Basic Mode b) Recent Receiver Mode c) Forward Path Mode.

directly A-D-A. Here, circular paths are priviledged since they might incorporate special semantic meaning whereas back-spreading of linear paths is impeded. Different modes are a measure that may impede extended oscillated spreading by means of a sophisticated spreading permission system.

In contrast to constraints, spreading modes can not be combined. Exactly one mode must be chosen, where the basic mode can be seen as a default mode.

IV. SEMANTIC NETWORK SKELETON

As stated before, proper configuration of a spreading activation algorithm is a challenging task. One important influencing factor for a good configuration is the structure of the underlying semantic network. Often however, semantic networks tend to be very large, and therefore hard to comprehend.

We propose a tool called *semantic network skeleton*, introduced in [1], which is supposed to summarize the structure of a semantic network. Therefore, using a skeleton shall make it easier to comprehend their structural properties and draw conclusions for configurations.

A. Skeleton Introduction

A skeleton of a semantic network is a directed graph that has been derived from a semantic network. We will call the semantic network from which the skeleton has been derived the *source (network)*.

Generally spoken, the skeleton shall represent the semantic structure of the source. Therefore, similar nodes and edges are grouped and represented by single node representatives and edge representatives in the skeleton. Thus, the skeleton hides all the parts of the source which are similar, and it makes the structural differences in the network more explicit.

Often, a semantic network contains also nodes and edges that carry little semantic value and therefore should be ignored by a spreading activation algorithm. An example from the RDF Specification are blank nodes, which by definition carry no specific meaning. Therefore, before creating a skeleton from a source, one first has to define the *semantic carrying* set of nodes and edges. This choice is very problem-specific, and therefore cannot be generalized. We call the semantic carrying subnetwork of the source the *spread graph*.

Since the skeleton is based on the spread graph, it represents only semantic carrying nodes and edges. The skeleton usually contains three types of node representatives: classes, instances, and literals. Since the relationships between instance node representatives carry the most structural information about the semantic network, we call this part the *skeleton core*.

B. Types of Semantic Network Skeletons

We distinguish between two types of skeletons regarding their completeness and detail level: the maximum and the effective skeleton of a network.

A *maximum skeleton* contains all potential nodes and relations of the source. It is comparable with a UML class diagram in the sense that it shows everything that is theoretically possible in that network. However, it does not transport any information about the actual usage of classes/instances in the source network. Therefore, the maximum skeleton might contain nodes and relationships that have never been instantiated in the source.

An *effective skeleton* represents the structure of a specific instance of a semantic network. Therefore, it contains only nodes and relations that are actually part of the source network. This means that a class that is part of an RDF schema, but that has not been instantiated in a concrete instance of that RDF schema would have a node representation in the maximum skeleton, but not in the effective skeleton.

By comparing maximum and effective skeletons, we find advantages and disadvantages for both of them: The maximum skeleton is the more generalized skeleton version, and therefore it applies to many different network instances of the same RDF schema. However, its generality also means that it carries less specific information about each single instance, and therefore, conclusions drawn from a maximum skeleton are weaker than those drawn from an effective skeleton. The effective skeleton is specific to one instance of a semantic network. Thus, it cannot be reused for other instances, but it results in more precise conclusions.

C. Annotations

While the skeleton structure helps to understand the basic structure of the source network, a detailed analysis often requires more information: It might be useful to know, how many node or edges are subsumed by a node or edge representative in the skeleton; The average number of incoming or outgoing edges for all represented nodes could indicate a certain spreading behaviour; Maybe there are 10.000 edges of the same type subsumed by one edge representative, but actually they all originate in only 10 different nodes. To capture such (often numerical) information, skeletons can be enhanced by annotations. Typically, there are four types of annotations: those that describe node or edge representatives and those that describe the source or target of an edge representative.

Since effective and maximum skeletons carry different information, this also applies to annotations on them. While annotations on an effective skeleton refer to a concrete network instance of an RDF Schema (e.g., the concrete count of instances of a node type), annotations on a maximum skeleton describe potential values. Thus, an instance count could have the value $*$, meaning that any number of instances is possible.

D. Syntax

Let L_S be a set of labels. A Semantic Network Skeleton S is defined by

$$S = (N_S, E_S, s, t, l, \omega),$$

where

- N_S is a non-empty set of *node representatives*,
- E_S is a set of *edge representatives*,
- $s : E_S \to N_s$ is the *edge source mapping*,
- $t : E_S \to N_S$ is the *edge target mapping*, and
- $l : N_S \cup E_S \to L_S$ is the labelling,
- $\omega : E_S \to \mathbb{R}$ is the edge weight mapping.

The node and edge representatives each represent a set of nodes/edges of the same type from the original semantic network. Each edge representative $e \in E_S$ has a source node representative $s(e)$ and a target node representative $t(e)$. Furthermore, all node and edge representatives have a label $l(n)/l(e)$ assigned.

Given a semantic network skeleton $S = (N_S, E_S, s, t, l, \omega)$, and let $n_1, n_2 \in N_S$, $e \in E_S$, $s(e) = n_1$, and $t(e) = n_2$. Then the triple

$$T_S = (n_1, e, n_2)$$

is called a *skeleton triple* of S. A skeleton triple represents all corresponding RDF triples of the source network.

For a skeleton S the *skeleton annotation* A_S is defined as

$$A_S = (A_n, A_e, A_s, A_t),$$

where

- $A_n : K \times N_S \to V$ is the *node annotation*,
- $A_e : K \times E_S \to V$ is the *edge annotation*,
- $A_s : K \times E_S \to V$ is the *edge source annotation*, and
- $A_t : K \times E_S \to V$ is the *edge target annotation*.

Here, K stands for a set of *annotation keys*, and V stands for a set of *annotation values*.

E. Graphical Notation

The graphical notation for the skeleton corresponds to the graphical notation of RDF Graphs. In Figure 2, the proposed graphical notation is depicted. A node representative $n \in N$ is represented by a circle with its label $l(n)$ denoted over the circle. An edge representative $e \in E$ is represented by an unidirectional arrow with its label $l(n)$ denoted next to the arrow center. An arrow must connect two circles, with the arrow start connecting to the circle that represents the source and the tip of the arrow connecting to the circle that represents the target. Annotations are denoted in the circles, or near the start, middle, or end of the arrow, depending on their annotation type (node, edge, edge source, or edge target annotation).

F. Formal Notation of Graphical Example

A skeleton $S = (N_S, E_S, s, t, l, \omega)$ that contains among others the node and edge representatives depicted in Figure 2 would be formally denoted by

- the labels *Function, Malfunction, hasMalfunction* $\in L_S$,
- two nodes $n_1, n_2 \in N_S$ with $l(n_1) =$ *Function*, and $l(n_2) =$ *Malfunction*,
- an edge $e \in E_S$ with $l(e) =$ *hasMalfunction*, $s(e) = n_1$, and $t(e) = n_2$.

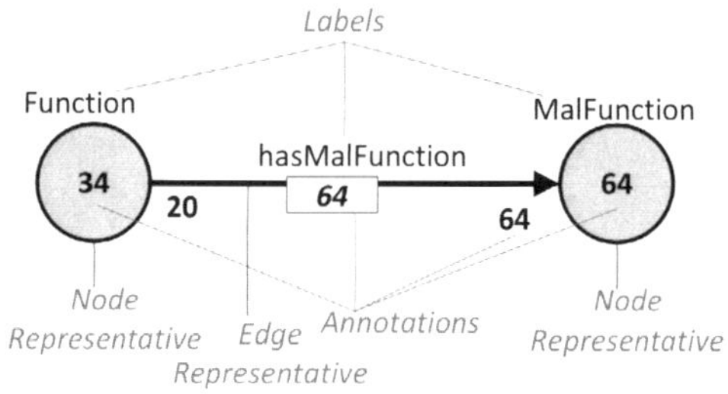

Figure 2. Graphical Notation for Skeletons.

Additionally, the skeleton annotation $A_S = (A_n, A_e, A_s, A_t)$ would contain the following mappings:

- $A_n(nc, n_1) = 34$,
- $A_n(nc, n_2) = 64$,
- $A_e(ec, e) = 64$,
- $A_s(src\_rep, e) = 20$, and
- $A_t(tgt\_rep, e) = 64$.

Here, nc and ec are the numbers of nodes/edges (node count and edge count) that have been subsumed by a node/edge representative. The source and target annotations src_rep and tgt_rep are the number of represented nodes that are part of represented RDF triples. Thus, 20 of the 34 nodes represented by n_1 are connected to nodes represented by n_2 via an edge represented by e. For the sake of brevity, we use the annotation keys similar as functions in the remainder of this article.

G. Skeleton Retrieval

Semantic network structures are as diverse as their potential applications and user-specific design decisions. Generally, skeletons can be retrieved from all kinds of semantic networks. However, transformation rules must guarantee that the semantic definition described in Section IV-A holds. We focus on retrieving skeletons from semantic networks based on RDF and RDF Schema. More specifically, we utilize the RDF statements from the corresponding RDF Graph. Technically, different approaches are possible from successively parsing RDF Statements to utilizing query languages such as SPARQL [19]. We offer an abstract retrieval description focusing on semantic compliance as introduced in [1].

H. Creating Effective Skeletons

For retrieving the effective node and edge representatives from the spread graph, we apply the following abstract method.

1) Each resource that is an RDF class becomes a node representative in the skeleton.
2) All instances of one class are subsumed by one node representative.
3) All literals are subsumed by one node representative in the skeleton.
4) For each statement, an edge representative is added (if not yet existent) for the predicate between the node representative of the statement's subject and the node representative of the statement's object in the skeleton.

Additionally, during the skeleton retrieval process, the desired annotation values can be computed. We propose to subsume all literals by one node representative in the skeleton. In RDF, the literals of the class rdfs:Literal contain literal values such as strings and integers. A literal consists of a lexical form, which is a string with the content, a datatype IRI, and optionally a language tag. It is, of course, possible to further distinguish depending on datatype, or even analyzing value equality instead of term equality. However, the content string of the lexical form seems to be most important and sufficient for the application.

I. Creating Maximum Skeletons

For creating a maximum skeleton, we apply the following method to retrieve node and edge representatives from a spread graph.

1) Each resource that is an RDF class becomes a node representative in the skeleton. Additionally, a node representative for instances of this class must be created. For resources that are classes themselves and subclasses of another class all properties must be propagated from its superclass.
2) Find all properties and their scope (range, domain). For each property add (if not existent yet) an edge representative from the node representative for the instances of the specified domain to the node representative for the instances of the specified range. For each subproperty p_1 of a property p_2 edge representatives must be created between all node representatives connected via p_2.

Again, required annotation values can be computed during the skeleton retrieval process.

V. SIMULATING SPREADING ACTIVATION BEHAVIOR WITH SEMANTIC NETWORK SKELETONS

Structural network properties as well as spreading activation constraints and configuration settings affect spreading activation results. Knowledge about spreading activation effects and their causes supports pre-configuration analyses in order to optimize the settings to retrieve the desired effects. Since semantic networks tend to be very large, an excessive examination of spreading behavior with a multitude of configuration settings can be a time-consuming task. Therefore, we utilize the comprised structural summary of semantic network skeletons to simulate the spreading activation behavior of its represented semantic network. In this section, we formally introduce the spreading activation simulation approach. For better comprehensibility, we apply selected simulation steps to an example.

A. Simulation Method

Spreading Activation on a network skeleton requires careful mapping of the algorithm to the new graph structure. Since the skeleton contains representatives for nodes and edges, we introduce an averaging approach in order to simulate the expected spreading behavior and approximate the activation strength and spreading strength for each simulation step.

In Figure 3, one challenge of this mapping can be observed. A spreading activation step on a skeleton triple needs to simulate spreading activation on the underlying bipartite graph. The explicit annotations are advantageous for the approach. We can identify how many represented nodes are not connected to a represented edge, and consequently can be identified as unreachable. Additionally, we can make estimations about the number of represented edges a represented node can be expected to be connected to. However, we do not have full

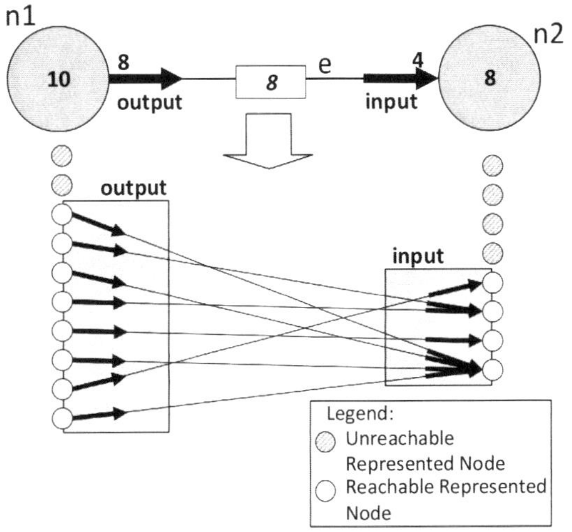

Figure 3. Spreading Activation on a Skeleton Triple.

information about the connectedness of the represented nodes and edges. Moreover, we have to pay attention to the actual state of expected activation in every pulse. For example, there is a difference for both input and output function if one node represented by $n1$ is expected to be already activated, or if all of the 10 represented nodes are expected to be activated. We refer to the ratio of activated nodes in the set of represented nodes as saturation. The overlapping of already activated nodes and newly activated nodes needs to be considered as well, e.g., how many of the new ones are expected to be contained in the set of the already activated nodes. Therefore, we include combinatorial considerations into our spreading activation function mapping.

1) Local And Global Simulation Steps: We distinguish between two kinds of spreading steps that we refer to as local and global simulation steps. This differentiation supports the comprehensibility of the required adaptations. Figure 4 depicts local and global simulation areas.

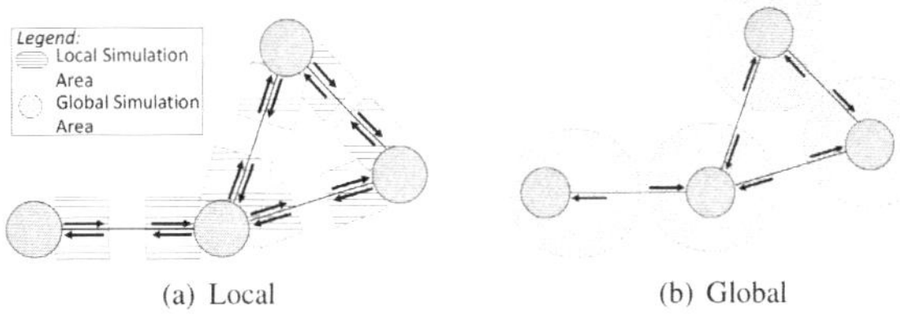

(a) Local (b) Global

Figure 4. Simulation Areas.

In a local simulation step, each node-edge pair of the skeleton is examined. For each of these pairs, the expected outgoing as well as expected incoming activation are calculated.

Since a node representative may receive activation via various edge representatives, a consolidation of incoming activation is necessary. In a global simulation step, each node is examined and the results from the local observations are consolidated. Thus, we obtain the expected and incoming activation as well as the new expected overall activation level for each node in the skeleton.

2) Simulation Input: Spreading activation simulation requires the corresponding semantic network skeleton to the source network that the spreading is simulated for. We additionally need the same configuration settings, e.g., selected from constraints and spreading modes presented in Section III-B and III-C. Starting point for the simulation has to be the node representative(s) of the starting node(s) in the source network.

3) Simulation Results: Two aspects of activation distribution are of special interest. First, the expected growth of the number of activated nodes represented by each skeleton node. It reveals the *spreading strength* and answers the questions how fast activation probably reaches representatives of skeleton nodes in the underlying semantic network. More importantly, it examines the pulse-wise growth of the number of activated nodes represented by each skeleton node and provides an estimation about the proportion of already activated nodes represented by its representative, which we call the activation saturation. Second, we are interested in expected growth of the activation values of the nodes represented by a skeleton node. This reveals the *activation strength* and answers the question how fast activation values can be expected to increase in the underlying semantic network. Therefore, we calculate for each skeleton node the expected number of activated nodes and the expected activation value for each simulated spreading activation step.

B. Mapping Spreading Activation Functions for Simulation Purposes

The basic idea is to adapt the beforementioned three components of the spreading activation computation, i.e., output activation, input activation, and activation level, to an averaging approach for approximating the activation value development. Therefore, we introduce the following spreading activation simulation functions along with the corresponding levels of expected activation. For $n \in N_S$, edge $e \in E_S$, pulse $p \geq 0$, for local simulation steps:

- the aggregated output function $\overline{out} : N_S \times E_S \times \mathbb{R} \rightarrow \mathbb{R}$ determines the expected total output activation of node n via edge e, denoted by $\overline{o}^{(p)}_{n,e}$,
- the counting output function $\hat{out} : N_S \times E_S \times \mathbb{R}^2 \rightarrow \mathbb{R}$ determines the expected number of nodes represented by n to be activated via edge e from node n, denoted by $\hat{o}^{(p)}_{n,e}$,
- the aggregated input function $\overline{in} : N_S \times E_S \times \mathbb{R} \rightarrow \mathbb{R}$ determines the expected total input activation of node n via edge e, denoted by $\overline{i}^{(p)}_{n,e}$,
- the counting input function $\hat{in} : N_S \times E_S \times \mathbb{R}^3 \rightarrow \mathbb{R}$ determines the expected number of nodes represented by n to be newly activated via edge e, denoted by $\hat{i}^{(p)}_{n,e}$,

and for global simulation steps:

- the aggregated input function $\overline{in} : N_S \times N \rightarrow \mathbb{R}$ determines the expected total input activation of node n via all connected edges of node n, denoted by $\overline{i}^{(p)}_{n}$,
- the counting input function $\hat{in} : N_S \times N \rightarrow \mathbb{R}$ determines the expected number of nodes represented by n to be newly activated via all connected edges, denoted by $\hat{i}^{(p)}_{n}$,
- the aggregated activation function $\overline{act} : \mathbb{R}^2 \times \mathbb{R} \rightarrow \mathbb{R}$ determines the expected total activation of node n, denoted by $\overline{a}^{(p)}_{n}$,
- the counting activation function $\hat{act} : \mathbb{R}^2 \rightarrow \mathbb{R}$ determines the expected number of nodes represented by n to be newly activated, denoted by $\hat{a}^{(p)}_{n}$.

The skeleton triple and its underlying bipartite graph depicted in Figure 3 reveal two important facts. First, we can obtain the *connection rate* of a node represented by $n \in N_S$ to be connected with a represented edge of $e \in E_S$. This connection rate $con : N_S \times E_S \rightarrow \mathbb{R}$ can be calculated as follows:

$$con(n,e) := \begin{cases} \frac{src\_rep(e)}{nc(n)} & \text{if } s(e) = n, \\ \frac{tgt\_rep(e)}{nc(n)} & \text{if } t(e) = n, s(e) \neq n, \\ 0 & \text{else.} \end{cases} \qquad (18)$$

We want to point out that loops are handled by the first case and restricted from the second case such that only one *con*-value per node and connected edge exists, i.e., in the reading direction of the edge's property.

Second, the expected spread factor $fac : N_S \times E_S \rightarrow \mathbb{R}$ denotes the number of edges represented by $e \in E_S$ that each connected node represented by $n \in N_S$ is expected to be connected to.

$$fac(n,e) := \begin{cases} \frac{ec(e)}{src\_rep(e)} & \text{if } s(e) = n, \\ \frac{ec(e)}{tgt\_rep(e)} & \text{if } t(e) = n \wedge s(e) \neq n, \\ 0 & \text{else.} \end{cases} \qquad (19)$$

Figure 5 depicts an annotated skeleton triple with two node-edge pairs, each for a local simulation step in the output and in the input direction. This will be the example for the following simulation step descriptions.

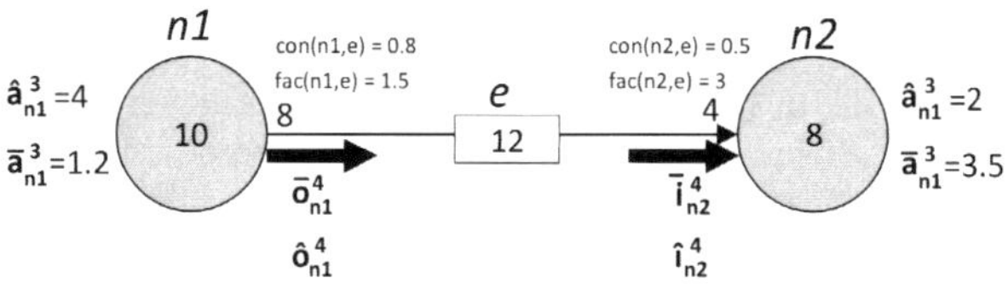

Figure 5. Annotated Skeleton Triple with expected activation levels assigned.

1) Local Calculation of Expected Total Activation: The expected total output activation can be calculated by an adapted constraints- and mode-aware output function. The spreading modes presented in this article and the associated permission function φ do not require adaptations when used for spreading activation simulation, as well as pulse decay and activation threshold. The fan-out constraint requires adapting the fan-out factor, since spreading in the skeleton follows an averaging approach. Here, we do not consider the degree of a node to be of interest but the expected spread factor of all edges connected to a node, defined by $\overline{fac} : N_S \rightarrow \mathbb{R}$. We define $\overline{o}_{n_1,e}$ to be the expected total activation that might be passed from the nodes represented by n_1 via the connected edges represented by e. Therefore, we need to consider the connectivity rate as well as the spread factor in the aggregated output function. The total output activation value is determined by:

$$\overline{o}^{(p)}_{n,e} = \overline{out}(n, e, \overline{a}^{(p-1)}_{n}), \qquad (20)$$

where

$$\overline{out}(n,e,a) := \begin{cases} d\cdot a\cdot con(n,e)\cdot fac(n,e) & \text{if } s(e)=n \vee t(e)=n, \\ & a\geq \tau, \neg fanout, \\ \frac{d\cdot a\cdot con(n,e)\cdot fac(n,e)}{\overline{fac}(n)} & \text{if } s(e)=n\vee t(e)=n, \\ & a\geq\tau, fanout, \\ 0 & \text{else,} \end{cases} \tag{21}$$

where

$$\overline{fac}(n) := \sum_{e\in E_S, s(e)=n\vee t(e)=n} fac(n,e). \tag{22}$$

The expected total input activation $\overline{i}_{n,e}^{(p)}$ for node $n, m \in N_S$ via edge $e \in E_S$ at each pulse $p > 0$ is determined by the input function without further adaptations:

$$\overline{i}_{n,e}^{(p)} = \overline{in}(n, e, \overline{o}_m^{(p)}) \tag{23}$$

where

$$\overline{in}(n,e,o) := \begin{cases} o\cdot\omega(e) & \text{if } t(e)=n, \\ o\cdot\omega(e) & \text{if } s(e)=n, \\ 0 & \text{else.} \end{cases} \tag{24}$$

The example in Figure 6 shows that without any constraints the assigned expected activation value of $n1$ is expected to be passed by 8 nodes represented by $n1$ where each is expected to be connected to 1.5 of the represented edges. Therefore, the total expected output activation can be expected to be 1.44. Since there is no edge weights assigned, in this example the total expected input activation can be expected to be the total output activation 1.44.

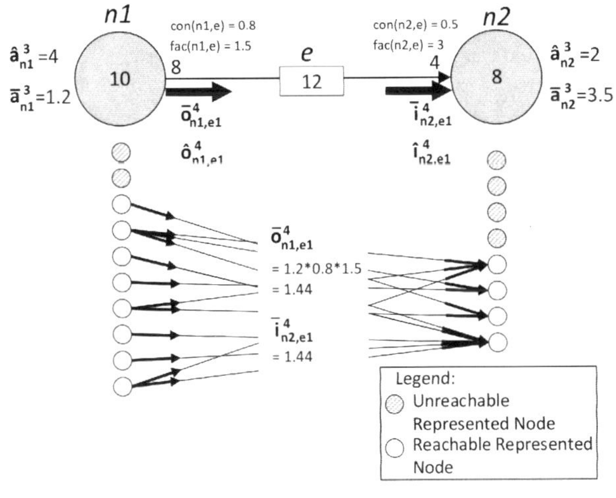

Figure 6. Example: Local Expected Total Activation.

2) Local Calculation of Expected Number of Activated Nodes : The expected number of activated output nodes can be calculated by an adapted mode- (and constraint) aware output function:

$$\hat{o}_{n,e}^{(p)} = \hat{out}(n, e, \hat{a}_n^{(p-1)}, \overline{o}_{n,e}^{(p)}), \tag{25}$$

where

$$\hat{out}(n,e,a,o) := \begin{cases} a\cdot con(n,e)\cdot fac(n,e) & \text{if } s(e)=n\vee t(e)=n, \\ & o>0, \\ 0 & \text{else.} \end{cases} \tag{26}$$

In contrast to the computation of expected total activation, the local expected number of activated nodes does not directly depend on the spreading activation constraints. Indirectly, the restriction in the first case requires an expected total output activation greater than zero to be transported via edge e, and input activation respectively (which indirectly may be influenced by the algorithm settings).

The expected input activation number can be calculated by an adapted and constraint aware input function.

$$\hat{i}_{n,e}^{(p)} = \hat{in}(n, e, \hat{a}_n^{(p-1)}, \hat{o}_{m,e}^{(p)}, \overline{i}_{n,e}^{(p)}) \tag{27}$$

The input function needs to take into account that we have no knowledge about the actual connections between represented nodes and edges. When a certain number of edges reaches nodes, there are several potential combinations. In order to estimate how many represented nodes are reached by a number of activation passing edges, we follow a combinatorial approach. The function $split$ determines how the number activation passing edges needs to be reduced regarding their receiving nodes. It represents a combinatorical approach to get the average number of buckets (y) that have a ball, when distributing x balls to them.

$$split(x,y) := \frac{1-(\frac{y-1}{y})^x}{1-(\frac{y-1}{y})} \tag{28}$$

$$\hat{i}_{n,e}^{(p)} = \hat{in}(n,e,a,o,i) := \begin{cases} split(o, src\_rep(e))\cdot(1-\frac{a}{nc(n)}) & \text{if } s(e)=n, i>0, \\ split(o, tgt\_rep(e))\cdot(1-\frac{a}{nc(n)}) & \text{if } t(e)=n, i>0, \\ 0 & \text{else} \end{cases} \tag{29}$$

Figure 7 depicts the example calculation for this simulation step. Only already activated and connected nodes can spread via the expected number of connected edges per node. After split reduction, the remaining nodes need to be checked for potential overlapping with already activated nodes. As a result, we can expect 2.25 nodes to be newly activated after this local simulation steps.

C. Global Simulation Step - Consolidation of Local simulation Steps

After examining each node-edge pair in the local simulation step, we must consolidate them for each node because one node may receive input via many edges.

1) Global Calculation of Expected Total Activation : The complete expected input activation value of a node n via all edges can be determined by the adapted input activation function:

$$\overline{i}_n^{(p)} = \overline{in}(n,p), \tag{30}$$

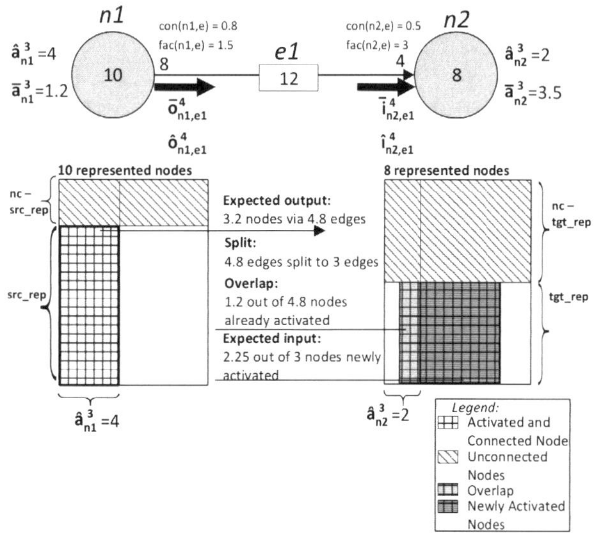

Figure 7. Example: Local Expected Number of Activated Nodes.

where

$$\overline{in}(n,p) := \sum_{e \in E_S} \bar{i}^{(p)}_{n,e}. \tag{31}$$

The complete expected activation level value of a node n via all edges can be performed by the activation function, no further adaptations needed:

$$\bar{a}^{(p)}_n = act(\bar{i}^{(p)}_n, \bar{a}^{(p-1)}_n). \tag{32}$$

Figure 8 depicts an example calculation. All expected input activation values for a node are aggregated and then used for the calculation of its new expected total activation.

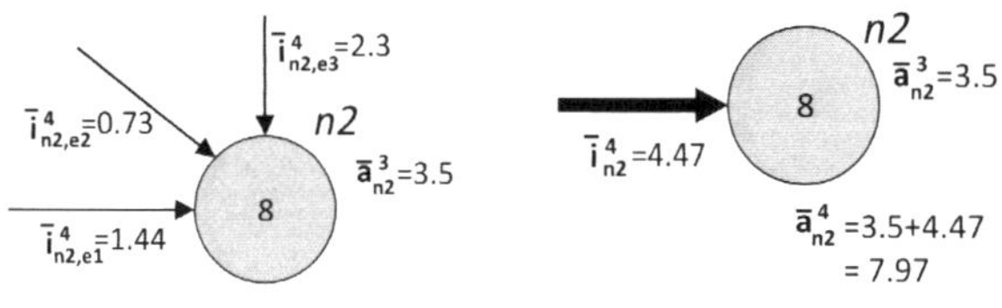

(a) Total Input Activation (b) Number of Activated Nodes

Figure 8. Example: Global Expected Activation.

2) Global Calculation of Expected Number of Activated Nodes: When consolidating, we have to take into account that the expected number of activated nodes transported via all connected edges to a node might contain overlap. First, a represented node that gets activated may already be contained in the set of activated nodes of the target node representative. Second, potentially newly activated nodes coming from different edges may have an overlap as well. Therefore, the consolidated expected number of potentially newly activated nodes should not contain the nodes that are expected to be not activated.

The number of non-activated represented nodes $non\_act : N_S \to \mathbb{R}$ of a node representative n in a pulse p is defined as

$$non\_act(n,p) := nc(n) - \hat{a}^{(p-1)}_n. \tag{33}$$

The number of represented nodes that are expected to be neither activated nor part of any overlap is denoted by $idle : N_S \to \mathbb{R}$:

$$idle(n,p) := non\_act(n,p) \cdot \prod_{e \in E_S} \left(1 - \frac{\hat{i}^{(p)}_{n,e}}{non\_act(n,p)}\right). \tag{34}$$

The expected input activation number via all edges is denoted by

$$\hat{i}^{(p)}_n = \hat{in}(n,p), \tag{35}$$

where

$$\hat{in}(n,p) := non\_act(n,p) - idle(n,p). \tag{36}$$

Computation of the complete expected number of activated represented nodes of a node n can be performed by the activation function, no further adaptations needed.

$$\hat{a}^{(p)}_n = act(\hat{i}^{(p)}_n, \hat{a}^{(p-1)}_n) \tag{37}$$

Figure 9 depicts an example calculation. All expected input activation values for a node are aggregated and then used for the calculation of its new expected total activation.

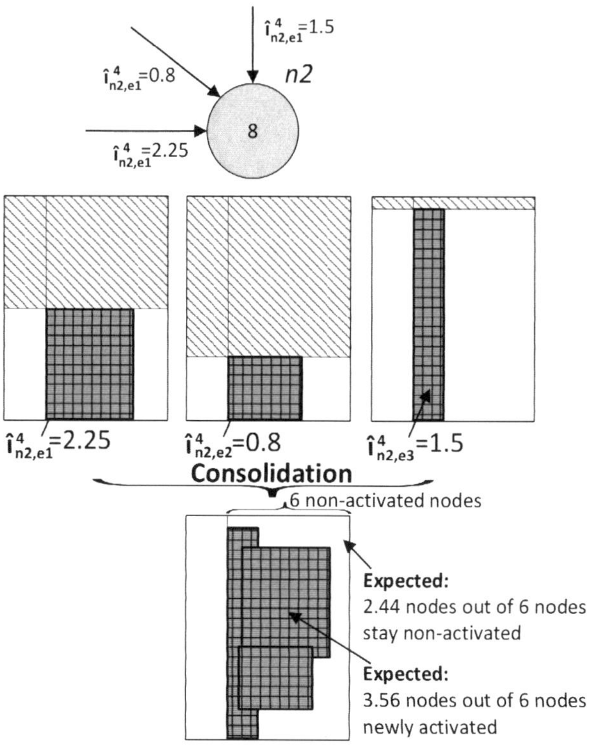

Figure 9. Example: Global Expected Number of Newly Activated Nodes.

VI. EXPERIMENTS

A. Appropriateness of Simulation Results

Predictive precision is a key property of a good simulation. Similarly, this should apply for spreading simulation on a semantic skeleton. To understand the quality of the predictions made by spreading simulation, we will compare pulses of a simulation on skeleton triples with real spreading pulses on the underlying network.

When simulating a pulse, we are mainly interested in a good prediction for the number of activated nodes and for the total activation of the receiving node representative. However, there are many other values that can be predicted by the simulation as well, such as the number of edges that transported activation from source to target and how much activation has been transported by them.

To compare simulation and spreading results, we generated 5000 pairs of skeleton triples $T_S = (n_1, e, n_2)$ with their corresponding underlying networks, and used each pair with the same activation values. To observe a high number of diverse cases, we decided for rather large triples with $A_n(nc, n_1) = 100$, $A_n(nc, n_2) = 130$, and $A_e(ec, e)$ being randomly generated, averaging at around 200. We kept the number of edges low in order to guarantee examples with connected and unconnected nodes, and therefore, to avoid trivial examples. On average, we assigned initial activation between 0.0 and 10.0 to 40% of the represented nodes of n_1. In order to observe the local consolidation, we assigned initial activation 0.0 and 10.0 to 20% of the represented nodes of n_2.

For our initial experiment, we decided to use pure spreading, i.e., a threshold of 0.0, a decay of 1.0, and no fanout. We collected the mean and standard deviation of the spreading results, the simulation results, and of the difference between spreading result and simulation result in Table I. Additionally, we calculated the difference mean as well as the difference standard deviation relative to the spreading result (shown as % diff).

Table I shows that total activation values can be predicted with high accuracy. The mean prediction error is far below 1% of the spreading average for total edge activation as well as right total activation. The standard deviation of the error is also very acceptable for simulating pulses. Predicting activated node counts is less precise, with up to -7% mean error. Nevertheless, this value improved at the end of the pulse to -4.7%. Altogether, the simulation shows a very good estimate of the total activation of n_2 after the pulse, and a good estimate of the number of activated nodes.

After the base experiment, we examine some variations in order to see if they affect the accuracy of the predictions. In the second experiment (see Table II), we activated the fanout constraint. Thus, nodes will spread less activation, depending on their connectivity. As we can see, the simulation also predicts this fanout parameter well. There is even an improvement on the standard deviation of the error, which is half the deviation of the base example.

In the third experiment (see Table III), we activated the decay factor and set it to 0.5. Thus, again, nodes will spread less activation, but this time independent of other factors. Again, the simulation predicts this parameter well, but there is no significant change compared to the base experiment.

In Experiment 4 (see Table IV), we set the activation threshold to 3.0. So, this times less nodes will spread activation. The experiment indicated that thresholds are a bit harder to predict, with a mean error of -0.3%. Still, this value is a very good prediction.

Experiment 5 (see Table V) combines the three parameters of experiments 2-4. The mean error didn't change too much, but interestingly, the standard deviation of the error dropped further to 2.6%

TABLE I. Experiment 1: Base

total edge activation $\bar{o}^p_{n1}$	**mean**	**standard deviation**
spreading	399.696	78.992
simulation	400.078	66.428
diff	0.382	42.684
% diff	0.095%	10.679%
active edge count $\hat{o}^p_{n1}$		
spreading	79.807	13.084
simulation	79.891	11.160
diff	0.083	6.753
% diff	0.105%	8.462%
right receiving node count $split(\hat{o}^p_{n1}, tgt\_rep(e))$		
spreading	59.758	7.724
simulation	55.389	5.460
diff	-4.369	4.659
% diff	-7.311%	7.797%
right new active node count $\hat{i}^p_{n2}$		
spreading	47.804	6.899
simulation	44.316	4.810
diff	-3.488	4.305
% diff	-7.297%	9.006%
right total activation $\bar{a}^p_{n2}$		
spreading	529.567	83.178
simulation	529.949	71.584
diff	0.382	42.684
% diff	0.072%	8.060%
right active node count $\hat{a}^p_{n2}$		
spreading	73.801	6.935
simulation	70.313	5.045
abs. diff	-3.488	4.305
% diff	-4.727%	5.833%

TABLE II. Experiment 2: Fanout

right total activation $\bar{a}^p_{n2}$	**mean**	**standard deviation**
spreading	303.203	39.914
simulation	303.273	38.196
diff	0.070	10.445
% diff	0.023%	3.445%
right active node count $\hat{a}^p_{n2}$		
spreading	73.912	7.034
simulation	70.356	5.092
abs. diff	-3.557	4.402
% diff	-4.812%	5.956%

TABLE III. Experiment 3: Decay

right total activation $\bar{a}^p_{n2}$	**mean**	**standard deviation**
spreading	330.468	48.010
simulation	330.159	43.124
diff	-0.309	21.607
% diff	-0.094%	6.538%
right active node count $\hat{a}^p_{n2}$		
spreading	74.037	7.152
simulation	70.365	5.146
abs. diff	-3.672	4.429
% diff	-4.959%	5.983%

TABLE IV. Experiment 4: Threshold

right total activation $\bar{a}^p_{n2}$	**mean**	**standard deviation**
spreading	495.542	83.702
simulation	494.037	70.426
diff	-1.504	44.059
% diff	-0.304%	8.891%
right active node count $\hat{a}^p_{n2}$		
spreading	62.666	7.351
simulation	60.187	5.038
abs. diff	-2.479	4.903
% diff	-3.956%	7.824%

TABLE V. Experiment 5: All Parameters

right total activation $\overline{a}^{p}_{n2}$	mean	standard deviation
spreading	209.716	31.117
simulation	209.390	30.425
diff	-0.327	5.580
% diff	-0.156%	2.661%
right active node count $\hat{a}^{p}_{n2}$		
spreading	62.527	7.362
simulation	60.152	5.101
abs. diff	-2.375	4.895
% diff	-3.798%	7.828%

Altogether, the results look promising, and it seems like using all parameters pushes the predictive power of the simulation.

B. Time-Related Advantages

Besides increased comprehensibility, another main motivation for the concept of semantic skeletons and spreading simulation is the expected time gain for potential applications. Of course, we do not aim at replacing spreading activation but propose bypassing potential applications whenever the averaging simulation results are sufficient. Therefore, we examined the run time of both spreading activation on a semantic network and spreading simulation on it's skeleton.

1) Experimental Setup: The semantic network under investigation is taken from our related research on an advisory system for decision-making support for hazard and risk analysis in the automotive domain [20]. This analysis is strongly expert-driven, and therefore expensive, time consuming, and dependent from the individual experts opinion. Therefore, the advisory system aims at providing useful recommendations for expert users when conducting such safety analyses. The semantic search within this network is performed by spreading activation. This advisory system will be utilized for our time-related experiments.

The network contains the knowledge taken from more than 150 concluded safety analyses from the domain. It contains more than 257.000 edges (representing 45 properties) connecting more than 61.800. The retrieved effective network skeleton only consists of 136 skeleton triple containing 45 node representatives and 136 edge representatives.

For the experiments, we examined 36 input variants using combinations of the different constraints and spreading modes presented in this article. Each input variant was executed for two different starting node situations. The experiments are conducted in the same running environment for both the spreading and the simulation approach.

2) Results: Figure 10 depicts the elapsed average time for the spreading activation runs as well as for the simulation runs. The simulation's lead in performance is obvious. The graph shows a gradual increase of run time over the pulses for the simulation runs. In contrast, the spreading activation graph reveals a sharp rise in execution time. One reason, why simulation can be performed faster is the smaller network size of a skeleton. We also observe differences regarding their configurations. Since both the simulation and the spreading runs are performed with the same input, we assume that it does not favor any of the both.

The results support our motivation to bypass the difficulties caused by extensive semantic network sizes by taking advantage of the skeleton's compactness. We conclude that whenever the averaging results from the simulation approach

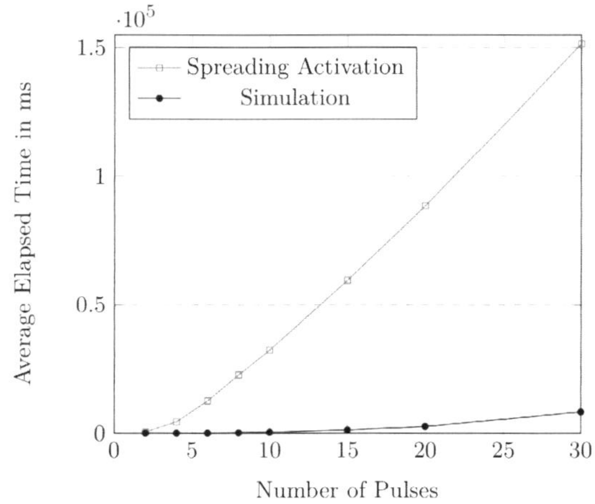

Figure 10. Average Elapsed Time for Spreading Activation and Spreading Simulation Runs.

are sufficient for a specific application or analysis, e.g., effect detection in pre-configuration analyses, the use of skeletons can save time.

VII. CONCLUSION AND FUTURE WORK

In this article, we extended previous work on the concept of semantic network skeletons by an approach that utilizes skeletons for simulating spreading activation. We presented a framework for spreading activation simulation that supports detailed observations of two basic properties: the expected pulsewise development of activation values, and the number of nodes that are expected to be activated, which is a measure for activation saturation in the semantic network. The approach is based on a careful mapping of the spreading activation functions to the specific characteristics of a skeleton. Averaging and combinatorial methods are used in order to estimate the spreading and activation behavior for the represented nodes and edges.

Through randomized experiments, we showed that the simulation results are good predictors for the actual spreading activation on the original network. We furthermore showed in time-related experiments that spreading simulation on a skeleton outperforms spreading activation on its represented semantic network.

We claimed that proper configuration is crucial and requires special attention for the useful application of spreading activation as a semantic search method in most application areas. Simulation results can reveal valuable information about spreading and activation behavior, e.g., the effects that may occur under certain influences from the algorithm and network settings. We showed that simulation can be performed on the comprised structure of a skeleton in a more efficient and sufficiently approximated way. Therefore, we conclude that it enables more efficient pre-configuration analyses.

The skeleton is not a tool to avoid spreading activation on semantic networks, but it poses an alternative to enhance working with vast networks that are difficult to manage. The objective is to use a skeleton's capabilities, i.e., time advantage and comprehensibility, to improve processes in the background in order to make spreading activation activities in the foreground easier to use with better results.

The semantic skeleton offers many opportunities for further applications and advanced extensions. Follow-up research can set up catalogs of potential structural and configurational influences as well as their effects in a systematic way in order to identify correlations and interdependencies. The resulting guidelines can be of direct use for finding proper configurations by including desired effects or excluding undesired effects. This may replace the momentary experience-driven controlling of such algorithms and may support a consistent rise in the quality of semantic search algorithms. Applicability and usability of spreading activation approaches may increase since manual adaptions often pose obstacles.

However, we have the futuristic vision of an adaptive self-configuration approach that automatically determines alleged good or bad configurations. For this long term goal, networks that change in size and structure should be treated flexibly such that disadvantages coming from hard-coding algorithm parameters can be discarded.

Skeletons can be valuable beyond utilization in the context of spreading activation. The compressed and summarized character of network skeletons might be useful for cognate disciplines also dealing with large semantic networks.

REFERENCES

[1] K. Hartig and T. Karbe, "Semantic Network Skeletons - A Tool to Analyze Spreading Activation Effects," in The Eighth International Conference on Information, Process, and Knowledge Management eKNOW 2016, C. Granja, R. Oberhauser, L. Stanchev, and D. Malzahn, Eds., 2016, pp. 126–131.

[2] F. Crestani, "Application of Spreading Activation Techniques in Information Retrieval," Artificial Intelligence Review, vol. 11, no. 6, 1997, pp. 453–482.

[3] M. R. Quillian, "Semantic Memory," in Semantic Information Processing, MIT Press, Ed., 1968, pp. 216–270.

[4] A. M. Collins and E. F. Loftus, "A Spreading-Activation Theory of Semantic Processing," Psychological Review, vol. 82, no. 6, 1975, pp. 407–428.

[5] J. F. Sowa, Principles of Semantic Networks: Exploration in the Representation of Knowledge, J. F. Sowa and A. Borgida, Eds. Morgan Kaufmann, Jan. 1991.

[6] "RDF 1.1 Concepts and Abstract Syntax," W3C, W3C Recommendation, Feb. 2014.

[7] J. R. Anderson, "A Spreading Activation Theory of Memory," Journal of Verbal Learning and Verbal Behavior, 1983, pp. 261–295.

[8] M. R. Berthold, U. Brandes, T. Kötter, M. Mader, U. Nagel, and K. Thiel, "Pure Spreading Activation is Pointless," in Proceedings of the 18th ACM Conference on Information and Knowledge Management CIKM 2009, New York, NY, USA, 2009, pp. 1915–1918.

[9] J. M. Álvarez, L. Polo, and J. E. Labra, "ONTOSPREAD: A Framework for Supporting the Activation of Concepts in Graph-Based Structures through the Spreading Activation Technique," Information Systems, E-learning, and Knowledge Management Research, vol. 278, 2013, pp. 454–459.

[10] J. M. Alvarez, L. Polo, W. Jimenez, P. Abella, and J. E. Labra, "Application of the spreading activation technique for recommending concepts of well-known ontologies in medical systems," in Proceedings of the 2nd ACM Conference on Bioinformatics, Computational Biology and Biomedicine - BCB 2011, R. Grossman, A. Rzhetsky, S. Kim, and W. Wang, Eds. New York, New York, USA: ACM Press, 2011, pp. 626–635.

[11] L. Grad-Gyenge, H. Werthner, and P. Filzmoser, "Knowledge Graph based Recommendation Techniques for Email Remarketing," International Journal on Advances in Intelligent Systems, vol. 9, no. 3&4, 2016.

[12] F. Crestani and P. L. Lee, "Searching the web by constrained spreading activation," Information Processing & Management, vol. 36, no. 4, 2000, pp. 585–605.

[13] C.-N. Ziegler and G. Lausen, "Spreading Activation Models for Trust Propagation," in IEEE International Conference on e-Technology, e-Commerce, and e-Services EEE 2004. Los Alamitos and Piscataway: IEEE Computer Society Press, 2004, pp. 83–97.

[14] K. Schumacher, M. Sintek, and L. Sauermann, "Combining Fact and Document Retrieval with Spreading Activation for Semantic Desktop Search," in Proceedings of the 5th European Semantic Web Conference, ser. Lecture Notes in Computer Science, S. Bechhofer, M. Hauswirth, J. Hoffmann, and M. Koubarakis, Eds. Springer, 2008, vol. 5021, pp. 569–583.

[15] J. Banks, Ed., Handbook of Simulation: Principles, Methodology, Advances, Applications, and Practice. New York, NY, USA: Wiley, 1998.

[16] J. A. Sokolowski and C. M. Banks, Eds., Principles of Modeling and Simulation: A Multidisciplinary Approach. Hoboken N.J.: John Wiley, 2009.

[17] M. D. Haselman, S. Hauck, T. K. Lewellen, and R. S. Miyaoka, "Simulation of Algorithms for Pulse Timing in FPGAs," IEEE Nuclear Science Symposium conference record. Nuclear Science Symposium, vol. 4, 2007, pp. 3161–3165.

[18] J. Polvichai, P. Scerri, and M. Lewis, "An Approach to Online Optimization of Heuristic Coordination Algorithms," in Proceedings of the 7th international joint conference on Autonomous agents and multiagent systems AAMAS 2008 - Volume 2, L. Padgham, D. C. Parkes, J. Mueller, and S. Parsons, Eds. Richland, SC: International Foundation for Autonomous Agents and Multiagent Systems, 2008, pp. 623–630.

[19] "SPARQL 1.1 Query Language," W3C, W3C Recommendation, Mar. 2013.

[20] K. Hartig and T. Karbe, "Recommendation-Based Decision Support for Hazard Analysis and Risk Assessment," in The Eighth International Conference on Information, Process, and Knowledge Management eKNOW 2016, C. Granja, R. Oberhauser, L. Stanchev, and D. Malzahn, Eds., 2016.

Optmized Preflight Planning for Successful Surveillance Missions of Unmanned Aerial Vehicles

Carlo Di Benedetto, Domenico Pascarella, Gabriella Gigante, Salvatore Luongo, Angela Vozella
Integrated Software, Verification and Validation Laboratory
CIRA (Italian Aerospace Research Centre)
Capua, Italy
e-mail: c.dibenedetto@cira.it, d.pascarella@cira.it, g.gigante@cira.it, s.luongo@cira.it, a.vozella@cira.it

Francesco Martone
Software Development and Virtual Reality Lab
CIRA (Italian Aerospace Research Centre)
Capua, Italy
e-mail: f.martone@cira.it

***Abstract*—This paper investigates the flight planning for surveillance missions of unmanned aerial vehicles. It proposes a prototype of preflight planner for different operative scenarios. The planner is able to provide an optimized route planning taking into account several constraints (e.g., the vehicle dynamics, the no fly zones, the endurance, the feasibility of the mission objectives, the terrain separation, etc.). It also provides a quantitative estimation of the air data link coverage and of the National Imagery Interpretability Rating Scale (NIIRS) index for the image quality. An overview of the prototype and of the planning approach is reported and some significant test results are discussed in order to show its features.**

Keywords-UAV; surveillance mission; optimal flight planning; payload management; NIIRS.

I. INTRODUCTION

This paper is an extended version of [1]. Compared with the previous work, here we provide a detailed survey of the background for the surveillance missions of Unmanned Aerial Vehicles (UAVs) and we add the design of a new functionality of the Route Planner module implementing the optimal allocation strategy of the sequence of targets.

UAVs are suitable to accomplish the D-cube (dull, dangerous and dirty) missions [2]. Dull operations are too monotonous or require excessive endurance for human occupants. Dirty operations are hazardous and pose a health risk to a human crew. Dangerous operations could result in the loss of life for the onboard pilot.

The D-cube terminology was originally defined within the military field, but is also applied to the civil sector. Examples of military applications include ISTAR (Intelligence, Surveillance, Target Acquisition and Reconnaissance) missions, such as visual detecting of enemy tanks and troop movements and surface-to-air missile launcher suppression. Civil applications include investigation in post-disaster areas for search and rescue operations and monitoring of environmental phenomenon in harsh scenarios (e.g., monitoring nuclear radiation). Moreover, recent advances in UAVs' technology allowed the emergence of a wide range of applications, such as for military operations [3], for disaster management [4], for urban terrain surveillance [5], and for agricultural surveillance [6].

A UAV is an aircraft with no human pilot onboard. It is the central element of an Unmanned Aerial System (UAS), which is the set of the aircraft and all the other elements supporting its service, including the Ground Control Station (GCS) and the payload.

Nowadays, UAVs are mostly Remotely Piloted Vehicles (RPVs) since their operations are performed by large teams of human operators, who remotely pilot the aircraft and control its actions. For RPVs, ground operators must be endowed with the proper expertise and this represents a substantial constraint, especially concerning costs. Dull missions particularly stress the training requirements. These considerations push the necessity to extend aerial platform capability related to autonomous flight. Therefore, one the main objectives of UAV research is to reduce the reliance on human operators in order to make UAVs a more economical and scalable technology. Indeed, tedious and repetitive tasks could relieve the task load of the remote pilots if they were autonomously performed and could provide a formal guarantee of the mission success. This approach would reduce the operators' workload with regard to system specific tasks, that are usually detailed and monotonous. Besides, it would allow the operator to focus on global situation awareness and emergency decision-making actions and it would limit their fatigue and lack of attention. A reduction of operational costs would also be achieved since the number of necessary members of the ground human team would be minimized.

This is also true for the tasks relating to mission preflight operation, such as the design of the flight path. In general, an integral part of UAV operation is the design of a flight path that attains the mission objectives. Flight planning shall ensure that the UAV operates in a safe and efficient way. Moreover, the mission effectiveness shall be ensured by verifying that all the required objectives are fulfilled by means of the design route.

This work deals with an offline flight planner, named PreFlight Planner (PFP), wherein the mission objectives concern the proximal sensing of geographical targets. The PFP is a Java software prototype, which is in charge of the 4D flight planning for different samples of UAVs. The 4D flight planning problem is concerned with finding a path that links a specified initial state and several goal states. These states are four-dimensional (three spatial and one time dimension). It is also a constrained problem. Thus, the proposed PFP is able to take into account the vehicle dynamics, the no-fly zones, the endurance, the data link coverage, the feasibility of the mission objectives, the terrain separation, etc.

The proposed software is an innovative UAV flight planner since it permits:

- a planning that is jointly based on the mission targets and the payloads;
- the insertion of emergency and termination routes;
- the verification of performances and constraints complying with surveillance mission objectives;
- an optimal allocation of the sequence of targets to cover.

The rest of this paper is organized as follows. Section II discusses the background. Section III provides an overview of the prototype and its software architecture. Section IV addresses a detailed analysis of the approaches for the flight plan verification. Section V details the approach for the route planning. Section VI presents some significant test results.

II. Background

This section provides some essential introductive concepts for the description of the PFP, such as the surveillance missions of UAVs, the related planning, the possible support tools and the image quality metrics for the evaluation of surveillance tasks.

A. *Surveillance Missions of UAVs*

A UAS is made up of [7]:

- **Airframe** – It is the mechanical component of the vehicle. It consists in the propeller(s) and the servos that actuate the control surfaces.
- **Flight Control System** (FCS) – It collects aerodynamic information by means of a set of sensors and controls the propulsion system and the servos.
- **Payload** – It is the specific equipment to accomplish a given mission. It may include cameras, infrared sensors, synthetic aperture radars, etc.
- **Ground Control Station** (GCS) – It is a network of computer systems on the ground, which monitor and control UAS operation.
- **Communications infrastructure** – It is the set of data links enabling communication between the aircraft and the GCS.
- **Launch and recovery systems** – They are special means to launch and recover the vehicle.

One of the most common applications of UAVs are surveillance missions or observations missions, which employ the UAS as an observation platform in order to locate a target entity within a Region of Interest (ROI). Thus, the UAS has to scan a given area, to track a fixed or mobile entity, to detect a predefined event and to monitor its evolution, etc. The surveying and reconnaissance capabilities of the vehicle depend on the sensor payload features.

A typical surveillance mission of a UAV includes a mission scenario with a number of geographically distributed targets in a given ROI. Hence, the UAV is in charge of visiting these targets and to perform the needed manoeuvres and the sensing activities for their observation, according to the requirements of the specific surveillance mission. Each target shall be observed for the UAV to accomplish the mission.

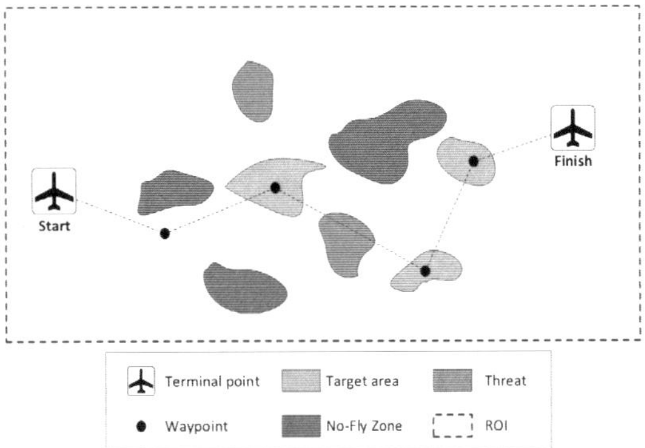

Figure 1. Two-dimensional graphical representation of a UAV surveillance mission.

Figure 1 graphically illustrates a two-dimensional description of the required mission.

Actually, the considered surveillance mission is an exploration mission since the UAV shall cover all targets once. Other instances of surveillance mission exist, such as the persistent surveillance mission (wherein all targets shall be continuously visited) and the coverage mission (wherein a certain ROI shall be completely covered). Anyway, the solution approach for the exploration mission may be easily extended to the other instances of surveillance mission.

In order to partially automatize the preflight operation for a surveillance mission of a UAV, an offline planner shall be introduced. Generally speaking, a planner is an abstract and explicit deliberative process that chooses and organizes actions by anticipating their expected outcomes. This process aims to achieve some predefined objectives as best as possible. Then, the planning of a surveillance mission of a UAV needs to generate a surveillance strategy for the vehicle that fulfills the requested mission objectives in an optimal way.

The planning of a surveillance strategy shall usually process two types of plans [8]:

- the flight plans, that allow the vehicle to reach the targets requested by the operator and to perform the manoeuvre for the successful sensing of the targets;
- the activity plans, that allow the boarded payloads to execute the necessary activities on a target for the successful fulfilment of the mission.

The proposed problem should be stated as an optimization problem since the planning is expected to produce plans which somehow maximize the mission effectiveness, accruing an utility and optimizing a convenient cost function. This optimization problem has to be constrained because the plans shall respect a set of constraints, which may be explicit (i.e., related to the mission definition) or implicit (i.e., related to the operative scenario, such as the configuration of the vehicle and the external context). Constraints may be further classified in:

- mission constraints, that are related to mission objectives;
- system constraints, that are related to the system configuration and state (the adopted vehicle model, the ground control station, the payloads, etc.);
- path constraints, that are related to the features of the region of interest (e.g., no fly zones).

Concerning the targets allocation for the flight planning, different approaches may be used. The spatial queue approach treats the target allocation problem as "customer" representing spatially distributed demands. Formally, spatial queues assume that a model of the exogenous component of the process exists, such as a stochastic model of the spatio-temporal distribution of the arrivals of customers. The graph theoretic approach, instead, represents the allocation problem as a search of the optimal path on the graph.

B. Support Tools for UAVs Missions

A UAV mission may be divided in two main parts: the flight and the fulfillment of the assigned objectives. Objectives are reached by means of onboard payloads. A typical UAV mission starts with the assignment of the objectives, goes on with the definition of the flight plan to reach them and the execution and control of the flight from take-off to landing, and it ends with the post flight analysis of collected data.

All such phases are supported by different types of software, that may be categorized in:

- **UAV Activities Management** – Software to manage the different activities of UAV fleets and related projects at business level, maintenance plans and pilot workload. Different platforms providing such services are going to be developed in Europe.
- **Flight Management** – Software allowing the execution of the flight from take-off to landing. This includes both Ground Control Station (GCS) software and onboard guidance, navigation and control software (autopilot). The autopilot works according to the flight plan and by means of sensing and actuating. The typical UAV ground control software receives telemetry data from the UAV and sends telecommands to it. It allows the aircraft operator to communicate the flight plan to onboard autopilot and/or to remotely control the UAV. It may support First-Person View (FPV) equipment to enhance the situational awareness of the remote pilot. In these fields, much research effort has been focusing on relevant aspects such as the perceptual and cognitive issues related to the interface of the UAV operator, including the application of multimodal technologies to compensate for the dearth of available sensory information. GCS software products usually allow to manage one UAV and they are combined to the UAV autopilot. For example, APM (ArduPilotMega) is the GCS of all UAVs with ArduPilot, a 3D robotics autopilot. Paparazzi GCS is the software employed in projects using the UAV Paparazzi platform [9]. It allows the design of the flight plan as well as the system configuration by means of a TCP-IP aircraft server. DJI provides a PC ground station for multi-rotor UAVs and manages the no-fly zones by means of a global list with a safety margin of 8 km [10]. The KopterTool is the ground software for the platform MikroKopter [11], whereas OpenPilot is an open platform [12]. Currently, it is possible to find commercial GCSs for multi-UAV systems ranging from the advanced proprietary and closed solution by Boeing for the X-45, Parrot SDK systems of PrecisionHawk, Draganfly, and Aeryon to open source solutions as QGroundControl Station and others [13]-[23].
- **UAV Payload Management** – Software enabling the management of the onboard payloads during the flight. This class allows the fulfillment of the assigned mission objectives. Payload management products may be integrated into ground control software or not. They strictly depend on the payload model and type. The payload usually provides its own control software.
- **UAV Post Flight Analysis** – Software producing evidences on the basis of data collected by the UAV during the flight. In the photogrammetry domain, companies such as Erdas or Inpho have been proposing solutions for UAV. APS from Menci Software has been one of the first platforms for UAV in Italy. It provides some additional functionalities, such as StereoCAD and Terrain Tools to enhance the cartographic data, and APSCheck for the check of the collected images. It also allows to validate and classify the collected data [24]. Pix4D from Pix4D Switzerland (a spin-off of Swiss university) provides Pix4Dmapper Capture App, which allows to display on tablets or smartphones the images from commercial UAVs, like the DJI Phantom. ENSOMosaic Suite and PIEneering ([25], [26]) offer different and integrated solutions from flight planning software to post flight photogrammetric analysis, including 3D models. The PhotoScan platform from Agisoft proposes the SFM (Structure For Motion) innovative approach. PhotoScan Professional and Standard Edition products are cheap and are open enough to accomplish the growing needs from applications [27]. Cloud services for UAV (like REDcatch GmbH [28], Agribotix [29], and the Maps Made Easy project [30]) may support UAV not only for planning, but especially for post flight elaboration of geo data. Additionally, a transversal category may be considered regarding the 3D modeling and vision digitalizing to realize 3D model and advanced visualization applications.

- **UAV Flight Planning** – Software implementing: the strategic planning, which occurs before take-off and takes a priori information about the environment and the mission goals to construct an optimal path for the given objectives; the tactical planning, which involves re-evaluation of the flight plan during flight.

Table I summarizes the types of support tools for UAVs missions and the related examples.

TABLE I. SUPPORT TOOLS FOR UAVS MISSIONS

Category	Tools Description
Activities Management	Management of the UAVs fleet
Flight Management	Execution of the flight from take-off to landing (APM, Paparazzi, KopterTool, OpenPilot, QGroundControl Station)
Payload Management	Management of the onboard payloads
Post Flight Analysis	Production of evidences on the basis of collected data (APS, Pix4D, ENSOMosaic Suite, PIEneering, PhotoScan, REDcatch GmbH, Agribotix, Maps Made Easy)
Flight Planning	Strategic and tactical planning of the UAV flight

Such software enables each UAV to properly flight followed by its own GCS, but two point seems to need further studies:

- to guarantee a successful mission, what about the flight plan and the clear sight of the targets associated to mission objectives?
- to guarantee the UAV flight according to airworthiness requirements, which ground station will cover the UAV?

A careful study of the market and of the existing products shows that very few products combine these aspects.

C. Images Quality Metrics

As regards the mission objectives, the first issue in devising a surveillance planner is to agree what it means to do a good surveillance job and to define a surveillance performance requirement. In particular, in any application where proximal sensing on a specific target is required, a variable that plays an important role is the quality of the set of pictures. Many image quality metrics have been proposed in the recent years [31].

The quality of images is expressed by several technical parameters, such as ground sampling distance (GSD), modulation transfer function (MTF), signal to noise ratio (SNR) and National Imagery Interpretability Rating Scale (NIIRS). However, these parameters may partially address interpretability. GSD is related to the spatial resolution of images and is probably the most popular parameter. This is not the ultimate parameter to describe quality of images. For example, images with a same GSD may have very different interpretability. MTF and SNR may specify some aspects of image quality.

For this reason, the NIIRS index has been proposed as a measure of image quality in terms of interpretability criteria. It has been applied with multiple types of imagery and offers a robust approach to developing an evaluation scale. It was formerly defined for intelligence and military use and extended to civilian use later on. The general approach is to use image analysis tasks to indicate the level of interpretability for imagery based on the detection of the object. The scale is defined so that when more information may be extracted from the image, the NIIRS rating increases. A set of standard image analysis tasks or "criteria" defines the levels of the scale. The NIIRS consists of 10 graduated levels (0 to 9), with several interpretation tasks or criteria forming each level. These criteria indicate the level of information that may be extracted from an image of a given interpretability level. All NIIRS rating levels are described in Table II.

TABLE II. NIIRS LEVELS [32]

Rating Level	Description
0	Interpretability of the imagery is precluded by obscuration, degradation or very poor resolution.
1	It is possible to: distinguish between major land use classes; detect a medium-sized port facility; distinguish between runways and taxiways at a large airport; identify large area drainage patterns by type.
2	It is possible to: identify large fields; detect large buildings; identify major road patterns; detect ice-breaker tracks; detect the wake from large ships.
3	It is possible to: detect large area contour ploughing, individual houses in residential areas, trains or strings of rolling stock; identify inland waterways navigable by barges; distinguish between natural forest and orchards.
4	It is possible to: identify farm buildings as barns, silos or residences; detect basketball or tennis courts in urban areas; identify individual tracks, rail pairs and control towers; detect jeep trails through grassland.
5	It is possible to: identify individual rail wagons by type; detect open bay doors of storage buildings; identify tents at recreational camping areas; distinguish between coniferous and deciduous trees during leaf-off conditions; detect large animals in grasslands.
6	It is possible to: identify cars as saloon or estate types; identify individual electricity or telephone posts in residential areas; detect footpaths through barren areas; distinguish between grain crops and row crops.
7	It is possible to: identify individual railway sleepers; detect individual steps on a stairway; detect tree-stumps and rocks in forest clearings and meadows.
8	It is possible to: identify vehicle grille detailing and/or the license plate on a truck; identify individual water lilies on a pond; identify the windscreen wipers on a vehicle; count individual lambs.
9	It is possible to: identify individual barbs on a barbed-wire fence; detect individual grain heads on small grain crops; identify an ear tag on livestock.

Because of different types of imagery support different types of interpretation tasks, individual NIIRS indexes have been developed for four major imaging types: Visible, Radar, Infrared, and Multispectral. It provides a simple, yet powerful, tool for assessing and communicating image quality and sensor system requirements and it has been used for our purposes to provide a direct criterion to validate the waypoint and the relative legs associated to mission targets objectives. In other words, a target will be considered successfully acquired or observed if the related payload image exhibits at least the requested NIIRS value.

III. High-Level Description of the UAV PreFlight Planner

This section provides a high-level description of the PFP, by detailing the concepts behind the prototype and the software architecture.

A. *PFP Concepts*

This work concerns the PFP, that is a strategic planner allowing the mission controller to plan (edit), validate and then upload the flight plan to the UAV. It proposes a solution of an offline flight plan validated against aspects related both to mission objectives (acquisition of targets) and path constraints (such as no fly zones) and system constraints (such as data link coverage). The effectiveness of the acquisition of targets is enabled by a quantitative assessment of the NIIRS index. The PFP does not include the planning of payload activities.

Research has focused on the identification of approaches and optimization algorithms which select the best route to guarantee the feasibility according to the vehicle performances, the compliance with the safety objectives, the endurance, the ability to return to base, and the terrain profile.

The problem of flight planning is an instance of the generic path and motion planning problem, regarding the synthesis of a geometric path from a starting position to one or more targets and of a control trajectory along that path that specifies the state variables in the configuration space of a mobile system. The adopted approach for the optimal targets allocation is graph theoretic.

B. *PFP Software Architecture*

The PFP is a Java software prototype which allows to plan a mission of a UAS, namely, to identify the mission objectives and to design the mission path to observe them. Furthermore, the PFP ensures the success of the planned mission. The success assurance of the mission is attained by guaranteeing the following properties for the designed plan:

- the dynamic feasibility from a 4D point of view by means of the selected vehicle;
- the terrain separation;
- the compliance with the no-fly zones, i.e., the 3D regions that shall not be entered by the UAV;
- the compliance with the safe zones, i.e., the 3D regions that are reserved for the UAV flight and that shall not be left by the UAV;
- the endurance, which requires that the boarded fuel level is enough to accomplish the mission;
- the air data link coverage at any point of the route;
- the visibility of the targets at the related route points.

The preflight verification of these properties is necessary to avoid potential and expensive mission aborts due to neglected offline checks. In particular, the visibility check of the targets is profitable in order to avoid online changes of the UAV flight plan for the achievement of the mission objectives. In this way, the PFP provides a flight plan that is entirely verified and approved to guarantee the success of the designed mission.

In detail, the PFP operation has been structured in three main phases, as shown in Figure 2:

- the setup phase, which allows for the setting of all the configuration data that are required for the planning;
- the planning phase, which identifies all the mission parameters and the actual route taken by means of the waypoints positioning;
- analysis, which allows for the necessary checks in order to verify and approve the designed plan and shows the related numerical results and diagrams.

Moreover, the software structure of the PFP is split into five modules:

- **User Database**;
- **Mission Data**;
- **Route Planner;**
- **Analysis**;
- **Export**.

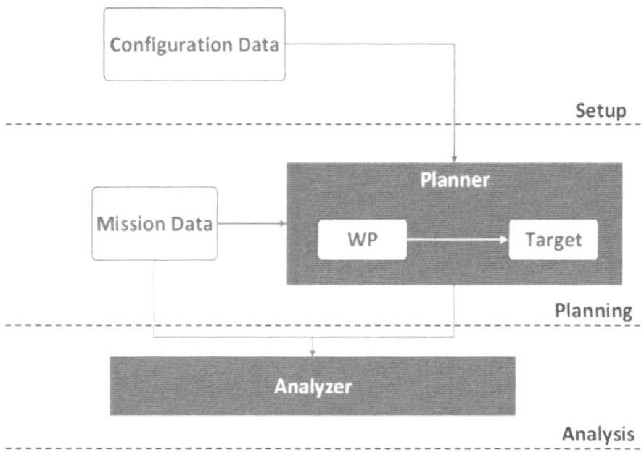

Figure 2. Operation phases of the PreFlight Planner.

The User Database and the Mission Data modules are employed in the setup phase, the Route Planner is used in the planning phase and the Analysis module performs the analysis phase.

Figure 3 shows a block diagram of the software architecture of the PFP. It also graphically depicts the data flow amongst the different modules.

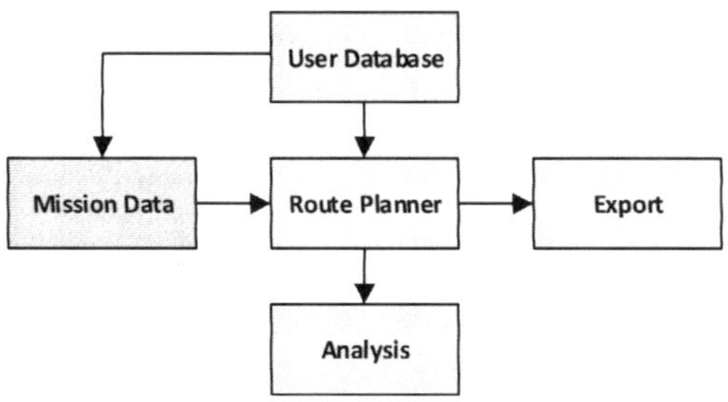

Figure 3. Data flow diagram of the PreFlight Planner.

1) User Database Module

The User Database is the module for the management of the database of the reusable data. Such data refer to objects that are used for the planning of a mission, but are not specific of a single mission. On the contrary, they may be defined and reused without modification in order to simplify the operator throughout the generation of a mission plan.

Some of the reusable entities are: aircrafts; airports; payloads that may be boarded; point targets, i.e., mission objectives without a significant size; area targets, i.e., mission objectives with a significant size; user waypoints, which are defined by the user; standard waypoints, which are standard aeronautic waypoints; air data links, i.e., the transmission/reception instruments that may be boarded; no-fly zones and safe zones; patterns, i.e., waypoint sequences that define significant route segments; contingency routes, i.e., standard routes that may be reused in case of failure in the air data link.

The databases used are described in Table III.

TABLE III. DESCRIPTION OF THE DATABASES

Database	Description
Aircraft	Database of the vehicles.
Payload	Database of the sensors that may be boarded on the vehicle.
Point Target	Database of the punctual targets, i.e., the mission objectives of interest that do not have a significant extension.
Area Target	Database of the extended targets, i.e., the mission objectives of interest that have a significant extension.
User Waypoint	Database of reference waypoints that are defined by the user.
Standard Waypoint	Database of reference aeronautical waypoints.
Map	Database of georeferenced images, which may be displayed in overlay on the map during the mission planning.
Air Data Link	Database of transmission/reception devices that may be boarded on a vehicle.
Data Link Station	Database of transmission/reception devices that may be used in the GCS.
No Fly Zone	Database of the regions that mark prohibited airspace for the flight of a vehicle.
Safe Area	Database of the reserved areas for the flight of a vehicle and from which the exit is prohibited.
Pattern	Database of waypoint sequences, which define reference route segments that may be reused for different missions.
Contingency	Database of standard routes, which have to be used in case of failures of the radio link between the vehicle and the GCS.
Airport	Database of the airports.

In detail, the Aircraft database contains the models of the vehicles that may be used for a mission. These models allow to verify that the planned route belongs to the flight envelope of the selected vehicle. The parameters of the models are grouped for homogeneous classes, which define the vehicle performances throughout the different flight phases: acceleration, cruise, climb, descent, take-off and landing.

The acceleration parameters describe the vehicle performances during the transition from a flight condition to another one (e.g., during a turn or during the passage from an altitude level to another one). Table IV reports the acceleration parameters of an aircraft model.

The cruise performance model includes a set of parameters which define the behaviour of the vehicle during the levelled flight phase. Table V reports the cruise parameters of an aircraft model.

TABLE IV. ACCELERATION PARAMETERS OF AN AIRCRAFT MODEL

Parameter	Description
Turn Rate	Turn rate of the vehicle in a levelled and coordinated turn.
Pull Up	Orthogonal acceleration with respect to the motion vector, which is used during a flight transition from a levelled flight or a dive to a nose-up.
Push Over	Orthogonal acceleration with respect to the motion vector, which is used during a flight transition from a levelled flight or a nose-up to a dive.
Roll Rate	Change rate of the bank angle of the vehicle during a turn.
Pitch Rate	Change rate of the pitch angle of the vehicle during a manoeuvre.
Yaw Rate	Change rate of the yaw angle of the vehicle during a manoeuvre.

The cruise performance model includes a set of parameters which define the behaviour of the vehicle during the levelled flight phase. Table V reports the cruise parameters of an aircraft model.

TABLE V. CRUISE PARAMETERS OF AN AIRCRAFT MODEL

Parameter	Description
Ceiling Altitude	Maximum altitude for the vehicle to hold up a levelled flight without resorting to accelerations.
Default Altitude	Cruise default altitude of the vehicle.
Minimum Speed	Minimum cruise speed (true airspeed), with the related fuel consumption.
Maximum Speed	Maximum cruise speed (true airspeed), with the related fuel consumption.
Maximum Endurance	Cruise speed (true airspeed) that allows for the maximum endurance of the flight, with the related fuel consumption.
Maximum Range	Cruise speed (true airspeed) that allows for the longest path of the flight, with the related fuel consumption.

Table VI reports the performance parameters of a vehicle for the climb flight phase and the descent flight phase.

TABLE VI. CLIMB/DESCENT PARAMETERS OF AN AIRCRAFT MODEL

Parameter	Description
Airspeed	Vehicle speed (true airspeed) in the climb/descent phase.
Altitude Rate	Altitude rate of climb/descent of the vehicle.
Fuel Flow	Fuel consumption during the climb/descent manoeuvre.

Table VII reports the performance parameters of a vehicle for the landing flight phase.

Table VIII reports the performance parameters of a vehicle for the take-off flight phase.

TABLE VII. CLIMB/DESCENT PARAMETERS OF AN AIRCRAFT MODEL

Parameter	Description
Airspeed	Vehicle speed (true airspeed) that is kept during the descent path towards the landing track.
Ground Roll	Covered on-ground distance until the stop.
Fuel Flow	Fuel consumption during the landing manoeuvre.

TABLE VIII. CLIMB/DESCENT PARAMETERS OF AN AIRCRAFT MODEL

Parameter	Description
Airspeed	Vehicle speed (true airspeed) during the taxiing.
Ground Roll	Covered on-ground distance until the take-off.
Departure Speed	Vehicle speed (true airspeed) at the take-off.
Climb Angle	Climb angle at the take-off.
Acceleration Fuel Flow	Fuel consumption during the acceleration for the take-off.
Departure Fuel Flow	Fuel consumption at the take-off speed.

As regards the point targets, they are generally objects (natural or artificial structures), with a negligible extension or non influential for the purposes of the planning. These targets shall be acquired by means of one or more payloads that are boarded on the vehicle. Table IX reports the parameters of a point target.

TABLE IX. PARAMETERS OF A POINT TARGET

Parameter	Description
Latitude	Target latitude.
Longitude	Target longitude.
Altitude	Target latitude.
NIIRS Level	Requested minimum NIIRS for the target acquired image by the sensors.
Date From	Starting validity date of the target.
Date To	Ending validity date of the target.
Info	Description of the target.

Besides, the managed waypoints are compliant with the ARINC (Aeronautical Radio INCorporated) 424 standard, which is the international standard file format for aircraft navigation data.

2) Mission Data Module

The Mission Data carries out the management and the insertion of the set of data that characterize a given mission throughout the planning phase. The module is invoked both for the creation and for the change of a mission.

It collects the following data from the user:

- the mission vehicle;
- the mission payloads;
- the air data links for the mission;
- the fuel level;
- the start time;
- the safe zone;
- the ground control stations that are active.

The Mission Data receives the contents of the following databases from the User Database: aircraft, safe area, payload, airport and data link station, and sends its own data to the Route Planner. The data that the operator submits by means of the Mission Data module are then sent to the Route Planner module in order to allow for the creation for the mission scenario.

3) Route Planner Module

The Route Planner is the module that accomplishes the flight planning (or route planning) phase. In the following, flight planning and route planning will be used with the same meaning.

Moreover, the Route Planner module performs the following functions by means of the interaction with a georeferenced 2D map:

- insertion of a new waypoint, both as a last waypoint of the route and as an intermediate waypoint between two preexisting waypoints;
- change of a the position and/or of the attributes of a previously inserted waypoint;
- removal of a previously inserted waypoint.

The crossing order of the waypoints may be also modified.

Each waypoint may be related to one or more targets, which shall be observable (i.e., shall exhibit a minimum specified NIIRS) along the route section between two consecutive waypoints. The user may request that a target is observable by means of one or more payloads within the set of boarded payloads.

Besides, every waypoint may be optionally related to one or two contingency routes, that shall be selected within the User Database. One contingency route may be defined as emergency route, whereas the other may represent a termination route: the former is the route to follow if the air data link is lost along the course starting from the chosen waypoint, while the system is waiting for the link recovery; the latter is the route to follow if the air data link is lost along the course starting from the chosen waypoint and it cannot be recovered. Hence, the match between a waypoint and the contingency routes is static.

During the insertion and the change/removal of the waypoints, the Route Planner executes some validity checks in order to ensure that the following two conditions always hold:

1. the vehicle is able to perform the necessary manoeuvres to reach the waypoints;
2. there are no ground impacts (i.e., collisions with the terrain).

If the first condition is violated, the system does not agree to the proposed modification of the route. If the second condition is violated, the system signals the problem to the user, who may also continue the planning without automatic modifications to the route. The module also handles a 3D view of the Earth, that may be invoked anytime and allows a realistic visualization of the mission execution.

Section V deepens the approach for the route planning.

4) Analysis Module

The Analysis module is in charge of the analysis of the flight (or route) plans as a function of the mission objectives. It verifies that all the mission constraints are fulfilled and ensures the success of the plan.

In detail, the following properties of the computed plan are checked:

- the vehicle never leaves the coverage region of the air data links, which is computed by taking into account the positions of the GCSs and the land orography;
- the targets are always visible along the route sections, by taking into account the boarded payloads and the land orography and by envisaging a minimum level of quality of the captured image; if some variable confocal optics are boarded, the visibility check is carried out with four different focal lengths, namely, minimum, 1/3 of the maximum, 2/3 of the maximum and maximum;
- the vehicle never leaves the safe zone, if this is included in the mission planning;
- there are no ground impacts; a minimum distance with the terrain is guaranteed for each point of the route along vertical, frontal and lateral directions;
- the boarded fuel is enough for the accomplishment of the whole flight plan.

The checks are performed starting from the data of the aircraft (i.e., its model parameters), of the payload and of the mission. The results of each check may be displayed both on a 2D map and on a 3D view, by highlighting the route segments wherein the test has passed and the ones wherein the test has failed.

The approach for the flight plan verification carried out by the Analysis module is examined in depth in Section IV.

5) Export Module

The Export module exports one or more planned missions in order to upload them in the Flight Management System (FMS) of the reference UAV.

The interchange format is based on XML (eXtensible Markup Language) and has been implemented by a configurable XML schema.

IV. FLIGHT PLAN VERIFICATION IN THE UAV PREFLIGHT PLANNER

Section III reports the high-level requirements of the Analysis module for the verification of a flight plan.

In detail, the coverage limit of the air data link is computed starting from the link budget equation, i.e.

$$P_{RX} = P_{TX} + G_{TX} - L_{TX} - L_{FS} - L_M + G_{RX}\,, \quad (1)$$

wherein P_{RX} is the power of the signal that arrives at the receiver, P_{TX} is the transmitted power, G_{TX} is the gain of the transmitter antenna, L_{TX} is the transmitter loss, L_{FS} is the loss due to the signal propagation in space, L_M is the safety link margin, and G_{RX} is the gain of the receiver antenna. All these parameters are known and are stored as data of the air data links in the User Database, except L_{FS}. The latter depends on the distance R that is covered by the wave and the wave length λ, which is derivable from the frequency of the transmission channel (also stored in the User Database). In detail, the relation between L_{FS}, R and λ is

$$L_{FS} = 20\,\ln\frac{4\pi R}{\lambda} P_{RX}\,. \quad (2)$$

In order to receive a signal, the condition $P_{RX} > 0$ must hold. This condition is equivalent to

$$20\,\ln\frac{4\pi R}{\lambda} < P_{TX} + G_{TX} - L_{TX} - L_M + G_{RX} = \alpha\,, \quad (3)$$

wherein α is equal to $P_{TX} + G_{TX} - L_{TX} - L_M + G_{RX}$.

Hence, the maximum coverage distance R_{MAX} is

$$R_{MAX} = \frac{\lambda}{4\pi} e^{\frac{\alpha}{20}}\,. \quad (4)$$

As regards the NIIRS quantitative assessment, the first step is the computation of the GSD, which is the dimension of the ground projection of a sensor pixel. If we assume the pixels to be square with dimension d and the acquisition to occur with an elevation angle that is different from $\pi/2$, the ground projection of the pixel is distorted in a rectangle. Starting from Figure 4, the following equations hold

$$x = \frac{d\cdot r}{f}\,, \quad (5)$$

$$y = \frac{d\cdot r}{f\cdot \sin elev}\,, \quad (6)$$

$$\mathrm{GSD} = \sqrt{x\cdot y} = \frac{d\cdot r}{f\cdot\sqrt{\sin elev}}\,. \quad (7)$$

The expected NIIRS may be computed as

$$\mathrm{NIIRS} = A + B\cdot \log_{10}\mathrm{GSD}, \quad (8)$$

wherein A and B are two constants, whose values have been set as $A = 10.251$ and $B = -3.32$ [33].

The structure of eq. (8) and the values of A and B are coherent with the General Image Quality Equation (GIQE). The GIQE is an empirical formula for calculating the image quality that is expected for a given optical system [33]. It is a model that was developed using statistical analysis of imagery analyst responses.

The coefficients A and B and the logarithmic structure were obtained by regression to fit the results of an image evaluation study. In detail, the logarithmic structure of eq. (8) embodies the notion that NIIRS changes by 1.0 for each factor of two in the spatial resolution is equivalent to one unit on the NIIRS scale, namely, a change of ±1 of the NIIRS is equivalent to halving or doubling the distance between the sensor and the observation point. This relationship was confirmed by visual observations [33].

More broadly, the GIQE predicts the NIIRS value as a function of other parameters in addition to the GSD (which is directly related to the spatial resolution). These supplementary parameters are: the Relative Edge Response (RER), which is indirectly associated to the point spread function and that estimates the effective slope of the imaging system's edge response; the SNR and the system post-processing noise gain, which quantify the noise in the post-processed imagery; the system post-processing edge overshoot factor, that measures the amount of edge ringing resulting from post-processing. Within this work, we consider only the spatial resolution (i.e., the GSD) as a parameter for the NIIRS estimation, whereas the other criteria are not considered since they are related to the post-processing phase and the aperture configuration.

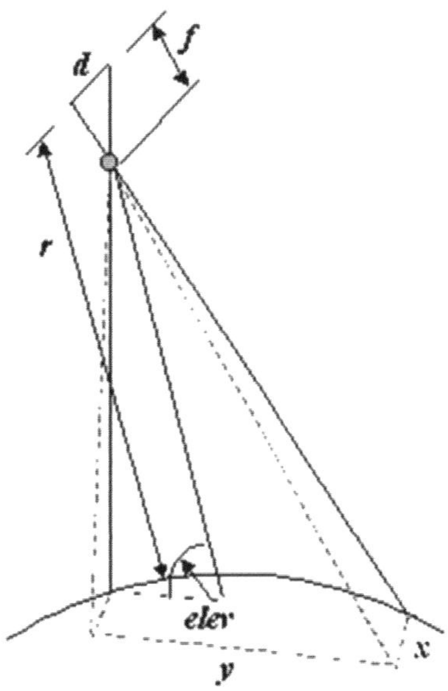

Figure 4. NIIRS quantitative estimation in the PreFlight Planner.

V. Route Planning in the UAV PreFlight Planner

As stated in Section III, the problem of flight planning has to be stated as a constrained optimization problem, whose solution is generally challenging from a computational point of view. A possible solution of this issue is the adoption of a hierarchical decomposition. Indeed, the original problem is a monolithic planning problem, namely, it consists of a single large problem and may be solved only by means of a single large algorithm, which examines all the factors at once. By contrast, a hierarchical decomposition splits the monolithic problem into smaller sub-problems, which are arranged in a hierarchical fashion. The decomposition is usually performed by reducing the degree of detail or the range of the single problems, which is named problem horizon. For instance, the top-level sub-problems may consist of the whole problem range with a small degree of detail, whereas the bottom-level sub-problems may have a small horizon with a high degree of detail. The hierarchical decomposition of the original problem in sub-problems is established by fixing a criterion for the problems horizon (i.e., the range of the single problems). Common horizons are temporal or spatial, wherein the problem is broken down by units of time or distance.

In our case, we use a temporal hierarchical decomposition for the partition of the joint mission planning problem. Therefore, a root planning problem is provided for the planning over the entire mission time and it acts over the total temporal horizon, but with a coarse degree of detail. Instead, the child sub-problems work on shorter temporal horizons and supply accurate plans. As regards the coordination of the hierarchical decomposition, given that the planning problem has to be stated as an optimization problem, we employ the multilevel optimization principle [8] in order to ensure that the system-wide objectives and constraints are respectively optimized and satisfied along the hierarchy.

In particular, the global optimization problem is broken in simpler problems, which are independently solved. Moreover, the upper levels coordinate the solutions of the decoupled problems of lower levels. In our case, the flight planning problem for the surveillance mission of a UAV is decomposed in the following sub-problems:

- the task planning problem, which works over the whole temporal horizon and aims at an optimal scheduling (assignment and ordering) of the targets to cover and at the generation of an optimal high-level (i.e., with a coarse degree of detail) trajectory;
- the trajectory planning problem, which works over a small temporal horizon and consists in the actual flight planning (i.e., the real trajectory) of the vehicle.

In the case of PFP, the trajectory planning problem has to generate a trajectory that allows the aircraft to reach the targets safely and on schedule. This problem is solved by the Route Planner module, which carries out the computations of the flight plan for the specific aircraft. It employs the performance model of the aircraft in order to ensure the realistic and optimized route. The performance model includes some well-known characteristic parameters, such as cruise airspeed, climb rate, roll rate, etc. The route is modeled by means of a sequence of curves and the state of the vehicle may be analytically computed at any given time. Moreover, this module provides a software geometry engine that accurately illustrates dynamic objects.

The Route Planner module is based on the STK (Systems Tool Kit) product of AGI (Analytical Graphics Inc.). It is a physics-based software geometry engine that accurately displays and analyzes dynamic objects in real or simulated time. It models moving objects and the dynamic relationships of those objects in space. Moreover, it provides the platform and tools for solving system level problems of motion and time.

Instead, as regards the task planning problem, it may be seen as a task allocation problem. Indeed, it produces the selection and the ordering of the waypoints (i.e., the reference points for navigation) for the mission accomplishment and it establishes the optimal ordered sequence of targets to cover. The produced list of waypoints is the reference input for the trajectory planner.

By taking into account the constraints that are handled by the PFP, the stated problem about the task planning for a UAV surveillance mission is surely NP-hard. Indeed, the Travelling Salesman Problem (TSP) and the Vehicle Routing Problem (VRP) are known to be NP-hard [34] and they may be regarded as a special case for the surveillance task planning.

Hence, we firstly make the following further assumptions to enable an approximate resolution: the UAV moves only in a plane (i.e., at a constant altitude); the targets always coincide with a single waypoint; the durations of an acquisition activity on a target by means of the payloads are left out. Under these assumptions, the stated task planning problem is a topological planning problem is a topological planning problem [35]. Here, the landmarks and the gateways are represented by the targets and some distinctive points for the no fly zones, such as their polygonal vertices. The search space may be built by orientation regions, which are defined by landmark pair boundaries. Every landmark pair boundary is a link between two landmarks and it partitions the world into orientation regions. Then, orientation regions are conceptually similar to neighbourhoods and typify the search space as a graph.

Figure 5 shows a graphical depiction of the topological view for task planning problem of a surveillance mission by means of a UAV.

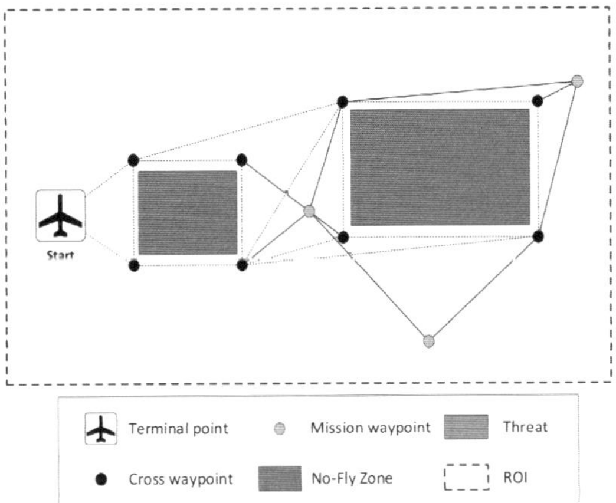

Figure 5. Topological view of the task planning problem for a surveillance mission of a UAV.

In light of these reflections, the total cost of a surveillance itinerary $\boldsymbol{\tau}$ will be related to the assessed time T_τ for its completion. The itinerary $\boldsymbol{\tau}$ is a sequence of allocated tasks (i.e., waypoint) for the UAV and can be described as an ordered sequence of points in the space domain (i.e., the region of interest) W that are assigned to the vehicle, i.e.,

$$\boldsymbol{\tau} = \{\boldsymbol{\tau}_0, \boldsymbol{\tau}_1, \boldsymbol{\tau}_2, \dots\}, \quad \boldsymbol{\tau}_i \in W, i \in \mathbb{N}\,. \tag{9}$$

The single points may coincide with the target areas and may be scheduled for their visitation or may be used for the avoidance of no fly zones. Furthermore, the times to targets are a decision variable and they should be coupled with the itinerary points $\boldsymbol{\tau}_i$. We ignore this and we assume that the UAV moves at a constant speed. Thus, the times to targets are only a consequence of the itinerary scheduling.

The task planning problem for the surveillance mission of a UAV may be formally stated as the search of a surveillance itinerary $\boldsymbol{\tau}_{opt}$ such that

$$\boldsymbol{\tau}_{opt} = \underset{\boldsymbol{\tau}}{\operatorname{argmin}}\, T_\tau\,. \tag{10}$$

Each itinerary may be described by a structure with the following attributes: the sequence of the traversed waypoints; the temporal cost T_τ. The behaviour of the planning algorithm has been designed with an iterative approach. At every step, the target with the shortest time to reach (from the current planned position) is selected as a next candidate for the itinerary. If more targets have the same shortest time to reach, they are all selected and an alternative itinerary is processed for each of them.

A new itinerary is computed for every candidate target with the shortest time to reach by invoking the same algorithm with different inputs, which plans an itinerary starting from the current candidate target. The pseudo-code for the task planning algorithm is the following:

```
function task_planning(route_id, residual_scans, start_visit_times, M)
root ← null
do
  if root ≠ null
    route_id ← root.id
    start_visit_times ← root.start_visit_times
    residual_scans ← root.residual_scans
    root ← root.next
  end
  next_targets ← findTargetsWithShortT(start_visit_times)
  start ← last(route_id)
  for k=1 to size(next_targets)
   current_next_target ← next_targets(k)
   route_to_current_target ← Dijkstra(start, current_next_target, M)
   new_start_r_times ← update_visit_times(start_visit_times)
   new_route_id ← update_route_id(itineraries, route_id)
   update_itineraries(route_id, route_to_current_target)
   if residual_time > 0
     new_root.route_id ← new_route_id
     new_root.start_visit_times ← new_start_visit_times
     new_root.residual_scans ← residual_scans – 1
     if root = null
       new_root.next ← null
     else
       new_root.next ← root
    end
 while root ≠ null
end
```

The *route_id* variable is the identifier of the local route into the planned itineraries set and start_visit_times is the array of targets local visit times. If there are some residual scans (residual_scans) to schedule, the planning strategy schedules the execution of a child process (planning spawns), which will look for an itinerary starting from the current candidate (i.e., the local next target). The candidates are saved on a linked list implementing a stack. The *route_id* needs to be updated because the planning could overwrite the current itinerary or could allocate a new itinerary depending on the number of candidates for the spawn point. Besides, the itinerary update involves the update of the related costs. The route for the next target is processed by the Dijkstra algorithm, which operates according to the adjacency matrix M of the topological graph.

The adopted search strategy is:

- best-first, because every spawn selects the next candidate among the most promising targets (the ones with the shortest time to reach);
- breadth-first, because the graph structure is explored starting from the current root node and by inspecting its neighbour nodes (the targets with the shortest times to reach).

The function may be used also in case of re-planning by updating the matrix M.

VI. Test Results

We have conducted a series of tests to verify the correct implementation of the software. The main entities have been tested by creating, modifying and deleting records in different databases and also checking their correct visualization during the planning process. The verification of the analysis has required the creation of a number of flight plans to test the software behavior on different situations. In the following, two test cases are reported.

The first test and the related check results are depicted in Figure 6. The flight takes place in a segregated area (the azure line), the route (the yellow line) consists of eight waypoints, three of which are loiter. The no-fly zone is reported in red. There is a single GCS, but the link coverage is not visible because the area of operations is much less extensive. Two targets are associated to loiter waypoints. As shown by the right side of Figure 6, the flight plan validation fails on two aspects: the targets visibility and the boundaries overcome of segregated flight zone. The PFP analysis module is able to provide other graphic evidences: the non compliance with safety objectives, the issues on target visibility (highlighted red path) and the report on the fuel consumption.

In the second test, the flight plan of the first test has been modified in order to violate the data link coverage, the fuel consumption and the terrain obstacles on a linear target. The outcomes of the analysis are shown in Figure 7, which provides: the evidence that the flight plan is not feasible due to the overcoming of all the considered constraints; finally, the evidence of the link coverage analysis, the problems of visibility on the linear target (a river).

It may be noted that the previous test cases have been discussed in order to highlight the verification and the analysis capabilities of the PFP. Indeed, the checking phase of the PFP is able to verify the compliance of the computed flight plan with all the reference constraints and to guarantee the success of the designed mission. However, some of these constraints are previously taken into account by the Route Planner, which processes the actual flight plan in order to reach the prescribed waypoints by means of the selected aircraft (i.e., the related dynamic model). Clearly, the other constraints are not considered in the planning phase since they do not directly involve the trajectory elaboration. Thus, they may be only evaluated by means of the PFP checks.

As regards the route planning algorithm, some specific tests have been performed in order to exclusively solicit it and to evaluate the time required for the processing of a route plan. The Arduino MEGA 2560 has been used as testing platform. It is a microcontroller board, based on the ATmega2560 microcontroller, with 16 MHz clock speed, 8 kB of SRAM and 2560 kB of flash RAM. Different scenarios have been used, with an increasing number of targets. Table X reports the test results of the route planning algorithm.

TABLE X. Test Results of the Route Planning Algorithm

Number of Targets	Planning Time [μs]
5	90728
10	195136
15	299200
20	366048
25	427223

VII. Conclusion and Future Work

This work proposes some new perspectives on UAV preflight panning by pursuing the idea that a flight plan should not only guarantee a successful flight, but also a successful mission. It analyses the typical UAV surveillance missions where proximal sensing is requested and their main requirements. Here, the quality of images is a critical aspect and an approach for its measurement is implemented in the PFP as a criterion to validate the flight plan. Once assured the achievements of the mission targets, the inclusion of other kind of constraints such as the link coverage, the no fly zones avoidance, the evaluation of the emergency and termination routes, etc., guarantees the safety of the produced plan.

The integration of the task allocation optimization in the Route Planner module enables the capability to support the operator in the waypoints identification.

Future enhancement will consider the planning of the route of a fleet of UAVs jointly cooperating to perform a surveillance mission.

References

[1] C. Di Benedetto, D. Pascarella, G. Gigante, S. Luongo, A. Vozella, and F. Martone, "A Preflight Planner for Succesful Missions of Unmanned Aerial Vehicles," In: Proceedings of The Twelfth International Conference on Autonomic and Autonomous Systems (ICAS 2016), IARIA, Lisbon, Portugal, 26-30 June 2016, pp. 18—24.

[2] L. A. Ingham, "Considerations for a roadmap for the operations of Unmanned Aerial Vehicles (UAV) in South African Airspace," PhD thesis, Electrical and Electronic Engineering, Universiteit Stellenbosch University, 2008.

[3] C. Schumacher, P. R. Chandler, M. Pachter, and L. S. Pachter, "Optimization of Air Vehicles Operations Using Mixed-Integer Linear Programming," CMU/SEI-95-TR-021 ESC-TR-95-021, Air Force Research Laboratory, 2006.

[4] M. Quaritsch, "Agent-oriented programming," Elektrotechnik & Informationstechnik, vol. 127, no. 3, 2010, pp. 56–63.

[5] D. Gross, S. Rasmussen, P. Chandler, and G. Feitshans, "Cooperative operations in urban terrain (COUNTER)," Proceedings of Society of Photo-Optical Instrumentation Engineers Conference, Vol. 6249, 2006, pp. 1–11.

[6] M. Israel, "A UAV-based roe deer fawn detection system," International Archives of the Photogrammetry, Remote Sensing and Spatial Information Sciences, Volume XXXVIII-1/C22, 2011, ISPRS Zurich 2011 Workshop, 14-16 September 2011, Zurich, Switzerland, pp. 51–55.

[7] E. S. Barnadas, "Formal Mission Specification and Execution Mechanisms for Unmanned Aircraft Systems," PhD thesis, Department of Computer Architecture, Technical University of Catalonia, 2010.

[8] S. E. Kolitz and R. M. Beaton, "Overall System Concepts in Mission Planning," In: New Advances in Mission Planning and Rehearsal Systems. Vol. 192. AGARD Lecture Series. Neuilly Sur Seine, France: Advisory Group for Aerospace Research & Development, 1993.

[9] P. Brisset, A. Drouin, M. Gorraz, P. S. Huard, and J. Tyler, "The Paparazzi Solution," Proceedings of MAV (Micro Air Vehicles) 2006.

[10] DJI, Fly Safe, [Online], Available from http://www.dji.com/fly-safe [retrieved: 02, 2017].

[11] MikroKopter, MikroKopter Tool, [Online], Available from http://www.mikrokopter.de/ucwiki/MikroKopterTool [retrieved: 05, 2016].

[12] OpenPilot, [Online], Available from https://www.openpilot.org [retrieved: 05, 2016].

[13] Easy Map UAV, Specification, [Online], Available from http://www.easymapuav.com/specification [retrieved: 02, 2017].

[14] APM, Mission Planner Home, [Online], Available from http://planner.ardupilot.com [retrieved: 02, 2017].

[15] 3DR, Free Groun Station Application, [Online], Available from http://3dr.com/download_software [retrieved: 02, 2017].

[16] mdCockpit, UAV Control, [Online], Available from http://www.microdrones.com/en/products/software/mdcockpit/flight-planning [retrieved: 02, 2017].

[17] UAV Navigation, Visionair GCS Software, [Online], Available from http://www.uavnavigation.com/products/visionair-ground-control-station-software [retrieved: 02, 2017].

[18] UAV-EA, Mission Planner Autopilot Software, [Online], Available from http://uaveastafrica.wordpress.com/mission-planner-autopilot-software [retrieved: 02, 2017].

[19] Orbit Logic, UAV Planner, [Online], Available from http://www.orbitlogic.com/products/uav.php [retrieved: 02, 2017].

[20] MAVinci, MAVinci Desktop, [Online], Available from http://www.mavinci.de/en/completesys/desktop [retrieved: 02, 2017].

[21] FAS, Tactical Control Station (TCS), [Online], Available from http://fas.org/irp/program/collect/uav_tcs.htm [retrieved: 02, 2017].

[22] Micropilot, Micropilot Ground Control Station, [Online], Available from http://www.micropilot.com [retrieved: 02, 2017].

[23] SAGEM, SAGEM Mission Planning Systems, [Online], Available from http://www.sagem.com/aerospace/military-aircraft/mission-planning-systems [retrieved: 02, 2017].

[24] Menci Software, Photogrammetry Software, [Online], Available from http://www.menci.com [retrieved: 02, 2017].

[25] MoasicMill, EnsoMOSAIC photogrammetry software and hardware for aerial image processing, [Online], Available from http://www.ensomosaic.com [retrieved: 02, 2017].

[26] PIEnnering, Parallel Image Engineering, [Online], Available from http://www.pieneering.fi [retrieved: 02, 2017].

[27] Agisoft, Ahisoft PhotoScan, [Online], Available from http://www.agisoft.com [retrieved: 05, 2016].

[28] REDcatch, Photogrammetric Cloud Service, [Online], Available from http://www.redcatch.it [retrieved: 05, 2016].

[29] Agribotix, Agricultural Intelligence Drone-Enabled, [Online], Available from http://www.agribotix.com [retrieved: 05, 2016].

[30] Maps Made Easy, Aerial Map Processing & Hosting, [Online], Available from http://www.mapsmadeeasy.com [retrieved: 05, 2016].

[31] R. Reulke and A. Eckardt, "Image quality and image resolution," In 2013 Seventh International Conference on Sensing Technology (ICST), 2013, pp. 682-68.

[32] The National Imagery Interpretability Rating Scale (NIIRS), [Online], Available from http://ncap.org.uk/sites/default/files/NIIRS.pdf [retrieved: 05, 2016].

[33] S. T. Thurman and J. R. Fienup, "Analysis of the general image quality equation," Proceedings of SPIE, Vol. 6978, Visual Information Processing XVII, 2008.

[34] J. K. Lenstra and A. R. Kan, "Complexity of the vehicle routing and scheduling problems," Networks, Volume 11, Issue 2, 1981, pp. 221–227

[35] J. Giesbrecht, "Global Path Planning for Unmanned Ground Vehicles," Technical Memorandum DRDC Suffield TM 2004-272, Defence R&D Canada – Suffield, 2004.

Figure 6. Results of the first test on the PFP.

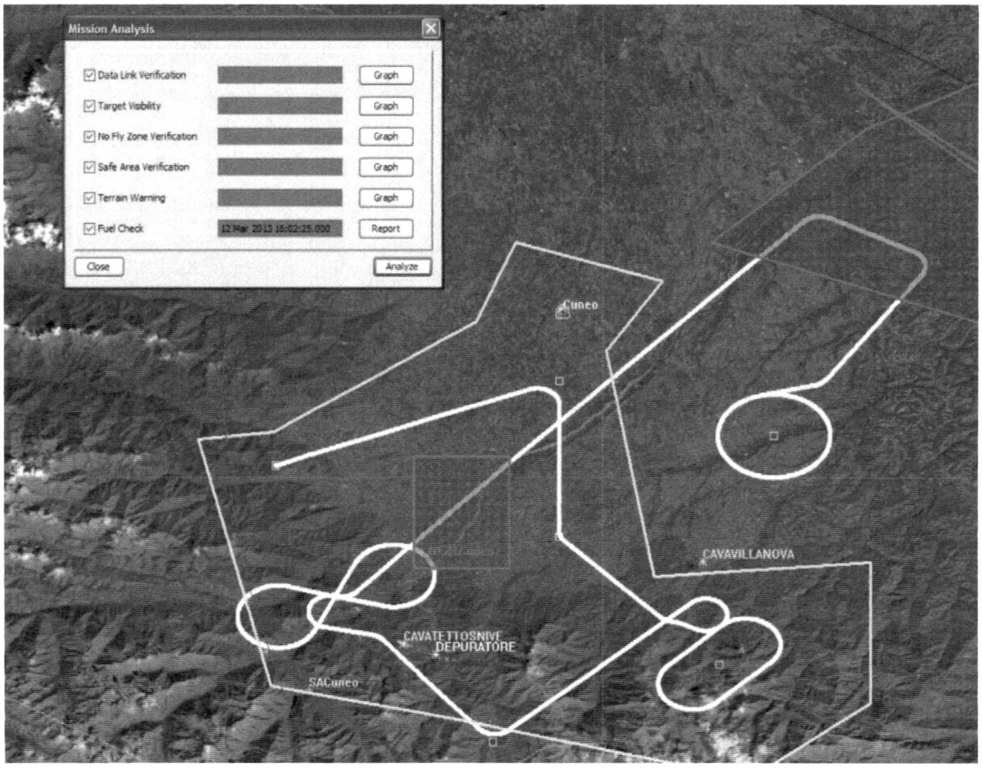

Figure 7. Results of the second test on the PFP.

Automated Infrastructure Management (AIM) Systems

Network Infrastructure Modeling and Systems Integration Following the ISO/IEC 18598/DIS Standards Specification

Mihaela Iridon
Cândea LLC for CommScope, Inc.
Dallas, TX, USA
e-mail: iridon.mihaela@gmail.com

Abstract— **Automated Infrastructure Management (AIM) systems are enterprise systems that provision a large number and variety of network infrastructure resources, including premises, organizational entities, and most importantly, all the telecommunication and connectivity assets. In 2016 the International Standards Organization released the ISO/IEC 18598 specifications that provide standardization and sensible guidelines for exposing data and features of AIM systems in order to facilitate integration with these systems. CommScope, the primary contributor in defining these standards, has implemented these specifications for their imVision system [1]. This paper elaborates primarily on the ISO-recommended infrastructure elements and how to design the resource models that represent them. It also discusses the layered architecture used to build CommScope's imVision AIM system, and briefly describes a possible integration scenario between two AIM systems. Additionally, this article intends to share design and technology-specific considerations, challenges, and solutions adopted by CommScope, so that they may be translated and implemented by other organizations that intend to build - or integrate with - an AIM system in general.**

Keywords-automated infrastructure management (AIM); system modeling; network infrastructure provisioning; data integration.

I. INTRODUCTION

Modeling network infrastructure elements (ports, modules, patch panels, servers, cables, circuits, etc.) and building effective network management systems is a rather challenging task due to the complexity and large variety of telecommunication assets [1] and vendor implementations. Such systems are also designed to model and automatically detect physical connectivity changes and manage infrastructure and data exchange with other systems.

Until recently, no common representation of such elements existed, so that network infrastructure management providers defined their own proprietary models. For this reason, the task of integrating with these systems posed a high degree of complexity, forcing integrators to define highly specialized solutions and models, and potentially unwieldy model and data transformations to enable compatibility between the integrating systems.

CommScope has identified the stringent need to create a unified representation of telecommunication assets to help build and integrate with Automated Infrastructure Management (AIM) systems and worked with the International Standards Organization towards achieving this goal. The result of this collaboration was the ISO/IEC 18598 standard [2], a set of guidelines for modeling and provisioning AIM systems. These specifications were captured and extended in [1] and are also the main focus of this paper, by including modeling details that bring more clarity, add context, and provide further guidelines to the information described in the standards document. Identifying and organizing AIM system's assets in a logical and structured fashion allows for an efficient access and management of all the resources administered by the system.

This paper is organized around six sections as follows.

Section II presents several resource models from the perspective of designing RESTful services [3] [4] [5], with focus on the telecommunication assets, as proposed and used by CommScope's imVision API. This section also presents a solution for handling a large variety of hardware devices while avoiding the need for an equally large number of URIs for accessing these resources.

Section III discusses system architecture, patterns and design-specific details, elaborating on a few practical challenges, followed by noteworthy technology and implementation aspects captured in Section IV.

Section V examines options for integrating two or more AIM systems, specifically two CommScope AIM systems: imVision and the Quareo Middleware API. A high-level solution employing a variant of the Normalizer integration pattern is presented along with a few data integration and data layer modeling objectives.

Finally, Section VI attempts to join and summarize the main ideas and analysis points presented in this paper.

II. AIM SYSTEM DOMAIN ANALYSIS AND RESOURCE MODELING

As with every software system – and more so with enterprise-level applications – domain modeling is of vital importance as it helps define, organize, and understand the business domain, facilitating the translation of requirements into a suitable design [6]. However, dedicated models can and should be designed for the various layers of a system's architecture [7]. Defining clean boundaries between the system's domain and the integration models [8] [9] as well as ensuring the stability of these models (via versioning) are imperative requirements for building robust and extensible systems, while allowing the domain models – both structural and behavioral – to evolve independently [3] [10].

The specification of the AIM resource model described here employed various design and implementation paradigms. However, all concrete resource types exposed by the system are simple POCOs (Plain Old CLR Objects for the .NET platform) or POJOs (Plain Old Java Objects for the Java EE platform). These models represent merely *data containers* that do not encapsulate any behavior whatsoever. Functional attributes are specific to the physical entities being modeled and are exposed only from the perspective of the system's connectivity they describe. The purpose of the AIM model described here and in [1] is to define a common understanding of the data that can be exchanged with an AIM system while any specific behavior around these data elements is left to the implementation details of the particular system itself.

As opposed to the design principles of stateful services (such as SOAP and XML-RPC-based web services) – where functional features and processes take center stage while data contracts are just means to help model those processes [9] [7], in RESTful services the spotlight is distinctly set on the transport protocol and entities that characterize the business domain. These two elements follow the specifications of Level 0 and 1, respectively, of the RESTful maturity model [11] [5]. The resources modeled by a given system also define the service endpoints (or URIs), while the operations exposed by these services are simple, few, and standardized (i.e., the HTTP verbs required by Level 2: GET, POST, PUT, DELETE, etc.) [4] [5]. Nonetheless, in both cases, a sound design approach (as with any software design activity in general) is to remain technology-agnostic [6] [8] [7].

A. *Resource Categories Overview and Classification*

The entities proposed in the Standards document [1] are categorized by the sub-domain that they describe as well as their composability features. This classification helps define a model that aligns well with the concept of separation of concerns (SoC), allowing common features among similar entities to be shared effectively, with increased testability and reliability.

The ISO/IEC Standards document proposes the classification of resources shown in Table I. While some elements listed here may not be germane to all AIM systems, the Standards document intends to capture and categorize *all elements* that could be modeled by such a system.

TABLE I. RESOURCE CATEGORIES AND CONCRETE TYPES

PREMISES	Geographic Area, Zone, Campus, Building, Floor, Room
CONTAINERS	Cabinets, Racks, Frames
TELECOM ASSETS	Closures, Network Devices, Patch Panels, Modules, Ports, Cables, Cords
CONNECTIVITY ASSETS	Circuits, Connections
ORGANIZATIONAL	Organization, Cost Center, Department, Team, Person
NOTIFICATIONS	Event, Alarm
ACTIVITIES	Work Order, Work Order Task

It also proposes a common terminology for these categories so that from an integration perspective there is no ambiguity in terms of what these assets or entities represent, where they fit within an AIM system, and what their purpose is. It defines, at a high-level, the ubiquitous integration language by providing a clear description and classification of the main elements of an AIM system.

This paper analyzes these recommendations, materializes them into actual design artifacts – following the exact nomenclature used in the Standards document, and proposes a general-purpose layered architecture for the RESTful AIM API system while addressing a few concerns regarding AIM systems integration in general.

B. *Common Model Abstractions*

Since all resources share some basic properties, such as name, identifier, description, category, actual type (that identifies the physical hardware components associated with this resource instance), and parent ID, it is a natural choice to model these common details via basic inheritance, as shown in Figure 1. In order to support a variety of resource identifier types, e.g., Globally Unique Identifier (GUID), integer, string, etc., the `ResourceBase` class is modeled as a generic type with the resource and parent identifier parameterized by the generic type `TId`.

Of particular interest are *telecommunication assets* – the core entities in all AIM systems – a class of resource types which all must realize the `IAsset` marker interface – as proposed in [1] and in this paper.

C. *Designing the AIM Resource Models*

AIM systems are comprised of elements that fall into seven main categories. The modeling of these elements will be described following this standard classification which also aligns with the way these entities are organized into a compositional hierarchy; this grouping also defines the granularity and association relationship among them.

1) *Premise Elements*

A given organization's network infrastructure can be geographically distributed across multiple cities, campuses, and/or buildings, while being grouped under one or more sites – logical containers for everything that could host any type of infrastructure element. At the top of the infrastructure-modeling hierarchy, there are premises, which model location at various degrees of detail: from geographic areas and campuses to floors and rooms. Composition rules or restrictions for these elements may be modeled via generic type constraints, unless these rules are not enforced by a given system. Figure 2 shows the standards-defined premise entities, their primary properties, and the relationships between them.

2) *Telecom Connectivity Elements*

The main assets of a network infrastructure are its telecommunication resources, from container elements, such as racks and cabinets, to switches and servers, network-devices (e.g., computers, phones, printers, cameras, etc.), patch panels, modules, ports, and circuits that connect ports via cables and cords.

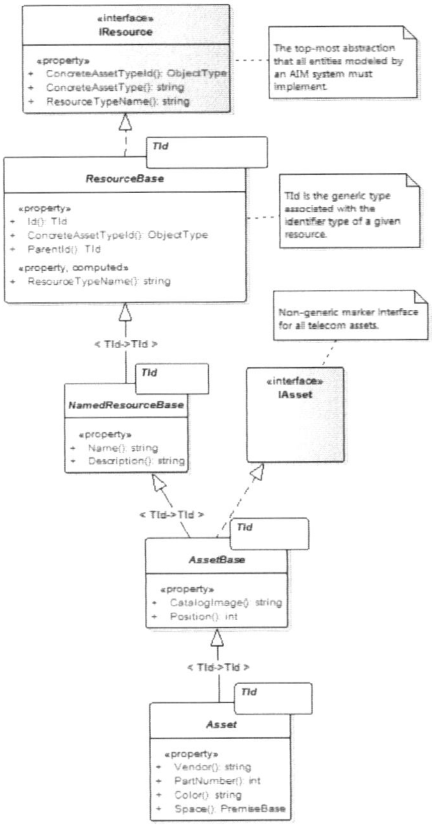

Figure 1. Resource Base Models

The diagram included in Figure 3 shows these asset categories modeled via inheritance, with all assets realizing the **IAsset** marker interface. As is the case for CommScope's imVision system, the type of the unique identifier for all resources is an integer; hence, all resource data types will be closing the generic type **TId** of the base class to **int**: **ResourceBase<int>**. This way, the RESTful API will expose these AIM Standards-compliant data types in a technology- and implementation-agnostic way that reflects the actual structure of the elements, while generics and inheritance remain transparent to integrators, regardless of the serialization format used (JSON, XML, SOAP). This fact is illustrated in Figure 5, which shows a sample Rack instance serialized using JSON. In addition to the elements shown in Figure 3 that support a persistent representation of the data center's telecom assets, there are those that describe the physical connectivity (i.e., circuits): cables, connectors, and cords. They play a chief role in defining the connectivity dynamics of the system. Figure 4 shows the primary resources for modeling this aspect of an AIM system.

3) Organizational Elements

Large AIM systems typically provision entities that describe the organization responsible for maintaining and administering the networking infrastructure. For example, tasks around the management of connectivity between panels and modules is usually represented by work orders and tasks which, in turn, are assigned to technicians.

4) System Notifications and Human Activity Elements

Hardware components of AIM systems, e.g., controllers, discoverable/intelligent patch panels and in some instances intelligent cords (e.g., CommScope's Quareo system) allow continuous/automatic synchronization of the hardware state with the logical representation of the hardware components.

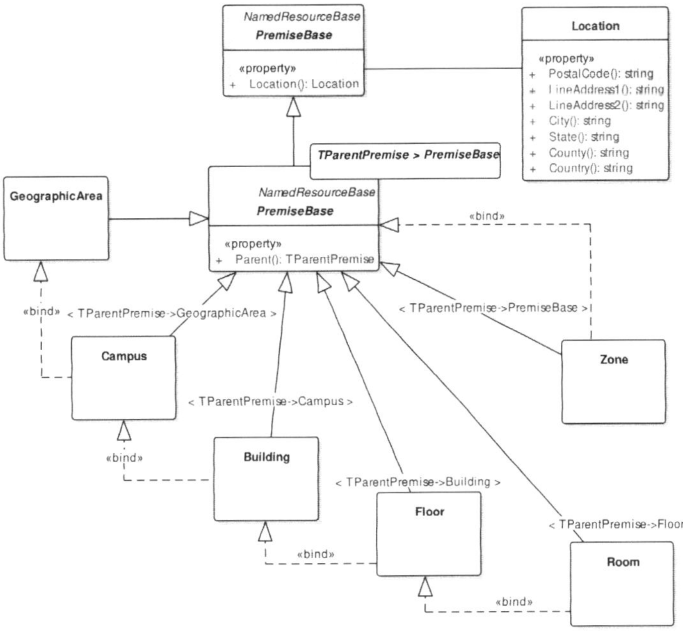

Figure 2. Premise Resource Models

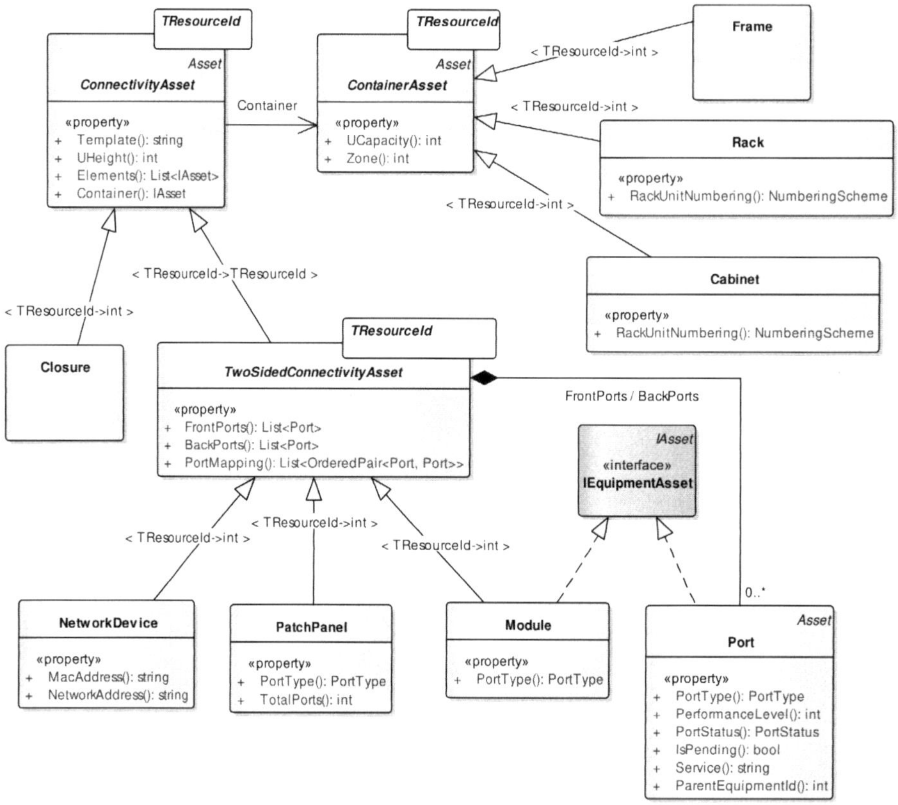

Figure 3. Telecommunication Assets Resource Models

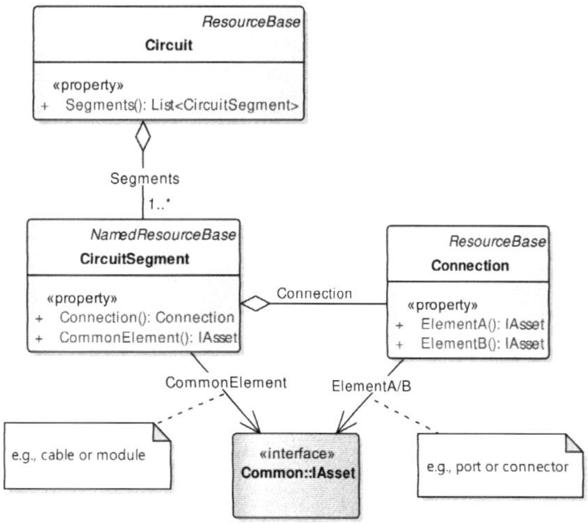

Figure 4. Connectivity Models


```
{
    "rackUnitNumbering": 140002,
    "uCapacity": 46,
    "zone": 1,
    "position": 2,
    "name": "Rack A123",
    "description": "Rack hosting instaPATCH panels",
    "concreteAssetType": "Rack (7 ft - 45U)",
    "concreteAssetTypeId": 10,
    "parentId": 26
}
```


Figure 5. A JSON Representation of a Rack Resource

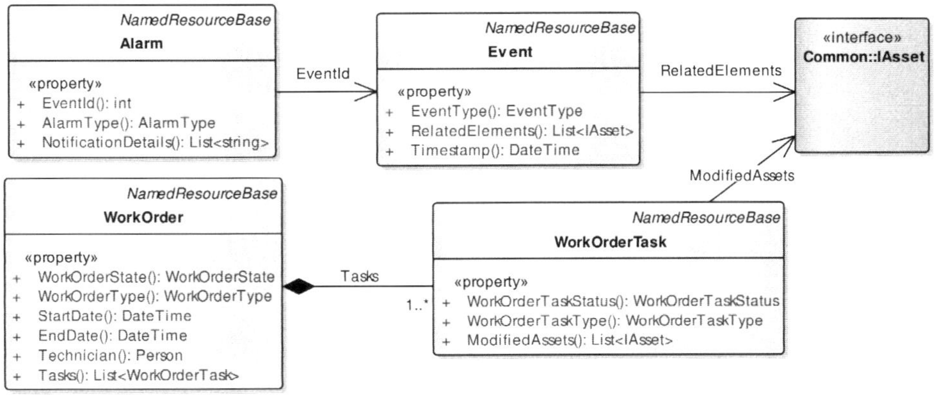

Figure 6. Notification and Activity Models

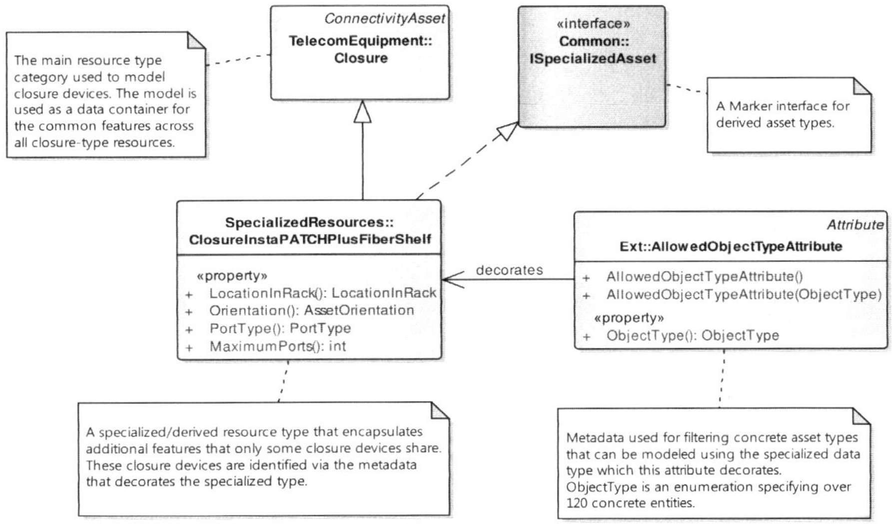

Figure 7. A Sample of a Specialized Closure with Additional Properties

This synchronization is facilitated by the concept of events and alarms that are first generated by controllers (**Alarm**) and then sent for processing by the management software (**Event**). These notification resource types are supported by the AIM Standards and are modeled as shown in Figure 6. This also includes activities that technicians must carry out, such as establishing connections between assets, activities that in turn trigger alarms and events, or are created as a reaction to system-generated events.

D. Modeling Large Varieties of Hardware Devices

The telecom asset model presented in Figure 3 depict the categories that define all or most physical devices seen in network infrastructure. However, actual hardware components have specialized features that are vendor-specific or that describe some essential functionality that the components provide. Such specialized attributes – like the ones shown in Figure 7 for a specific type of Closure – must be incorporated in the model for supporting the Add (POST) and Update (PUT) functionality of the RESTful services that expose these objects to the integrators. The main challenge then is: how to support such a large variety of hardware devices without having to expose too many different service endpoints, one for each of these specialized types?

According to the Richardson Maturity Model for REST APIs [11] – which breaks down the principal ingredients of a REST approach into three steps – Level 1 requires that the API be able to distinguish between different resources via URIs; i.e., for a given resource type there exists a distinct service endpoint to where HTTP requests are directed. For querying data using HTTP GET, we can easily envision a service endpoint for a given resource *category* – as per the models described above. For example, there will be one URI for modules, one for closures, one for patch panels, etc. However, when creating new assets, one must specify which *concrete* entity or device type should be created, and for this, the device-specific data must be provided. Since these supplementary features are not intrinsic to all objects that belong to that category, specialized models must be created – e.g., as *derived* types inheriting from the category models that encapsulate all relevant device-specific features.

For example, one of CommScope's connectivity products that falls under the category of Closures is the SYSTIMAX 360™ Ultra High Density Port Replication Fiber Shelf, 1U, with three InstaPATCH® 360 Ultra High Density Port Replication Modules [12] – a connectivity solution for high-density data centers that provides greater capacity in a smaller, more compact footprint. These closures come in a variety of configurations and aside from the common closure attributes (position, elements, capacity, etc.) other properties are relevant from a provisioning, connectivity, and circuit tracing perspective. Such properties include Orientation of the sub-modules, Location in Rack, Maximum Ports, and Port Type, as shown in the class diagram in Figure 7.

An alternative to using an inheritance model would be to create distinct types for each individual physical component that could be provisioned by the AIM system, but given the significant overlap of common features they can be consolidated and encapsulated in such a way that derived specialized models can be employed in order to increase code reusability, testability, and maintainability. The distinction between the various hardware components that map to the same specialized type can be managed, for example, via custom metadata associated with that data type (e.g., the **AllowedObjectTypeAttribute** in Figure 7).

E. Benefits of the Proposed Model

The models proposed in this paper are closely following the categories and elements outlined in the ISO/IEC standards. However, given the structural models presented here and taking advantage of certain technology-specific constructs and frameworks, there are some notable advantages resulting from the design of these models, related to their usage, and the integration capabilities for the services that expose them, with direct impact on performance, maintainability, testability, and extensibility.

✓ *Simplified URI scheme based on resource categories rather than specialized resource types.* This allows clients to access classes or categories of resources rather than having to be aware of - and invoke - a large number of URIs dictated by the large variety of hardware devices modeled. This also confers the API a high degree of stability, consistency, and extensibility even when the system is enhanced to provision new hardware devices.

✓ *Reduced chattiness between client application and services when querying resources* (**GET**). This benefit is directly related to the URI scheme mentioned above, since a single HTTP request can retrieve all resources of that type (applying the Liskov substitution principle [13]), even when multiple sub-types exist.

✓ *Reduced chattiness between client application and services when creating complex entities* (**POST**) *by supporting composite resources.* In some cases, the hardware device construction itself requires the API to support creating a resource along with its children in a single step (see Section IV.B for details). Child elements can be specified as part of the main resource or they can be omitted altogether while custom composition and validation frameworks resolve the missing sub-resources based on predefined rules.

Table II captures metrics regarding the request counts and sizes for creating a **PatchPanel** object.

✓ *Ample opportunity for automation when creating and validating composite resources.* Aside from considerably reducing the size of the request body given the option to omit child elements when adding new entities - as is the case for the imVision API – by employing frameworks that support metadata-driven automation, the API will ensure that the generated resource object reflects a valid hardware entity, with all the required sub-elements.

For the API consumers, this reduces the burden of knowing all the fine details about how these entities are composed and constructed. In some cases, the number of child elements to be created in the process depends on properties that the main resource may expose (e.g., **TotalPorts**) – which client applications will have to specify if the corresponding property is marked as [**Required**].

✓ *Extensible model as new hardware devices are introduced.* New models can easily be added to the existing specialized resources or as a new subtype. The interface for querying the data (**GET**) will not change. Adding/updating resources follows the Open/Closed principle [13] such that new types, properties, and rules can be added/extended without changing the already defined ones, thus ensuring contract stability.

TABLE II. POST REQUEST METRICS FOR QUATTRO PANEL (A PATCHPANEL RESOURCE)

Metric	Scenario	Value
Number of POST Requests	Without Support for Composite Resources	**31**: 1 for the Panel, 6 for the child Modules, and 6x4 for the ports
	With Support for Composite Resources	**1**: a single request for the Panel with its Modules (under **Elements**), with each Module being itself a composite resource containing 4 ports each, specified under the **FrontPorts** property of each Module
POST Request Body Size	With Explicit Children Included	21,449 bytes
	With No Children Specified (i.e., relying on the Framework to populate default elements)	572 bytes

III. A Proposed Layered Architecture for AIM API Integration Services

A. *Adding Integration Capabilities to an AIM System*

As per the Standards document guidelines [2], the AIM Systems should follow either an HTTP SOAP or a RESTful service design. Regardless of the service interface choice, there are several options for designing the overall AIM system. A common yet robust architectural style for software systems is the layered architecture [7] [8], which advocates a logical grouping of components into layers and ensuring that the communication between components is allowed only between adjacent or neighboring layers. Moreover, following SOLID design principles [13], this interaction takes place via interfaces, allowing for a loosely coupled system [14], easy to maintain, test, and extend. This will also enable the use of dependency injection (DI) or Inversion of Control (IoC) technologies such as Microsoft's Unity and MEF, or any other DI/IoC containers, to create a modular, testable, and coherent design [15].

CommScope's imVision system was built as a standalone web-based application, to be deployed at the customer's site, along with its own database and various middleware services that enable the communication between the hardware and the application. Relying on the current system's database, the RESTful Services were added as an integration point onto the existing system. The layered design of this new sub-system is shown in Figure 8 with the core component – the resource model discussed earlier – shown as part of the domain layer. The system also utilizes (to a limited extent) a few components from the legacy imVision system that encapsulate reusable logic. The diagram shows the actual design used for CommScope's imVision system.

Several framework components were used, most notably the *Validation* component, which contains the domain rules that specify the logic for creating and composing the various entities exposed by the API. These rules constitute the core module upon which the POST functionality relies. Along with the resource composition and validation engines, they constitute in fact a highly-specialized rule-based system that makes extensive use of several design and enterprise integration patterns that will be cataloged next.

B. *Patterns and Design Principles*

The various patterns and principles [8] [13] [14] employed throughout the design and implementation of the imVision API system are summarized in Table III. The automation capabilities built into imVision API mentioned earlier, that support creating composite object hierarchies, are a direct realization of the Content Enricher integration pattern used together with the Builder, Composite, and Specification software design patterns. From a messaging perspective, all requests are synchronous and only authorized users (Claim Check pattern) are allowed to access the API.

Design principles such as IoC/DI have been heavily used to deploy concrete implementation components (e.g., repositories, data access, etc.) to various layers of the application.

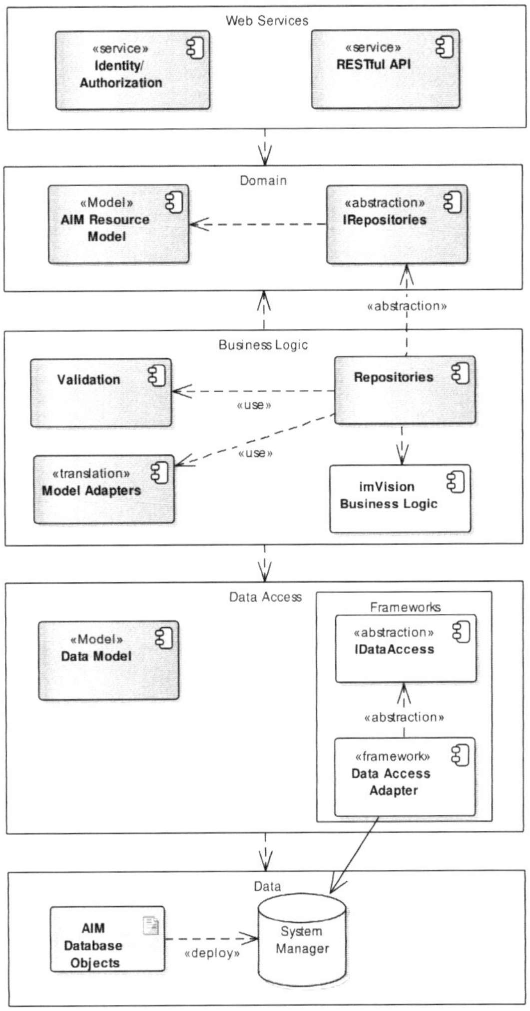

Figure 8. The Layered Architecture of the imVision AIM API

TABLE III. Design Patterns and Principles Employed

Design Patterns		
Type	***Category***	***Pattern Name***
Design Patterns	Creational	Abstract Factory, Builder, Singleton, Lazy Initialization
	Structural	Front Controller, Composite, Adapter
	Behavioral	Template Method, Specification
Enterprise Application Patterns	Domain Logic	Domain Model, Service Layer
	Data Source Architectural	Data Mapper
	Object-Relational Behavioral	Unit of Work
	Object-Relational Metadata Mapping	Repository

	Web Presentation	Front Controller
	Distribution Patterns	Data Transfer Object (DTO)
	Base Patterns	Layer Supertype, Separated Interface
Enterprise Integration Patterns	Messaging Channels	Point-to-Point Channel Adapter
	Message Construction	Request-Reply
	Message Transformation	Content Enricher Content Filter Claim Check Canonical Data Model
	Composed Messaging	Synchronous (Web Services)
Design Principles		
SOLID Design Principles	**S**ingle Responsibility Principle (SRP) **O**pen/Closed **I**nterface Segregation **L**iskov Substitution (in conjunction with co- and contra-variance of generic types in .NET) **D**ependency Inversion (Data Access and Repositories are injected using MEF and Unity)	

IV. A Few Challenges and Solutions

This section captures a few interesting aspects that surfaced during the design and implementation of the API.

A. *Handling POST Requests for Large Numbers of Specialized Resource Types with Few URIs*

Simplified URI schemes have the benefit of providing a clean interface to consumers, without having to introduce a myriad of URIs, as would be the case of one URI per actual hardware device supported by the AIM system. The different representations of these resources are grouped by category, while specific details are handled using *custom* JSON *deserialization* behavior injected in the HTTP transport pipeline [3] [5]. Since all resources must specify the concrete entity type they represent (under the `ConcreteAssetTypeId` property), the custom deserialization framework can easily create instances of the *specialized* resource types based on this property, and pass them to the appropriate controller (one per URI/resource *category*) for handling.

The impact on performance is negligible given the use of a lookup dictionary mapping asset type ID to resource type, which is created only once (per app pool lifecycle) based on *metadata* defined on the model. Even if new specialized resource types are added, the lookup table will automatically be updated at the time the application pool is (re)started.

For example, a "360 iPatch Ultra High Density Fiber Shelf (2U)" and a "360 iPatch Modular Evolve Angled (24-Port)" [12] – two hardware devices that map to two different specialized types in the imVision API resource model, are both resources of type `PatchPanel`. Therefore, a POST request to create either of these will be sent to the same URI: `http://[host:port/app/]PatchPanels`.

This means that the same service components (controller and repository – and even stored procedure) will be able to handle either request but the API would also be aware of the distinction between these two different object instances, as created by the custom deserialization component.

B. *Adding Support for Composite Resources*

Hardware components are built as composite devices, containing child elements, which in turn contain sub-child entities. For example, the Quattro Panel contains six Copper Modules with each module containing exactly four Quattro Panel Ports. To realize these hardware-driven requirements and avoiding multiple POST requests, while preserving the integrity and correctness of the device representation, a rule-based composition representation model was used in conjunction with the Builder design pattern applied recursively down the object hierarchy. The composition rules for the Quattro Panel and its module sub-elements are shown in Figure 9 (using C#.NET). The strings represent optional name *prefixes* for the child elements.

C. *A Functional and Rule-Based Approach for Default Initializations and Validations of Resources*

Given the considerable number of specialized resources to be supported by CommScope's imVision API and the even larger number of business rules regarding the initialization and validation of these entities, a functional approach was adopted. This rendered the validation engine into a rule-based system: there are *composition rules*, default *initialization rules*, and *validation rules* – which apply to both simple as well as complex properties that define a resource. Following the same example of Quattro Panel used earlier, an important requirement for creating such resources is the labeling of ports and their positions, which must be continuous across all six modules of the panel.

Figure 10 shows a snapshot of the rules defined for this type of asset. Figure 10 (a) shows the initialization rules whereas Figure 10 (b) shows a few of the validation rules. In both cases, the programming constructs like the ones shown make heavy use of lambda expressions as supported by the functional capabilities built into the C#.NET programming language [16], demonstrating the functional implementation approach adopted for the imVision AIM API.

```
//...
{ ObjectType.QuattroPanel24Port, new CompositionDetail<ModuleCopperModule, int, ModuleValidator>(ObjectType.CopperModule, "Module", 6) },
//...
{ ObjectType.CopperModule, new CompositionDetail<PortBasicPort, int, PortValidator>(ObjectType.QuattroPanelPort, "Port", 4) },
//...
```

Figure 9. Composition Rules for Quattro Panel and Its Child Elements of Type Copper Module

```
result[ObjectType.QuattroPanel24Port] = new Lazy<Dictionary<string, IPropertyInitDetail>>(() =>
        new Dictionary<string, IPropertyInitDetail>
        {
          [nameof(PatchPanel.UHeight)] = new PropertyInitDetail<int>(() => 1),
          [nameof(PatchPanel.TotalPorts)] = new PropertyInitDetail<int>(() => 24),
          [nameof(PatchPanel.PortType)] = new PropertyInitDetail<PortType>(() => PortType.Rj45),
          [nameof(PatchPanel.Elements)] =
            new PropertyInitDetail<IEnumerable<IAsset>, PatchPanel>((r) =>
            DefaultElementsFactory.GenerateElements(ObjectType.QuattroPanel24Port,
            6, r, new List<Action<Module, PatchPanel>>
            {
              (module, panel) => module.FrontPorts.ForEach(x =>
              {
                x.Name = ((module.Position - 1)*4 + x.Position).ToString("00");
                x.Position = ((module.Position - 1)*4 + x.Position);
              }),
            })),
        });
```

Figure 10. (a) Default Initialization Rules Sample

```
result[ObjectType.QuattroPanel24Port] = new List<IValidationRule>
{
  new ValidationRule<PatchPanelPreTermCopperPanel>(nameof(PatchPanelPreTermCopperPanel.TotalPorts),
                  x => x.TotalPorts == 24, "Total ports must be equal to 24."),
  new ValidationRule<PatchPanelPreTermCopperPanel>(nameof(PatchPanelPreTermCopperPanel.PortType),
                  x => x.PortType == PortType.Rj45),
  new ValidationRule<PatchPanelPreTermCopperPanel>(nameof(PatchPanelPreTermCopperPanel.Elements),
                  x => x.Elements != null && x.Elements.Count() > 1 && x.Elements.Count() <= 6,
                  "Invalid ELements Count: There must be at least one but no more than 6 modules."),
  new ValidationRule<PatchPanel>(nameof(PatchPanel.Elements),
                  x => x.Elements.OfType<ModuleCopperModule>().Select(
                        y => y.Position).Distinct().Count() == x.Elements.Count,
                  "Invalid Module Positions"), //distinct positions of modules validation
  new ValidationRule<PatchPanel>(nameof(PatchPanel.Elements),
                  x => x.Elements.OfType<ModuleCopperModule>().SelectMany(
                        y => y.FrontPorts.Select(z => z.Name)).Distinct().Count() == x.Elements.Count * 4,
                  "Non-distinct port names."),
  //more rules ...
};
```

Figure 10. (b) Validation Rules Sample

Among some of the reasons worth mentioning for embracing the functional model are:

- ✓ a more robust, concise, reusable, and testable code
- ✓ minimizing side effects from object state management and concurrency.

Explicit goal specification – central to the functional programming paradigm – confers *clarity* and *brevity* to the rule definitions, as seen in the code samples provided here.

V. Integration with Other AIM Systems

As stated in the introduction, one of the main goals of the API is to allow easy integration between AIM systems. This section presents a theoretical approach to such an integration.

A. *Quareo Middleware API*

CommScope's Quareo physical layer management solution is a real-time physical connectivity provisioning system with a dual hardware and software implementation [17]. Using an eventing mechanism, Quareo provides immediate feedback on all network connection elements, while enabling technicians to efficiently and accurately respond to address a variety of infrastructure connectivity concerns and responsibilities.

Originally, Quareo was developed under one of TE Connectivity's units – which was acquired by CommScope in 2015. Now, two similar yet different systems provide comparable services to CommScope's clients and, not surprisingly, the need to unify the two systems' functionality of provisioning managed connectivity data has become a recognized necessity and focus for the company.

The Quareo Middleware API exposes networking infrastructure elements via a RESTful API but the focus is exclusively on telecom assets. It is also using a more generic approach to modeling these elements than does imVision.

The next sub-section briefly describes the main resource models as designed and implemented for the Quareo system.

B. *Quareo Resource Models*

A more generic representation of telecom assets makes the API more flexible and extensible. However, this puts a burden on the model itself to allow for this generalization – requiring potentially a more complex *mapping* of concrete assets to generic elements which may or may not be able to describe all the attributes of the assets in a straightforward and strongly-typed fashion. Additional complexities may arise on the consumer end; integrators must have sufficient detail as of how to restore specialized hardware information from the generalized representation and how new hardware elements will be represented by the system.

From a high-level perspective, some of the main entities of the resource model employed by the Quareo Middleware API are shown in Figure 11. Since the hardware assets that the middleware provisions feature the Connection Point Identification (CPID) technology [18], all assets (including the most granular of elements, i.e., `Port`) inherit from the base class `CpidComponent`, which encapsulates a large array of hardware-specific attributes – modeled as simple or complex types, such as color, connector type, copper/fiber cable category/rating/polarity, manufacturer Id, hardware revision, insertion count, catalog, etc.

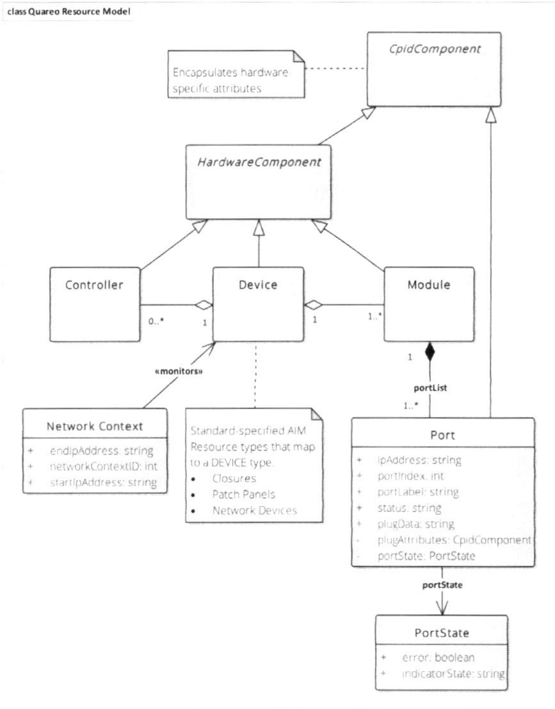

Figure 11. Simplified View of Quareo's Telecom Assets Resource Model

C. *AIM Software Systems Integration Scenarios*

1) One-way Integration

Assuming one of the systems as the system-of-record, or primary infrastructure provisioning system, a one-way integration solution could be devised such that telecom assets provisioned by the secondary system can be retrieved via RESTful GET API requests by the designated primary system. Consequently, the infrastructure elements managed by the secondary system become visible to the primary system. Given that imVision currently provisions more than just the telecom assets, it would be an obvious choice for being considered as the primary system in this proposed integration solution. This would include having its resource model become the canonical model for all data exchange – as described later.

Pulling the data managed exclusively by Quareo into imVision can either be (a) a one-time operation - which would then require managing connectivity via imVision only, or (b) a periodic process which would allow the Quareo system to continue managing telecom assets while imVision would only be allowed to report on these assets.

Figure 12 shows the general integration scenario and the data flow between these two systems.

2) Bidirectional Integration

If a unified collection of networking resources is to be managed by more than one software system, assuming that each system enables some highly-specialized set of features that would be prohibitively expensive to migrate to the other system, then data – and (to a lesser extent) functional – integration concerns would be applicable at both ends. If only two systems are considered, then a direct point-to-point integration mechanism via the already exposed integration APIs is possible and recommended.

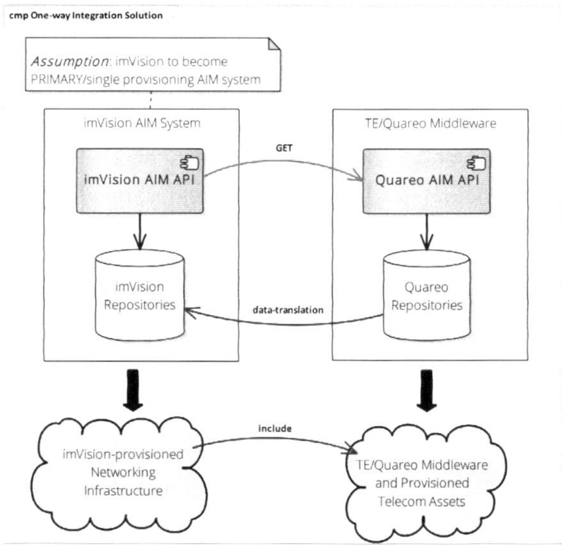

Figure 12. A Straightforward One-Way Integration Scenario

However, adding even one more system to the mix, an integration infrastructure would be required in order to reduce complexity and isolate the integration responsibilities and models. A similar problem, where multiple business domains required both data and functional integration across the enterprise, has been presented and discussed in [19]. For the CommScope integration scenario, a comparable framework based on messaging and eventing communication mechanisms would also be appropriate, especially given the real-time nature of Quareo's solution as opposed to the offline update features of imVision.

D. Data Integration Approach and Challenges

The following discussion assumes the adoption of the first integration option, where imVision system will be provisioning the entire infrastructure using a persistent representation of all the telecom assets, as well as the premise, organizational, and container elements.

1) Data Model Refactoring

In order to support specialized hardware attributes featured by the CPID technology specific to Quareo [18], the data layer currently used to model assets managed by the imVision system must be refactored and enhanced accordingly. For example, Table IV shows the additional Quareo attributes that were extended to the imVision data model for Port and Cable assets. They can also be seen in the Entity Relationship Diagram (ERD) in Figure 13, which defines these attributes under the two corresponding tables.

As part of a comprehensive architectural effort, a set of data model updates were designed and recommended. Figure 13 highlights a *sample* output of such data model refactoring – more precisely, the models corresponding to the main asset connectivity elements (ports and cables).

TABLE IV. QUAREO-SPECIFIC CABLE AND PORT ATTRIBUTES

Entity	*Required Attributes*
Port Detail	Color Insertion Count Indicator State Is Managed
Cable Detail	Color Hardware Revision Serial Number Country of Manufacture Date of Manufacture Manufacturer Part Id Material Tracking Number

While the data models capture all relevant attributes of the hardware assets that they represent, other essential data layer design requirements and concerns were addressed as part of this effort. To provide a few pointers as to what this effort entailed, the list below highlights some of the data layer refactoring tasks that were undertaken:

- ✓ Appropriate entity relationship modeling (realized by adding the missing foreign keys)
- ✓ Data integrity and referential integrity (also done via foreign keys and unique constraints)
- ✓ Careful data type selection/updates
- ✓ Lookup data specification for modeling essential domain attributes
- ✓ Normalization and vertical partitioning of tables to reduce data redundancy among entities that share similar attributes
- ✓ Refactoring of functions and procedures; moving stored procedure implementations to table-valued functions where no data mutation was involved
- ✓ Proper schema partitioning, associations and object renaming, while creating synonyms for these objects in order to reduce the impact on the application layer
- ✓ Data cleansing required to remove *existing* invalid data or data that would not conform to the added constraints.

2) Representation and Identification of Telecom Assets

Both AIM systems use integer-valued surrogate keys to identify the provisioned entities but – in order to migrate data from one system to the other, or to continuously exchange data between the two – it is imperative to identify attributes that uniquely identify concrete hardware asset types. Fortunately, the ISO/IEC standards document has accounted for such *natural* keys based on serial numbers, manufacturer details, and component identifiers. Since these attributes have been included into the various models (data, domain, resource), an integration solution would no longer require a resolution framework where cross-domain asset identifiers would be stored and looked up. Serial numbers and perhaps manufacturing data will represent the business domain identifiers that integration adapters on both sides of the integration boundary would use when adding, updating and deleting asset data from the corresponding repositories.

However, model translators/adapters are required on both sides since the asset representations are quite different, but not irreconcilable – given the semantics imposed by the Standards specification and the extent to which they are implemented by each system participating in the integration.

To alleviate the constant need for updating these adapter components whenever new hardware must be handled by the AIM systems, extensible models and intelligent mapping frameworks could be created; ideally, these would be encapsulated under distributable and reusable model brokers that are capable of bi-directional data translation and consistent asset type resolution.

Schematically, this brokered adaptive integration layer would look similar to the one depicted in Figure 14. The AIM systems will not depend directly on each other's asset representation but rather delegate the translation task to the adapter component.

Given that only two systems are involved in the message exchange, there is no need for designing a common model to normalize the two representations of assets. However, to facilitate future integration needs, it would be beneficial to designate the more comprehensive model as the *canonical representation* of telecom assets, expose it to all integrating systems, and use it as the *ubiquitous integration language* across the enterprise, analogous to the approach described in [19], following a pattern quite similar to the *Normalizer* messaging EIP (Enterprise Integration Pattern) [14].

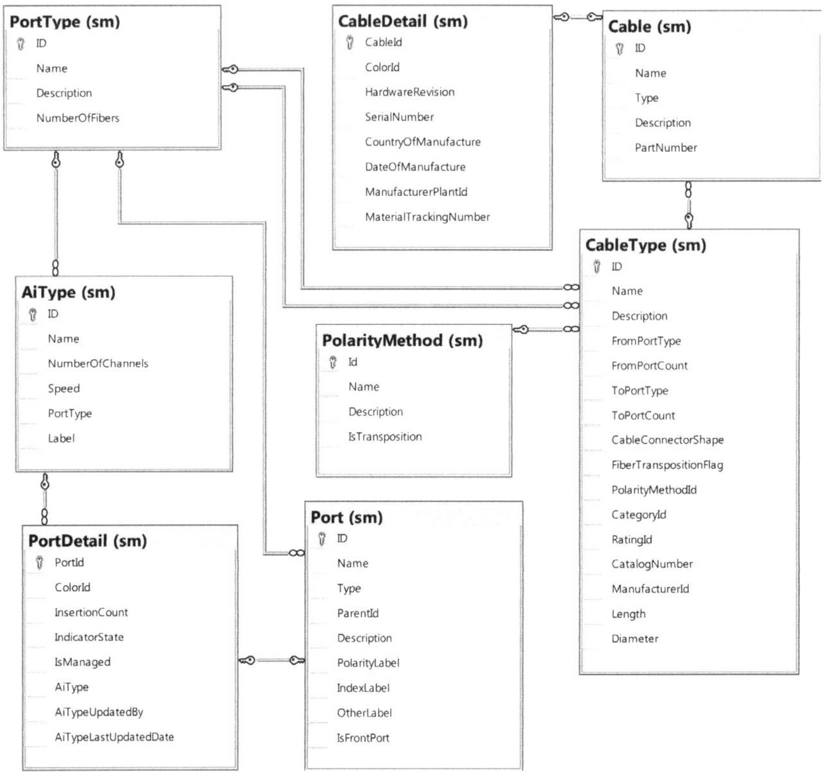

Figure 13. The Entity Relationship Diagram (ERD) Including the Refactored Connectivity Elements

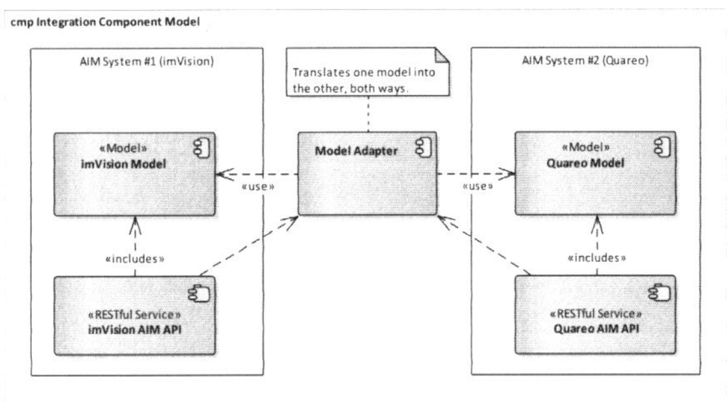

Figure 14. Enabling Data Exchange via a Model Adapter

VI. CONCLUSION

Modeling large varieties of telecommunication assets can be a challenging task, even more so if other applications intend to integrate with one or more systems that automate the management of such complex telecommunication enterprise infrastructure and their physical connectivity.

The benefits entailed by the model standardization of the entities managed by such systems are significant and can be summarized as follows:

- ✓ Standardized models facilitate a common understanding of the AIM systems in general and of the elements that such systems expose and provision;
- ✓ The common model is divorced from any proprietary representation of telecommunication assets while still allowing the inclusion of vendor-specific details;
- ✓ The ISO/IEC specifications define a true domain model of the physical layer connectivity;
- ✓ The model is technology-agnostic;
- ✓ By omitting unnecessary detail, the model is highly flexible, allowing both present and future network hardware specification in a unified fashion;
- ✓ The ISO/IEC standardization enables and ensures a systematic, consistent, and unified modeling of AIM systems;
- ✓ Functional features of AIM systems, such as connectivity provisioning and asset management, can easily be described and modeled in terms of the structural elements introduced by the Standards document;
- ✓ Integrating with AIM systems is a considerably less complex undertaking, given the standardized model that systems can now use to communicate with each other.

This paper took further steps to elaborate on these models and the relationships between them via concrete design artifacts developed using UML (Unified Modeling Language). Inheritance, composition/aggregation, and generic typing were used in designing a hierarchical resource model shown to be extensible and fit for representing telecommunication assets, connectivity features and activities, premises, organizational elements, and system notifications – as they relate to any AIM-centric domain.

Although the primary focus of the 18598/DIS draft ISO/IEC Standards document is to address the representation of network connectivity assets, the motivation behind this specification is to facilitate custom integration solutions with AIM systems. Given the challenging nature of software systems integration in general, building AIM systems with the right quality attributes that support such integration is essential. Extensibility, scalability, rigorous and stable interface and model design, and performance through adequate technology adoption are important goals to consider. For this reason, the present paper also introduced the layered architecture adopted by CommScope's imVision API, targeting the management of telecommunications infrastructure.

Emphasis was placed on the Standards-recommended RESTful architectural style, while technology specifics were succinctly described to show how they helped align the system's design and functionality with the AIM standards requirements. Various design and implementation aspects were elaborated along with a selection of key benefits, such as dynamic resource composition, custom serialization to support consistent handling of similar resources, efficient POST request construction and network traffic, and a simple URI scheme despite large varieties of specialized resources.

Delving into a few technology-specific facets, a brief overview of a rule-based engine and supporting frameworks designed for resource initialization and validation was described. Interesting implementation details that highlight aspects of the functional programming paradigm employed by key components of CommScope's imVision API were also shared.

Considering the imVision and Quareo resource models, the AIM API architecture, and exposed features of the CommScope's networking infrastructure provisioning system, integration-related aspects were also addressed. Data integration concerns were considered for the imVision software system as they were tackled as part of the data layer refactoring effort prompted by non-functional requirements such as extensibility, robustness, and – last but not least – organizational data integration needs.

A straightforward integration candidate solution between CommScope's imVision AIM API and Quareo API RESTful services was presented – one based on model normalization and point-to-point messaging. Both one-way/one-time and two-way integration scenarios were discussed, concluding with a brief debate regarding the need for a canonical model to allow the AIM systems to efficiently communicate with each other.

VII. REFERENCES

[1] M. Iridon, "Automated Infrastructure Management Systems. A Resource Model and RESTful Service Design Proposal to Support and Augment the Specifications of the ISO/IEC 18598/DIS Draft," FASSI 2016 : The Second International Conference on Fundamentals and Advances in Software Systems Integration, ISBN: 978-1-61208-497-8, pp. 8-17, Nice, France, July, 2016.

[2] Automated Infrastructure Management(AIM) Systems– Requirements, Data Exchange and Applications, 18598/DIS draft @ ISO/IEC.

[3] G. Block et. al., "Designing Evolvable Web APIs with ASP.NET," ISBN-13: 978-1449337711.

[4] J. Kurtz and B. Wortman, "ASP.NET Web API 2: Building a REST Service from Start to Finish," 2nd Edition, 2014, ISBN-13: 978-1484201107.

[5] J. Webber, "REST in Practice: Hypermedia and Systems Architecture," 1st Edition, 2010, ISBN-13: 978-0596805821.

[6] E. Evans, "Domain-Driven Design: Tackling Complexity in the Heart of Software," 1st Edition, Prentice Hall, 2003, ISBN-13: 978-0321125217.

[7] Microsoft, "Microsoft Application Architecture Guide (Patterns and Practices)," Second Edition, Microsoft. ISBN-13: 978-0735627109. [Online] Available from: https://msdn.microsoft.com/en-us/library/ff650706.aspx [retrieved: March 2016].

[8] M. Fowler, "Patterns of Enterprise Application Architecture," Addison-Wesley Professional, 2002.

[9] T. Erl, "Service-Oriented Architecture (SOA): Concepts, Technology, and Design," Prentice Hall, 2005, ISBN-13: 978-0131858589.

[10] R. Daigneau, "Service Design Patterns: Fundamental Design Solutions for SOAP/WSDL and RESTful Web Services," Addison-Wesley, 1st Edition, 2011, ISBN-13: 078-5342544206.

[11] M. Fowler, "The Richardson Maturity Model". [Online]. Available from http://martinfowler.com/articles/richardsonMaturityModel.html [retrieved: March 2016].

[12] CommScope Enterprise Product Catalog. [Online] Available from: http://www.commscope.com/Product-Catalog/Enterprise/ [retrieved March 2016].

[13] G. M. Hall, "Adaptive Code via C#: Agile coding with design patterns and SOLID principles (Developer Reference)," Microsoft Press, 1st Edition, 2014, ISBN-13: 978-0735683204.

[14] G. Hohpe and B. Woolf, "Enterprise Integration Patterns; Designing, Building, and Deploying Messaging Solutions," Addison-Wesley, 2012, ISBN-13: 978-0321200686.

[15] M. Seemann, "Dependency Injection in .NET," Manning Publications, 1st Edition, 2011, ISBN-13: 978-1935182504.

[16] T. Petricek and J. Skeet, "Real-World Functional Programming: With Examples in F# and C#," Manning Publications; 1st edition, 2010, ISBN-13: 978-1933988924.

[17] CommScope Quareo Physical Layer Management System. [Online] Available from: http://www.commscope.com/Docs/Quareo-Physical-Layer-Management-System-BR-319828-AE.pdf [retrieved February 2017].

[18] CommScope NG4access ODF Platform [Online] Available from: http://www.commscope.com/Docs/NG4access_ODF_Platform_Quareo_CO-319580-EN.pdf [retrieved February 2017]

[19] M. Iridon, "Enterprise Integration Modeling – A Practical Enterprise Integration Solution Featuring an Incremental Approach via Prototyping," International Journal on Advances in Software, vol. 9 no. 1&2, 2016, pp. 116-127.

Evaluating a Recommendation System for User Stories in Mobile Enterprise Application Development

Matthias Jurisch, Maria Lusky, Bodo Igler, Stephan Böhm

Faculty of Design – Computer Science – Media
RheinMain University of Applied Sciences
Wiesbaden, Germany
Email: {matthias.jurisch,maria.lusky,bodo.igler,stephan.boehm}@hs-rm.de

***Abstract*—Mobile application development is characterized by a higher market volatility and shorter development cycles than traditional desktop application development. Developing mobile applications in large enterprise contexts (mobile enterprise applications) requires additional effort to adapt to new circumstances, since complex processes, user roles and enterprise-specific guidelines need to be taken into account. This effort can be reduced by reusing artifacts from other projects, such as source code, wireframes, documentation, screen designs or requirement specifications. We propose a recommendation system based on user stories in order to make artifacts accessible without requiring users to formulate an explicit search query. We present a prototype implementing this approach using standard methods and tools from information retrieval and evaluate it using different components of user stories as well as taking into account varying user story quality. The results show that using only user story text for calculating recommendations is the most promising approach and that user story quality does not affect the efficiency of recommendations.**

Keywords–Mobile Enterprise Applications; User Stories; Recommendation Systems; Pattern Inventories.

I. INTRODUCTION

The market for mobile applications (mobile apps) is characterized by the high volatility of platforms, devices and requirements. Hence, mobile app development projects require a shorter development cycle than traditional desktop applications. Consumer application development has been adapted to these circumstances by using agile methods and prototyping to accelerate app development. In the context of *mobile enterprise applications* (MEA), these adaptions require additional effort. Enterprise-specific guidelines, business processes and complex user roles need to be taken into account, which slows down the development process.

We proposed to approach this problem by building a repository with artifacts from past MEA-projects in the same enterprise and using this repository to accelerate and simplify the development process [1]. Project artifacts are screen designs, source code, requirements and technical documentation as well as all other documents created during the development process. Being able to reuse parts of these artifacts, using them for inspiration or for getting familiar with similar projects could help speeding up development.

In order to access the artifact repository efficiently, a method for user-friendly navigation of artifacts is required. Short, user-centered descriptions of usage scenarios called *User Stories* are common in requirements documentation in mobile app development. Since all other artifacts are in some way related to a user story, we consider user stories to be a reasonable starting point for navigating an artifact repository. Showing artifacts related to similar user stories to a user of the artifact repository should provide her with possible solutions to her problem. The solutions derive from best practices that had been used in previous projects that are similar to the one at hand. This can be realized through a recommendation system for project artifacts.

In this paper, we present a first step towards this recommendation system. When relating user stories to artifacts of similar user stories, the similarity computation between user stories is an important task. We present an approach for a recommendation system for user stories using standard information retrieval techniques and a prototypical implementation. We also evaluate in how far this approach fits the recommendation of user stories, which parts of user stories are relevant to the recommendation computation and how user story quality influences the accuracy of recommendations.

The remainder of this work is structured as follows: Section II describes the context of our research. Related work and its relation to our results are discussed in Section III. Section IV presents the architecture of a user story recommendation prototype. We discuss the evaluation methodology, the corpus used and two experiments to assess our prototype and approach in Section V. Section VI presents the results of the experiments. Implications from the results and potential shortcomings of our experiments are presented in Section VII. A conclusion and an outlook to future work is given in Section VIII.

II. BACKGROUND

According to Flora et al. [2] mobile apps are "... compact programs developed to work on smartphones, tablets, and feature phones." Thus, an important characteristic of this type of software is that it has to be adapted to the specific requirements of mobile devices, mobile networks and mobile usage contexts. Besides this more technical perspective, the term mobile app has a specific meaning from the user perspective as well. It represents a bit of software that can be obtained from a distribution platform, i.e., an app store, and installed at the device by the user herself. Based on these characteristics, a more comprehensive definition of mobile apps can be given: Mobile apps are application software to run on mobile and network-connected devices, such as smartphones, to solve user-specific problems. They are provided by distribution platforms and consist of programs and data installed by the end user as an important element of handset personalization.

The origins of mobile apps are to be found in the consumer domain and closely related with the introduction of Apple's App Store in 2008. Since then, especially smaller enterprises have entered this emerging market and tried to exploit the business opportunities provided by the new app ecosystem. Even today, the app developer market is dominated by small companies. A global app developer report by Inmobi [3] from 2016 revealed that only eight percent of the participating firms had more than 20 employees. This suggests that most of the app development is carried out in small groups enabling a very direct communication amongst involved employees and characterized by short communication channels. As a result, app development tools and processes are often aligned to the requirements of lean or startup-like companies with agile and flexible structures, but they are less tailored for collaborative work environments within the complex structures and processes of large enterprises with a very high division of work and responsibilities.

However, large enterprises will not be able to evade the growing external demand for mobile apps. They need to adapt and adopt development tools and processes from the consumer segment to their own requirements and needs. For example, large enterprises need to find ways to prevent duplicate work across the entire enterprise and stimulate collaboration and knowledge sharing across teams when shifting to a more decentralized software development approach with agile and independent teams.

Besides the external challenges mentioned above, mobile apps are becoming more and more important for the corporate environment from the internal enterprise perspective. This trend is often discussed in the context of a *consumerization of IT*. As a result, Andriole [4] observes "... a reverse technology-adoption life cycle at work: employees bring experience with consumer technologies to the workplace and pressure their companies to adopt new technologies (with which many corporate technology managers might be only barely familiar)". This also has an impact on the processes and technologies used in enterprises by generating a shift towards the adoption of more consumer-driven approaches [5].

To sum up, large enterprises need to develop frameworks of processes and tools adapted to both, providing the flexibility of lean and consumer-driven approaches (coming from the consumer segment and smaller firms) by taking into account the high complexity of organizational structures within the context of large corporations. With this regard, the contribution of this paper is the evaluation of a user story based recommendation system as an element of a prototyping framework for MEA design in large enterprises. Our approach is based on the analysis of user stories linked to artifacts of MEA projects in a enterprise-wide repository. An identification of similar user stories could not only lead to reusable project artifacts but also foster cross-project communication and cooperation (e.g., by identifying the User Experience designer or developer of existing artifacts derived from completed projects) or help reducing uncertainty by providing reference points or estimates based on the learnings of completed projects (e.g., cost estimates for screen designs or software components). Before we provide an overview on the related work in this field, we will close this section with a brief discussion and conceptualization of the core elements of our approach.

A. Mobile Enterprise Applications

An exact definition of the term mobile enterprise app (MEA) is still missing [6] and it is used here in a wider sense. We are using the term to refer to any mobile app developed or deployed in the context of (large) enterprises and thus not only to mobile front-ends for existing enterprise software applications (EAS).

Mobile enterprise applications are often categorized by target groups into business-to-customer (B2C), business-to-business (B2B), and business-to-employee (B2E) [7], [6]. All the three types of MEA are in the scope of our study, as the challenges described before do not depend too much on the intended target group or user, but more on the organizational characteristics of the enterprise managing the app development process (by internal organizational units or subcontracting external suppliers).

B. Artifact and Repositories

The idea of an artifact repository is inspired by some longer-established concepts of (1) the usage of patterns in software engineering and human-computer interface design [8], (2) the asset reuse as promoted by the product-line approach[9], and (3) the design science research approach to evaluate artifacts for relevance and rigor in a systematical and iterative way [10]. As mentioned before, artifacts can comprise technical as well as non-technical aspects. The artifacts itself can be linked to organizational information or other details relevant for the development process (e.g., responsible developer or development costs).

A repository of all project-relevant information provides the underlying data for further analysis. The repository can be a common knowledge base within a project management software used for MEA development (e.g., Jira). In this respect, one of our main research objectives is to provide an approach to identify reusable project artifacts within this knowledge base to facilitate mobile app prototyping and development in large enterprises.

C. Recommendations

Based on a definition proposed by the organizers of the 2009 ACM International Conference on Recommender Systems (as cited in Robillard et al. [11]) recommendation systems for software engineering (RSSEs) are "... software tools that can assist developers with a wide range of activities, from reusing code to writing effective bug reports." According to this conceptuality, our aim is to evaluate an approach to identify similar project artifacts based on a sample repository. These similarities can then be used to provide a recommendation to UX designers or developers to consider aspects of existing artifacts for reuse or facilitate knowledge transfer across development teams.

However, one problem not mentioned before is the high complexity of MEA implementations, e.g., due to interfaces to back-end systems within the enterprise IT infrastructure. Some artifacts (e.g., login screens) might be characterized by a high level of similarity, but an incompatible implementation. This is why – as a first step – we decided to abstract from more implementation-oriented artifacts and defined an approach based on user stories.

D. User Stories

In the context of software engineering, requirements specify necessary functions and features of software. In traditional software engineering, requirements are recorded in text documents that are difficult to grasp completely. In agile software development, user stories are user centered requirements expressed in one sentence, as described by Cohn [12].

A user story typically consists of three components: (1) a *role*, (2) a *desire* and (3) a *benefit*. While the role expresses, which kind of person wants the requirement, the desire and benefit describe the feature itself, for example: *As a user I want to mark and select favorites in order to receive information about my daily bus and train connections as fast as possible*. Each user story is associated with *acceptance criteria* that specify required properties for the implementation of the requirement described by the user story, for example: *The favorites should be ordered alphabetically*. Furthermore, Wake [13] defined the INVEST criteria for good user stories. According to his model, a user story should be *independent* from other user stories, *negotiable*, *valuable* with a benefit for the user that is clearly identifiable, *estimable* regarding its cost, *small* and *testable* or verifiable. These guidelines enable developers to easily write user stories that are meaningful on the one hand and comparable on the other hand. Creating user stories complying these criteria is a common practise in agile development.

III. Related Work

Regarding the general question of how enterprises should develop MEAs, according to [14] and [15], many enterprises still lack experience concerning their development. While there are no established process models for MEA development, first research approaches can be found in related literature. Dugerdil [16] presents an approach for transforming enterprise applications to mobile applications. An instrumentation framework that tries to ease the maintenance of MEAs is proposed in [17]. The management perspective of this problem is also represented in literature. Badami [18] examines this aspect from an organizational viewpoint and proposes the concentration of MEA development into "Mobile Centers of Excellence" that focus on competences of mobile experts inside enterprises.

Mobile app prototyping is supported by various tools. Existing prototyping tools (Kony, Verivo, Akula, SAP Mobile Platform) allow rapid prototyping. However, they can not always be used in the context of MEA, since they are focused on predefined use cases or the integration of existing enterprise products.

No processes or tools that specifically support the development of MEAs can be found in literature or in practice. Key questions that need to be answered are how an approach can take into account the specifics of MEAs and how time and effort for development can be decreased. Our approach is to reuse artifacts from existing MEA projects and to utilize recommendation systems in order to relate artifacts in pattern repositories and ease artifact reuse.

Leveraging information from user stories to recommend related artifacts has not been addressed in the literature until 2016 [19]. User stories are often stored in issue management systems that are normally used for bug tracking. Issues as used in issue management share some similarities with user stories. Both usually contain a short description formulated from a user perspective and are related to artifacts that are created to implement the changes required by the issue respectively the user story. A significant difference is that bug descriptions often contain a more technical language and provide less information about why a change is important and what the reason is for a change from an application domain perspective. While user stories have not been in the focus of scientific work regarding artifact recommendation, bug reports from issue management systems have been studied to support issue triage and issue-based project navigation.

In issue triage, systems find duplicates for bug reports. In this way, systems can automatically mark a bug report as a duplicate, minimizing the effort required to manually managing bug reporting systems. An approach by Runeson et al. [20] proposes using information retrieval techniques to detect duplicate bug reports. This approach has been combined with considering other artifacts like execution information [21]. Anvik and Murphy [22] have presented a framework for supporting developers building project-specific recommendation systems that help with assigning bugs to developers and linking them to project components. The framework allows the combination of several techniques for the construction of recommendation systems. Approaches from issue triage are primarily focused on bug reports and removing duplicates. Recommending useful solutions to similar issues, like in our case, is not considered.

Issue-based project navigation uses recommendation systems to support the navigation of projects. Hipikat [23] is a system that gathers information from mailing lists, documents and bug reports to ease the navigation of a source code repository. No quantitative evaluation of this approach exists and the applicability to other domains than issue management is not clear. Nevertheless, an evaluation of our similar approach to user-story-based recommendation systems seems promising.

Work in this direction has been conducted by Pirzadeh et al. [19]. Their approach recommends source code files based on user-story-similarity using standard information retrieval technologies. Connections between issues and source code are discovered based on tagged issue ids in commit messages of a version control system. While an evaluation shows a good performance of recommending source code artifacts in terms of precision, accuracy and specificity, it is not evaluated whether these results are actually caused by user story similarity. Relevant recommendations could also be a consequence of the general importance of some artifacts. Further aspects that are not investigated are which parts of the user stories should actually be used for the recommendation computation and how user story quality affects the recommendations.

In practice, plugins for the issue management system Atlassian JIRA that use information retrieval techniques to find similar issues exist [24]. These Plugins focus on duplicate detection and are not tailored to user story similarity. Also, they do not provide an API to programmatically access recommended similar issues and lack an evaluation. Especially no evaluation of the performance regarding the similarity computation and recommendation for user stories exists.

After reviewing the presented literature, we can conclude that several research questions have not been addressed in the literature: It is unclear to which degree textual user story similarity can be leveraged for getting useful recommendations. It has also not been studied, which parts of user stories are relevant to computing similarities and how user story quality affects the performance of the recommendation systems.

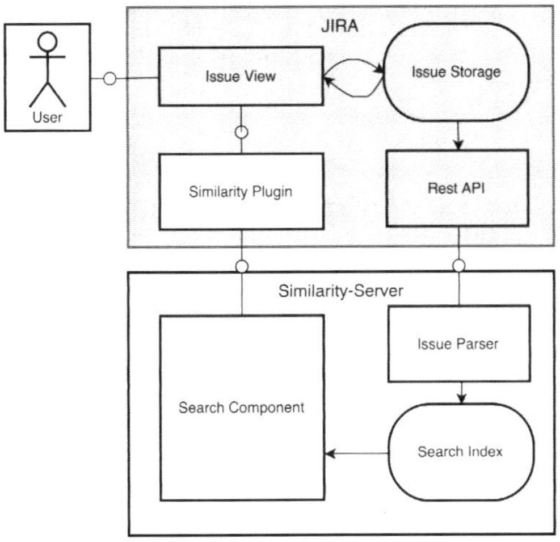

Figure 1. Prototype Architecture.

IV. PROTOTYPE

To support the construction of an artifact repository, a basis for a recommendation system has been implemented. The recommendation system will later interlink existing artifacts from several projects and different domains (e.g., user stories, source code, requirements, technical and organizational documentation) to help those involved in the software project. The foundation for our system that supports the interlinking of artifacts in general is a recommendation system for user stories. Given a user story as an input, the first iteration of the system will output the most similar and therefore relevant user stories. Later, several kinds of artifacts will be regarded.

To compute the similarity between user stories, we use standard procedures from information retrieval [25], in particular the vector space model (VSM), a representation of text documents, and term frequency-inverse document frequency (TF-IDF), a weighting method for terms in search queries and documents. First, all user stories are preprocessed. The documents are tokenized into collections of terms. All stopwords (e.g., "the", "it") are removed. Of the remaining terms, only a stemmed form is stored. User stories are represented in the vector space model (VSM), a common feature representation for natural language documents. In the VSM, each vector component refers to the term frequency of a term in the document.

To find similar user stories to a story, the text of the story is used as a query. The terms are weighted using TF-IDF term-weighting, which is calculated by multiplying the term frequency with the inverse document frequency of a term. The inverse document frequency is $\log \frac{N}{|t|}$, where N is the number of all documents (here user stories) and $|t|$ is the number of occurrences for a term in all documents. The query vector and all user story vectors are compared using the cosine similarity (i.e., the cosine of the angle between two vectors is used as the similarity measure). This process is implemented by Apache Lucene that uses several optimization strategies to improve the search performance. More details regarding these optimizations can be found in the Apache Lucene documentation [26].

User stories are stored as issues in Atlassian Jira [27], an issue management system. To allow easy developer access, our user story recommendation platform is integrated into Jira using the Jira plugin API. An FMC-Diagram of the implementation is given in Figure 1. Gray components are provided by Jira and hence did not need to be implemented. The *User* has access to an *Issue View* that is used to display and edit issues. Issues are persisted using an *Issue Storage* that can be accessed via a Rest API [28]. A *Similarity Server* is used to compute recommendations. The server is separated from Jira to improve the independences between recommendation generation and representation of user stories. In this way, other issue management systems as well as other similarity computation approaches can be used without too much adaption required. As a part of the server, the *Issue Parser* parses the user stories from the *Rest API* to a *Search Index*. A *Search Component* uses the index to answer requests from a *Similarity Plugin* that asks for recommendations for user stories currently displayed by the Jira *Issue View*. This architecture has been implemented as a prototype.

V. EVALUATION

In order to evaluate the performance of the prototype and the feasibility of the overall approach we conducted two experiments that focused on different aspects of user story recommendation.

- Does the usage of different components of user stories affect the usefulness of the recommendations?
- Does the quality of user stories affect the usefulness of the recommendations?

Therefore, the first experiment investigated the quality of recommendations with respect to different components of a user story that were used as a query on the one hand and as part of the corpus on the other hand. The second experiment took into account different levels of user story quality.

A. Corpus

For conducting both experiments, we built a corpus that consisted of 84 user stories for generating recommendations and 60 additional user stories to account for noise effects. We needed different user stories with acceptance criteria, whereas a part of them should describe the same use case. Thus, we created two different use cases *A - favorites* and *B - location* for a popular public transport app and made two short video films of about 20 seconds each that showed typical interactions of each use case. The two video films were then shown to a group of German-speaking students. Each student created a user story and three acceptance criteria per use case, resulting in 42 user stories for each use case A and B. Since our user stories described only two different use cases, we added 60 more user stories from an external data set [29] that were translated into German via a semiautomatic procedure.

If all user stories from the corpus were used as a query and as a part of the set of documents that was searched, the first recommendation would always be the user story used as the query, which would skew the results. To address this issue, the user stories were randomly separated into a query and a search corpus set. Only user stories for use cases A and B were allowed as a part of the query set, since no relevant recommendations could be generated for user stories from the external data set. The query set contained 30 user stories, so it comprised about 25% of the overall document corpus.

Recommendations were generated only for user stories in the query set. Only elements of the search corpus set were used as recommendations.

B. Metric

For each user story, recommendations are calculated based on textual similarity. A recommendation is regarded as "correct", when the recommended user story relates to the same use case A or B as the query. In the context of this work we consider a recommendation system the more *useful*, the higher the precision of the result is. *Precision* and *recall* are standard metrics for evaluating these kinds of scenarios [30]. Since a recommendation system will provide the user with only the first few recommendations, the usage of overall precision and recall is not an appropriate metric in this case. A metric that is more useful regarding recommendation systems in our case is *precision at rank* [25, p.161]:

$$PR = \frac{TP}{SR}$$

TP is the number of true positives (i.e., recommendations of the correct use case) and SR a fixed number of search results. This metric only evaluates the SR best search results. The two experiments were conducted for each rank from one to ten. To get an overview of the overall performance, the average of the precision for each user story was calculated. We therefore measured the average precision at rank for ranks one to ten.

C. Experiment 1: User Story Components

For the first experiment we defined several variants of our data sets: user stories along with their associated acceptance criteria (USAK), user stories only (US) and acceptance criteria only (AK). These are the smallest possible variants that are sensible. Separating the user stories into smaller components would result in parts of very few words, which would not allow meaningful processing using IR techniques. Each variant can be used as a query set on the one hand and as a corpus set on the other hand. We combined each variant as a query with each variant as a corpus and therefore conducted the first experiment nine times with all nine combinations of our data. Since no acceptance criteria were available for the external data set, the same artificial acceptance criteria were added to each of these user stories. Hence, it is less likely to retrieve user stories as recommendations from the external data set while the corpus set consists of user stories with acceptance criteria (USAK) or only acceptance criteria (AK). This would lead to a better average precision at rank for these cases. Effects of this shortcoming will be further discussed in Section VII.

D. Experiment 2: User Story Quality

A second experiment was conducted to evaluate if user story quality affects the effectiveness of a text-similarity based recommendation system. For this purpose we categorized the user stories into three quality groups.

First, the quality of all user stories was rated based on a five point scale. We defined five quality criteria and assigned one point to the user story for each criterion that was satisfied: (1) The user story had to have exactly one *role*. (2) The user story had to express exactly one *desire*. (3) The user story had to have exactly one *benefit*. (4) The user story had to be written in only one sentence. (5) The user story's *benefit* had to be verifiable, as defined by the INVEST-criteria.

Then the user stories (written by students and from the external data source) were categorized into three quality classes: User stories with five points were assigned to quality class 1, user stories with four points were assigned to quality class 2 and user stories with three or less points were assigned to quality class 3, resulting in class 1 comprising 95 user stories, while classes 2 and 3 contained 26 respectively 23 user stories.

To evaluate the effect of user story quality on recommendations, datasets with different user story quality were needed. Using the previously described categories, the data was split into three sets: (1) user stories of all quality classes, (2) user stories of quality classes 1 and 2, (3) user stories of only the high quality class 1. For each of these sets, the precision at all ranks from one to ten was calculated. For this experiment, only the combination of user story parts from experiment 1 with the best results regarding precision was used.

VI. Results

We implemented a small evaluation application that initiates the recommendation-process, gathers user story recommendations, automatically calculates the average precision at rank by evaluating class labels (e.g., corresponding use case) according to the approach presented in Section V and stores results in a CSV file. The results of the experiments performed using this application are discussed in the following subsections.

A. Experiment 1: User Story Components

The results from the first experiment are shown in Figure 2. Each data series represents one combination of corpus and query sets, whereas the first part of the data series label denotes the query set and the second part denotes the corpus type (e.g., *AK/US* represents queries that contain only acceptance criteria and a corpus consisting of user stories without acceptance criteria).

The data series can be split into two categories: (1) Experiments where user story text is used as query *and* corpus and (2) experiments where either the query or the corpus consists *only* of acceptance criteria. With one exception (*USAK/USAK* at rank 1), members of the first category in general have a higher average precision than members of the second. For readability purposes, only representatives of these categories with highest and lowest average precision at rank in the respective group are shown in the data series. Note that *AK/US* and *AK/AK* are representatives with lowest average precision for their group at different ranks. Therefore two data series are displayed as lower bounds for the second category. The data series that are not displayed (*USAK/US* and *US/USAK* in the first group; *AK/USAK* and *US/AK* in the second group) are always between the upper and lower bounds of their respective groups.

The combination using only user stories (*US/US*) shows the highest average precision. The precision for rank 1 is 1.0 and drops to 0.88 when considering the first 10 recommendations. The data series of the combined user stories along with acceptance criteria (*USAK/USAK*) has a lower precision that ranges between 0.71 and 0.79. The data shows that the precision differs widely between these combinations.

In the category of the experiments where either the query or the corpus consists of acceptance criteria only, the combination *USAK/AK* showed the highest precision at rank that ranged from 0.54 to 0.75. The two combinations of *AK/US* and *AK/AK* resulted in the lowest precision varying between 0.58 and 0.63 for *AK/US* and between 0.53 and 0.65 for *AK/AK*. However, the

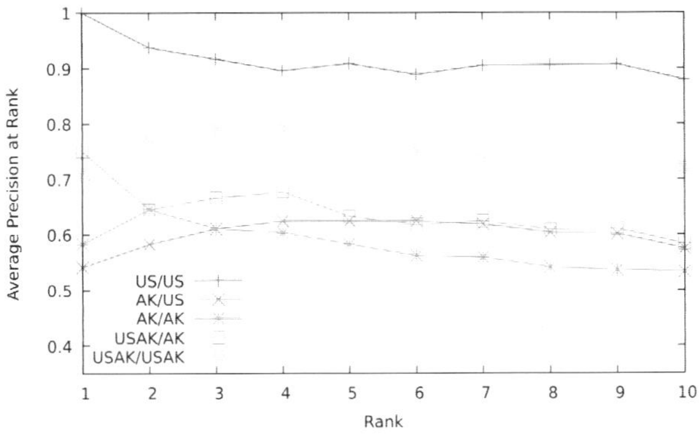

Figure 2. Evaluation results for combinations of query and corpus data.

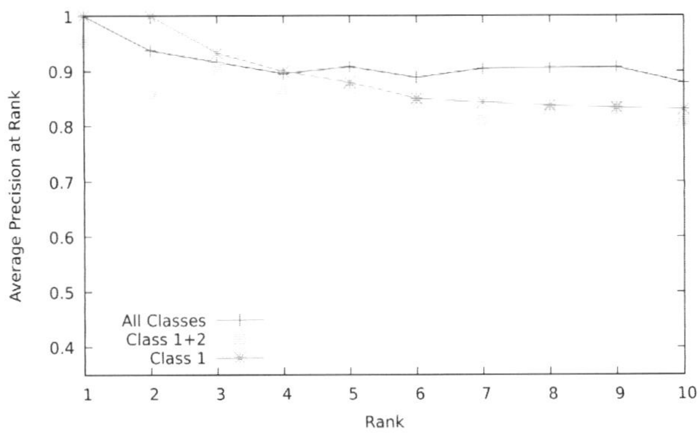

Figure 3. Comparison of results when filtering user story quality.

results show only small differences between all combinations in this group.

In general, data series that use only user stories either in the query or the corpus set have a higher average precision than the data series applying acceptance criteria only in either query or corpus. The three data series with the lowest average precision all use only acceptance criteria as queries. Average precision of these data series is between 0.53 and 0.65 varying in dependence of the rank, while the average precision of the data series of the other category varies between 0.71 and 1.0.

B. *Experiment 2: User Story Quality*

The results of the second experiment are shown in Figure 3. The data series *Class 1* contains only high quality user stories of class 1, as described in Section V-D. *Class 1 + 2* are medium- and high-quality user stories, while *All Classes* refers to user stories of all quality classes.

Average precision values for all data sets are between 0.8 and 1.0. While class 1 user stories show the best results at ranks 1, 2 and 3, the precision lowers at the following ranks. The precision with data of all quality classes varies between 1.00 and 0.88 and receives the highest values at ranks 5 and following. However, the precision values of quality classes 1 and 2 are the lowest at all ranks.

VII. Discussion

The results we received from our experiments provided us with information about the precision of text-based recommendations for user stories and acceptance criteria. Based on these results we aim to answer our two research questions:

- Does the usage of different components of user stories affect the usefulness of recommendations?
- Does the quality of user stories affect the usefulness of recommendations?

A. *Experiment 1*

The results from experiment 1 showed that the highest precision is received using the combination US/US. The precision of the other combinations is not only lower, but by far lower. Also, after a decrease from rank 1 to rank 2, the precision of the US/US combination remains relatively stable. Out of all remaining combinations, the ones that use user stories in both the query and the corpus produced the higher precision values. All combinations that use only acceptance criteria in the query and/or the corpus show the lowest precision that is by far lower than the highest received precision.

Based on our results we can therefore answer our first research question positively. Different components of user stories do affect the usefulness of recommendations. We discovered that the usage of acceptance criteria deteriorates the precision of the recommendation system, since these combinations received the lowest precision values. Corresponding to that, the combination that contained only user stories and no acceptance criteria led to the highest precision values. While it is difficult to define limits for the precision of a recommendation system, we believe the observed precision is sufficient for recommendation systems in the context of mobile enterprise application development. We therefore conclude that using only user story text as a basis for recommendation computation in this context seems to be the most promising alternative.

B. *Experiment 2*

The results from experiment 2 show that the usage of all quality classes leads to a higher precision from rank 4 onward. However, at ranks 1, 2 and 3 the usage of only high quality user stories received the best precision values. Furthermore, it is especially notable that average precision is lower for user stories of quality classes 1 and 2 combined than for all kinds of user stories.

Based on this data, we can not ascertain any impact of user story quality on recommendation precision and therefore, our second research question is to be answered negatively.

C. *Thread to validity*

One weakness of our experimental setup may be the small number of user stories in our corpus. However, the distribution of user stories to primarily two use cases compensates this shortcoming. Although the quality rating of the user stories did not follow a common model for user story quality, it is based on the main and most popular user story models. Furthermore, to our knowledge there is no established model for quality measurement of user stories on an individual level.

As mentioned in Section V-A, we used data from an external source that did not contain acceptance criteria. One could assume that this would distort the results in favor of the combinations that use acceptance criteria. However, these combinations gained lower precision than the other combinations, despite the lack of acceptance criteria. Therefore, our conclusion that the usage of user stories has a positive effect on precision still holds.

VIII. Conclusion

In this paper we have presented foundation work for an artifact repository to support the development of MEA. The foundation is built on a recommendation system for artifacts based on user-centered requirement specifications called "User Stories", in order to allow the user of the artifact repository an efficient navigation. Standard information retrieval techniques were used to build the recommendation system. We evaluated which parts of the user stories should be used for recommendation computation and how user story quality affects the performance of the system.

Our experiments have shown that the most valuable part for requirement computation from a user story is the user story text. Including acceptance criteria into recommendation computation has a negative impact on recommendation performance. In our experiment data, we could not find a positive correlation between user story quality and quality of recommendations.

As future work, we plan to use our results to extend our recommendation system that includes development artifacts from several domains. Collecting and evaluating methods for connecting different artifact types to user stories will be the next step to reach this goal. In addition, the artifacts will be enriched with further information, such as cost and benefit information or process and workflow data.

Acknowledgments

This work was funded by the German Federal Ministry of Education and Research, grant no. 03FH032PX5; the PROFRAME project at RheinMain University of Applied Sciences. All responsibility for the content of this paper lies with the authors.

References

[1] M. Jurisch, B. Igler, and S. Böhm, "PROFRAME: A Prototyping Framework for Mobile Enterprise Applications," in CENTRIC 2016, The Ninth International Conference on Advances in Human-oriented and Personalized Mechanisms, Technologies, and Services, 2016, pp. 7–10, 2016.

[2] H. K. Flora, X. Wang, and S. V. Chande, "An investigation on the characteristics of mobile applications: A survey study," International Journal of Information Technology and Computer Science, vol. 6, no. 11, pp. 21–27, 2014. [Online]. Available: https://doi.org/10.5815%2Fijitcs.2014.11.03

[3] Inmobi, "State of mobile app developers 2016: Based on a survey of 1000+ app developers," http://www.inmobi.com/insights/download/whitepapers/state-of-mobile-app-developers-2016/, accessed: 2017-03-02.

[4] S. J. Andriole, "Managing technology in a 2.0 world," IT Professional, vol. 14, no. 1, pp. 50–57, 2012. [Online]. Available: https://doi.org/10.1109%2Fmitp.2012.13

[5] B. Niehaves, S. Köffer, and K. Ortbach, "The effect of private it use on work performance: Towards an it consumerization theory," in 2013 11th International Conference on Wirtschaftsinformatik. Institute of Electrical and Electronics Engineers (IEEE), 2013, pp. 39–53, 2013. [Online]. Available: http://aisel.aisnet.org/wi2013/3/

[6] A. Giessmann, K. Stanoevska-Slabeva, and B. de Visser, "Mobile enterprise applications–current state and future directions," in 2012 45th Hawaii International Conference on System Sciences. Institute of Electrical and Electronics Engineers (IEEE), 2012, 2012. [Online]. Available: https://doi.org/10.1109%2Fhicss.2012.435

[7] R. C. Basole, "The emergence of the mobile enterprise: A value-driven perspective," in International Conference on the Management of Mobile Business (ICMB 2007). Institute of Electrical and Electronics Engineers (IEEE), 2007, 2007. [Online]. Available: https://doi.org/10.1109%2Ficmb.2007.63

[8] J. O. Borchers, "A pattern approach to interaction design," AI & Society, vol. 15, no. 4, pp. 359–376, 2001. [Online]. Available: https://doi.org/10.1007%2Fbf01206115

[9] K. Kang, J. Lee, and P. Donohoe, "Feature-oriented product line engineering," IEEE Software, vol. 19, no. 4, pp. 58–65, 2002. [Online]. Available: https://doi.org/10.1109%2Fms.2002.1020288

[10] A. Cleven, P. Gubler, and K. M. Hüner, "Design alternatives for the evaluation of design science research artifacts," in Proceedings of the 4th International Conference on Design Science Research in Information Systems and Technology - DESRIST '09. Association for Computing Machinery (ACM), 2009, 2009. [Online]. Available: https://doi.org/10.1145%2F1555619.1555645

[11] M. Robillard, R. Walker, and T. Zimmermann, "Recommendation systems for software engineering," IEEE Software, vol. 27, no. 4, pp. 80–86, 2010. [Online]. Available: https://doi.org/10.1109%2Fms.2009.161

[12] M. Cohn, User stories applied: For agile software development. Addison-Wesley Professional, 2004.

[13] B. Wake, "INVEST in good stories, and SMART tasks," blog post, [retrieved: 2017.05.10], 2003. [Online]. Available: http://xp123.com/articles/invest-in-good-stories-and-smart-tasks

[14] A. Giessmann, K. Stanoevska-Slabeva, and B. de Visser, "Mobile enterprise applications–current state and future directions," in System Science (HICSS), 2012 45th Hawaii International Conference on, Jan 2012, pp. 1363–1372, Jan 2012.

[15] Gartner, "Gartner says demand for enterprise mobile apps will outstrip available development capacity five to one," website [retrieved: 2017.05.10], 2015. [Online]. Available: https://www.gartner.com/newsroom/id/3076817

[16] P. Dugerdil, "Architecting mobile enterprise app: A modeling approach to adapt enterprise applications to the mobile," in Proceedings of the 2013 ACM Workshop on Mobile Development Lifecycle, ser. MobileDeLi '13. New York, NY, USA: ACM, 2013, pp. 9–14, 2013.

[17] M. Pistoia and O. Tripp, "Integrating security, analytics and application management into the mobile development lifecycle," in Proceedings of the 2Nd International Workshop on Mobile Development Lifecycle, ser. MobileDeLi '14. New York, NY, USA: ACM, 2014, pp. 17–18, 2014.

[18] S. A. Badami and J. Sathyan, "micE Model for Defining Enterprise Mobile Strategy," Int. J. on Recent Trends in Engineering and Technology,, vol. 10, no. 1, p. 9, Jan 2014.

[19] H. Pirzadeh, A. D. S. Oliveira, and S. Shanian, "ReUse : A Recommendation System for Implementing User Stories," in International Conference on Software Engineering Advances, no. c, 2016, pp. 149–153, 2016.

[20] P. Runeson, M. Alexandersson, and O. Nyholm, "Detection of duplicate defect reports using natural language processing," Proceedings - International Conference on Software Engineering, pp. 499–508, 2007.

[21] X. Wang, L. Zhang, T. Xie, J. Anvik, and J. Sun, "An Approach to Detecting Duplicate Bug Reports using Natural Language and Execution Information 1 2," Proceedings of the 30th international conference on Software engineering, pp. 461–470, 2008.

[22] J. Anvik and G. C. Murphy, "Reducing the Effort of Bug Report Triage: Recommenders for Development-Oriented Decisions," ACM Transactions on Software Engineering and Methodology (TOSEM), vol. 20, no. 3, 2011.

[23] D. Cubranic and G. C. Murphy, "Hipikat: Recommending Pertinent Software Development Artifacts," 25th International Conference on Software Engineering, no. Section 2, pp. 408–418, 2003. [Online]. Available: http://dl.acm.org/citation.cfm?id=776816.776866

[24] D. Oguz, "Similar issues finder," website, [retrieved: 2017.05.10], 2017. [Online]. Available: https://denizoguz.atlassian.net/projects/SIF/summary

[25] C. D. Manning, P. Raghavan, and H. Schütze, Introduction to Information Retrieval. New York, NY, USA: Cambridge University Press, 2008.

[26] Apache Foundation, "TFIDF Similarity (Lucene 4.6.0 API)," website, [retrieved: 2017.05.10], 2017. [Online]. Available: https://lucene.apache.org/core/4_6_0/core/org/apache/lucene/search/similarities/TFIDFSimilarity.html

[27] Atlassian, "JIRA Software - Issue & Project Tracking for Software Teams," website, [retrieved: 2017.05.10], 2017. [Online]. Available: https://www.atlassian.com/software/jira

[28] Atlassian Developers, "JIRA REST APIS," website, [retrieved: 2017.05.10], 2017. [Online]. Available: https://developer.atlassian.com/jiradev/jira-apis/jira-rest-apis

[29] Open Knowledge International, "Frictionless data: User stories," website, [retrieved: 2017.05.10], 2016. [Online]. Available: http://frictionlessdata.io/user-stories/

[30] D. M. W. Powers, "Evaluation: From Precision, Recall and F-Factor to ROC, Informedness, Markedness & Correlation," Tech. Rep. December, 2007.

The DynB Sparse Matrix Format Using Variable Sized 2D Blocks for Efficient Sparse Matrix Vector Multiplications with General Matrix Structures

Javed Razzaq, Rudolf Berrendorf, Jan P. Ecker,
Soenke Hack, Max Weierstall
Computer Science Department
Bonn-Rhein-Sieg University of Applied Sciences
Sankt Augustin, Germany
e-mail:{javed.razzaq, rudolf.berrendorf, jan.ecker,
soenke.hack, max.weierstall}@h-brs.de

Florian Mannuss
EXPEC Advanced Research Center
Saudi Arabian Oil Company
Dhahran, Saudi Arabia
e-mail: florian.mannuss@aramco.com

Abstract—**The Sparse Matrix Vector Multiplication is an important operation on sparse matrices. This operation is the most time consuming operation in iterative solvers and therefore an efficient execution of that operation is of great importance for many applications. Numerous different storage formats that store sparse matrices efficiently have already been established. Often, these storage formats utilize the sparsity pattern of a matrix in an appropiate manner. For one class of sparse matrices the nonzero values occur in small dense blocks and appropriate block storage formats are well suited for such patterns. But on the other side, these formats perform often poor on general matrices without an explicit / regular block structure. In this paper, the newly developed sparse matrix format DynB is introduced. The aim is to efficiently use several optimization approaches and vectorization with current processors, even for matrices without an explicit block structure of nonzero elements. The DynB matrix format uses 2D rectangular blocks of variable size, allowing fill-ins per block of explicit zero values up to a user controllable threshold. We give a simple and fast heuristic to detect such 2D blocks in a sparse matrix. The performance of the Sparse Matrix Vector Multiplication for a selection of different block formats and matrices with different sparsity structures is compared. Results show that the benefit of blocking formats depend – as to be expected – on the structure of the matrix and that variable sized block formats like DynB can have advantages over fixed size formats and deliver good performance results even for general sparse matrices.**

Keywords–Sparse Matrix Vector Multiplication; SpMV; Blocking; Vector Units; Autotuning

I. Introduction

Sparse matrices arise in many applications of natural science and engineering. The characteristic of sparse matrices is that almost all matrix values are zero and only very few entries (usually less than 1%) have a nonzero value. This sparseness property is used in special storage formats for such matrices to store only / mainly nonzero values along with index information. A performance critical operation on such matrices is the multiplication of a sparse matrix with a dense vector (SpMV) $\vec{y} \leftarrow A\vec{x}$ that may be executed many times, e.g., at each iteration step of an iterative solver. The efficiency of the SpMV operation highly depends on the used sparse matrix format, the matrix structure and how the SpMV operation is implemented and optimized according to the format. Many techniques are known to store a sparse matrix and perform the SpMV operation that take advantage of the nonzero structure of the matrix. One class of formats are block formats. Block storage formats exploit block structures of nonzero elements in a matrix and store dense blocks of values [1]. Block formats have several advantages for efficient SpMV executions. Storing nonzero values together in a block can lead to an improved spatial data locality and, by addressing more than one nonzero value by one index entry, the overall index structure, the memory indirections and the memory bandwidth demand are reduced [2] [3]. Another advantage of block formats is the use of the processor's Single Instruction Multi Data (SIMD) extension [4], i.e., the vector units of a processor. Such a block approach works for dense nonzero block structures in sparse matrices and increases the performance of the SpMV operation significantly, even if explicit zeros are used to fill the blocks [5].

There are two groups of blocking formats: fixed size blocking formats that use the same fixed block size for the whole matrix and variable sized block formats that use the structure of the matrix to build variable sized blocks. The advantages of fixed sized blocking formats are the possibility of optimizing the SpMV for certain, at compile time known, block sizes and the rather simple building of blocks by allowing and storing explicit zeros. The advantages of variable blocking formats are the exploitation of a non-regular matrix structure and the ability to store different sized blocks for a matrix. Furthermore, the two types can be combined with different other optimization techniques, like using bitmaps [6] [7] or relative indexing [8] [9]. There are also some block formats that do not fit in either of these categories or use both techniques [10].

Sparse matrices with an inherent block structure usually arise from a regular 2D / 3D geometry associated with the original problem. Such matrices can certainly benefit from blocking techniques [11]. A question is whether rather general matrices without a clear block structure can also benefit from blocking techniques.

Additionally, for different block sizes different implementations of the SpMV kernel may be optimal. Selecting an implementation among a set of different implementations for a large amount of different block sizes may be a task that can hardly be handled manually, due to the large parameter space. Thus, using an autotuning approach for this task may be beneficial.

The paper is structured as follows. In Section II, an overview on related work is given. In Section III, our own newly developed block format DynB is described, including the description of a low overhead algorithm for block detection, implementation issues of the specific SpMV operation and optimizations. In Section IV an autotuning approach for selecting optimal SpMV kernel implementations for different 2D block sizes is presented for the new format. The following Section V describes the experimental setup. Section VI shows performance results, which compare and evaluate relevant blocking formats on matrices without an explicit block structure. At last, in Section VII a conclusion is given.

II. Related Work

In this section, a comprehensive overview of block formats is given, including formats where blocks are used aside with other optimization techniques. Then, a short overview on further block detection methods is given. At last, autotuning methods are discussed.

As an introduction we start with a brief discussion of rather general sparse matrix formats. The Coordinate format (COO) [12] is the most simple and basic format to store a sparse matrix. It consists of three arrays. For a nonzero value, the value as well as the row and column index is stored explicitly at the i-th position in the three arrays, respectively. The size of each array is equal to the number of nonzeros. The order of values stored is of no concern. The Compressed Sparse Row format (CSR) [13] [12] [14] is one of the most used matrix format for sparse matrices. The index structure in CSR is in relation to COO reduced by replacing the row index for every nonzero value with a single index for all nonzero values in a row. This row index indicates the start of a new row within the other two arrays. As a consequence and in difference to COO, all values in a row must be stored consecutively.

For blocked formats, the Block Compressed Sparse Row format (BCSR) [14] [2] is similar to the CSR format. But instead of storing single nonzero values, the BCSR format stores blocks, i.e., dense submatrices of a fixed size. The matrix is partitioned into blocks of fixed size $r \times c$, where r and c represent the number of rows and columns of the blocks.Then, only submatrices with at least one nonzero element are stored. The optimal block size differs for different matrices and even different processor platforms. Advantages of the BCSR format are a possible reduction of the index structure, possible loop unrolling per block, using vector units through automatic compiler vectorization or using explicit intrinsics [15] and many other low level optimization techniques [16]. However, it may be necessary to store explicit zero values for blocks that are not fully filled with nonzero values. In the worst-case, this could lead to the same index structure as with CSR, but with additional zeros stored for each nonzero value.

The Mapped Blocked Row format (MBR) [6] is similar to the BCSR format. Like BCSR, MBR uses blocks of a fixed size $r \times c$. In addition to BCSR, bitmaps are stored that encode the nonzero structure for each block. An advantage of this bitmap array is, that only actual nonzero values need to be stored in the `values` array, even though filled-in zeros exist. In exchange for the reduced memory use, additional computation time is needed during the SpMV operation.

The Blocked Compressed Common Coordinate format (BCCOO) [17] uses fixed size blocks. It is based on the Blocked Common Coordinate (BCOO) format, which stores the matrix coordinates of a fixed sized block to address the value. BCCOO relies on a `bit_flag` to store information about the start of a new row. By using a bit array instead of an integer, a high compression rate of the index information is archived. One disadvantage of the `bit_flag` array is, that an additional array is needed to execute the SpMV operation in parallel with partition information.

The Unaligned Block Compressed Sparse Row format (UBCSR) [5] [18] removes the row alignment of the BCSR format by adding an additional array. However, this optimization appears to be only applicable to a special set of matrices where blocks occur in a recurring pattern in a row and are all shifted.

The Variable Block Row format (VBR) [5] analyses rows and columns that are next to each other. Their nonzero values are stored in blocks, if they have the identical pattern of nonzero values in a row or in a column. Hereby, only completely dense blocks are stored by VBR. It is possible to relax the analyses of rows and columns by the use of a threshold, which allows VBR to store explicit zeros to build larger blocks [18].

The Variable Block Length format (VBL) [3] [19] [11], which is also referred as Blocked Compressed Row Storage format (BCRS), is likewise similar to the CSR format. But, rather than storing a single value, all consecutive nonzero values in a row are stored in 1D blocks. The blocks of the VBL format do not have a fixed size and only nonzero values are stored. VBL may reduce the index structure depending on the stored matrix, but compared to CSR an additional loop inside the SpMV is required to process all blocks in a row and to proceed all elements in a block.

The aim of the Compressed sparse eXtended format (CSX) [10] is to compress index information by exploiting (arbitrary but fixed) substructures within matrices. CSX identifies horizontal, vertical, diagonal, anti-diagonal and two-dimensional block structures in a pre-process. The data structure, which is used by CSX to store the location information, is based on the Compressed Sparse Row Delta Unit format (CSR-DU) [20]. The advantages of CSX are the index reduction by using the techniques of CSR-DU and, at the same time, the provision of a special SpMV implementation for each substructure. However, implementing CSX seems to be rather complex and to determine appropriate substructures in a matrix may cause perceptible overhead.

The Pattern-based Representation format (PBR) [7] aims to reduce the index overhead. Instead of adding fill-in or relying on dense substructures in a matrix, PBR identifies recurring block structures that are sharing the same nonzero pattern. For each pattern that covers more nonzero values than a certain threshold, PBR stores a submatrix in the BCOO format plus a bitmap, which represents the repeated nonzero pattern. For each of these patterns, an optimized SpMV kernel is provided or generated. Belgin et al. state in their work [7] that it is possible to use prefetching, vectorization and parallelization to optimize each kernel individually. Advantages of PBR are the possibility of providing special SpMV kernels for each occurring block pattern as well as low level optimization for these SpMV kernels.

The Recursive Sparse Blocks (RSB) format [21] [22] aims to reduce the index overhead while keeping locality. By building a quadtree, which represents the sparse matrix, the matrix is recursively divided into four quadrant submatrices, until a certain termination condition is reached. The termination condition for the recursive function is defined in detail by Martone et al. in [23] [24]. The submatrix is stored in the leaf node of the quadtree in COO or CSR format. All nodes before the leaf node do not contain matrix data and are pointers, which build the quadtree.

The Compressed Sparse Block format (CSB) [8] [9] aims to reduce the storage needed to store the location of a value within a matrix by splitting the matrix into huge square blocks. Further, row and column indices of each value are stored relatively to each block. Due to the relative addressing of the values, it is possible to use smaller data types for the row and column index arrays, which leads to an index reduction per nonzero. It is possible to order the values inside the `values` array to get better performance of the SpMV operation. The authors of the original work suggest a recursive Z-Motion ordering to provide spatial locality. The parallel SpMV implementation of CSB uses a private result vector per thread, but the implementation also provides an optimization in case the vector is not required for a block row [8].

In [25] it is shown that finding optimal nonoverlapping dense blocks in a sparse matrix is a NP complete problem. Here, the proof is given by using a reduction of the maximum independent set problem, which is known to be NP complete [26]. Moreover, [25] gives a greedy algorithm for finding 2×2 blocks within a sparse matrix. This algorithm is based on a decision tree for finding only dense blocks, allowing no fill-in within these blocks.

Other methods that can be used for blockfinding are for example the kd-tree [27] and r-tree [28] data structure / algorithm known from spatial databases. Both build (search) tree data structures using spatial location of points or objects within a search region.

Various other publications [29] [30] [31] [32] [33] discuss the use of autotuning approaches, which can be used for a wide range of optimizations. E.g., the selection of format parameters, specific optimization techniques or the selection of the best suited formats. Sophisticated auto-tuning approaches are based on complex models [31] [32] or mathematical and machine learning concepts [33].

In [29] Byun et al. present an auto-tuning framework for optimizing the CSR format, e.g., by fixed-sized blocking. This framework is used to find the optimal blocking for the resulting BCSR format for a given input matrix and used hardware platform.

III. Development of a 2D Variable Sized Block Format

In this section, a newly developed variable sized block format, called DynB, is described. The goal of DynB is, to find rectangular 2D blocks within a matrix to efficiently utilize a processor's vector units for the SpMV. At first, a simple and fast algorithm for the detection of variable sized 2D blocks is introduced. Then, the overall structure of the format is given. Afterwards, the SpMV kernel is presented and at last code optimization techniques are considered.

A. Finding Variable Sized Blocks

As described in Section II, the CSX format uses a sophisticated but time consuming algorithm to find even complex nonzero substructures within the entire matrix. Although the speedup of the SpMV operation may be high, many SpMV operations may be neccessary to compensate the cost of the detection algorithm. In contrast, the VBL format uses a simple and fast algorithm to find just 1D blocks within each row of a matrix. However, the speedup of the SpMV may not be as high as for CSX. For the introduced DynB format a fast algorithm

Input: $A[\,][\,]$, T, S_{max}
Output: $B[\,][\,]$
for $i \leftarrow 1, nRows$
  for $j \leftarrow 1, nColumns$
    if $A[i][j] \neq 0 \wedge A[i][j] \notin B$
      $r \leftarrow 1,\ c \leftarrow 1,\ rr \leftarrow 0,\ cc \leftarrow 0$
      $added \leftarrow TRUE$
      while $added$
        $added \leftarrow FALSE$
        $rr \leftarrow r-1,\ cc \leftarrow c-1$
        $search$(next column n with $A[i:i+rr][n] \neq 0$)
        $search$(next row m with $A[m][j:j+cc] \neq 0$)
        if $r*(n+1-j) \leq S_{max} \wedge t(A[i:i+rr][j:n]) \geq T$
          $c \leftarrow n+1-j$
          $added \leftarrow TRUE$
        end if
        if $(m+1-i)*c \leq S_{max} \wedge t(A[i:m][j:j+cc]) \geq T$
          $r \leftarrow m+1-i$
          $added \leftarrow TRUE$
        end if
      end while
      $B \leftarrow B + A[i:i+rr][j:j+cc]$
    end if
  end for
end for

Figure 1: Fast Heuristic for the Detection of 2D Blocks.

to find rectangular 2D blocks over the entire matrix should be developed. With these 2D blocks, a reasonable runtime improvement for the SpMV operation should be achieved, by using advantages similar to BCSR, while possibly generating less fill-in.

The algorithm we developed to find 2D block structures of nonzero elements is a fast greedy heuristic. It tries to find possible block candidates that should be as large as possible, even if nonzeros are not direct neighbors, i.e., fill-ins of explicit zeros are allowed up to a certain amount per block. Consequently, a threshold T is used that indicates how dense a block candidate, which has been found by the heuristic, needs to be in order to be stored as a block. That means T is a measure for how many fill-in is allowed in a block. The nonzero density $t(block)$ of a block has to satisfy the relation

$$\begin{aligned} t(block) &= nnz_{block}/blocksize \\ &= nnz_{block}/(nnz_{block}+zeros) \\ &= nnz_{block}/(r*c) \\ &\geq T \end{aligned}$$

where nnz_{block} represents the number of nonzero values in the block and r, c the number of rows, columns of that block.

The algorithm shown in Figure 1 describes a simplified version of the heuristic, which is used to find the blocks in a matrix. The heuristic takes a sparse matrix $A[][]$, the desired threshold T (maximum portion of nonzero values in a block) and a maximum blocksize S_{max} (usually according to the size of the vector units) as an input. It gives the converted blocked Matrix $B[][]$ as output. The algorithm iterates rowwise over the nonzero elements of the original matrix. If a nonzero value of the original matrix is not already assigned to a block, a new 1×1 block will be created. Then this block will be

$$A = \begin{pmatrix} 0 & a_1 & a_2 & 0 & 0 & 0 & 0 & 0 \\ 0 & a_3 & a_4 & 0 & 0 & 0 & 0 & 0 \\ 0 & 0 & a_5 & 0 & 0 & 0 & a_6 & a_7 \\ 0 & 0 & a_8 & 0 & 0 & 0 & a_9 & a_{10} \\ a_{11} & 0 & 0 & a_{12} & a_{13} & a_{14} & 0 & 0 \\ a_{15} & 0 & 0 & a_{16} & 0 & a_{17} & 0 & 0 \\ a_{18} & 0 & 0 & a_{19} & a_{20} & a_{21} & 0 & 0 \\ 0 & a_{22} & 0 & 0 & 0 & 0 & 0 & 0 \end{pmatrix}$$

$$\begin{aligned}
\texttt{values} &= \{a_1, a_2, a_3, a_4, 0, a_5, 0, a_8, \\
&\quad a_6, a_7, a_9, a_{10}, \\
&\quad a_{11}, a_{15}, a_{18}, \\
&\quad a_{12}, a_{13}, a_{14}, a_{16}, 0, a_{17}, a_{19}, a_{20}, a_{21}, \\
&\quad a_{22}\} \\
\texttt{block_start} &= \{0, 8, 12, 15, 24\} \\
\texttt{row_index} &= \{0, 2, 4, 4, 7\} \\
\texttt{column_index} &= \{1, 6, 0, 3, 1\} \\
\texttt{block_row} &= \{4, 2, 3, 3, 1\} \\
\texttt{block_column} &= \{2, 2, 1, 3, 1\}
\end{aligned}$$

Figure 2: The DynB Format storing Matrix A with a Threshold of 0.75.

expanded successively with new columns and rows in each iteration of the while loop. Adding a new column or row means adding the column/row with the next nonzero element and all fill-in columns/rows with zeros that are located between the outermost block column/row and the column/row with the next nonzero. Column/rows are only added to the block if the nonzero density of the block after adding these columns/rows would be large enough. If not enough nonzero elements would be added, i.e., the **if** statements for both column and row fail, the heuristic will finish the block. After all blocks are found, the memory for the DynB data structure is allocated and filled with the actual values and index structure. This data structure is described in the following section.

B. Structure of the Format

The DynB format relies on six arrays. In the `values` array the nonzero values (plus fill-in zeros) are consecutively stored in block order and rowwise within a block. The `block_start` pointer stores the starting position of each block in the `values` array. The `row_index` and the `column_index` store the location of the upper left corner of each block. This is similar to the COO format for single values, but here, fewer indices are stored explicitly, because the indices are used to address a whole block of values. Finally, the `block_row` and `block_column` arrays store the column and row size of each two dimensional block, i.e., the block size is variable. Below, the purpose of the six arrays are described as well as why certain data types were chosen and how many entries they contain:

- `values[nnz+zeros]` : **double** contains the values of the matrix.
- `rowIndex[blocks]` : **int** stores the row index in which a block starts.
- `columnIndex[blocks]` : **int** stores the column index in which a block starts.
- `blockStart[blocks]` : **int** stores the start point of each block inside the `values` array.

```
for (int i = 0; i < nonZeroBlocks; ++i){
  //general SpMV for any blocksize
  for (int ii = 0; ii < blockRow[i]; ++ii){
    double s = 0.0;
    int jj =  blockStart[i] + (blockColumn[i]*ii) ;
      for (int j = 0 ; j < blockColumn[i]; ++j, ++jj){
        s += values[jj] * x[columnIndex[i]+j];
      }
      y[rowIndex[i]+ii]+=s;
  }
}
```

Figure 3: SpMV implementation of DynB for general blocks.

- `blockRow[blocks]` : **unsigned char** stores the number of rows a block contains. The unsigned char data type is used because the maximum allowed block size is 64, according to the size of vector units, which means that $blockRow \times blockColumn \leq 64$ must hold.
- `blockColumn[blocks]` : **unsigned char** stores the number of columns a block contains.
- `nonZeroBlocks` : **int** stores the quantity of blocks.
- `threshold` : **float** needs to be set prior to the conversion of a matrix into the DynB format. The threshold needs to be positive and smaller or equal to 1.0 (e.g., $1.0 = 100\%$ nonzero values, $0.5 = 50\%$ nonzero values in a block are allowed).

All data types are choosen as small as possible to reduce memory bandwidth demands, which are critical in SpMV operations. Figure 2 shows in an example how a matrix A is stored using the DynB format.

C. SpMV Kernel

The SpMV implementation of DynB iterates over the blocks, which have been build before. A general and simplified code version is shown in Figure 3. Initially, beside a generic code version able to handle arbitrary block sizes, we implemented additionally optimized code versions for special and often found block structures (single nonzero values, horizontal and vertical 1D blocks and the general case of all other 2D block sizes). Further block kernels were implemented for the autotuning (see Section IV-A).

D. Code Optimization

It was already shown in [34] that using vector intrinsics to address the vector units of a processor can lead to a performance gain for the SpMV operation. However, with this technique the programmer needs to write code on an assembler level, which can be tedious and error prone. Another approach, which showed good results in [34], is to leave the utilization of vector units solely to the compiler. For the Intel Compiler icc/icpc, automatic compiler vectorization is enabled for the optimization level `-O2` and higher levels [15]. The compiler can use various optimization techniques and auto-vectorize code, where possible. To achieve this, the compiler has to be provided with appropriate information. E.g., by using the `-x` compiler option the information on the target processor architecture / instruction set can be provided [15]. Without this option, the compiler uses a default (older) instruction set that can not utilize abilities of current vector units. A programmer can give the compiler additional hints, e.g., where data can be assumed as aligned, if the compiler is not able to

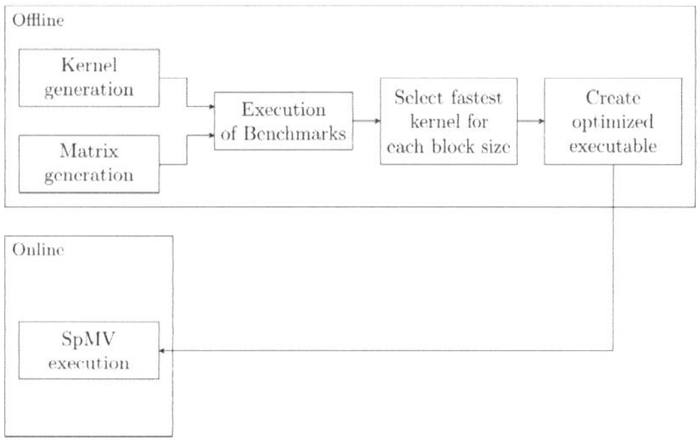

Figure 4: Simplified Process of the DynB Autotuning.

detect this automatically [15]. Furthermore, different `pragmas` exist to force the compiler to execute different actions. With `#pragma simd` a compiler is requested to vectorize a loop even if the compiler ascertains that this is not a good idea. There are many other possible optimizations as well for the blocked SpMV. Loop unrolling can be executed manually by the programmer, if the blocksizes are known beforehand. With `pragma unroll`, the compiler can be forced to unroll a loop. Furthermore, special cases of the blocked SpMV can be considererd, e.g., for 1D blocks, resulting in single loops instead of nested loops.

IV. Autotuning for 2D Blocks

By enabling variable block sizes, many blocks of different sizes may be found. Due to the design decision (and optimization) of using `unsigned char` and therefore 8 Bits to code a block size, the DynB format supports 280 different block sizes. It would be possible to compute the SpMV operation using one general kernel code for arbitrary block sizes that iterates over both dimensions of the blocks (see Figure 3 for such a general code version). This very simple implementation is not expected to deliver the optimal performance, as it contains two additional loops with unknown iteration counts, which can not easily be optimized by a compiler. It is expected that the optimal implementation for each block size is at least slightly different. E.g., the use of vector units may be beneficial for larger, but not for very small blocks, e.g., single values. Additionally, the optimal strategy to handle specific block sizes is processor specific. Finding the optimal implementation for each possible block size manually may be time consuming. Thus, an autotuning approach is used for the DynB format to find offline optimal implementations. The focus of the developed autotuning approach is on the optimization of the SpMV operation for the DynB format, which uses dynamic block sizes.

A. Description of the Autotuning Approach

The developed autotuning approach for the DynB format has similarities to the pOSKI framework [29]. This framework is used for finding the optimal blocking for a given input matrix and used hardware platform. The autotuning approach developed in this work focuses on the identification of optimal implementations for all possible block sizes of the DynB format.

The basic idea of the autotuning approach is to identify the optimal implementation for each block size individually, using a large set of possible implementations and synthetic benchmark matrices with different sparsity pattern. The simplified process of the autotuning is presented in Figure 4. In a first step, the possible SpMV kernels and the benchmark matrices have to be generated. A large set of matrices is thereby created, with each matrix containing only one specific block size. Afterwards, the SpMV is executed using all kernels and the benchmark matrices, while the execution time is measured. The gathered information can then be used to identify the fastest implementation for each specific block size. These implementations are then used to generate an optimized executable, which is used to execute the actual SpMV operation. The complete autotuning is required only once for the specific hardware platform and can be executed offline. This means there is no overhead for the the SpMV operation applied on an actual matrix, caused by the autotuning. In the following, the different steps are explained in more detail.

In the first step, the kernel generation, the required SpMV kernel source code for the for all possible block sizes is generated. Many kernels can be generated automatically, because they follow a fixed pattern. There are additional kernels of relevance, e.g., implementations using intrinsics, that can not easily be generated automatically and therefore hand-tuning is necessary is this cases. The following list shows the set of kernels used for most block sizes:

- **normal**: The default kernel, normally used in the general case. Consists of two loops with variable loop count.
- **loop**: Very similar implementation as the **normal** kernel. Instead of variable loop counts, the known block sizes are used as static loop counts.
- **singleLoop**: Special kernel for one dimensional blocks only. Implementation is identical with the **loop** kernel, but only using one of the loops. The other loop is not required, as its iteration count would be 1.
- **unroll**: Identical loop implementation as the **loop** kernel. Additionally the `#pragma unroll` directive is used to generated unrolled code with different unroll factors.
- **novec**: Identical loop implementation as the **loop** kernel. Additionally the `#pragma novector` directive is used to prevent a vectorization of the code.
- **simd**: Identical loop implementation as the **loop** kernel. Additionally the `#pragma simd` directive is used to force vectorization of the code.
- **plain**: The kernel is implemented without any loops. All operations are manually unrolled.
- **intrinsic**: Similar to the **plain** kernel, the kernel is implemented without loops. The calculation is implemented using low level intrinsic functions. The kernels have to be written manually.

In the basic DynB format the elements of every block are stored in row-major order. For the autotuning every kernel is additionally generated for a column-major order organization of the blocks. The creation of the format has been changed as well to allow both block types. This may allow a more efficient vector unit utilization.

Figure 5 shows the usage of vector units with a column-major order and row-major order. In column-major order, vector units are used to process multiple rows at once, which allows a very efficient calculation. Memory accesses can be easily aligned and consecutive. Furthermore, after calculating

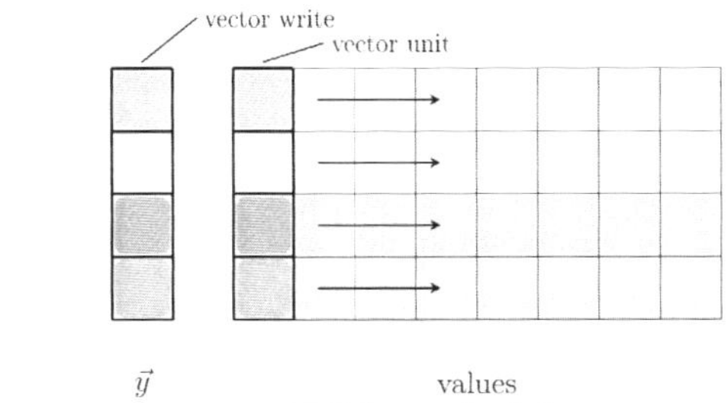

(a) Column-major Order

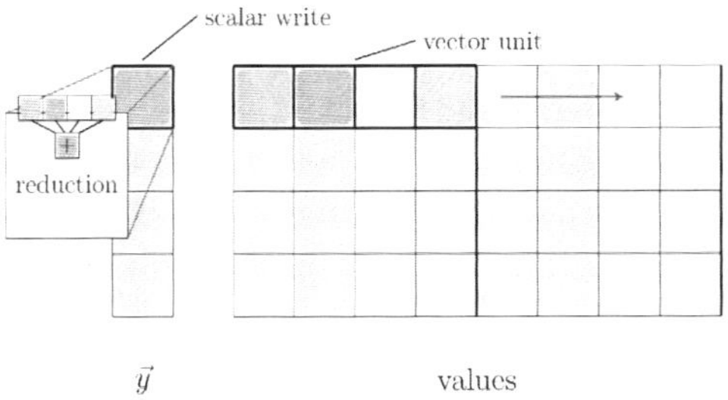

(b) Row-major Order

Figure 5: Calculation of 2D Blocks using Vector-Units.

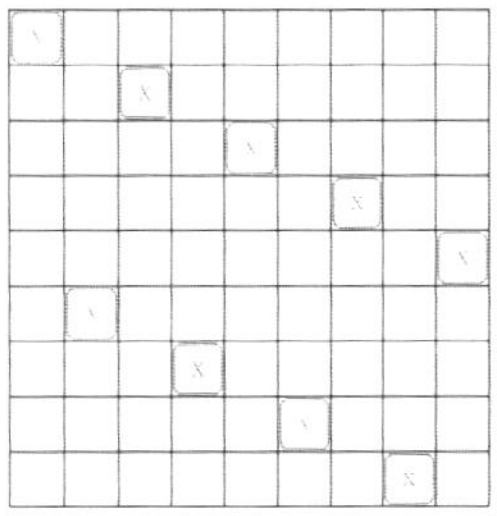

(a) Round Robin

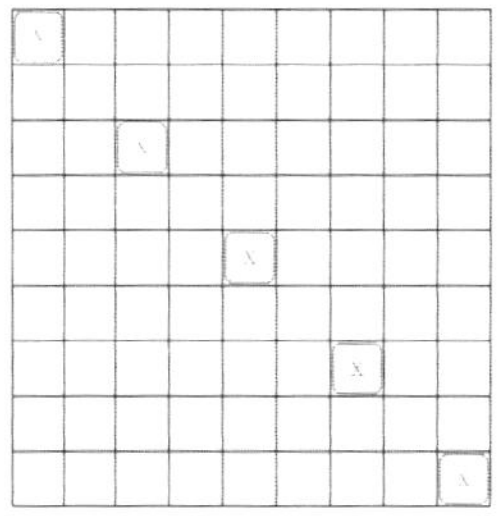

(b) Diagonal

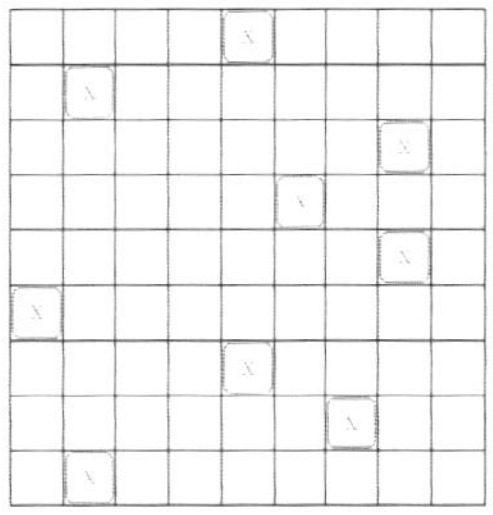

(c) Random

Figure 6: Illustration of the three different structures used for the synthetic matrices of the DynB autotuning. Every red square represents a block in the DynB format.

the last elements of the rows, the result of the vector unit is simply written to the $\vec{y}$ vector.

On the other hand, in row-major order, vector units process elements of the same row. This requires an additional reduction operation at the end of every row, as the partial results of the vector unit lanes have to be combined.

The matrix generation for the benchmark matrices is also done in the first autotuning step. For each block size a set of synthetic benchmark matrices is generated. Thereby, the matrices contain one specific block size only. Furthermore, for each block size three different distributions of the elements and two different nonzero densities are created. This is done to analyze, if the matrix structure has an impact on the individual kernel performance.

Figure 6 presents the three used distributions. In every distribution the blocks are placed with a safety margin around them, to prevent the greedy block finding algorithm of the DynB format to combine multiple blocks into one bigger block. The first structure is called round robin and it distributes the elements evenly over the columns of the matrix. Starting in the first row and column, the blocks are placed in increasing columns. When the end of the matrix is reached, the column index is reset. The resulting patterns resamble squashed diagonals. The second structure is a simple diagonal pattern, because of the safety margin there is not an element in every row. The last structure selects the column index of the blocks randomly. The number of entries per row is still fixed, also the safety margin is still be respected.

The second step of our autotuning uses the generated kernels and matrices and measures the SpMV execution time. Furthermore, for each kernel multiple versions should be used, using different compilers, optimization levels and inlining of code.

In the third step the fastest kernel for each individual block size has to be identified. This can simply be achieved by comparing the measured runtimes of all kernels for one specific block size. Further complexity is introduced by the different matrix structures used, which may require a comparison over a larger data set.

The last step of the offline autotuning is the creation of an optimized executable for the SpMV execution. The kernels identified in the previous step are combined into one large SpMV kernel, to provide a proper implementation for every possible kernel. Further analysis may be required to identify if it is suitable to provide an implementation for every of the 280 possible kernels. For each block in a matrix, the proper kernel has to be selected at runtime. The selection of the kernel has therefore to be very efficient, to prevent excessive branching. This will be described in more detail in the following Section IV-B, where the implementation is described.

The developed autotuning potentially can increase the performance of the DynB format. The default implementation does handle most of the block sizes identically. For small blocks the loop overhead of the general implementation might be too high, while for larger blocks the use of vector units may be beneficial. One possible problem with the use of individual kernels is the introduced branching that is necessary to handle the different sizes. For every block the correct kernel has to be identified and executed, which can potentially slow down the SpMV. Furthermore, the amount of program code could result in problems with the instruction caches. If a large number of different kernel implementations is used, the required code could not fit in the available caches.

Another problem may occur because of the developed autotuning process itself. The initial assumption of the autotuning is, that the performance result of the individual kernels and synthetic matrices can be used to determine the proper kernel for a real matrix. It is also assumed, that the performance numbers of the sequential execution can be used to find the optimal kernels for a parallel executions. It is possible that these assumptions do not hold true, which would result in wrong findings.

B. Implementation

The autotuning approach can be automated using scripts (e.g., we used Python) in combination with the SpMV implementation. As described in the previous section, most of the kernels can be generated automatically. These kernels have one basic pattern, which can be adapted to different block sizes. This is different for some more specialized kernels, which need to be written by hand. One example for this are implementations using intrinsics. The kernel creation scripts take manually written kernels and the general templates to create the source code for the kernels for every block size.

The benchmarking script uses the kernel source code to compile a special version of the DynB SpMV operation. The SpMV operation is executed using the synthetic matrices and the execution time is measured. The results can ce stored, e.g., in a database. This step is repeated several times for every kernel using different compilers and optimization options. Finally, the selection of the fastest kernels and the creation of the optimized executable can also be automated using scripts.

An important part of the implementation is the integration of the optimized block kernels into the SpMV operation of the DynB format. As already discussed in the previous section, 280 different block sizes and kernels are possible, which potentially introduces a lot of additional branching. To handle this efficiently a jumper table should be used either by function pointer arrays generated by a programmer or by a switch case that is handled by the compiler. Many compilers are able to create a jumper table from a switch case if certain limitations are respected, e.g., the number of states are within a certain limit. This behavior has been verified for the Intel compiler, by analyzing the generated assembler code. The analysis also showed, that the optimization can be applied in the case that not only consecutive numerical values are used. In this case, the missing values are filled with jump directives to the default case of the switch case statement.

V. Experimental Setup

The experiments to evaluate block formats were run on a system with an Intel Xeon E5-2697 v3 CPU (Haswell architecture) [35] and the Intel C++ Compiler version 2017 [15]. A set of 78 large test matrices from the Florida Sparse Matrix Collection [36] and SPE reference problems [37] was taken as test matrices. Most of the chosen matrices do *not* have an overall explicit block structure of nonzeros. Compiler optimization and AVX2 instruction set were used, if possible. The following block matrix formats were chosen to be compared in the experiments. They represent a selection of 1D and 2D block formats with fixed and variable sizes as well as more arbitrary pattern (CSX) which have shown to be well performing, at least on matrices with an explicit block structure. In parentheses is shown whether fixed or variable sized blocks can be used.

- DynB (variable): own implementation according to Section III, threshold T varied from 0.55 (slightly more nonzeros than fill-in) to 1.0 (only nonzeros, no fill-in).
- VBL (variable): own implementation according to [3].
- CSX (variable): library taken from the authors of the original work on CSX [10] [38], no influence on implementation.
- BCSR (fixed): own implementation according to [14], block dimensions: 2×2, 3×3, 4×4

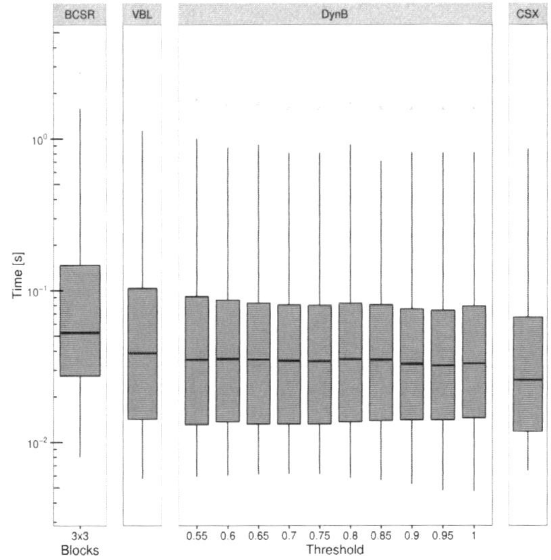

Figure 7: SpMV with all Blocking Formats, Best implementation.

TABLE I: Count of minimal SpMV execution times

BCSR	VBL	DynB	CSX
0	4	32	42

Moreover, the autotuning approach for the DynB format was measured for selected block kernels. The other block kernels were chosen to be optimized by the compiler, giving it in all cases of the switch statement the exact block dimensions as constants. For all experiments, the SpMV operation was executed 100 times and the median of these execution times was taken as the resulting execution time, to exclude uncertainty of the measurements. Subsequently, this is referred to as execution time.

VI. Results

In this section we present selected results of the executed experiments. When boxplots are shown, the quartiles over the results for all matrices are given, whiskers extend to the last datapoint within 1.5 × *interquartile range* and outliers are drawn as points.

A. Comparison of the Formats

Figure 7 shows the execution times of the SpMV for the formats of interest. Different optimizations were applied and the on average best implementation was chosen (for DynB optimizations see Section III-D). For BCSR different blocksizes are possible. In the figure, the results for the 3×3 blocks are shown which have shown the best results over all supported blocksizes.

The base BCSR version showed the weakest performance of all formats. An explanation is the introduced fill-in of

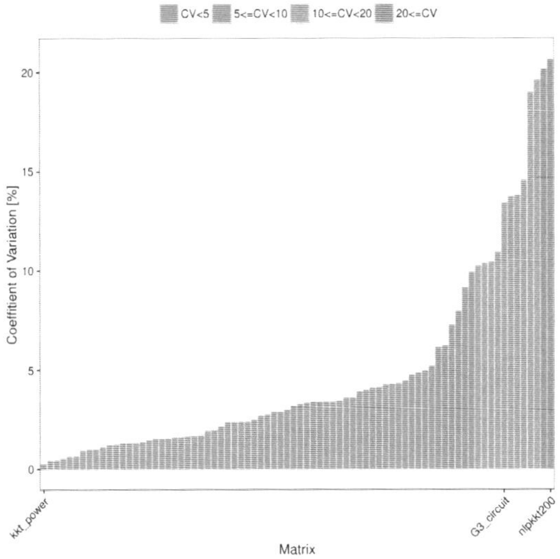

Figure 8: Coefficient of Variation of SpMV with DynB over all Thresholds per Matrix.

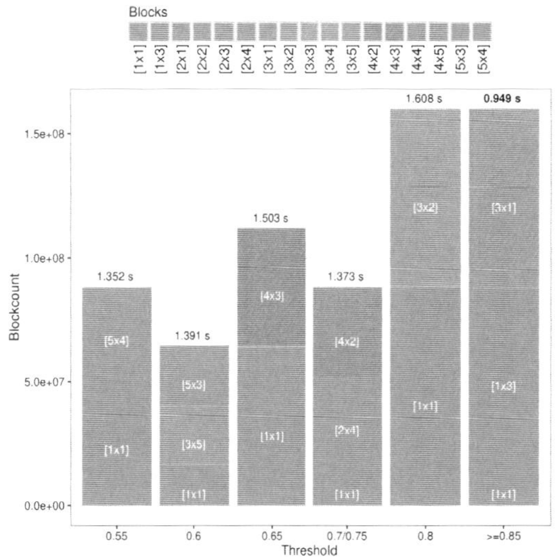

Figure 9: Blocks Found for DynB with Different Thresholds, *nlpkkt200* Matrix.

nonzero values of the format for the fixed 2D block sizes for the rather general matrices used (i.e., without regular block structures). Therefore, a first conclusion is already that the BCSR format should be used only for matrices where an appropriate nonzero pattern exists in the matrix.

Comparing VBL, DynB and CSX shows that these formats are on a similar SpMV performance level. However, the (one-time) creation times for the VBL format were much shorter than the complex detection algorithm for the CSX format, due to the simpler heuristics used in VBL. For the DynB format, there seem to be onyl minor differences dependent on the threshold T.

Table I summarizes the best ranking of the examined formats, i.e., when a format with any setting resulted in the minimal execution times of the SpMV operation. It can be seen that the DynB is the second best format for this setting behind the CSX. However, the algorithm for block detection in the CSX is much more complicated than the detection of the rectangular blocks for the DynB format. Additionally, parallelizing the CSX format is difficult, for example as it is possible that blocks overlap over a row which is circumvented in the creation process of the DynB format. Overlapping blocks in rows computed by different threads requires some form of (costly) synchronization, e.g., atomic operations or reductions on private buffers which can be quite costly.

B. Analysis of the DynB Format

In this subsection the DynB format is analyzed in more depth regarding the influence of the threshold T and the autotuning.

1) Influence of the Threshold T: Here, we begin initially with the standard / base version of the DynB and used compiler optimization level `O3` and the AVX2 instruction set. Figure 8 shows the coefficient of variation of the SpMV execution time for the DynB format for the test matrices, over all thresholds T for the allowable fill-in of a block. It can be seen that, for some matrices varying the threshold T has a significant impact on the execution time. This is due to the different blocks that were found by the heuristic. Figure 9 shows the found blocks and their execution times according to the threshold for the example matrix *nlpkkt80*. The class of *nlpkkt* matrices have shown the highest coefficient of variation. It can be seen that, for several different thresholds the same block sizes were found. Consequently, the execution times for the same block sizes do not differ significantly. Moreover, when blocksize 1×1 is predominant (i.e., such blocks consist of a single nonzero value), the execution times are highest. Here, a lot of overhead arises due to the indices that have to be stored for only single values. The best execution times are achieved, when the threshold is higher, i.e., less fill-in occurs, and (for

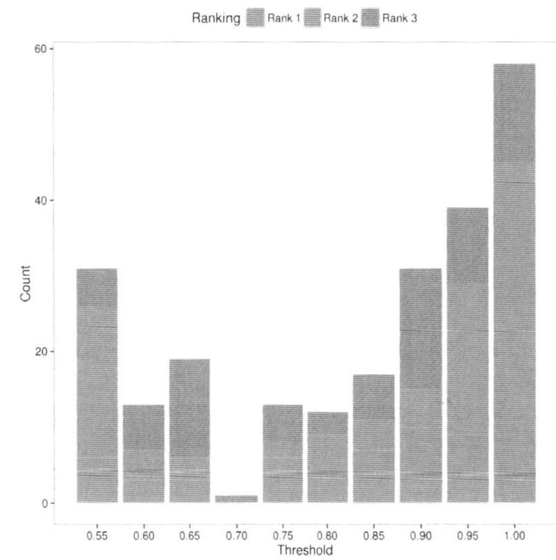

Figure 10: Ranking of DynB Thresholds.

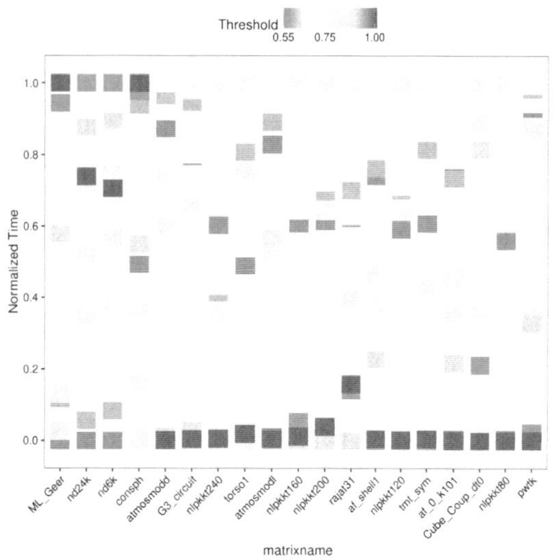

Figure 11: Normalized Times for selected Matrices with DynB, Different Thresholds.

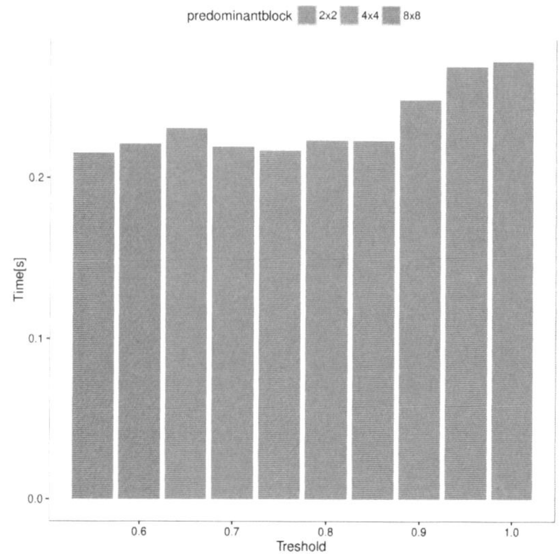

Figure 12: SpMV of ML_Geer for different Threshold.

this matrix) a lot of 1D blocks are found.

For the *G3_circuit* matrix the results are similar (not explicitly shown here), but its coefficient of variation is lower, what can be explained by the lower number of nonzeros, so execution time is primarily lower. The matrix with the lowest coefficient of variance is the *kkt_power*. For this matrix, changing the threshold did not result in different blocks, due to the structure of the matrix. Hence, the execution time was the same for all thresholds.

Figure 10 shows the count of the ranking (rank 1 to rank 3, related to time) of the thresholds across all matrices, i.e., how often a threshold resulted in the fastest, 2nd fastet and 3rd fastest time. Overall, it can be seen that higher thresholds (less or no fill-in) could lead mostly to a good ranking. Medium threshold did not result in a good ranking for the test matrices. However, in some cases, a low threshold (sufficient amount of fill-in) result in better rank counts again.

This is further shown in Figure 11. Here, the normalized times ($Time \in [0.0, 1.0]$) for selected matrices with different structures is given for different thresholds. It can be seen that not for all matrices a higher threshold leads to short execution times of the SpMV operation. For example, the matrices *ML_Geer*, *nd24k* and *nd6k* show the best results with a low threshold (thus more fill-in). Figure 12 shows the absolute results for the matrix *ML_Geer*. With a higher amount of fill-in it is possible to find more larger blocks (8×8 or 4×4). Moreover, when many small blocks are found the use of the AVX2 instruction set is even disadvantegous. With this instruction set the vector size of 4 with the Haswell architecture is assumed. Thus the shortest SpMV execution times can be achieved with different settings, dependent on the threshold.

2) Influence of the Autotuning: The results of the autotuning approach can be seen in Figure 13. Here, the autotuning described in Section IV-A was used. Four different settings are shown:

1) autotuned transposed
2) autotuned untransposed
3) comp. transposed
4) comp. untransposed

Items 1 and 2 are partially autotuned kernels, with 30 autotuned blocks and the rest of the kernels transposed or untransposed and optimized by the compiler (see Section IV-A). Compiler guided (comp.) denotes that the compiler is provided with the constant block sizes per kernel (constant propagation is therefore possible at compile time) and the compiler is thus able to optimize these kernels. The compiler guided version was also executed with transposed and untransposed blocks. It can be seen that all approaches mostly lead to a reasonable speedup. However, the compiler guided optimization, i.e., providing the Intel compiler with the information about (constant) blocksizes at compile time, results in the best speedup, even compared to the code version proposed by autotuning. This is consistent with the results presented in [34], where different optimization setting where examined.

3) Possible Applications: As described in Section I the SpMV is a central operation in iterative solvers, such as Conjugate Gradient (CG) or Generalized Minimal Residual (GMRES) [12]. Finding dense subblocks with the algorithm described in Figure 1 can be used in a one time preprocessing step before executing the actual solver. Then, the SpMV operation can be executed repeatedly with the same matrix within the iterative solver. Matrices where 1×1 blocks are *not* the predominant block size found by the algorithm are most suitable for the use with the DynB format. There are 44 matrices from our testset for which this is true. These matrices mostly arise from 2D / 3D problems with different origin, e.g., *RM07M* (CFD problem) [36], *Serena* (gas reservoir FEM problem) [36], *Geo_1438* (geomechanical problem) [36], *SPE* matrices (reservoir simulation problems) [37]. But there are also matrices that arise from other problems, like *TSOPF_RS_b2383* (power network problem) [36], *nlpkkt* matrices (optimization problems) [36] that are suitable for the DynB format. Spyplots of some of these matrices are given

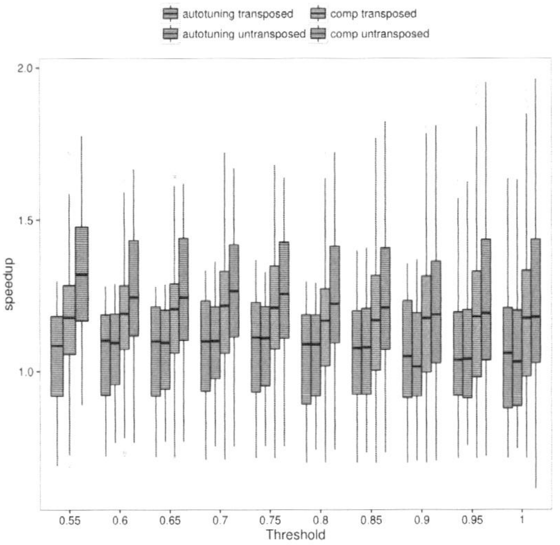

Figure 13: SpMV with DynB Format, Different Optimizations.

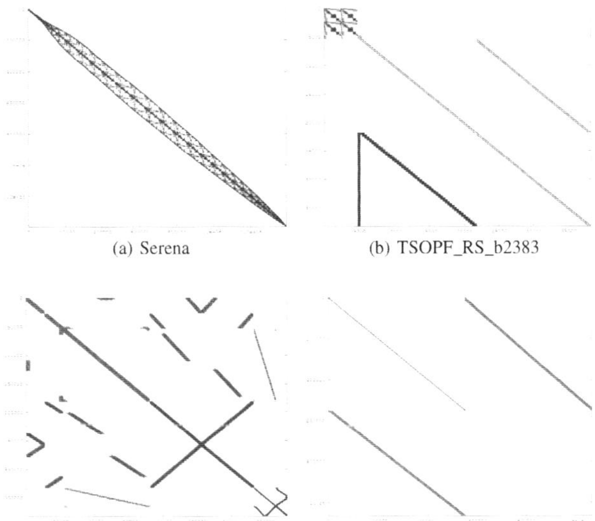

(a) Serena (b) TSOPF_RS_b2383

(c) RM07R (d) nlpkkt80

Figure 14: Example Matrices from the Testset.

in Figure 14. It can be seen that the matrices may have very different structures and they also have different properties, such as positive definiteness or symmetry. However, they all have a lot of densely packed regions, i.e., arbitrary grouped nonzero entries that can be exploited by the block finding alogorithm.

VII. Conclusions

In this paper, a new matrix format DynB for storing variable sized 2D blocks was introduced. The aim of the new format is to utilize *any* nonzero block structures in sparse matrices, because dense blocks can be handled efficiently with current and even more future processor architectures. For the DynB format, a simple and fast algorithm for finding blocks of different size and a related implementation of the SpMV operation was presented. Furthermore, several code optimization techniques, such as using vector intrinsics and using autotuning, were examined.

The execution of the SpMV operation on a large set of sparse matrices with different nonzero structures was examined and compared to other known block formats. Here, the formats with variable sized blocks had an advantage over the BCSR with fixed size blocks. For the DynB format, the structure of the matrix can have a significant impact on the dimension of the found blocks and thus on the execution time of the SpMV operation. Moreover, the choice of an appropiate threshold for DynB is dependent on the matrix structure. Several optimization approaches were introduced and combined in an autotuning technique for the DynB format. However, results showed that, when constant propagation is used for the block dimensions for every block kernel, the compiler optimizations showed the best results. Future work on the DynB format will include improvements in finding variable sized rectangular blocks and examining different parallelization techniques.

Acknowledgements

Simon Scholl at Bonn-Rhein-Sieg University helped us in many discussions. We would like to thank the CMT team at Saudi Aramco EXPEC ARC for their support and input. Especially we want to thank Ali H. Dogru for making this research project possible.

References

[1] J. Razzaq, R. Berrendorf, S. Hack, M. Weierstall, and F. Mannuss, "Fixed and variable sized block techniques for sparse matrix vector multiplication with general matrix structures," in Proc. Tenth Intl. Conference on Advanced Engineering Computing and Applications in Sciences (ADVCOMP 2016), pp. 84–90, 2016.

[2] E.-J. Im, K. Yelick, and R. Vuduc, "Sparsity: Optimization framework for sparse matrix kernels," The International Journal of High Performance Computing Applications, vol. 18, no. 1, pp. 135–158, 2004.

[3] A. Pinar and M. T. Heath, "Improving performance of sparse matrix-vector multiplication," in Proc. ACM/IEEE Conference on Supercomputing (SC'99), pp. 30 – 39. IEEE, Nov. 1999.

[4] S. Williams et al., "Optimization of sparse matrix-vector multiplication on emerging multicore platforms," in Proc. ACM/IEEE Supercomputing 2007 (SC'07), pp. 1–12. IEEE, 2007.

[5] R. W. Vuduc, "Automatic performance tuning of sparse matrix kernels," Ph.D. dissertation, University of California, Berkeley, 2003.

[6] R. Kannan, "Efficient sparse matrix multiple-vector multiplication using a bitmapped format," in Proc. 20th International Conference on High Performance Computing (HiPC), pp. 286–294. IEEE, 2013.

[7] M. Belgin, G. Back, and C. J. Ribbens, "Pattern-based sparse matrix representation for memory-efficient smvm kernels," in Proc. 23rd International Conference on Supercomputing (SC'09), ser. ICS '09, pp. 100–109. ACM, 2009.

[8] A. Buluc, J. T. Fineman, M. Frigo, J. R. Gilbert, and C. E. Leiserson, "Parallel sparse matrix-vector and matrix-transpose-vector multiplication using compressed sparse blocks," in Proc. 21th Annual Symp. on Parallelism in Algorithms and Architectures (SPAA'09), pp. 233–244. ACM, 2009.

[9] A. Buluc, S. Williams, L. Oliker, and J. Demmel, "Reduced-bandwidth multithreaded algorithms for sparse matrix-vector multiplication," in Proc. Intl. Parallel and Distributed Processing Symposium (IPDPS'2011), pp. 721–733. IEEE, 2011.

[10] V. Karakasis, T. Gkountouvas, K. Kourtis, G. Goumas, and N. Koziris, "An extended compression format for the optimization of sparse matrix-vector multiplication," IEEE Transactions on Parallel and Distributed Systems, vol. 24, no. 10, pp. 1930–1940, Oct. 2013.

[11] V. Karakasis, G. Goumas, and N. Koziris, "A comparative study of blocking storage methods for sparse matrices on multicore architectures," in Proc. 12th IEEE Intl. Conference on Computational Science and Engineerging (CSE-09), pp. 247–256. IEEE, 2009.

[12] Y. Saad, Iterative Methods for Sparse Linear Systems, 2nd ed. SIAM, 2003.

[13] ——, "Sparskit: a basic tool kit for sparse matrix computations," http://www-users.cs.umn.edu/~saad/software/SPARSKIT/, 1994, [retrieved: August, 2016].

[14] R. Barrett et al., Templates for the Solution of Linear Systems: Building Blocks for Iterative Methods, 2nd ed. SIAM, 1994.

[15] User and Reference Guide for the Intel C++ Compiler 17.0, https://software.intel.com/en-us/intel-cplusplus-compiler-17.0-user-and-reference-guide ed., Intel Corporation, 2017, [retrieved: February, 2017].

[16] R. Berrendorf, M. Weierstall, and F. Mannuss, "SpMV runtime improvements with program optimization techniques on different abstraction levels," Intl. Journal On Advances in Intelligent Systems, vol. 9, no. 3 & 4, pp. 417–429, 2016.

[17] S. Yan, C. Li, Y. Zhang, and H. Zhou, "yaSpMV: yet another SpMV framework on GPUs," in Proc. 19th ACM SIGPLAN Symposium on Principles and Practice of Parallel Programming (PPoPP'14), pp. 107–118. ACM, 2014.

[18] R. W. Vuduc and H.-J. Moon, "Fast sparse matrix-vector multiplication by exploiting variable block structure," in Proc. First Intl. Conference on High Performance Computing and Communications (HPCC'05), pp. 807–816. Springer-Verlag, 2005.

[19] V. Karakasis, G. Goumas, and N. Koziris, "Performance models for blocked sparse matrix-vector multiplication kernels," in Proc. 38th Intl. Conference on Parallel Processing (ICPP'09), pp. 356 – 364. IEEE, 2009.

[20] K. Kourtis, G. Goumas, and N. Koziris, "Optimizing sparse matrix-vector multiplication using index and value compression," in Proc. 5th Conference on Computing Frontiers (CF'08), pp. 87–96. ACM, 2008.

[21] M. Martone, S. Filippone, S. Tucci, P. Gepner, and M. Paprzycki, "Use of hybrid recursive csr/coo data structures in sparse matrix-vector multiplication," in Computer Science and Information Technology (IMCSIT), Proceedings of the 2010 International Multiconference on, pp. 327–335. IEEE, 2010.

[22] M. Martone, S. Filippone, M. Paprzycki, and S. Tucci, "Assembling recursively stored sparse matrices." in IMCSIT, pp. 317–325, 2010.

[23] ——, "On the usage of 16 bit indices in recursively stored sparse matrices," in Symbolic and Numeric Algorithms for Scientific Computing (SYNASC), 2010 12th International Symposium on, pp. 57–64. IEEE, 2010.

[24] M. Martone, S. Filippone, S. Tucci, M. Paprzycki, and M. Ganzha, "Utilizing recursive storage in sparse matrix-vector multiplication-preliminary considerations." in CATA, pp. 300–305, 2010.

[25] A. Pinar and V. Vassilevska, "Finding nonoverlapping dense blocks of a sparse matrix," Electronic Transactions on Numerical Analysis, vol. 21, pp. 107 – 124, 2004.

[26] M. R. Garey and D. S. Johnson, Computers and Intractability: A Guide to the Theory of NP-Completeness. W. H. Freeman & Co., 1979.

[27] J. L. Bentley, "Finding nonoverlapping dense blocks of a sparse matrix," Commun. ACM, vol. 18, no. 9, pp. 509 – 517, 1979.

[28] A. Guttman, "R-trees: A dynamic index structure for spatial searching," SIGMOD Rec., vol. 14, no. 2, pp. 47 – 57, 1984.

[29] J.-H. Byun, R. Lin, K. A. Yelick, and J. Demmel, "Autotuning sparse matrix-vector multiplication for multicore," EECS Department, University of California at Berkeley, Tech. Rep. UCB/EECS-2012-215, Nov. 2012.

[30] Y. Kubota and D. Takahashi, "Optimization of sparse matrix-vector multiplication by auto selecting storage schemes on GPU," in Proc. Computational Science and Its Applications - ICCSA 2011, vol. 6783, pp. 547–561. Springer-Verlag, 2011.

[31] J. W. Choi, A. Singh, and R. W. Vuduc, "Model-driven autotuning of sparse matrix-vector multiply on GPUs," in Proc. Principles and Practices of Parallel Programming (PPoPP'10), pp. 115–125. ACM, Jan. 2010.

[32] A. Elafrou, G. I. Goumas, and N. Koziris, "A lightweight optimization selection method for sparse matrix-vector multiplication," arXiv.org, vol. abs/1511.0249, Dec. 2015.

[33] C. Lehnert, R. Berrendorf, J. P. Ecker, and F. Mannuss, "Performance prediction and ranking of SpMV kernels on GPU architectures," in Proc. 22th Intl. European Conference on Parallel and Distributed Computing (Euro-Par 2016), ser. LNCS, P. Dutot and D. Trystram, Eds., no. 9833, pp. 90–102. Springer, 2016.

[34] R. Berrendorf, M. Weierstall, and F. Mannuss, "Program optimization strategies to improve the performance of SpMV-operations," in Proc. 8th Intl. Conference on Future Computational Technologies and Applications (FUTURE COMPUTING 2016), pp. 34–40. IARIA, 2016.

[35] Intel® Haswell, Intel, http://ark.intel.com/products/codename/42174/Haswell, [retrieved: August, 2016].

[36] T. A. Davis and Y. Hu, "The University of Florida Sparse Matrix Collection," ACM Trans. Math. Softw., vol. 38, no. 1, pp. 1:1–1:25, Nov. 2010.

[37] SPE Comparative Solution Project, Society of Petroleum Engineers, http://www.spe.org/web/csp/, [retrieved: August, 2016].

[38] V. Karakasis, T. Gkountouvas, and K. Kourtis, CSX library v0.2, https://github.com/cslab-ntua/csx, [retrieved: August, 2016].

Data Mining: a Potential Research Approach for Information System Research

A Case Study in Business Intelligence and Corporate Performance Management Research

Karin Hartl, Olaf Jacob
Department of Information Management
University of Applied Sciences Neu-Ulm (HNU)
Neu-Ulm, Germany
karin.hartl@hs-neu-ulm.de, olaf.jacob@hs-neu-ulm.de

***Abstract*—This paper investigates the opportunities of Data Mining applications for Information System research. Data Mining is a data driven statistical approach for knowledge discovery. Hypotheses and models do not have to be developed at the beginning of the research, which allows the detection of new and otherwise undiscovered patterns in a given dataset. Consequently, current challenges in Information System research can be investigated from a different angle. The Data Mining results may provide additional, surprising and detailed insights to an Information System problem. To prove these assumptions, this study applies Association Rule Discovery and cluster analysis to a questionnaire based data set. This data set has been collected to investigate the relationship between Business Intelligence and Corporate Performance Management. Even though this relationship has been explored at several stages in the Information System research literature, the results are often short on detail. This paper explores, if Data Mining methods can provide additional information to the subject. Both of the applied Data Mining methods provide promising results. Association rules and clusters have been identified, providing a different view on the connection between Business Intelligence and Corporate Performance Management. Therefore, Data Mining techniques offer an option to reuse questionnaire-based data and to gain new insights in Information System research.**

Keywords-Information Systems; Data Mining; Association Rule Discovery; Cluster Analysis; Business Intelligence.

I. INTRODUCTION

This research discusses the potentials of explorative Data Mining techniques for Information System (IS) related research and is the extended version of the previously published work of Hartl and Jacob [1] at the Data Analytics Conference 2016 in Venice.

In IS research, Explanatory Factor Analysis (EFA) and Structural Equation Modelling (SEM) are the commonly used research approaches. Before conducting any analysis, research assumptions and hypotheses are developed and afterwards confirmed with data collected for this specific research purpose. This approach has one major limitation, its reliance on human imagination for generating research theories and assumptions [2]. The theories and assumptions are typically based on findings and research results already accomplished in the field. To prove the pre-defined research assumptions, data sets are collected. These data sets may hold even more information regarding a research subject than anticipated and analysed. Nevertheless, non-logical connections are generally not investigated.

With Data Mining methods, interesting information and patterns can be discovered from various data types [3]. Instead of testing previously defined hypotheses, Data Mining applications are working up from the data [4]. This opens the opportunity to detect non-anticipated connections and hidden information in a given data set.

This research is a first approach in exploring the potentials of Data Mining methods for Information System research subjects [1]. Two descriptive Data Mining techniques are applied to a questionnaire-based data set, exploring the impact of Business Intelligence (BI) on Corporate Performance Management (CPM) [5]. Aim of the questionnaire was to make the business value of BI tangible. CPM is a suitable concept to explore the business value of BI, since a successful CPM requires data and up-to-the-minute information [1][5][6]. In recent researches, the business value of BI for CPM has been explored by extracting assumed connections from the literature and a subsequent testing of these connections with data collected from industry. Several pre-defined connections and interdependencies between BI and CPM have been proven. However, these results are often generic and lack detail.

As a result, the above mentioned research subject presents an interesting case study to investigate, if Data Mining techniques provide more insights to IS research subjects.

Association Rule Discovery and cluster analysis are renowned Data Mining methods and therefore have been identified as a suitable first approach in exploring the value Data Mining has for IS research. Association Rule Discovery searches for structural connections in a data set, formulates If-Then-Statements and can consider all available research criteria. For the presented case study, the results of the association analysis could allow conclusions on the specific BI capabilities accounting for a successful CPM. This may allow researchers and practitioners to focus on the most important BI features in order to improve CPM.

Cluster analysis explores the similarities between cases in a data set. The case study results could facilitate a better understanding of the connection between BI and CPM. Besides analysing the research variables – e.g., BI and CPM characteristics – cluster analysis facilitates the consideration of descriptive items - e.g., annual turnover, company size. This makes conclusions on the actual development of BI and CPM in German companies possible. Furthermore, the results could reveal whether companies with a well-established BI solution likewise have a well-functioning CPM. In addition, the findings may allow conclusions on the impact, the successful use and implementation of BI systems has on a company's CPM.

The paper is structured as follows. Section II discusses the motivation for this research. It points out, why IS research can profit from Data Mining applications. In Section III, the research approach is discussed. Section IV describes the case study. First, the research background is introduced. The terms BI and CPM are described and the relationship between these two areas is discussed. An investigation of the subject related research highlights the opportunities of the Data Mining approach. Second, the data selection and pre-procession is described for both Data Mining analysis – FP-Growth and k-means clustering. Third, the analysis process is described, before the results are presented. Section IV closes with a discussion on the case study results and on how they can be useful in practice. In Section V, it is discussed if Data Mining presents itself as a suitable research method for IS research topics. Section VI points out the next steps and future research opportunities.

II. Motivation for the Data Mining Approach

In the IS research field regarding the connection between BI and CPM first EFA and second PLS-SEM are the commonly used approaches. The starting point of these two analysis is always an empirically provable theory, which is developed based on assumptions [7]. Afterwards, hypotheses and a theoretical model are developed. To empirical investigate the proposed research model, typically, a questionnaire is developed and real-life data collected. Subsequent, these data are organized by an EFA analysis. The EFA groups correlating items and joins them together in a factor [8]. Data can be structured and reduced this way.

Next, the structured data are analysed with the PLS-SEM method by seeking the optimal predictive linear relationship to assess the previously defined causal relationship [1][9][10]. The characteristics (items) evaluated in the questionnaire built the measurement construct of the PLS model [10]. Mainly reflective PLS models are used in IS research. This means that the measurement model, also called the outer model, is caused by the construct [11]. The measurement items are then interchangeable and generally, a further investigation of the connections between the separate items is missing.

The creation of factors for compacting information might be the right approach for many research subjects, but it must not be the only correct approach to explore connections in IS research. It is assumed that Data Mining can highly contribute to the subject. Data Mining methods can include all available research criteria and has no need for compacting questionnaire data. This may lead to research result that are more detailed.

Data Mining can be understood as an extension of statistical data analysis and statistical approaches [12]. Both approaches aim to discover structure in data, but Data Mining methods are generally robust to non-linear data, complex relationships and non-normal distributions [13]. Data Mining is a data driven approach and supports the discovery of new and sometimes unexpected knowledge [2]. Instead of only testing assumed hypotheses, with Data Mining otherwise undiscovered data attributes, trends and patterns can be explored [14]. Especially with explanatory Data Mining techniques, a good understanding of connections in the data set can be achieved [15].

Although Data Mining is often only considered suitable for large data sets, Natek and Zwilling [16] illustrate in their research that small data sets are not limiting the use of the tool. They even applied a predictive Data Mining model to a relatively small data set. Prediction needs the division of the data set into a training set and a testing set. For exploratory Data Mining methods, this division is not necessary. All available data cases can be part of the analysis. Therefore, exploratory Data Mining methods should be applicable to small data sets.

III. Research Approach

The Data Mining literature describes various approaches to Data Mining problems [3][15]. The Cross Industry Standard Process for Data Mining (CRISP-DM) is a well-known procedure and the methodology chosen for this research [17]. As the data set is comparatively small, no selection of the appropriate data set was considered necessary. Therefore, the starting point for the data analysis was the pre-processing of the data. Fig. 1 shows the steps followed in the case study.

Each Data Mining analysis is conducted to answer a specific research question. This research question is then the basis for the chosen data and analysis method. In general, this research asks for the information gain in IS research through the application of Data Mining methods.

Exploratory Data Mining methods analyse given data and extract information and patterns from this data. In particular, association analysis allows to take all available items of a data set into account and to identify co-occurrence relationships on item basis. Cluster analysis groups the cases in the data set according to their similarity. The results identify structures in the data, which allow conclusions on dependencies.

In the data selection phase, the questionnaire data has been evaluated and missing values identified. Afterwards, the data has been pre-processed by calculating the missing values and addressing conflicting values. Han et al. [3] and Cleve and Lämmel [15] suggest alternatives for dealing with missing values, depending on the data structure. The important items of the questionnaire used for the case study are formatted as Likert scale items and can be interpreted as metric data. Metric data can be pre-processed by replacing the missing values in the sample by the mean value of all item-based compiled answers. Alternatively, the mean values can be stated by contemplating the data case closest to the data case with the missing value. This idea follows the k-nearest neighbours (kNN) approach. Joenssen and Müllerleite [18] assess the kNN approach as practicable imputation method for missing Likert scale values in small data sets. Therefore, the missing values in the data set were imputed using the kNN approach.

After dealing with the missing values, the data needs to be transformed in the required format for the applicable Data Mining technique. The applied Association Rule Discovery algorithm - FP-Growth - needs binary data [15].

Consequently, the Likert scale items have been transformed into binary variables. This has been directly done in the RapidMiner Data Mining tool. The information loss created by transforming the data into binary variables has been accepted at this point of the research. The goal was to apply Data Mining techniques to a questionnaire based data set for the first time in IS research. A wide range of IS researchers should understand the results. Therefore, the results ought to be elementary and understandable.

The results are then evaluated and interpreted. As in every research, not all findings are valuable and of real-life meaning. Accordingly, interpretation and evaluation presuppose a subject knowledge background to ensure that only sensible research results are discussed and interpreted.

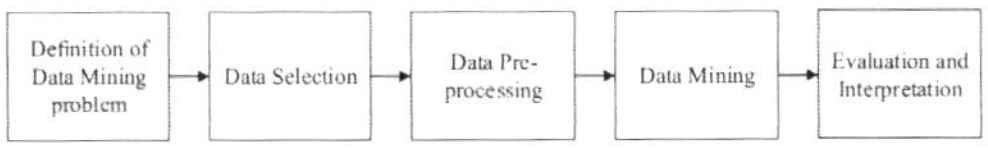

Figure 1. Research Approach (based on CRISP-DM) [17].

IV. Case Study

The case study focuses on a currend IS research topic which investigates the relationship between BI and CPM. The aim of the initial research was to investigate how the business value of BI can be made tangible [5]. Therefore, a context model has been identified by conducting a in-depth literature study. To pove the context model, data has been collected with the help of a questionairre. This data set and this research study background are used as the basis for the following case study.

A. *The Relationship Between BI and CPM*

Nowadays, companies have to face a more challenging and continuously changing environment each day. Especially, globalization intensifies the competition and the struggle for success and existence. Additionally, the digitalization confronts companies with immense amounts of data. Transforming these data into information and using these information for the management of a company are assumed to retain a company's survival in these challenging times. BI is a process including applications for storing data and systems as well as methods for analysing these data and the business environment. The usage of BI promises companies support in their decision making process by acquiring, analysing and disseminating information from data significant to the business activities [4][19][20]. Consequently, BI is a source for data of high quality and actionable information. This indicates that the proper use and application of BI systems supports the successful management of companies [5].

IT investments are necessary, but since there are increasing continuously their return on investment is evaluated critically in companies. Therefore, BI projects and implementations need to be justified. Accordingly, the measurement of the BI business value is an important topic [21]. But capturing the business value of BI is a strategic challenge, due to the diverse nature of BI [22]. Generally, BI systems are not strictly amortized by saving costs after implementation. Instead, the main BI benefits are of an intangible nature and therefore hard to measure [21]. Williams and Williams [22] see the BI business value in the usage of the system and the contained data within the management processes of a company. Miranda [23] then put BI and CPM into context and identified CPM as the appropriate framework to prove the value proposition and benefits of BI.

CPM is defined by the Gartner Group as "an umbrella term that describes all processes, methodologies, metrics and systems needed to measure and manage the performance of an organization" [24]. Therefore, CPM presents the strategic deployment of the BI solutions and is born out of a company's need to proactively manage business performance [1][25]. Inferentially, CPM needs BI to work effectively on accurate, timely and high quality data and BI needs CPM for a purposeful commitment [1][24]. As a consequence, it is expected that the effectiveness of CPM increases with the effectiveness of the BI solution and therefore the company success improves as well [1][6].

B. *Subject Related Research*

The relationship between performance management and BI has been investigated in several studies during the last couple of years.

Williams and Williams [22] are one of the first to expose the necessity to investigate the usage of BI within a company, for the purpose of exploring and measuring the business value of BI. The authors show that the value created through the implementation and usage of BI is to be found particularly within the management processes of a company, which affect the operational processes. Additionally, the research suggest that the return on BI investment can be measured on the increased revenues and reduced costs within a company [1][22]. However, the value created through successful BI solutions is more than just monetary benefits. BI is a complex process and the quest to make the business value of BI tangible needs an in-depth evaluation of the connection between BI and a company's management processes.

Miranda [23] suggested that CPM is an appropriate framework for BI applications. The authors describe the concept of CPM as a business management approach using business analysis to support the success and management of a company. Accordingly, CPM presents itself as a suitable framework to explore the business value of BI. Although, the research of Miranda [23] does not provide an empirical investigation of the subject, the article can be considered as the foundation for more detailed research in the field, including the following.

The connection between BI and CPM has been of research interest and empirically investigated mainly within the past 10 years. The differences and similarities between BI and CPM have been discussed by Aho [19] in form of a literature study and an action oriented research. The results support the conclusions of Miranda [23] and point out once more that BI and CPM need to be connected for an effective and efficient application. However, the empirical background does not deliver details on the configuration of the relationship between BI and CPM.

Yogev et al. [26] explore the business value gained through BI using a process-oriented approach. In the research model, key BI resources and capabilities are identified, which can explain the value created through the implementation and usage of a BI system. A hypotheses based theoretical model has been formulated and tested by the authors using EFA and SEM. The results demonstrate positive effects of BI on the strategic and the operational company level. Nevertheless, the empiricism does not provide any details about the BI related resources creating this positive effect.

Saed [27] investigates the relationship between BI and business success using regression and correlation analysis. First, hypotheses have been developed based on a literature review. Second, data has been collected and descriptively evaluated before correlation and regression analysis have been applied for hypotheses evaluation. Some of the hypotheses could be confirmed, but while these statistical techniques provide room for detailed results, only casual explanations have been provided [1].

Richards et al. [6] explore the connection between BI and CPM using EFA and PLS-SEM. Literature based hypotheses and a research framework have been developed. The framework supposes that BI directly influences and supports measurement, planning and analytics. The effectiveness of planning, measurement and analytics, again, influences the effectiveness of the company's processes. Through a large-scale survey, sample data has been collected. The number of variables in the questionnaire has then been reduces by applying an EFA. Afterwards, the factors have been converted into latent variables. The connections between these variables have then been evaluated with a Confirmatory Factor Analysis (CFA) using SmartPLS. Three of the seven hypotheses have been confirmed. Consequently, the research identifies a direction on how BI influences CPM, but the specific mechanisms who do so are not discussed or defined.

Hartl et al. [5] also developed a hypotheses based research framework. The framework assumed detailed relationships between BI and CPM. They expected that data quality and provision as well as pre-defined data analysis on the BI side of a company have a positive impact on the existence of closed-loop business processes on the CPM side of a company. Furthermore, technical data and method integration on the BI side of a firm is believed to have a positive impact on organizational alignment within the CPM. Eventually, the usage of extended collaborative and analytical functions is positively influencing CPM process effectiveness and process efficiency. All of these hypotheses have been confirmed, using an EFA first and a PLS-SEM analysis with SmartPLS second. Nevertheless, the detailed characteristics collected in the questionnaire regarding the development of BI and CPM in a company have only been used as the measurement construct of the PLS model. More detailed information contained in the data is not investigated.

This research project complements the subject related work and uses the questionnaire based data of Hartl et al. [5]. Instead of proving a pre-defined construct and compacting information from the collected data, this research considers all the research criteria. The aim is to get detailed insights on the relationship between BI and CPM on questionnaire item basis. This allows the identification of specific BI characteristics, which support a successful CPM. A first approach has been presented in the research of Hartl and Jacob [1]. The authors present an association rule analysis, which is extended in this research.

The aim of this case study is once more, to identify detailed information on the connection between BI and CPM. Exploratory Data Mining techniques are the used approach. As an alternative to SEM and grouping the questionnaire characteristics and measurement items describing BI and CPM together, all items are considered separately. It is supposed that this identifies patterns and structures that can explain the relationship between BI and CPM in more detail.

C. Defintion of the Data Mining Problem

Two main problems have been identified regarding the research project. Challenge number one is to identify the BI characteristics, which have a strong influence on CPM. Vice versa, it would be interesting to identify the CPM characteristics, which are strongly connected to BI.

The second challenge is to identify if companies with a high BI development also have a high CPM development. Additionally, it would be interesting to identify extra factors – e.g., company size, BI provider used –, which influence the development of CPM and/or BI in German companies.

Therefore, the following two research questions are defined:

Research question 1: Which specific BI characteristics are most influential on CPM and which specific CPM characteristics are most affected by BI?

Research question 2: Is a high development of BI related to a high development of CPM and are their certain characteristics that support a high development in both?

According to the defined research questions, two Data Mining methods have been identified for analyses – Association Rule Discovery and cluster analysis.

D. Data Selection

This research is based on the findings of Hartl et al. [5], where a set of criteria that is seen as suitable to represent CPM on one hand, and BI on the other hand, has been identified (Table I). A study has been conducted in Germany, to bring the criteria of both fields together and to clarify the relationship between BI and CPM. Therefore, the identified criteria have been transformed into questionnaire items, which had to be answered on a five-point Likert scale. The anchor points at the ends of the scale have been "does not apply" and "fully applies" and an additional definition "applies half and half" for the mid stage has been defined. The data collection has taken place from December 2014 until March 2015 using telephone interviews and an online questionnaire. Subjects were German companies who use BI for supporting their performance management. For this reason, decision makers from management, controlling and IT were addressed. In total 169 questionnaires were completed resulting in a response rate of 11.3%. The participating companies are mainly mid-sized

TABLE I: OVERVIEW OF THE BI AND CPM ITEMS [5]

BI items	CPM items
BI1_1: Clear roles and responsibilities for operating the BI systems	CPM1_1: Business management processes are transparent and traceable for managers
BI1_2: Data consistency ("Single Version of the Truth")	CPM1_2: Business management process are documented throughout the company
BI1_3: 24/7 operation of the BI systems	CPM1_3: Business management processes are communicated throughout the company
BI1_4: Only compulsory BI tools are used	CPM2_1: Business management processes base on a common database
BI1_5: Data integrity during simultaneous use	CPM2_2: Management methods are fully automated and linked without manual support
BI1_6: Clear roles and responsibilities for the BI-development between the company's departments and the IT throughout the whole enterprise	CPM2_3: Data in business management processes are complete
BI1_7: BI-architecture is documented	CPM2_4: Decision makers manual expenditure to edit reports is marginal
BI1_8: Master data changes are traceable	CPM3_1: Data in business management processes are relevant
BI1_9: BI relevant master data can be saved in various versions	CPM3_2: Data in business management processes are current
BI2_1: Use of feature set for predictive forecasting	CPM3_3: Effective use of external data (market data)
BI2_2: Use of feature set for describing data analysis	CPM4_1: Alignment of business management processes across all business functions
BI2_3: Use of feature set for information visualization	CPM4_2: Alignment of business management processes across all business units
BI3_1: Use of applications for scenario modelling	CPM4_3: Alignment of strategic and operational planning
BI3_2: Use of applications for statistical analysis	CPM5_1: Use of measurable indicators in all business functions
BI4_1: Each BI project is carried out using a standardized procedure model	CPM5_2: Use of measurable indicators in all business units
BI4_2: Each BI project bases on a standardized design method	CPM5_3: Use of measurable indicators in all operational business processes
BI4_3: Documentation standards for BI projects are clearly defined	CPM5_4: Use of measurable indicators in all strategic business processes
BI4_4: BI projects use agility	CPM6_1: Existence of feedback loops in operational business processes (e.g., complaint management)
BI5_1: Use of applications for adding describing comments	CPM6_2: Existence of feedback loops in strategy development (adjustment of vision, mission and the company's strategy to environmental changes)
BI5_2: Use of applications for sharing comments throughout the enterprise	CPM6_3: Existence of feedback loops in strategic planning processes
BI5_3: Use of applications for automatic text processing and Text Mining	
BI6_1: Denotations and spellings are standardized in the BI databases	
BI6_2: BI tools for strategic business management are interoperable	
BI6_3: Manual expenditures for ensuring standardized spelling and denotations are marginal	
BI7_1: Applications for mobile usage of the BI Systems are available	
BI7_2: Applications for the mobile usage of the BI Systems are used	
BI8_1: Use of BI applications for implementing alerts linked to automated workflow data in operational business processes	
BI8_2: Use of BI applications for implementing alerts linked to automated workflow data in strategic business processes	

E. Data Pre-processing and Data Mining

Before applying the analysis, the data has been screened for outliers and missing values. In total, the proportion of missing values is at 12%. As the dataset contains of many items and the missing values are balanced across the data set, it was decided to impute the missing values using the kNN approach. The procedure described in Section 3 has directly been implemented in RapidMiner. Additionally, no severe outliers have been detected and all cases in the data set could be included in the analysis.

1) Association Analysis [1]: Association Rule Discovery is a popular pattern discovery method [2]. With association rules, co-occurrence relationships between data items can be discovered, taking into account as many research items as needed and available [15]. This indeed can lead on the upside to results that are more detailed and on the downside to an enormous amount of discovered association rules. Unmanageable amounts of association rules easily can be organized by instating measures to evaluate and select rules based on their potential interestingness for the researcher [2]. These interestingness measures include *Lift*, *Support* and *Confidence* [15][28].

To generate association rules, many algorithms are available. The FP-Growth algorithm is the classic procedure used in RapidMiner. The algorithm works in two main steps [3]. In the first step, an FP-tree is generated. The FP-tree has a root node, which is usually marked by Null. Then, a separate node is built for each item. The algorithm calculates the relative frequency of the occurrence of the items in the data set. Afterwards, all cases are viewed and the items are ordered in a tree structure. In the second step, frequent item sets are directly extracted from the FP-tree. For each item a separate FP-tree is generated, which is evaluated from the leaves towards the tree root. Only items meeting the previously defined minimum *Support* are then recapped as a rule (please refer to Han et al. [3], pp. 257 for a detailed graphical description of the FP-Growth algorithm). After generating the frequent item set, association rules can be generated through a Rapid Miner operator. The overall rule interestingness is measured through the *Confidence* measure [15].

The FP-Growth algorithm needs binary data. Therefore, the data has to be transformed into binary variables. RapidMiner can do this transformation directly. The questionnaire characteristics "does not apply" to "applies half and half" (1-3) have been transformed to *does not apply* and "does apply" and "fully applies" (4-5) to *does apply*.

Furthermore, the minimum levels for the interestingness measures have been defined. Only association rules (X→Y) with a minimum *Support*≥0.6 have been considered as interesting. This means that in at least 60% of all the cases in the data set the rule has to show [28]. The confidence level has been set at *Confidence*≥0.7. This determines that in at least 70% of the cases in the data set where the first part of the rule (X) is shown, the second part of the rule (Y) has to show as well [16]. The measure *Lift* needs to be *Lift*>1 to indicate a positive correlation between the items of a rule [3]. Regarding the minimum settings of the measures, 103 association rules have been discovered.

Association rules do not imply causality. They find items that imply the presence of other items [2]. As the research focus is on the benefits of BI for CPM, the attention lies on association rules beginning with BI items, leaving 52 association rules for evaluation. The association rules with the highest *Support* are shown in Table II.

It is conspicuous that especially the CPM items *Data in business management processes are relevant* and *Data in business management processes are current* apply in a company, if specific BI items apply too. In more detail, these two CPM items most likely apply in a company, if in addition to the items in Table II the following BI items apply as well:

- *Data consistency ("Single Version of the Truth"),*
- *Only compulsory BI tools are used,*
- *Master data changes are traceable,*
- *Clear roles and responsibilities for the BI-development between the company's departments and the IT throughout the whole enterprise.*

In addition, the BI item *Use of applications for automatic text processing and Text Mining* is found in combination rules with the item *Clear roles and responsibilities for operating with the BI system* and *Data integrity during simultaneous use* (Table III). Different from these two, *Use of applications for automatic text processing and Text Mining* has the characteristic does not apply. Still, the CPM items *Data in business management processes are relevant* and *Data in business management processes are current* apply, indicating that data currency and relevance is not influences by the usage of Text Mining and context processing tools.

Furthermore, the association rules illustrate that:

- *Use of BI applications for implementing alerts linked to automated workflow data in strategic business processes* does not apply,
- *Use of applications for sharing comments throughout the enterprise* does not apply,
- *Use of applications for adding describing comments* does not apply,
- *Use of applications for automatic text processing and Text Mining* does not apply

TABLE II: STRONGEST ASSOCIATION RULES (RULE BODY CONTAINS OF BI ITEMS ONLY) [1]

BI items		CPM items	Interestingness
Data integrity during simultaneous use=**applies**	→	Data in business management processes are relevant=**applies**	Support=0.83 Confidence=0.92
Clear roles and responsibilities for operating the BI systems=**applies**	→	Data in business management processes are relevant=**applies**	Support=0.80 Confidence=0.93
Data integrity during simultaneous use=**applies**	→	Data in business management processes are current=**applies**	Support=0.78 Confidence=0.86
Data integrity during simultaneous use=**applies** *AND* Clear roles and responsibilities for operating the BI systems=**applies**	→	Data in business management processes are relevant=**applies**	Support=0.76 Confidence=0.93
Data integrity during simultaneous use=**applies**	→	Data in business management processes are relevant=**applies** *AND* Data in business management processes are current =**applies**	Support=0.74 Confidence=0.83
Clear roles and responsibilities for operating the BI systems=**applies**	→	Data in business management processes are current=**applies**	Support=0.74 Confidence=0.86
Clear roles and responsibilities for operating the BI systems=**applies**	→	Data in business management processes are relevant=**applies** *AND* Data in business management processes are current =**applies**	Support=0.73 Confidence=0.84
24/7 operation of the BI systems=**applies**	→	Data in business management processes are relevant=**applies**	Support=0.70 Confidence=0.91

the CPM item *Management methods are fully automated and linked without manual support* does not apply as well (Table III).

2) Cluster Analysis: Clustering attempts to find patterns and groups in research criteria [2]. The data are organized without previous knowledge of potential groups and are arranged by means of their similarity [15]. The objects belonging to one group are as much as possible homogenous [15]. The groups, however, are as heterogeneous as possible [15]. In clustering, all attributes available can be used in parallel. This offers a detailed view of the cluster features and enables a thorough view on the relations between BI and CPM. Clustering can be done by defining a similarity and distance measure, which is also known as proximity measure. Interesting results regarding the research data are believed to be accomplished by using the k-means algorithm as it is a well-known partitioning algorithm [29]. The algorithm works in 5 main steps [3][30].

1. From a data set k ojects are identified as the centre of k clusters. Each k object is one data case (k is the number of clusters to be estracted from a data set).
2. Every other data case from the dataset is then assigned to the k object - also calles cluster centre - it is most similar to. This can be measured based on the Euclidean distance between the data case and the cluster mean (for further details on the Eucledian Distance or alternative proximity measures, please refer to Han et al. [3] or Cleve and Lämmel [15]).
3. After assigning each data case to one cluster, a new cluster centre is calculated.
4. All data cases are then reassignes to one of the new cluster centres and new clusters are built.
5. The above process is continued until there are no more changes in the cluster centres and the compilation of the clusters.

The number of clusters k is to be chosen beforehand by the researcher.

In the case study, the k-means algorithm has been applied using k=2, k=3 and k=4, resulting in the most interesting output using k=3. Regarding, the data set has been divided into 3 clusters – Cluster 1, Cluster 2 and Cluster 3. An extract of the results is visually displayed in Fig. 2. The horizontal axes of the graph shows the items evaluated in the questionnaire. The vertical axes shows the encoded answers to these questions. For the Likert scale formatted BI and CPM items, number 1 is encoded as "does not apply", 3 as "applies half and half" and 5 as "totally applies". The numbers in between stand for middle stages. For the supporting questions, each number encodes an answering option. Table IV explains the codes and their meaning in detail.

Cluster 1 contains of 43 cases. The status and development in CPM and BI is assessed as mainly positive. Besides the characteristic *Management methods are fully automated and linked without manual support (CPM2_2)* CPM is weighed as continuously well developed and only the BI areas

TABLE III: SECOND AND THIRS SET OF STRONG ASSOCIATION RULES (RULE BODY CONTAINS OF BI ITEMS ONLY)

BI items		CPM items	Interestingness
Second Set of Association Rules			
Use of BI applications for implementing alerts linked to automated workflow data in strategic business processes=**does not apply**	→	Management methods are fully automated and linked without manual support=**does not apply**	Support=0.64 Confidence=0.85
Use of applications for sharing comments throughout the enterprise=**does not apply**	→	Management methods are fully automated and linked without manual support=**does not apply**	Support=0.63 Confidence=0.85
Use of applications for adding describing comments=**does not apply**	→	Management methods are fully automated and linked without manual support=**does not apply**	Support=0.60 Confidence=0.85
Use of applications for aromatic text processing and Text Mining=**does not apply** *AND* Use of applications for sharing comments throughout the enterprise=**does not apply**	→	Management methods are fully automated and linked without manual support=**does not apply**	Support=0.60 Confidence=0.86
Third Set of Association Rules			
BI items		**CPM items**	**Interestingness**
Clear roles and responsibilities operating the BI system=**applies** *AND* Use of applications for automated text processing and Text Mining=**does not apply**	→	Data in business management processes are relevant=**applies**	Support=0.68 Confidence=0.92
Clear roles and responsibilities for operating the BI systems=**applies** *AND* Data integrity during simultaneous use =**applied** AND Use of applications for automated text processing and Text Mining=**does not apply**	→	Data in business management processes are relevant=**applies**	Support=0.64 Confidence=0.92
Clear roles and responsibilities operating the BI system=**applies** *AND* Use of applications for automated text processing and Text Mining=**does not apply**	→	Data in business management processes are relevant=**applies** *AND* Data in business management processes are current =**applies**	Support=0.61 Confidence=0.82

- *Use of applications for adding describing comments (BI5_1),*
- *Use of applications for sharing comments throughout the enterprise (BI5_2)* and
- *Use of applications for automatic text processing and Text Mining (BI5_3)*

are evaluated with a critical tendency. Over 55% of the

TABLE IV: CODING OF THE SUPPORTING VARIABLES

Pos	Position in the company	1 – Management 2 – Middle Management 3 – Lower Management
Ber	Area of work in the company	1 – Company Management 2 – Managerial Accounting 3 – Financial Accounting 4 – Sales and Distribution 5 – Information Technology
Um	Company revenue	1 – Below 10 million € 2 – Between 10 and 50 million € 3 – Between 50 and 125 million € 4 – Between 125 and 500 million € 5 – Above 500 million €
Ma	Number of full-time Employees	1 – Below 50 Employees 2 – Between 50 and 250 Employees 3 – Between 250 and 1000 Employees 4 – Between 1000 and 5000 Employees 5 – Above 5000 Employees
ERP	Throughout the company, ERP software from the same provider	1 – Yes 2 – No
BI	Throughout the company, BI software from the same provider	1 – Yes 2 - No

questioned companies in the cluster stated to have above 1000 full-time employees. Almost half of these 55% even have above 5000 full-time employees. The annual turnover is exceeding 125 million Euro. The ERP and BI software used in the companies is primarily from the same producer and over 70% of the cases only use BI software from the same producer across the whole enterprise.

Cluster 2 can be described as the least developed in both BI and CPM. It contains of 36 cases. The CPM items *Data in business management processes are current (CPM3_1)* and *Data in business management processes are relevant (CPM3_2)* have a positive tendency in their development. The other CPM items are rather not distinctive. The same can be found in regards to the BI items. Only the items *Clear roles and responsibilities in operating with the BI Systems (BI1_1), 24/7 operation of the BI Systems (BI1_3)* and *Data integrity during simultaneous use (BI1_5)* are positively distinctive in the sample. The cases of this cluster comprise companies of all sizes. The same can be said for the annual revenue:

- 22% of the cases have an annual revenue below 125 million Euros,
- 33% of the cases have an annual turnover between 125 million - 500 million Euro,
- 33% have an annual revenue above 500 million Euro and
- 11% did not specify their annual turnover.

Predominantly, this cluster shows non-uniform BI software throughout the company. The ERP and BI software used throughout the company are mainly from different producers as well.

Cluster 3 consists of 90 cases. The situation and development of BI and CPM in the companies is assessed more critically than in Cluster 1 but more positively than in Cluster 2 (Figure 2). The items are continuously ranked as medium developed, but with a positive tendency. Especially the first couple of BI items (item *BI1_1* until *BI1_9*), which can be grouped under the topic Data Quality and Provision

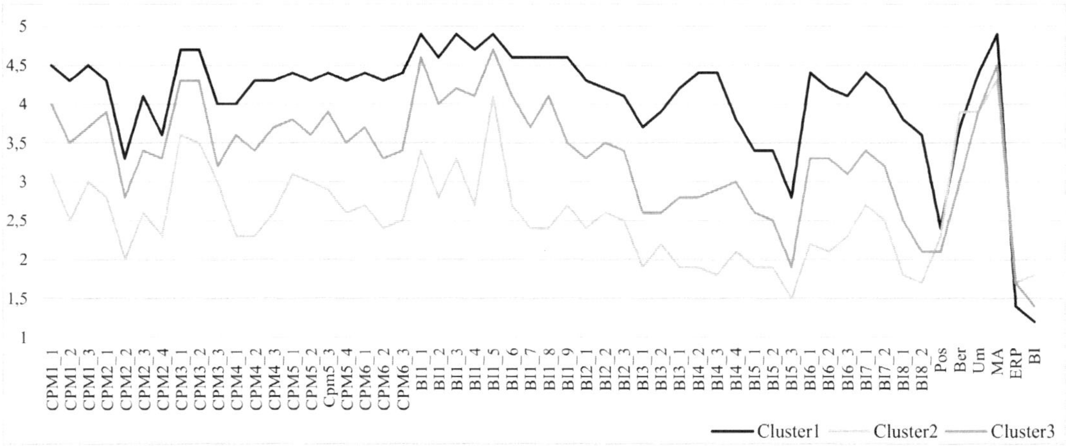

Figure 2. 3-Cluster solution using k-means clustring in RapidMiner

have an obvious positive tendency in their distinction. The BI items measuring

- Flexible Modelling and Analysis (items *BI3_1* and *BI3_2*),
- Rule-based implementation of BI-projects (items *BI4_1* to *BI4_4*),
- Information enrichment through unstructured Data (item *BI5_1* till item *BI5_3*) and
- Event-driven flow of Information (items *BI8_1* and *BI8_2*)

are weighted below *applies half and half.* They can be identified as the BI problem areas in Cluster 3. In CPM, an obvious problem area is the item *Management methods are fully automated and linked without manual support (CPM2_2).* The cluster concentrates together medium-sized and big companies, with more than 70% of them having between 500 and 5000 employees. The enterprises in the cluster mainly use the same BI software throughout the company, but almost 65% specified that their ERP systems and their BI systems are not from the same producer.

F. Result Evaluation and Interpretation

CPM is a management strategy for decision support [31]. This support is achieved by using measures and Key Performance Indicators (KPI's) from data. Decision makers and managers use the information gained from data to monitor the companies target achievements. If necessary, the strategy, the processes and the goals are adjusted to ensure the company's survival and success.

1) Association Analysis [1]: Data is the quintessence in CPM but only useful if provided when needed and of high quality. The association rules show that if BI items related to the subject of data quality and data provision (e.g., *Data consistency, Data integrity during simultaneous use*) are well established in a company the *Data in the business management processes are relevant* and *current.* The rules illustrate the connection between data and the business management processes and therefore the connection between BI and CPM. Supported with high quality data, decision makers can act and rely on actionable information to manage the enterprise. The rules underline the function of BI as a decision support tool needed for a successful CPM. The concentration on business management processes as the CPM part of the rule highlights the understanding of CPM as a multiplicity of business management processes connected and integrated into each other [30]. If the processes in a company are managed, based on needed high quality data, it is the initial point for an overall effective CPM.

Nevertheless, a CPM strategy is not implemented in one run. The implementation is a slow process carried out in sub-steps [31]. The focus of the association rules on *Data in business management processes is relevant* and *current* supports this. The rules indicate that initially the attention has to lie on each management processes separately. Once a company is working on high quality data when needed, a good connection of the management processes throughout the enterprise is possible. The lack of association rules containing further CPM items might be an indicator for companies in Germany still working on implementing a thorough performance management.

The second set of association rules discovered that if no opportunity to use and share comments within an enterprise and no opportunities to use unstructured data are given, a full automation and linkage of the company's management methods without manual support is not given either. Management methods are ideally accepted process descriptions for dealing with certain issues (e.g., Balanced Scorecard) [31]. These methods can only be successful if goal-oriented, understood and used continuously [31]. Consequently, management methods need defined measures and data analysis. For all measures to be useful, a reference magnitude is needed, which can be supplied by adding and sharing comments. Furthermore, the association rules imply that fully automated management and planning methods are dependent on the use of comments for ensuring transparency as well. Only if supported by describing comments, automated management processes and planning methods are understandable throughout a company and the need for manual support is minimalized.

Text Mining enables knowledge discovery from semi-structured or unstructured data. This is a rather advanced analysis method of BI and the rules indicate that if there is no or not much *usage of automatic text processing and Text Mining, Data in business management processes* are still *relevant* and *current* but the *Management methods* are not fully *automated or linked without manual support.* Text Mining is an advanced research method used to gain new information from texts. The association rules suggest that this feature of BI is not important for data currency and relevance in business management processes. Therefore, it might to be ignored in the establishment process of CPM. However, it seems to be interesting once an automation of management methods without manual support wants to be achieved.

The association rules discovered only comprise 3 different CPM related items *Data in business management processes are current, Data in business management processes are relevant* and *Management methods are fully automated and linked without manual support.* This awakes the awareness that BI is not the only information-technological support in companies. Enterprise Resource Planning Systems (ERP), Customer Relationship Systems (CRM) and Supply-Chain-Management System (SCM) also play an important role for a successful performance management. Before focusing on implementing a BI solution, the predominant step might be to focus on existing software first and afterwards built an effective BI solution on top.

2) Cluster Analysis: The cluster analysis divided the data set into 3 clusters. Cluster 1 contains the companies, which show a high development in both BI and CPM. The companies in this group mainly have above 1000 full-time employees and are considered as big. The BI systems throughout the company are primarily uniform.

Cluster 3 incorporates medium-sized to big companies, but generally with less employees then the ones in Cluster 1. The BI and CPM development is mediocre. The BI systems are uniform but ERP and BI software are mostly from different manufacturers.

Cluster 2 comprises of a mixture of all company sizes but mainly medium-sized enterprises. They have by trend a less developed BI and CPM in common. BI and ERP software as well as the BI software generally are not uniform within the company.

The results imply a connection between BI and CPM. Clusters with a bad development in one discipline also show a low distinction in the other discipline and vice versa. It seems that long established big companies are further in implementing both CPM and BI. Usually, companies with more resources invest earlier in new technologies than other enterprises. As well, they can employ experts to help them implement and use new technologies. This might be an explanation for the high development in both BI and CPM in Cluster 1.

The results further show that medium-sized companies are generally not as experienced in BI. BI characteristics dealing with data quality and data provision are well developed as well, but the medium to low distinction of characteristics including supportive BI techniques and tools indicate no current usage. This is reflected on the CPM side with a low development of the overall connection between the business management processes.

In addition, the patterns in the data set also indicate that in Germany, there are companies of all sizes who struggle with CPM and BI. All clusters discovered differ in the handling of BI and ERP software, which could be a reason for the struggle. Companies in Cluster 2 use different software from various manufacturers for BI and CPM. Additionally, the majority of the cases in this cluster declared that they are not using uniform BI software throughout the company (more than 76%). Instead, the majority of companies in Cluster 1 claimed to use ERP and BI software from the same brand as well as uniform BI software across the whole enterprise. Uniform BI software reduces unnecessary interfaces and ensures that throughout the company the same data and numbers are used for decision support. Inferentially, this facilitates advantages for CPM by providing transparency, which supports the formation of feedback loops in operational and strategic processes.

The results of the Data Mining analysis answer the research questions and can support practitioners in building a successful BI solution. The identified association rules point out the BI characteristics, which are most related to a high development of certain CPM characteristics. The cluster analysis identified three different clusters with a different distinction of BI and CPM development. Therefore, a clear connection between BI and CPM can be recognized as well as additional items influencing a high development of both – BI and CPM.

V. Discussion

The main goal of the previously published research by Hartl and Jacob [1] and this extended version has been to explore if Data Mining techniques can provide more detailed insights to IS research subjects. Association Rule Discovery and cluster analysis have been applied to the questionnaire based data set collected by Hartl et al. [5]. The aim was to explore, if these Data Mining procedures can extract even more information from the given data set.

In fact, information that is more detailed has been extracted from the data set. While in a PLS analysis all research items seem to matter equally, the association rule analysis showed that there are a handful of characteristics on BI and CPM side, which seem to be most related. For example, the business management processes do profit especially from a well-functioning BI - in detail, the existence of clear roles and responsibilities for operating the BI system and data integrity during simultaneous use. With this background, companies can analyze and improve their regarding BI development to ideally support the organizational alignment of their business processes. The results indicate that this is one of the first steps to a well-functioning CPM supported through BI.

In addition, the cluster analysis offered interesting results contained in the data set. Besides the BI and CPM related characteristics, the questionnaire contained general information about the company too (e.g., company size, software difference and similarities between ERP and BI systems used throughout the company). With cluster analysis, this information can be put into context with the CPM and BI characteristics evaluated. The results showed that a good development in BI and CPM is rather given, if the BI and ERP tools used within a company are from the same software developer.

In comparison to the subject related research, the results of the Data Mining approach show different and more detailed information about the connection of BI and CPM. Besides simply proving a positive relationship, the research outcomes allow conclusions on a path of action for practitioners. Although these inferences still need further investigation in practice, it has been possible to identify the BI and CPM items with the strongest connection. Furthermore, an already collected data set has been re-used and more insights could be gained about a previously investigated subject.

The Data Mining approach presents itself as a suitable addition to exploring the connection between BI and CPM. Inferentially, the results support the assumption that Data Mining methods are in general suitable for IS research subjects. In addition to reanalyze previously collected questionnaire data, Data Mining could support IS research without collecting data especially for the research purpose.

Data Mining methods like Text Mining and Web Mining might allow a totally different approach to IS research topics.

VI. CONCLUSION AND FUTURE RESEARCH

The Data Mining approach to the research area of BI and CPM has been successful. Nevertheless, this research still presents an early attempt in exploring the usage of Data Mining in IS research. It might be possible, that different clustering and/or association algorithms are a better fit to explore data in a Likert scale format. Hence, future research should evaluate and compare the results of different algorithms when applying Data Mining to questionnaire based data sets. Additionally, this research only applies Association Rule Discovery and cluster analysis to a relatively small data set. Due to the nature of Data Mining it is well possible that even slightly bigger data sets (200 and more cases) could lead to improved and even more results.

A next step in continuation of this research will be the application of Data Mining to other IS related research topics. It will be interesting to see, if similar results can be obtained. Therefore, given data sets will be evaluated using similar Data Mining applications. If indeed more information can be extracted from each given data sets, many existing researches can benefit.

Another interesting future research will be the application of Data Mining applications as a first approach towards an IS research topic. Text Mining and Web Mining offer the extraction of information from existing sources. In Text Mining the goal is to extract high quality data from texts [3]. In the IS research field the major part of information is available in text form, for example in the form of articles, digital libraries and books. The use of Text Mining could help to gain an overview of a research topic, structure information and detect new research fields. With Web Mining techniques, structured as well as unstructured online data can be analyzed [3]. Existing websites, media data and web usage data can be explored. Both applications offer IS researchers a huge opportunity by providing insights to IS related subjects without relying on test persons and questionnaires. Therefore, Text Mining and Web Mining applications should be tested to search for answers regarding current research questions.

REFERENCES

[1] K. Hartl and O. Jacob, "Using Data Mining Techniques for Information System Research Purposes - An Exemplary Application in the Field of Business Intelligence and Corporate Performance Management," The Fith Conference on Data Analytics (Data Analytics 2016) IARIA, Oct. 2016.

[2] K.-M. Osei-Bryson and O. Ngwenyama, eds. Advances in Research Methods for Information Systems Research. Springer-Verlag: New York, 2014.

[3] J. Han, M. Kamber, and J. Pei, Data Mining: Concepts and Techniques. vol. 3. Waltham, USA: Morgan Kaufmann Publishers, 2012.

[4] S. Rouhani, A. Ashrafi, A. Z. Ravasan, and S. Afshari, "The Impact Model of Business Intelligence on Decision Support and Organizational Benefits," Enterprise Information Management, vol. 29(1), pp. 19-50, 2016.

[5] K. Hartl, O. Jacob, F.H. Lien Mbep, A. Budree, and L. Fourie, "The Impact of Business Intelligence on Corporate Performance Management," The 49th Hawaii International Conference on System Science (HICSS 2016), Jan. 2016, pp. 5041-5051.

[6] G. Richards, W. Yeoh, A.Y.L. Chong, and A. Popovič, "An Empirical Study of Business Intelligence Impact on Corporate Performance Management," The Pacific Asia Conference on Information Systems (PACIS 2014), 2014, Paper 341.

[7] R. Weiber and D. Mühlhaus, Structural Equation Modelling. 2nd ed., Berlin Heidelberg: Springer-Verlag, 2014.

[8] K. Backhaus, B. Erichson, W. Plinke, and R. Weiber, Multivariate Analysis Methods. An Application-oriented Introduction. vol. 13. Berlin Heidelberg: Springer-Verlag. 2011.

[9] N. Urbach and F. Ahlemann, "Structural Equation Modeling in Information Systems Research Using Partial Least Squares," Journal of Information Technology Theory and Application, vol. 11(2), Article 2, 2010.

[10] E. Vinzi, W. W. Chin, J. Henseler and H. Wang, eds. Handbook of Partial Least Squares: Concepts, Methods and Applications. Berlin: Springer-Verlag, 2010.

[11] J. F. Hair, M. Sarstedt, L. Hopkins, and V.G. Kuppelwieser, "Partial leats squares structurl equation modeling (PLS-SEM)," European Business Review, vol. 26(2), 2014.

[12] J. Jackson, "Data Mining: A Conceptual Overview," Communications of the Association for Information Systems, vol. 8, 2002. 8: pp. 267-296.

[13] A. J. Stolzer and C. Harlford, "Data Mining Methods Applied to Flight Operations Quality Assurance Data: A Comparison to Standard Statistical Methods," Journal of Air Transportation, vol. 12(1), pp. 6-24, 2007.

[14] M. L. Gargano and B.G. Raggad, "Data mining - a powerful information creating tool," OCLC Systems & Services: International digital library perspectives, vol. 15(2), pp. 81-90, 1999.

[15] J. Cleve and U. Lämmel, Data Mining. vol. 2. Berlin: Walter de Gruyter GmbH, 2016.

[16] S. Natek and M. Zwilling, "Data Mining for Small Student Data Set – Knowledge Management Sytem for Higher Education Teachers," The International Conference for Management, Learning and Knowledge, Jun. 2013, pp. 1379-1398.

[17] P. Chapman, J. Clinton, R. Kerber, T. Khabaza, T. Reinartz, C. Shearer, et al., "CRISP-DM 1.0," SPSS Inc., 2000, Available from: https://www.the-modeling-agency.com/crisp-dm.pdf.

[18] D. W. Joenssen and T. Müllerleile, "Missing Data in Data Mining," HMD Praxis der Wirtschaftsinformatik, vol. 51(4), pp. 458-468, 2014.

[19] M. Aho, "The Distinction between Business Intelligence and Corporate Performance Management - A Literature Study Combined with Empirical Findings," The Mini Conference on Scientific Publishing (MCSP 2010), 2010.

[20] M. Hannula and V. Pirttimäki, "Business Intelligence: Empirical Study on Top 50 Finnish Companies," Journal of American Academy of Business, vol. 2(2), pp. 593-599, 2003.

[21] S. Negash, "Business Intelligence," Communications of the Association for Information Systems, vol. 13(1), pp. 177 - 195, 2004.

[22] S. Williams and N. Williams, "The Business Value of Business Intelligence," Business Intelligence Journal, vol. 8, pp. 30-39, 2003.

[23] S. Miranda, "Beyond BI: Benefiting from CPM Solutions," Financial Executive, vol. 20(2), 2004.

[24] J. Becker, D. Maßing, and C. Janiesch, "An evolutionary process model for introducing Corporate Performance Management Systems," Data Warehousing, pp. 247-276 2006.

[25] F. H. Lien Mbep, O. Jacob, and L. Fourie, "Critical Success Factors of Corporate Performance Management (CPM): Literature Study and Empirical Findings," The Sixth International Conference on Business Intelligence and Technology (BUSTECH 2015), March 2015.

[26] N. Yogev, L. Fink, and A. Even, "How Business Intelligence Creates Value," The European Conference on Information Sytems (ECIS 2012), Paper 84, 2012.

[27] R. A. Saed, "The Relationship between Business Intelligence and Business Success: An Investigation in Firms in Sharjah Emirate," American Journal of Business and Management, vol. 2(4), pp. 332-339, 2013.

[28] R. M. Müller and H.-J. Lenz, Business Intelligence. Berlin Heidelberg: Springer-Verlag, 2013.

[29] B. Liu, Web Data Mining: Exploring Hyperlinks, Contents, and Usage Data. vol. 2. Berlin Heidelberg: Springer-Verlag, 2011.

[30] M. Lang, ed. Handbook of Business Intelligence: Potentials, Strategies, Best Practices. vol. 1. Düsseldorf: Symposium, 2015.

[31] K. Oehler, Corporate Performance Management with Business Intelligence Tools. Carl Hanser Verlag: München, 2006.

Learning Method by Sharing Activity Histories in Multiagent Environment

Keinosuke Matsumoto, Takuya Gohara, and Naoki Mori
Department of Computer Science and Intelligent Systems
Graduate School of Engineering, Osaka Prefecture University
Sakai, Osaka, Japan
email: {matsu, gohara, mori}@cs.osakafu-u.ac.jp

Abstract*—Applications of multiagent systems are expected for parallel and distributed processing. Reinforcement learning is used as an implementation method for learning the actions of the agent. However, when systems must control many agents, the speed of learning becomes slower. Hence, Modular Q-Learning is proposed to solve this problem. Given that it deals with partial states, the number of states is reduced to avoid exponential increases. However, if n agents exist, they need n ($n-1$) learning tables, and therefore require a lot of memory. To solve the problem, Centralized Modular Q-Learning is proposed. In this method, the agent has only one learning table. Given that agents do not distinguish other agents, the number of learning tables is reduced. This study improves these methods and proposes a new reinforcement learning method that can learn quickly by using the past actions of its own and other agents. The proposed method can learn good actions in fewer trials. However, if agents continuously learn, the learning efficiency will deteriorate. The method reduces the effects of the actions of other agents in the late stage of learning. Therefore, agents are able to learn suitable actions. In experiments, agents are able to find a good strategy in a small number of trials than the conventional methods. In addition, agents learn actions in hunter games in various environments. The results show that the proposed method is an efficient reinforcement learning method.

***Keywords*—machine learning; Q-learning; sharing of activity histories; agents; hunter game**

I. INTRODUCTION

This paper is based on the study [1] presented at the ADVCOMP 2016. In recent years, information has distributed and increased largely due the rapid development of the Internet and multimedia. Systems also become larger and complicated. It is difficult for centralized systems, which judge by bringing information in one place, to deal with a lot of information and process it. From the viewpoint of parallel and distributed processing, the application of multiagent systems [2] that exchange information between agents [3] is expected.

It is difficult to follow environmental changes that humans could not forecast beforehand, and they do not carry out suitable actions. It is most important for each agent in a multiagent system to learn by itself. Each agent needs to learn a suitable judgment standard from its experience and information collected from other agents. Reinforcement learning [4][5] attracts attention as an implementation method for multiagent systems. It can be very effective means because it autonomously learns by setting the only reward, if a goal has been given.

A hunter game [6] is widely used as a cooperative problem solving [7][8] under multiagent environment as a benchmark of reinforcement learning. If a hunter game becomes complicated and the number of agents increases, the number of states increases exponentially. The speed of learning slows down. Ono et al. proposed Modular Q-Learning (MQL) [9] to solve this problem, but it had a disadvantage of using a lot of memory. Knowledge sharing methods [10][11][12][13] were also proposed. Reference [12] needs to build a tree structure model and [13] consumes a considerable amount of memory to store auxiliary variables that are used to record the trajectory of states, action, and rewards. With respect to memory, another method that reduced memory [14] was proposed. In this method, each agent has only one Q-value table by not distinguishing each agent with the same purpose.

Based on these methods, this paper proposes a new method that increases learning efficiency by using each agent's activity history of hunter agents. The method does not need preparation of any special model or communication algorithms between agents, strategies to exchange information [15][16], special exploration agents [17][18][19] and others according to various situations. This method saves only activity histories and updates the Q-value using its own or other hunters' activity histories. In this manner, the method shares experiences between agents simply by adding other hunters' activity histories to the Q-value table and picks up learning speed, which makes collective intelligence efficient.

This paper is organized as follows. In Section II, the explosion of the number of states in the reinforcement learning is explained. In Section III, conventional methods are described. In Section IV, the proposed method is explained. In Section V, the results of application experiments confirm the validity of the proposed method. Finally, in Section VI, the conclusion and future work are presented.

II. Hunter Game

This section describes a hunter game and the explosion of the number of states.

A. Definition of Hunter Game

A hunter game is one of the standard problems in multiagent systems. It is a game where multiple hunters catch a prey (runaway) by chasing in a two-dimensional field. The definition of a hunter game in this study is shown below.

-A field is a two-dimensional lattice and torus space as shown in Fig. 1.

-It is possible for multiple agents to take one lattice space.

-Each agent can take five actions of moving, such as right, left, up, down or stop.

-A hunter has perfect perception, and it recognizes a prey and other hunters in relative coordinates from itself.

-A unit of time that each agent takes one action is called a time step, and a period from an initial state to a goal (i.e., hunters catch a prey) is called an episode.

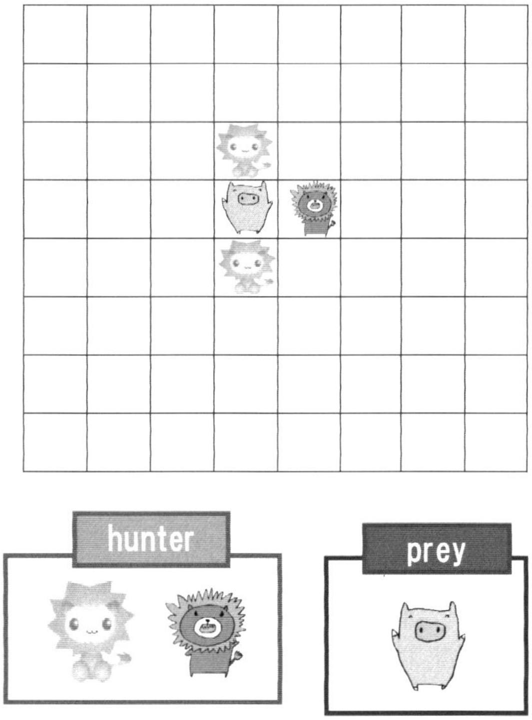

Figure 1. Hunter game.

TABLE I. Number of states m^{2n}.

$n \backslash m$	3	5	7	9
1	9	25	49	81
2	81	625	2401	6541
3	729	15025	117649	531441
4	6561	390625	5764801	43046721

B. Explosion of the Number of States

Q-Learning [20] is one of the bootstrap-type reinforcement learning. In Markov decision process, which is similar to Q-Learning, if the learning rate is appropriately adjusted, convergence to an optimal solution in infinite time has been proven [21].

In Q-Learning of the hunter game, an action is evaluated on a pair (s, a) considering all observable states S ($S \ni s$) and possible actions A ($A \ni a$). The evaluated value is utilized for the same pair of state and action. It requires a lot of information on (s, a) to make Q-Learning effective. For example, if the size of the field is $m \times m$ and the number of hunters is n, one hunter can see m^{2n} identifiable states (positional combinations of other hunters and prey). Table I shows the number of states for each number of hunters n and field size m. Given that each state has five kinds of actions, the state and action pair is $5m^{2n}$.

In the hunter game with multiple hunters, state explosion cannot be avoided because the exponent includes n. The explosion of the number of states results in slower learning speed. Therefore, in Q-Learning in multiagent environment, how the number of states is reduced is an important subject.

III. Conventional Methods

This section describes related work of this study.

A. Modular Q-Learning

Ono et al. [9] proposed MQL to solve the state explosion in hunter games. Completely Perceptual Q-Learning (CPQL) [22] is a perfect perception learning, and it uses relative coordinates of all hunters to define states. Moreover, MQL uses a partial state that consists of a hunter and another one. The number of states of field size $m \times m$ and n hunters is m^4. Given that the exponent is a constant and is not influenced by the number of hunters, it can prevent the state explosion.

Learning accuracy of MQL deteriorates because of imperfect perception by the observing partial states. In addition, if n hunters exist, the number of partial states becomes n-1, and n-1 learning machines are prepared per hunter. A total of $n(n$-1) learning machines are needed. The size of the Q-value tables tends to increase, and the amount of memory will increase.

B. Centralized Modular Q-Learning

Matsumoto et al. [14] proposed a Centralized Modular Q-Learning (CMQL) to solve the memory problem of MQL. In a hunter game, hunters should just surround a prey. It is not necessary to recognize the kind of hunters that surround the prey. Therefore, CMQL does not distinguish the characteristics of each hunter, and n-1 learning machines that the hunter has in MQL can be reduced to one learning machine. In CMQL, a hunter has only one Q-value table of the partial state. Given that the number of Q-value tables becomes one per hunter, only n Q-value tables are required in all if n hunters exist.

The number of states will increase, and the speed of learning will become slow in the hunter games of three or more hunters. To solve this problem, CMQL is introduced. CMQL improves the degradation of learning by parallel and switching learning [22]. The increase of memory is reduced by one learning machine per hunter.

1) Parallel learning

Imperfect perception learning is used to make learning quicker in the early stage and to accelerate learning processes to some extent. We switch to a perfect perception at a time. Owing to imperfect perception, the learning accuracy of CMQL is lowered, and the action selection will change for the worse in the later stages. A long-term performance is inferior compared with CPQL. The influence of lowered accuracy in early stages does not disappear, and the accuracy of action selection cannot be kept perfect.

Parallel learning is a method of using CMQL that excels in early short-term learning and CPQL that excels in long-term learning simultaneously. A decent action series is found by CMQL, and it is made to converge, where further convergence is expected by switching to CPQL at a suitable time. To obtain the suitable switching time for parallel learning, the mean unlearning entropy is defined. The probability $P(s, a)$, which chooses action a at the time of state s and the unlearning entropy $I(s)$ are shown below. I is an average of $I(s)$, which is averaged for all the states contained in episode E and all agents.

$$P(s,a) = \frac{Q(s,a)}{\sum_{i \in A} Q(s,i)} \quad (1)$$

$$I(s) = -\frac{1}{\log n_a} \sum_a P(s,a) \log P(s,a) \quad (2)$$

$$I = \frac{1}{n_p |E|} \sum_{s \in E} I(s) \quad (3)$$

where $Q(s, a)$ is the Q-value of action a in state s, A is a set of all possible actions, n_a is the number of actions that can be chosen, n_p is the number of hunters, and $|E|$ is the number of states contained in episode E. I comes close to 0 when the learning progresses. Moreover, it is 1 if no learning is carried on.

2) Switching learning method

If parallel learning of CMQL and CPQL are used at the same time, the amount of memory will increase because the two learning methods must use a lot of memory. Before switching learning, only the learning machine of CMQL is in the memory; and after switching, only the learning machine of CPQL is in the memory. By this process, learning can always be carried out under the memory of CPQL before and after switching.

The delivery technique of Q-value at the time of switching is shown: Three hunters (s_1, s_2, s_3) exist with states of $s_1(x_1, y_1)$, $s_2(x_2, y_2)$, and $s_3(x_3, y_3)$. Hunter s_1's Q-value of CMQL is $Q_m(s_1, T, a)$. Moreover, the Q-value of CPQL is $Q_c(s_1, s_2, s_3, a)$. Where T is a state of another hunter, and a is one of the actions. The Q-value cannot be copied easily because the expression forms are different. Q-value is delivered in the following formula:

$$Q_c[x_1][y_1][x_2][y_2][x_3][y_3][a] = \frac{Q_m[x_1][y_1][x_2][y_2][a] + Q_m[x_1][y_1][x_3][y_3][a]}{2} \quad (4)$$

This formula can deliver the same Q-value to all combinations from CMQL to CPQL. The difference between both expression forms is absorbed in this manner.

3) Preliminary experiments

Some preliminary experiments have been conducted to investigate the influence of mean unlearning entropy on learning. The problems that the preliminary experiments deal with are shown below. Each hunter carries out Q-learning individually, and a prey acts at random without learning in hunter games. The number of hunters is three, the field size is 7 × 7, and the cost per one-time step is 0.05. Q-value may become zero or less. To prevent this case, δ is defined as follows, and δ is added to $Q(s, a)$.

$$\delta = |\min_a Q(s,a)| + 0.01 \quad (5)$$

In both CPQL and CMQL, learning and discount rates are set to 0.5. Thresholds of mean unlearning entropy are set to 0.500, 0.840, and 0.947. These values correspond to switching times at 45,000, 15,000, and 3000 episodes. The resulting graphs are shown in Fig. 2. Every plot shows the average time steps to catch a prey of every 300 episodes. Given that the mean unlearning entropy comes close to 0 as the learning progresses as described in sub-section *1)*, the larger the thresholds are, the quicker it switches in the early stages of learning.

When it is switched at threshold 0.500, the number of steps to catch a prey has leaped up abruptly at the time of switching. Furthermore, it has also converged on the number of steps worse than that of CPQL. This means that the action patterns learned by CMQL is delivered to CPQL, but the deteriorated action patterns are not corrected. When the threshold is 0.840, it switches earlier than that of the threshold 0.500, but it switches similarly and the number of steps to catch a prey has leaped up abruptly. The convergent number of steps to catch is almost the same as that of CPQL. When it switches at the threshold 0.947, it has switched just before the learning accuracy of CMQL deteriorates. Change of learning machines can be performed, and the number of steps does not leap up abruptly. After the switching, the

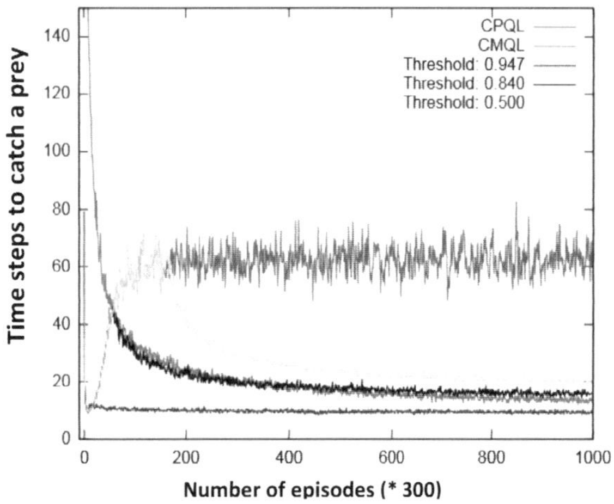

Figure 2. Learning graphs for various thresholds.

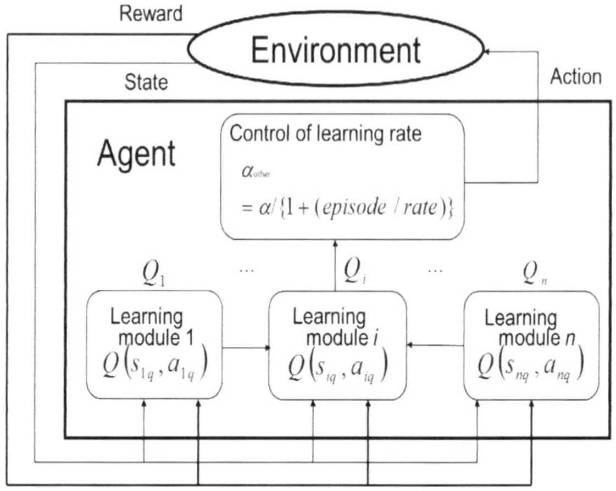

Figure 3. Architecture of the proposed method.

number of steps converges better than that of CPQL.

These results show that CMQL obtained a fewer steps solution and fewer amount of memory than those of CPQL when it switched at the threshold 0.947. Therefore, the efficiency of reinforcement learning in hunter games can be increased by CMQL. However, if the learning rates and discount rates are changed, the results will change. The inability to determine automatically an optimum switching time is a problem.

IV. Proposed Method

In this section, a method that raises learning efficiency is described based on MQL and CMQL. Fig. 3 shows the basic concept of the proposed method. The method for defining the partial state of CMQL in a hunter game in a maze environment is examined.

A. *Redefinition of the Partial State by the Relative Coordinate Change*

In MQL and CMQL, the definition of perceptual information is made by a relative coordinate from the prey. This study uses the relative coordinate from each hunter. If the coordinates of other hunters s_1: (x_1, y_1), s_2: (x_2, y_2), and the prey s_p: (x_p, y_p), the partial state of the method is $<s_p, s_1>$, $<s_p, s_2>$. Therefore, perceptual information of some hunters can be constituted based on information equal to the partial states of CMQL.

B. *Perception Method of Walls*

Conventional CMQL constitutes partial states based on hunter and prey coordinates. It is necessary to consider the walls in a hunter game in a maze environment. An effect seems to come out in learning results by way of defining the partial states. Given that the positions of the walls do not change in this study, all walls are grasped by the absolute coordinate system. The partial states that consider the walls using this absolute coordinates are constructed. The walls are blocks where each agent could not go through.

C. *Explorative Experiment*

Two kinds of partial states are considered in this experiment. In hunter games, one partial state consists of a pair of any hunter and prey, and another pair of a wall and prey (Method 1). Another partial state is considering a hunter, prey, and wall at the same time (Method 2). Figures 4 and 5 show partial states for Methods 1 and 2, respectively. The number of states of Method 2 is larger than that of Method 1, but their memory consumption is equal. Experimental conditions were as follows:

- Size of field: 12 × 12
- Number of walls in the mazy field: 43
- Number of hunters: $n = 3$
- Action selection strategy: ε-greedy ($\varepsilon = 0.01$)
- Prey's action: random action
- Capture state: Four lattices in left, right, top, and bottom of a prey's position are surrounded by hunters or walls.
- Cost per one time step: 0.05
- Learning rate: $\alpha = 0.2$
- Discount rate: $\gamma = 0.8$
- Maximum number of learning episodes: 300000

The comparison results are shown in Fig. 6. The number of steps of Method 2 to catch the prey decreases when the learning advances. Good learning is possible. Comparing Method 1 with Method 2, the learning speed of Method 1 is rapid, but the number of steps to catch increases. The positions of walls are considered in all partial states of Method 2. Method 2 can choose an action that bypasses walls between the hunter and prey. Some partial states of Method 1 disregard the walls, and Method 1 could not choose a good action that accesses the prey. If an element to be newly considered in the environment increases, each partial state seems to have to consider the new element at the same time.

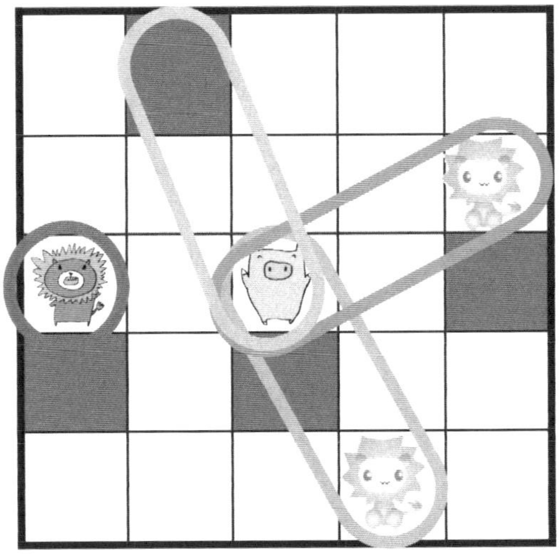

Figure 4. Partial states for Method 1.

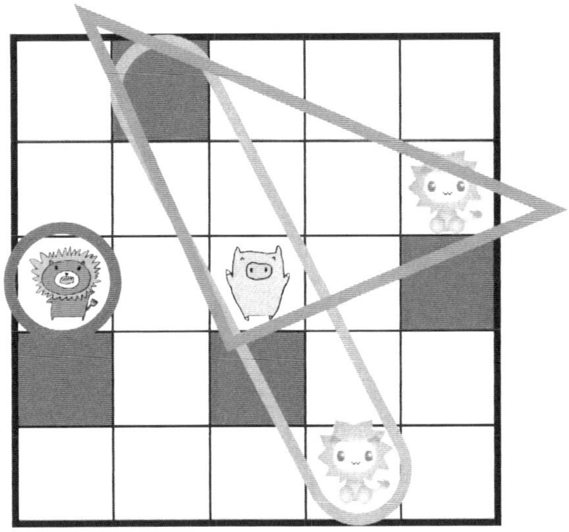

Figure 5. Partial states for Method 2.

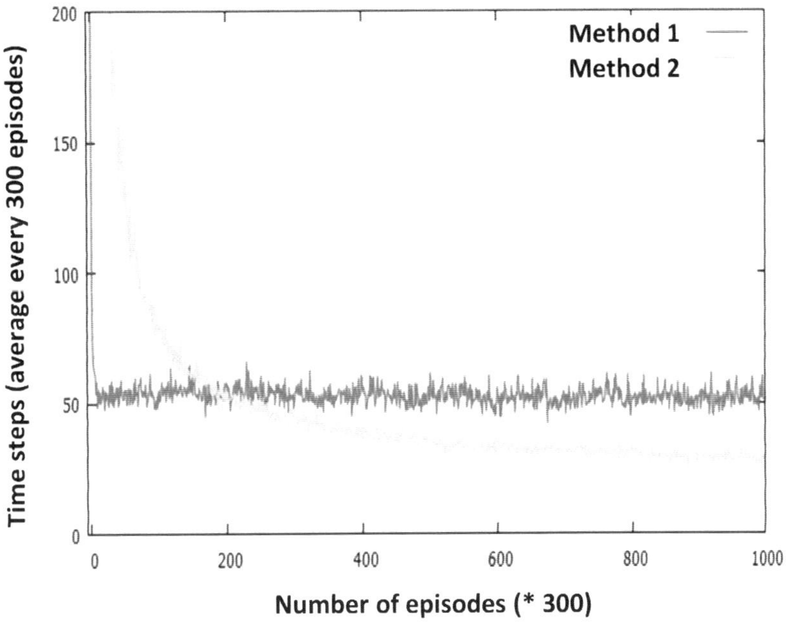

Figure 6. Results of the proposed method for maze task.

D. Learning Method by Sharing Activity Histories

In the hunter game, all hunters have the common purpose of catching the prey. In this environment, the learned actions of other hunters to catch the prey are useful. Appropriate actions can be learned with fewer trials by learning actions of other hunters. In this study, a method of updating the Q-value based on other hunters' activity histories is proposed. The number of times of updating for every episode increases, but the method raises the learning efficiency for every episode. The algorithm of the proposed method is shown below.

The number of hunters is n and a prey is caught at q steps. Each hunter is observing states s_1, s_2, ---, s_n and actions are a_1, a_2, ---, a_n.

(1) In each episode, save the hunters' coordinates and actions for every step, and for up to t steps. These are activity histories.
(2) Give awards to all hunters' Q-value Q (s_1, a_1), Q (s_2, a_2), ---, Q(s_n, a_n) if the prey is caught.
(3) $i = q$
(4) $Q(s_{i-1}, a_{i-1}) \leftarrow (1\text{-}\alpha)\, Q(s_{i-1}, a_{i-1}) + \alpha\, [r + \gamma \max_a Q(s_i, a_i)]$
(5) Replace i by i-1 and repeat (4) until $i \leq q\text{-}t$ or $i \leq 1$.

In the algorithm mentioned above, t is t = 1000. Combining this algorithm with CMQL makes a more efficient learning method. Parameter t is determined by the complexity of the applied problems to cover almost all states at the initial setting [23][24][25][26].

Although learning has become early in the proposed method, final learning results tend to deteriorate compared with the conventional methods without sharing activity histories. The learning accuracy of the proposed method becomes worse by learning actions of other hunters at the final learning stage. For this reason, the learning rate using other hunters' actions is decreased according to the number of episodes. Influence on learning by other hunters' actions is lessened as learning progresses. This will be an approach that utilizes other hunters' activity histories at the early learning stages and uses only each hunter's history at the final learning stage.

E. Control of Learning Rate

It is difficult to find an optimal action if a hunter learns other hunters' actions in the final stage of learning. The learning rate of learning other hunters' activity histories should be decreased in proportion to the number of episodes. If other hunters' activity histories are used at the last stage of learning, learning accuracy will reduce slightly. It does not become bad by learning only for one's history, and the learning rate at the time of updating for other hunters' activity histories should be gradually made small.

The influence of other hunters' activity histories on learning was reduced with the number of times of learning. This method (hereinafter referred to as Turned Experience CMQL (TECMQL)) is a learning approach that utilizes other hunters' activity histories in the early stage of learning and only its own history in the final stage.

The following formula defines the learning rate at learning other hunters' activity histories.

$$\alpha_{other} = \frac{\alpha}{1 + (episode\,/\,rate)} \tag{6}$$

where, α_{other} is a learning rate the updates the Q-value using other hunters' activity histories and *rate* is a constant that determines reduction rate of the learning rate. The learning rate at learning using other hunters' actions should be decreased according to the number of episodes. The value of parameter *rate* is determined to eliminate the effect of other hunters' actions in proportion to the number of episodes.

V. EXPERIMENTS

In this section, the proposed method was applied to hunter games to confirm its validity.

A. Outline of Experiments

Experiments compare learning efficiency of the following three methods.

- Proposed method: CMQL using other hunters' activity histories (referred to as Sharing Experience CMQL (SECMQL)).

- Compared method: CMQL using only each hunter's history (referred to as Own Experience CMQL (OECMQL)).

- Conventional method: CMQL that does not use activity histories.

These three methods were applied to a hunter game in a maze environment and two-prey hunter game.

B. Experiment 1: Hunter Games in Maze Environment

The performances of the three methods mentioned above were compared in the hunter game in a maze environment. In this case, hunters learn ways of bypassing walls in the maze and leading a prey to the place where it is easy to catch using the walls. The positions of the walls do not change from the beginning of this experiment. Walls are grasped by the absolute coordinate system. In this experiment, a partial state of CMQL consists of a relative coordinate from a hunter to any other hunter, a relative coordinate from the hunter to a prey, and an absolute coordinate of the hunter itself. Actions can be learned considering the positions of walls in each partial state.

Experimental conditions were as follows:

- Size of field: 8 × 8
- Number of walls in the mazy field: 21 (cf. Fig. 7)
- Number of hunters: $n = 3$
- Action selection strategy: ε-greedy ($\varepsilon = 0.01$)
- Prey's action: It escapes from hunters.
- Capture state: Four lattices in left, right, top, and bottom of a prey's position are surrounded by hunters or walls.
- Cost per one time step: 0.05
- Learning rate: $\alpha = 0.2$
- Discount rate: $\gamma = 0.8$
- Maximum number of learning episodes: 300000

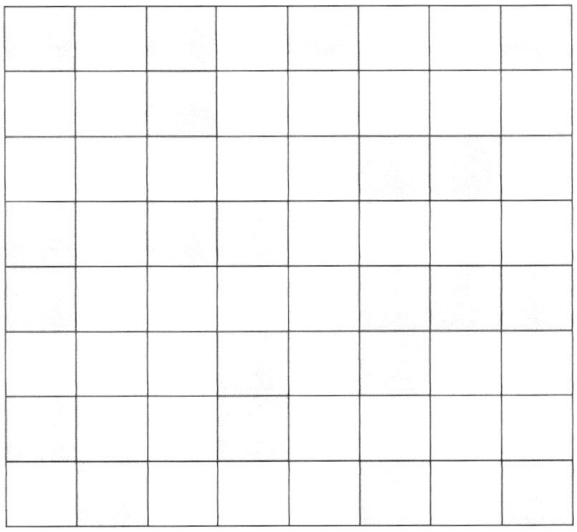

Figure 7. Maze environment.

- Reward of hunter that caught a prey directly: 5
- Reward of hunter that did not caught the prey directly: 4

In this experiment, only three hunters cannot catch a prey without making use of walls. Hunters will learn actions that guide the prey near walls and catch it using the walls. At least two or fewer hunters can catch a prey if they use walls. In this case, one hunter could guide the prey for the other two hunters to catch it. A slightly reduced reward was given to the hunter that did not catch the prey directly for its contribution to the catching.

Results are shown in Fig. 8. The horizontal axis indicates the number of episodes and the vertical axis indicates the time steps to catch a prey from an initial state. Every plot shows the average time steps to catch a prey of every 100 episodes. The fewer the time steps results in better action patterns that can be learned.

The learning of SECMQL became earlier until near episode no. 5000 than other methods, but the final learning result was bad compared with other methods. On the other hand, OECMQL could catch with fewer steps compared with CMQL. SECMQL's learning accuracy was deteriorated by learning other hunters' actions in the final stage of learning.

C. Experiment 2: Two-Prey Hunter Games

The performances of the three methods mentioned above were compared in a hunter game that has two preys. In this game, the hunters' purpose is to catch one of the two preys. Given that the candidate actions of a hunter increases in number, learning becomes difficult compared with the problem of one prey. In this experiment, a partial state of CMQL consists of a relative coordinate from a hunter to any other hunter and two relative coordinates from the hunter to two preys. Given that the positions of both preys can be seen, actions can be learned considering the two preys.

Experimental conditions were as follows:

- Size of field: 8 × 8
- Number of hunters: $n = 3$
- Action selection strategy: ε-greedy ($\varepsilon = 0.01$)
- Prey's action: It escapes from hunters.
- Capture state: At least two hunters exist in left, right, top, and bottom of one prey.
- Cost per one time step: 0.05
- Learning rate: $\alpha = 0.2$
- Discount rate: $\gamma = 0.8$
- Maximum number of learning episodes: 300000
- Reward of hunter that caught a prey directly: 5
- Reward of hunter that did not catch the prey directly:4

In this experiment, preys observe all hunters' positions and they escape from hunters based on the hunters' coordinates. A slightly reduced reward was given to the hunter that did not catch a prey directly for its contribution to catching.

Results are shown in Fig. 9. In this experiment, the learning efficiency of SECMQL is the best in the early stages of learning. Given that action patterns that lead to catching in the early stages of learning by only one hunter are insufficient, it is useful to use other hunters' activity histories for learning.

However, OECMQL found good action strategies over 100000 episodes. Obtaining good action strategies improves the way a hunter individually learns in the final stage.

D. Experiment 3: Hunter Games in Maze Environment after Control of Learning Rate

Performance was compared with the cases where they are with or without reducing learning rate of hunter games in a maze environment. TECMQL was added to the three methods of Experiments 1 and 2 as a compared method. Experimental conditions were the same as Experiment 1, and the *rate* of TECMQL was 500.

Results are shown in Fig. 10. In this experiment, OECMQL shows the best learning result. TECMQL also showed almost equivalent learning result to that of OECMQL, while TECMQL maintained good efficiency in the early stage of learning.

E. Experiment 4: Two-Prey Hunter Games after Control of Learning Rate

Performance was compared with the cases where they are with or without reducing learning rate of hunter games that have two preys. The compared method was the same as Experiment 3. Experimental conditions were the same as Experiment 2, and the *rate* of TECMQL was 10000. The results are shown in Fig. 11.

In this experiment, TECMQL discovered a strategy that could catch a prey with fewer steps than other methods. From these results, it seems to be effective to assemble a rough action strategy using actions of other hunters in the early stages of learning, and then to learn the action strategy that is suitable for each hunter by individual learning.

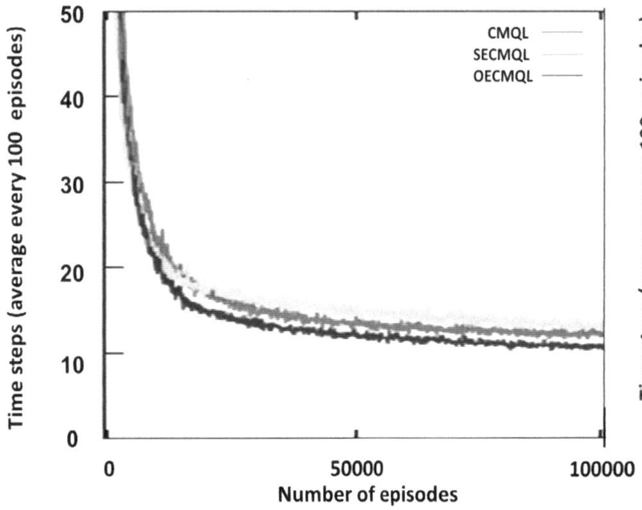

Figure 8. Results of the proposed method for maze task.

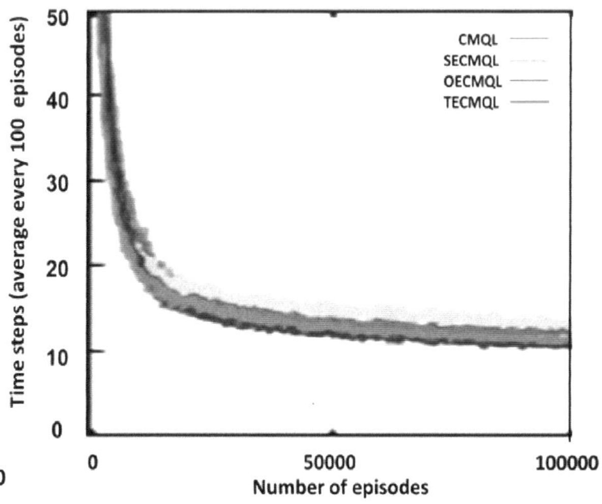

Figure 10. Results of the proposed method for maze task after control of the learning rate.

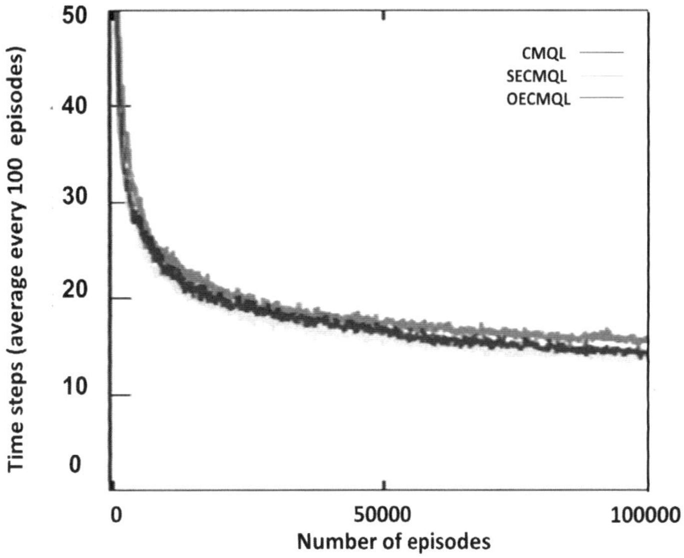

Figure 9. Results of the proposed method for two-prey game.

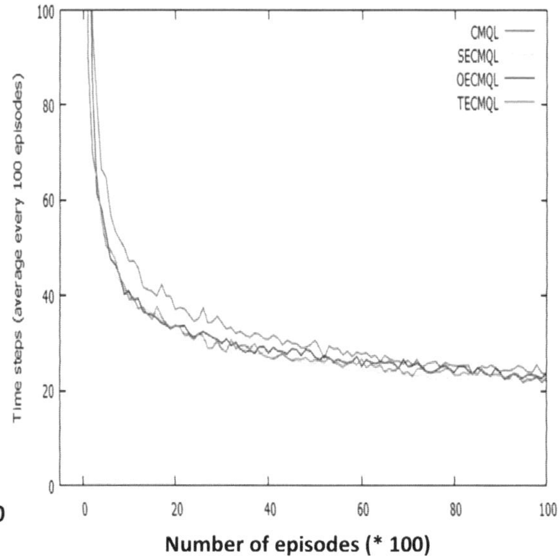

Figure 11. Results of the proposed method for two-prey game after control of the learning rate.

In addition to Experiment 3, TECMQL found actions that were easy to catch a prey rather than the conventional methods in different environments. However, it is necessary to adjust the learning rate according to the environments.

TABLE II. Convergent average steps.

Average number of steps	Maze task game	Two-prey game
TECMQL	9.6	10.6
SECMQL	11.5	12.1
OECMQL	9.4	11.3
CMQL	10.6	13.6

F. Convergent Average Number of Steps for Each Method

Table II shows the convergent average steps for each method after each method has finished learning. TECMQL obtained the best average number of steps for the two-prey game. For the maze task game, it obtained nearly the best number of steps.

VI. Conclusion

In this study, some Q-learning algorithms were applied in the hunter game of maze and two-prey environments. The composition of appropriate partial states was examined. This paper proposed a method that can learn in fewer trials by sharing activity histories among hunters. The method is based on MQL and CMQL, which are methods that prevent an explosion of the number of states. The performance of the proposed method was compared with CMQL. To solve the problem of deteriorating learning performance of the proposed method in the later stage of learning when using other hunters' activity histories, the learning rate is decreased according to the number of episodes. The proposed method can be generalized to other multiagent environment other than hunter games because it uses a general Q-learning algorithm.

At the present method, the control of learning rate is dependent on the number of episodes, but it is not controlled by the contents of learning. In future study, an index should be established to control the learning rate according to Q-value during learning. In addition, it is considered that the internal states of agents will be optimized by clustering.

Acknowledgment

This work was supported in part by JSPS KAKENHI Grant Number JP16K06424.

References

[1] K. Matsumoto, T. Gohara, and N. Mori, "Learning method by sharing activity logs in multiagent environment," Proc. of the Tenth International Conference on Advanced Engineering Computing and Applications in Sciences (ADVCOMP 2016), IARIA, October 2016, pp. 71-76, ISBN: 978-1-61208-506-7.

[2] G. Weiss, Multiagent Systems: a modern approach to distributed artificial intelligence, MIT Press, 1999.

[3] S. J. Russell and P. Norving, Artificial intelligence: a modern approach, Prentice-Hall, Englewood Cliffs, 1995.

[4] R. S. Sutton and A. G. Barto, Reinforcement learning: an introduction, MIT Press, 1998.

[5] H. Van Hasselt, "Reinforcement learning in continuous state and action spaces," in Reinforcement Learning, Springer Berlin Heidelberg, pp. 207-251, 2012.

[6] M. Benda, V. Jagannathan, and R. Dodhiawalla, On optimal cooperation of knowledge sources, Technical Report, BCS-G 2010-28, Boeing AI Center, 1985.

[7] I. Nahum-Shani, M. Qian, D. Almirall, W. E. Pelham, B. Gnagy, G. A. Fabiano, and S. A. Murphy, "Q-learning: A data analysis method for constructing adaptive interventions," Psychological methods, vol. 17, no. 4, p. 478, 2012.

[8] S. Shamshirband, A. Patel, N. B. Anuar, M. L. M. Kiah, and A. Abraham, "Cooperative game theoretic approach using fuzzy Q-learning for detecting and preventing intrusions in wireless sensor networks," Engineering Applications of Artificial Intelligence, vol. 32, pp. 228-241, 2014.

[9] N. Ono and K. Fukumoto, "Multi-agent reinforcement learning: a modular approach," Proc. of AAAI ICMAS-96, pp.252-258, 1996.

[10] M.Tan, "Multi-agent reinforcement learning : independent vs. cooperative agents," Proc. of the 10th International Conference on Machine Learning, pp. 330-337, 1993.

[11] R. M. Kretchmar, "Parallel reinforcement learning," Proc. of the 6th World Conference on Systemics, Cybernetics, and Informatics, vol. 6, pp. 114-118, 2002.

[12] K. Hwang, W. Jiang, and Y. Chen, "Model learning and knowledge sharing for a multiagent system with Dyna-Q learning," IEEE Transactions on Cybernetics, vol. 45, no. 5, pp. 978-990, 2015.

[13] Z. Zhang, D. Zhao, J. Gao, D. Wang, and Y. Dai, "FMRQ-A multiagent reinforcement learning algorithm for fully cooperative tasks," IEEE Transactions on Cybernetics, vol. 47, no. 6, pp. 1367-1379, 2017.

[14] K. Matsumoto, T. Ikimi, and N. Mori, "A switching Q-learning approach focusing on partial states," Proc. of the 7th IFAC Conference on Manufacturing Modelling, Management, and Control (MIM 2013) IFAC, pp. 982-986, ISBN: 978-3-902823-35-9, June 2013.

[15] H. Iima and Y. Kuroe, "Swarm reinforcement learning algorithm based on exchanging information among agents," Transactions of the Society of Instrument and Control Engineers, vol. 42, no. 11, pp. 1244-1251, 2006 (in Japanese).

[16] S. Yamawaki, Y. Kuroe, and H. Iima, "Swarm reinforcement learning method for multi-agent tasks," Transactions of the Society of Instrument and Control Engineers vol. 49, no. 3, pp. 370-377, 2013 (in Japanese).

[17] T. Tateyama, S. Kawata, and Y. Shimomura, "Parallel reinforcement learning systems using exploration agents," Transactions of the Japan Society of Mechanical Engineers Series C vol. 74, no. 739, pp. 692-701, 2008 (in Japanese).

[18] Y. M. De Hauwere, P. Vrancx, and A. Nowe, "Future sparse interactions: A MARL approach," Proc. of the 9th European Workshop on Reinforcement Learning, pp. 1-3, 2011.

[19] H. Igarashi, M. Handa, S. Ishihara, and I. Sasano, "Agent control in multiagent systems – Reinforcement learning of weight parameters in particle swarm optimization," The Research Reports of Shibaura Institute of Technology, Natural Sciences and Engineering vol. 56, pp. 1-8, 2012 (in Japanese).

[20] C. J. C. H. Watkins and P. Dayan, "Technical note Q-learning," Machine Learning, vol. 8, no. 3, pp. 279-292, 1992.

[21] S. J. Bradtke and M. O. Duff, "Reinforcement learning method for continuous-time Markov decision problems," Advances in Neural Information Processing Systems, vol. 7, pp. 393-400, 1994.

[22] A. Ito and M. Kanabuchi, "Speeding up multi-agent reinforcement learning by coarse-graining of perception — hunter game as an example—," IEICE Trans. Information and

Systems D-I, vol. J84-D-I, no. 3, pp. 285-293, 2001 (in Japanese)

[23] G. Giannakopoulos and P. Themis, "Revisiting the effect of history on learning performance: The problem of the demanding lord," Knowledge and information systems, vol. 36, no. 3, pp. 653-691, 2013.

[24] I. Koychev and R. Lothian, "Tracking drifting concepts by time window optimisation," Proc. of the twenty-fifth SGAI International Conference on Innovative Techniques and Applications of Artificial Intelligence, pp. 46–59, 2005.

[25] I. Koychev and I. Schwab, "Adaptation to drifting user's interests," Proc. of ECML2000 Workshop: Machine Learning in New Information Age, pp. 39–45, 2000.

[26] J. Patist, "Optimal window change detection," Data Mining Workshops, pp. 557–562, 2007.

Potential and Evolving Social Intelligent Systems in a Social Responsibility Perspective in French Universities: Improving Young Unemployed People's Motivation by Training for Business Creation Integrating Emotions around Mediator Artifacts

Christian BOURRET

Research Team DICEN IDF (Information and Communication Devices in the Digital Era)
University of Paris East Marne-la-Vallée (UPEM)
Marne-la-Vallée, France
e-mail: christian.bourret@u-pem.fr

Abstract - **In France, with the economic crisis and the huge rate of unemployment, the role of Universities has changed in the recent years with a new challenge of social responsibility. They try to promote the creation of new economic activities to attract new people, especially coming from disadvantaged areas in great town suburbs, particularly unemployed young people. We present the experiment of Creators of Activities University Degrees (DUCA) around cooperative devices or Creators' Groups (GC). These DUCA / GC correspond to an individual project, part of a global dynamics in a collective approach. In a perspective of helping disadvantaged people to rebuild their life in a project dynamics of creation of economic activity, information and communication issues are central. These DUCA / GC areas of interactions and cooperations constitute socio-technical devices progressively evolving to potential Social Intelligent Systems. We propose to analyze these cooperative devices through two Mediator Artifacts developed in the DUCA / GC areas of cooperations: the business plan of the activities' creators and the training serious game "Solutia". They help to better master the emotions and feelings of activities' creators to develop their self-confidence, their motivations, their entrepreneurship skills and their individual and collective knowledge. These areas of projects constituting potential and evolving Social Intelligent Systems correspond to a specific way of sustainable development to try to build "democratic solidarity" on territories.**

Keywords – intelligent systems; socio-technical devices; unemployed people; social responsibility; economic activities creation; entrepreneurship; mediator artifacts; disadvantaged areas.

I. INTRODUCTION

In a period of social crisis and of huge unemployment, particularly for non-graduated young people in disadvantaged areas [1], Serge Paugam pointed the importance of "social links" [2] and of solidarity. These evolutions correspond to the need of repositioning the Universities in a new perspective of Social Responsibility (RSU) but also other organizations with public service missions, such as Local Missions / *Missions Locales* (ML) or Centre for Information and Orientation / *Centres d'Information et d'Orientation* (CIO) in National Education Ministry.

According to Hervé Azoulay [3], "there are talents in the suburbs but they need to be discovered and developed in different manners". We must give confidence to potential activities' creators and enable their talents to flourish, and also to promote "innovation in everyday life" according to Norbert Alter [4] and especially social innovations.

The first Creators' Groups (GC) and Creators of Activities University Degrees (DUCA) have been created in 2000 by a partnership between the University Institute of Technology (IUT) of Melun-Sénart belonging to the University of Paris East Créteil (UPEC) and the Local Mission (*Mission Locale*) of Melun-Sénart. A Local Mission is an intervention space to help young people under 25 years of age. Each young person is given a personalized follow-up, to help him on employment, on training but also on housing or health problems.

The University of Paris East Marne-la-Vallée (UPEM,) through its component IUT has managed since 2006 several groups of Creators of Activities University Degrees (DUCA) recently become TPE (Very Small Business) Entrepreneur, supported by training partnerships devices, the Creators' Groups (GC). These GC (15 in 2016) are federated in a national association: National Association of Creators' Groups (ANGC).

We first present the global context of the unemployment challenges in France, Social Responsibility of the Universities (RSU) and Social and Solidarity Economy (SSE), particularly for young people in disadvantaged areas. Then we explain our researcher's position and the methodology used. We show the specificity of the DUCA / GC devices, pointing particularly on their Information and Communication issues and the question of emotions and feelings to improve their motivation. We present two emotions' Mediator Artifacts: first a training "serious game" (Solutia) and a second, the Business Plan used as the framework of the economic activity project. We explain how DUCA / GC devices may be considered as potential and evolving Social Intelligent Systems. Finally, we show the importance of the DUCA / GC in a Social Solidarity Economy perspective before giving some examples of success stories of activities' creations and mention some possibilities of evolution of the DUCA / GC.

II. Unemployment Challenges, Social Responsibiliy of Universities in a Social and Solidarity Economy

The challenge of unemployment is particularly strong in France. At the end of November 2016, there were 6,238,400 people registered in the Unemployment Office (*Pôle Emploi*) in mainland France (without overseas areas), including 3,447,000 people without any activity. France also has about 8,000,000 people living below the poverty level. The situation is particularly worrying for young people. Nearly 2 million young people are unemployed, without a diploma or training and, in particular, 19% of young people under the age of 25: the "neets" (not in education, employment or training), according to the Anglo-Saxon expression [5].

The situation has worsened since 2008. For the Minister of Labor, Myriam El Khomri (DUCAs' Graduation Ceremony, Paris, December 12, 2016): "we cannot miss no skill or talent".

In this context, in the recent years, the role of University has changed. It is no longer just only to build and transfer knowledge, but also to welcome new people and promote their vocational integration, including the creation of new economic activities. We speak of Social Responsibility of Universities (RSU). There is also the new position of "entrepreneur student" [6], concerning all the students and not only those coming from disadvantaged areas or being unemployed.

Eric Dacheux defined Social and Solidarity Economy (SSE) as "seeking to develop links, rather than making profits" [7]. In the same seminar, Florine Garlot, highlighting the work of Jean-Louis Laville and Alain Yvergniaux (2009), stressed the difference between two types of solidarity: "philanthropic" solidarity and "democratic" solidarity. With the profound changes of capitalism over the last thirty years and in particular the financialization of the economy, Laville and Yvergniaux propose another project based on "democratic solidarity". While for them philanthropic solidarity corresponds to a liberal political project aimed at calming the tensions of a system by nature egalitarian, democratic solidarity is centered on emancipation and the reduction of inequalities [8].

Our approach to the RSU corresponds to this social and solidarity economy perspective, thus articulating the notions of link or interaction (reliance) to promote the sustainable development of territories through the interactions and solidarity of all the actors, and especially in disadvantaged areas (resilience).

III. Researcher's Position and Methodology

The author of this paper manages DUCAs in the IUT / UPEM and is also member of GC Coordination Committees.

From a methodological perspective, the author of this article belongs to the French University's interdisciplinary field of Information and Communication Sciences, according to the approach proposed by Françoise Bernard [9] with the convergence of four aspects: meaning, link (relationships, interactions), knowledge and action. He positions in a research action perspective mixing theory and practice to build knowledge for action. His analysis corresponds to the research position described by Françoise Bernard as "engaging communication" [10].

Insisting on the primacy of action, Françoise Bernard proposed the paradigm of "engaging communication" to organize communication of societal action and utility, which is the case of the social and solidarity economy, as defined by Eric Dacheux. It is a question of apprehending the change in actions and the complex time of the various actors. Information corresponds to the time of knowledge, the urgency of action to the time of change. The articulation of the four major issues of action, link, knowledge and meaning, makes it possible to reconcile these different times to build a new civic responsibility. F. Bernard outlines the dimensions of "engaging position" and that of projects, which is the case for DUCA / GC.

According to Nicole D'Almeida [11], organizations move "between projects and stories." The projects correspond to two types of devices: first is the organizational one, and the second she calls "symbolic narrative" part where "stories" (symbolic devices) are essential. Organizations or organizational devices build their own imaginary stories. To take an example in a presentation's leaflet of Val de Marne Creators' Group: "Creators' Groups help to switch from dream to reality." They are based on two core values: "everyone is an asset for the territory", "everyone expressing the desire to create an activity is heard".

In this work, we met several concepts. The first concept met is that of "device" (in French, "*dispositif*"), that we consider, according to Michel Foucault [12], with all its socio-technical dimensions. For him, "What I'm trying to identify with that name, is first a decidedly mixed space, with speeches, institutions, architectural arrangements, regulatory decisions, laws, administrative measures, scientific statements, philosophical propositions, moral, philanthropic, in short: the words, as well as the unspoken, are mere elements of the device. The device in itself is the network that can be established between all these elements. Secondly, that I would identify in the device, is precisely the nature of the relationship that may exist between these heterogeneous elements."

In a socio-constructivist perspective, we also rely on the concept of "mediator artifact": "the tools provided by the environment do not only play a role of mediator but also of artifact in that they organize (or reorganize) cognitive functioning" [13] with all the importance of project dynamics as especially developed by Jean-Pierre Boutinet and Gino Gramaccia [14] [15]. We also rely on the concepts of situations and interactions [16], defined by Manuel Zacklad as a logic of "cooperative transactions" [17].

Afterwards we analyze these DUCA / GC socio-technical devices as potential and evolving social Intelligent Systems [18] built by the cooperative knowledge of all their actors.

IV. The DUCA – GC as Socio-technical Devices

In this section, we will show how DUCA / GC correspond to socio-technical devices as interactions' areas with important Information and Communication Issues.

A. *DUCA and GC as interactions' areas*

According to ANGC, "The Creators Groups seek autonomy and professional integration of unemployed people, including school leavers, based on their desires to undertake as a catalyst". The main goal of the DUCA / GC devices is to restore confidence, especially for young school leavers by leveraging their creativity in a project approach from an individual project based on training (DUCA), developed in training and group work, but also with an individual coaching (GC).

The GCs (Creators' Groups) aim to transform the desire for entrepreneurship into catalysts for professional integration through support and coaching based on entrepreneurship and project pedagogy. And this coaching is proposed without judging on the feasibility of the idea of the potential creator of activity or on the capacity to create or rescue an activity.

So this is an individual project, part of global dynamics, in a collective approach.

We have pointed the two key values of the DUCA / GC: "everyone is an asset for the territory", "everyone wanting to develop an economic activity is heard". These values are highlighted by the National Association of Creators' Groups (ANGC).

The potential creator of activity is in the center of the DUCA / GC devices, initiator and co-constructor of his project. Integration and autonomy are the aims of the coaching. The support or coaching correspond to a public service approach and the GC services are offered free of charge [19].

Since 2006, UPEM / IUT proposed several DUCAs in partnership with different Creators Groups: Val de Marne Department (94), Val Maubuée (Torcy, 77) and, during three years, with the Paris 20th GC.

We will analyze how a new kind of training (DUCA) is based on cooperative processes and may be regarded as a "device" or an "organizational form" created by all the interactions between all the actors, to develop new opportunities for job seekers coming from disadvantaged areas, especially young school leavers. This process creates a new dynamics among all the actors, combining the individual dimension of each project with a collective dynamics.

A DUCA / GC device brings together partners including: 1) A federative structure (*Mission Locale*, Local Plan for Economic Insertion (PLIE), House of Employment (*Pôle Emploi*), other associations, etc.), 2) a University, often through an IUT, 3) a consultancy team in business creation (management shop or *boutique de gestion*, cooperative, industry and trade chambers, etc.).

B. *Importance of Information and Communication Issues*

Eric Dacheux, already mentioned [7], characterized Social and Solidarity Economy (SSE) as "seeking above all to build links". This approach corresponds to the main goals of Communication Sciences, as stressed by both Françoise Bernard [10] and Daniel Bougnoux [20], emphasizing the importance of the links and the relationship. It is the question of "living connected" or "reliance" that, for us, joins that of the "resilience" of territories in difficulty.

In a perspective of helping people to rebuild their life [21] in a project dynamics, information collect and communication issues are central. Their analysis will constitute a main part of our grid to consider awareness and management of emotions and feelings as levers of creating economic activities. And so their management included in these activities' creation may help people in difficult situations to rebuild their life.

Firstly, candidates to DUCA / GC are searching in leaflets on business and crafts, books and numerous documents offered by the Local Missions and Centre for Information and Orientation (CIO), specialized websites, etc., information to better formalize their projects. They are helped in their information and documentation work by members of ML or of CIO.

The personal reconstruction of the learner / creator is based on an innovative process of creating an activity that is formalized in an oral mid-term and an end-of-year presentation. This process involves many exchanges and a strong research activity for information and documentation with the help of people resources belonging to Local Mission, CIO, or different local associations. It is driven by Mediator Artifact such as Business Plan of each student or meetings around a training "serious game".

This paper corresponds to a complementarity of views. We have met, observed and interviewed: DUCA teachers, GC leaders, trainers, facilitators from Local Missions, members of *boutiques de gestion*, psychologists, and, of course, students-learners and potential creators of their economic activity.

We propose some ways to analyze emotions and feelings of these actors, especially of young people creating activities around two Mediator Artifacts: a training serious game (Solutia) and the business plan of each activity's creator. In a first step, these two Mediator Artifacts constitute for us socio-technical devices.

V. Two Emotions' Mediator Artifacts

DUCA / GC devices correspond to societal innovative areas to promote interactions. Two Mediator Artifacts may act to reveal emotions and feelings and so help to improve activities creators' skills and their creativity.

A. *A training "Serious Game" (Solutia) as first Mediator Artifact to develop ludic interactions*

The main goal of DUCA / GC is to help increase creativity spirit and skills of creators of potential economic activity and especially young people. The DUCA / GC training teams try to invent new ways to interest the potential activities' creators in being involved and so changing their life. One specific way consists in a training game: "Solutia". It is actually a form of "serious game", but not developed on Internet interactions but on real exchanges in face-to-face situations between some creators (five to eight) with the help (a form of coaching) of a ML member.

This game constitutes a Mediator Artifact to develop ludic interactions to improve interest for cooperation and to create a project dynamics. This training "serious game" may also help converge the representations and develop confidence by creating collective dynamics and some form of pride around a personal project which may be also that of a whole family and, sometimes, of a larger community.

First, this game has been thought and created by Marie Beauvais – Chevalier, member of ML of Marne-la-Vallée / Torcy, coordinator of the GC in Val Maubuée. Solutia's game corresponds to a sort of Monopoly and Game of the Goose (*Jeu de l'Oie*) for learning how to manage company's creation and its traps and opportunities.

In a second step, Solutia has been developed and marketed by a student of UPEM University with the creation of a new company through a new device "Students poles for Innovation, Transfer and Entrepreneurship" (PEPITE) [22].

This business creation by a student around Solutia's serious game illustrates the important evolution of the French Universities, and especially UPEM University. UPEM University tries to develop a new spirit of entrepreneurship through various devices and especially with times of exchanges and interactions between teachers and students such as the "All Creative Day, *Tous Créatifs*" (this year on June 22 [th]). It also corresponds to interactions between civil society and local actors and Universities members.

B. *A second Mediator Artifact: the Business Plan of the creators' projects*

We have also observed the emotions and feelings of the actors of DUCA / GC Devices around another Mediator Artifact, the Business Plan of each creator of potential economic activity. The business plan is the main framework of the entire process of monitoring the development of the economic activity of the potential creator. It is a crystallizer of interactions from the beginning of the process (emergence phase) to the final presentation of the project.

The emergence phase allows the potential activity creators to better define their ideas and formalize them. It includes four steps: 1) better knowing their potentiality as project's leaders, 2) better defining the main idea of activity to develop, 3) discover the environment of the project, 4) define the suitability of their personality to the project and its environment. After this phase, the future creator formalized a file, which is the basis for presentation and is defending before a jury for admission to the DUCA degree. The interview is always conducted sympathetically to give confidence to the future creator and help to validate his idea.

The training phase (DUCA) allows future creators to receive specific knowledge to develop skills necessary to manage any activity (company, association, etc.): management, information and communication, legal and tax information, sales management, market survey, project management, etc., and to check the feasibility of the proposed project, specifying the business plan (market survey, financing, cost calculations, etc.). The "case" is finalized and presented before a jury. Pedagogy emphasizes the collective dimension and the practical application of the teachings around creative projects.

VI. Interactions Analysis around Mediator Artifacts Integrating Emotional Dimensions

The two presented Mediator Artifacts enable us to observe the emotions and feelings expressed in particular by young potential entrepreneurs: a phase of interactions between them in a playful position (Solutia Game) and also with interactions with the teaching team: the Business Plan. Both Mediator Artifacts converge to help to build an individual project in a collective dynamics.

Finally, our findings highlight an analysis process with the transition from the initial and spontaneous emotions of the actors, especially young creators of economic activity, to more lasting feelings, attitudes and behaviors over a long period, in relation with their personality.

We promote a dynamic dimension of integration (integrative approach) of changing emotions and feelings in the situation analysis and interactional approach proposed by Alex Mucchielli (Situational and Interactionist Semiotics) [23] for economic activity creativity, apprehended in a grid of informational and communicational integration of actors' views. Different contexts constituting a situation for the actors are considered: respective positions, goals, references or norms, interactions, values, etc. The set of meanings found provides access to the "global meaning" of the phenomenon, which is therefore the synthesis of the meanings taken in the different contexts and for the different actors.

For us, it is also the challenge of development of a dynamics (process) around control of emotions and feelings on a rather long term process.

Alain Caillé presented the quest for recognition as a new total social phenomenon in the second half of the XXth century, notably for minorities or some social groups, but also for populations of sensitive areas. For him, until the 1980s, the emphasis was rather on levels of remuneration, (wages), social protection and working conditions, in particular with the development of trade unions [24]. Recognition by others and the reconstruction of self-esteem are very linked according to Gerard Lefebvre [21].

The DUCA / GC devices are also a space for converging management of project approaches [14], [15], and quality approaches. We propose to consider this convergence through three types of processes that exists in any organization or project: the objective to compliance (control), the desire to implement changes and so the commitment to promote creativity and innovation [25]. For us, DUCA / GC devices constitute interesting areas of cooperation to observe this convergence. The challenge is to promote a culture of change and innovation in the French society based for example on validated and reproducible experiments. It can be first developed betting on the capacity for innovation and creativity in small structures that promote initiatives. But it is also a question of answering the reality of markets and needs of local consumers or funding institutions.

The emotional skills of young creators are the central element of an emotional intelligence, in our opinion, not sufficiently taken into account. The human body is both the mediator from which the individual can sensitize his affects and constitutes a communication support of them, according to Fabienne Martin-Juchat [26].

By helping to set the individual project of business creation in a collective dynamics, the two studied Mediator Artifacts may help to favor a first awareness among activity creators; they are never completely alone and there are levers, networks that they must know how to use to get the right information at the right time and in the right place (informational and communicational skills). This awareness may help activities' creators to restore their confidence and to overcome their shyness.

The serious game Solutia also promotes situational skills: it allows students to discover a number of problem situations they can find in their creative activity and so help to overpass them. It can give awareness of their personal evolution, especially of their new skills and some pride of their activity's project: importance of self-esteem, often built through the eyes of others, especially their friends and their families.

The goal of the Mediator Artifacts, particularly Solutia serious game is to (re) give confidence, to raise awareness that everyone has met difficulties in his entrepreneurship's pathway and that they can be overcome. It is good to know how to go beyond emotions such as fear of failure, withdrawal, frustration, anger, etc. Understanding and better managing emotions by relativizing them may help to recreate a positive dynamics of trust. It is also important to train the activities' creators to be aware of their emotions and feelings, so they are not paralyzed by them, and, therefore, to better manage them and to succeed in their creation of activity process.

VII. From Socio-tchnical Devices to Potential and Evolving Social Intelligent Systems

DUCA / GC constitute spaces for cooperation in order to develop an individual project in a collective process of building knowledge based on Mediator Artifacts fostering exchanges and cooperation among all their actors, notably creators of economic activity.

As a first step, we proposed to consider them as socio-technical devices based in particular on interactions around two Mediator Artifacts. In a second step, we propose to consider the DUCA / GC as potential and evolving Social Intelligent Systems by placing us notably in the constructivist approach (the social reality is "construct" by the actors) of the complexity analysis proposed by Edgar Morin [27] and Jean-Louis Le Moigne [28]. Particularly, Jean-Louis Le Moigne proposes an approach to the elaboration of a General System, which gradually emerged from the 1950s with the cybernetic, structuralist and structural-functionalist approaches ([18].

J.-L. Le Moigne stresses the importance of modeling: "modeling a complex system is modeling a system of actions". In the formalisms of the systemic modeling, he relies on Edgar Morin, who proposed the concept of organiz-action corresponding to principles of eco - auto - re - organization with information, communication and computational dimensions.

For J.-L. Le Moigne, it is an organizational or informed system: "the information forming the organization that forms it", with all the importance of documentation and information resources, as we have pointed out for the DUCA / GC [28].

From the communicational point of view, Alex Mucchielli proposed [29] a "Systemic and Communicational Approach of Organizations" (2002). He presents an Information and Communication Sciences approach based on the paradigm of complexity in relation with systemism and constructivism, referring to the works of the invisible college at Palo Alto, where "communication is always conceived as a participation in a communicative ensemble or a system of relations (the "orchestra" model). It is a matter of bringing to light the meaning of the different interactions in a global system, in order to create a collective sense of the relational system itself for all actors. It proposes a method leading to model the relations. It begins with an observation of relations, and continues with an effort to diagram the exchanges (including implicit communications) of the actors and to finish with the description of the functioning of the whole system. The final analysis must reveal the emerging "values" of the system, which, implicitly, can be regarded as "leading the game", almost unknown to the actors.

He will confirm and extend these propositions a few years later in his "situational and interactional semiotic" approach (2010) already mentioned in an interactionist analysis of the DUCA / GC [23]. This perspective joins that of the Communication as Constitutive of Organizations proposed by Linda L. Putnam and Anne M. Nicotera [30], considering organizations as organizational systems as Edgar Morin.

After the informational and communicational dimensions of his modeling approach, J.-L. Le Moigne evokes a third "computational" dimension. In this perspective of computational analysis of players' relations in the case of game situations, such as for the Mediator Artifact Solutia game, we can refer for example to the works of Mossakowski and Mandziuk in the case of the bridge game [31].

At this stage of our analysis, we are at the first two levels of modeling information and communication situations around interactions between DUCA / GC actors in a perspective of social systemic approach in a shared knowledge building perspective.

DUCA / GC considered as potential social Intelligent Systems correspond also to an approach of building collective intelligence in specific situations. We are then in the perspective of management of collective intelligence (CI) proposed by Olivier Zara [32]. According to him, "Collective Intelligence is the intelligence of the link, of the relationship defined by some as a connective intelligence or "global brain"... The heart of the collective intelligence is the harmony in the links... These links induce the cooperation and collective intelligence would ultimately be the consequence of intellectual co-operation, their materialization. He refers to Pierre Lévy, for whom "the best thing that can be done with new technologies is not Artificial Intelligence (AI), but, on the contrary, Collective Intelligence ... Computers do not mimic humans, but help them to think and collectively evolve their ideas. CI helps people to think together, while AI seeks to substitute for humans to limit their mistakes ".

All this from a perspective of social systemic that J.C. Lugan proposes to develop in a pragmatic approach "concerned to confront the available systemic tools with concrete social formations" [18], for us DUCA / GC.

VIII. Through an Individual Dynamics in a Collective Approach

To use a formula coming from an ANGC document: "To dare it is already to move forward". It is a question of helping to "overcome the preconceived ideas that prevent change": "I have no money", "I am too young", "It is too complicated", "I have no idea", "I feel alone ","I have a disability", "I do not have a diploma", etc. [19].

We think that learning to better manage the emotions can become a collective goal to develop cooperation and improve skills. It is on this aspect that we propose to the other partners of the DUCA / GC to insist with a view of continuous improvement of existing devices.

Social sharing of emotions is also important for encouraging awareness of group membership [16]. This group is essential to promote the personal development of each potential creator. This integration of emotions and feelings can help to better integrate an individual project of creation of activities in a collective dynamics of exchange of experiences and feelings (Group of Creators) to better understand and support in times of doubt and (re) motivate them. We wish to analyze their mechanisms to best promote these periods of interactions and information sharing for improvement of their projects.

Our observations lead us to propose a broadening of perspectives of Situational and Interactionist Semiotics defined by Alex Mucchielli [23] with the integration of the experiences of the actors and their emotions and feelings according to Daniel Goleman [33], particularly for creators of activity.

Another approach to consider is the Sociology of Actor-Network (SAR) proposed by Michel Callon [34], even if the business plan and the serious game Solutia are not full technical devices, but rather social and managerial devices. The idea that the collective activity ("acting elements") can be considered as a "black box" ("*boîte noire*") seems to match our approach of the business plan as the idea of "hybrid reality composed of successive translations" and the fact that the SAR "has been designed to follow the collective in their making process", which is the case of DUCA / GC devices.

In the perspective developed by Aurélia Dumas and Fabienne Martin-Juchat [35], through situations of participatory observations or interviews with young creators of activities, in particular around the uses of the two mediating artifacts, we tried to understand their emotional culture, their emotional language and their mechanisms of emotional regulation. By privileging the vision of these actors, in a rather ethnographic approach, we considered the two mediating artifacts as "communicative objects".

We can then consider a dynamic relational semiotics approach to a certain length: global (approach by the complexity theory in a constructivist way), based on the search for meaning in the interactions' situations between all the actors (including socio-technical artifacts), and of course also including emotions, feelings, experiences of all the actors in a dynamic approach (convergence of the management of project approaches and the process approaches of quality management) to create a dynamic of change, creativity and innovation, mixing individual and collective dimensions.

IX. A Success to Better Socially Integrate People By Creating New Economic Activities for the Sustainable Development of Disadvantaged Territories

A very recent study on Creators' Groups [36] clearly highlights the impact of GCs, corresponding to "an integration program through project pedagogy". DUCA / GC students are both better paid (29 % more than other young unemployed people) and can take back studies in better conditions and with motivation. By enabling young people to rebuild themselves, to regain their confidence and to think about a project, the DUCA / GC are thus two-fold integration mechanisms: both by activity (60% of DUCA graduates) and by training.

Since 2000, the GCs, mostly through Local Missions, have received over than 15,000 people, mainly young people, coached 7,500 people in the project emergence phase and more than 1,300 people in the training phase or DUCA [19]

For the University of Paris East Marne-la-Vallée (UPEM), since 2006, 305 activity creators and, especially, young people, have been trained in the IUT of UPEM and 157 graduated, that is to say more than 50%, which is considered as a very positive result by the Ile-de-France Regional Council (CRIF), the main public collectivity giving funds to the DUCA / GC devices.

More globally, nearly 500 people, especially young people, have been sensitized to business creation and reality of the economic constraints of companies. Nearly 35% of the graduated students have created their business or taken over an existing activity; others have been inserted as employees in existing companies (often trade or food activities). Activities creations successes particularly concern the services sector in very different aspects. First, we have food activities such as free gluten bakeries, food to all tastes and cuisines possible, particularly Afro-Asian. Secondly, we have clothes manufacturing companies corresponding to different countries (Japan and Asia fashion, North Africa, etc.) and shops of different types of clothes. We have also organic cleaning companies, communication companies to organize special events (marriage, etc.), production of video games, jewelry creations, home automation companies, etc. We have also more usual activities such as nurseries, gardening, public writers, different ways of home help, beauticians, hairdressers, sometimes with itinerant projects. But also, with the reform of school times (2013), we have animation's projects to provide stimulating activities or sports for children after school time, etc.

A great satisfaction during the graduation ceremonies for the DUCAs in December 2015 and 2016 was to see some graduated of previous years come to offer jobs to those who had just come into training.

DUCA / GC can also correspond to an intergenerational perspective that may be part of the Silver Economy (markets linked to ageing and well-ageing). Young retired volunteers could thus help young creators or young rescuers of activities to develop their activity: aids in management but also according to the different types of jobs (baker, car repair, gardener, etc.) giving a sense of solidarity and transmission in the early years of the often difficult transition from an intense activity to the breaking, not always wanted, to retired new life. These retired people may act as supports or coaches for young and inexperienced creators of activities. This form of intergenerational solidarity on the territories also corresponds to the articulation of the challenges of "reliance" and "resilience".

X. Conclusion

Since 2006, DUCA / GC socio-technical devices developed in UPEM / IUT, in cooperation with federated partners in the DUCA / GC have progressively constituted potential and evolving Social Intelligent Systems. They have trained over than 500 students in the creation of activity, including a majority of young school leavers. The challenge is now finding additional funding to the specific aid the Regional Council of Ile-de-France. We hope in European subsidies.

In the cooperation areas developed around DUCA / GC devices, the position of "committed researcher" has really, for us, taken all its meaning and corresponds to a personal approach to the RSU, revisited as "societal responsibility of the researcher", in a perspective of "engaging communication" proposed by Françoise Bernard for societal responsibility [10]. We have gradually become convinced that the future can be built from micro actions on the territories and on daily innovative practices.

For us, beyond the figures and examples of activities successes creations in various sectors (gardening, personal computers, clothing, cleaning, food, restaurants, personal services, etc.), the more important part is to have renewed hope through a project dynamics to allow potential creators of economic activities, especially school young leavers, to take charge of their destiny, in taking the risk of action for hope to promote a new business vision, resolutely different from "destructive innovation" discussed by Luc Ferry [37], with the disasters of the financial and speculative capitalism. We insist on a first goal, that people dare to do the first step and also meeting the words of George Mallory starting to climb to Everest Mountain (1924): "Where there is a will, there is always a way." We also meet Stéphane Hessel and Edgar Morin who proposed new paths towards "the way of hope" in the same perspective of Economic Social and Solidarity where we try also to walk [38].

This approach focuses on the integration and management of emotions and feelings of all the actors of DUCA / GC devices, particularly those of the potential creators of economic activities. It also incorporates the concepts of "resilience" (ability to move again in a crisis situation), both with individual and collective aspects, of "sustainable development" of territories. Territories are then considered as built by a synergy of local projects, both individual and collective, all these projects building new links or interactions and solidarity, especially in disadvantaged areas [39] in order to create a collective dynamics and give capacity for innovation and creativity [40]. For us, they constitute potential and evolving Social Intelligent Systems progressively built by all the knowledge and skills of all their actors and especially the creators of activity.

It is a question of trying to "catalyze" the energies to contribute to a new territorial dynamics, training being an essential element in helping to broaden territorial social capital by relying on projects of motivated young people. It is also in a certain manner an element of the perspective proposed by B. Carayon [41] of the French Economic Intelligence approach insisting on associating competitiveness of companies and social cohesion in a new territorial dynamics linking stakes of economic or competitive intelligence and territorial intelligence.

Potential and Evolving Social Intelligent Systems, DUCA / GC also correspond to new ways of "democratic solidarity" on territories, promoting new links between unemployed people with existing companies, local authorities or retired people acting as supports or coaches to invent new ways of local citizenship. They then contribute to the "relationship economy" proposed by Nicole D'Almeida in a communication perspective [42] and the "economies of conviviality and transactions" defined by Manuel Zacklad [17].

REFERENCES

[1] C. Bourret, "Tracks to Analyze Emotions around Mediator Artifacts to Improve Training and Business Creation for Unemployed People in French Universities," *Proceedings / The Second International Conference on Human and Social Analytics*, HUSO 2016 – IARIA, Barcelona November 13 – 16, pp. 9-13, ISBN : 978-1-61208-517-7

[2] S. Paugam, The social link / *Le lien social*, Paris: PUF, 2010.

[3] H. Azoulay, "Social Intelligence. The case of suburbs : use networks to go gout crisis / *L'intelligence sociale. Le cas des banlieues : utiliser les réseaux pour sortir de la crise,*" in M.-A.Duval dir., New territories of Business Intelligence / *Les nouveaux territoires de l'Intelligence Economique*, Paris: ACFCI – IFIE Ed., pp. 119-146, 2008.

[4] N. Alter, Ordinary Innovation / *L'innovation ordinaire*, Paris: PUF, Coll. Quadrige, 2005.

[5] Available on: http://www.lefigaro.fr/social/2015/03/25/09010-20150325ARTFIG00325-pres-de-2-millions-de-jeunes-sont-sans-emploi-ni-diplome-en-france.php. Retrieved 2017, February 5th.

[6] Available on : http://www.enseignementsup-recherche.gouv.fr/cid79926/statut-national-etudiant-entrepreneur.html. Retrieved 2016, June 26th.

[7] Seminar "New forms of cooperation for the Digital Age / New Civic Sociability", ISCC, Paris, December 1st, 2016.

[8] J.L. Laville and A. Yvergniaux, "Tags for a left project. Democratic solidarity, sustainable development, plural economy / *Balises pour un projet de gauche. Solidarité démocratique, développement durable, économie plurielle,*" Institut Polanyi / France, 2009, Available on: http://institutpolanyi.fr/balises-pour-un-projet-de-gauche-solidarite-democratique-developpement-durable-economie-plurielle/. Retrieved 2017, February 5th.

[9] F. Bernard, "The SIC, a Disciplinary of Openness and Decompartmentalization / *Les SIC, une discipline de l'ouverture et du décloisonnement* ", in A. Bouzon dir., op. cit., Paris : L'Harmattan, pp. 33 – 46, 2006.

[10] F. Bernard, "Organize communication for societal action and utility. The paradigm of engaging communication / *Organiser la communication d'action et d'utilité sociétales. Le paradigme de lacommunication engageante,*" Communication and Organization / *Communication et organisation* , 29 | 2006. Available on http://communicationorganisation.revues.org/3374. Retrieved February 2017, 6th.

[11] N. D'Almeida, "Organizations between projects and stories / *Les organisations entre projets et récits*", in A. Bouzon dir., Organizational Communication in debates. Fields, Concepts and Prospects / *La communication organisationnelle en débats. Champs, concepts et perspectives,*" Paris : L'Harmattan, p. 145 – 158, 2006.

[12] "The game of Michel Foucault / *Le jeu de Michel Foucault*" (interview), Ornicar ?, n° 10, July, pp. 62-93, 1977.

[13] Available on : http://www.edu-tice.org/approche-th%C3%A9orique/glossaire/concepts-5/. Retrieved 2016, June 26th.

[14] J.-P. Boutinet, Psychology of Project Conducts / *Psychologie des conduites à projet*, Paris: PUF, 1999.

[15] G. Gramaccia, "Quality, Project, Digital : three symbolic variations of Managerial Effectiveness / *Qualité, projet, numérique : trois variations symboliques de l'efficacité gestionnaire,*" in C. Batazzi dir., Communication, organisation, symboles, Revue MEI, n° 29, Paris : L'Harmattan, pp. 55-67, 2008.

[16] L. Bègue and O. Desrichard dir., Treaty of Social Psychology. Science of Human Interactions / *Traité de psychologie sociale. La science des interactions humaines*, Bruxelles: De Boeck, 2013.

[17] M. Zacklad, "Economies of Conviviality in Information and Services Societies / *Les économies de la convivialité dans les sociétés de l'information et des services,*" Inaugural Lecture / *Leçon inaugurale*, Paris: CNAM, 2009 June 17th.

[18] J.-C. Lugan, Social Systemic / *La systémique sociale*, Paris : PUF, 2012.

[19] Creators Groupments Network / *Le réseau Groupement de Créateurs*, Undertake his future / *Entreprendre son avenir*, Paris, Available on: www.groupement-de-createurs.fr

[20] D. Bougnoux, Introduction to sciences of communication, Paris: La Découverte, 2006.

[21] G. Lefebvre, Identitary Reconstruction and Insertion / *Reconstruction identitaire et insertion*, Paris: L'Harmattan, 1998.

[22] Available on : http://www.enseignementsup-recherche.gouv.fr/cid79223/pepite-poles-etudiants-pour-innovation-transfert-entrepreneuriat.html. Retrieved 2016, June 26th.

[23] A. Mucchielli, Situation and Communication, Nice : Les éditions Ovadia, 2010.

[24] A. Caillé dir., The quest for recognition new total social phenomenom / *La quête de reconnaissance nouveau phénomène social total*, Paris : La Découverte, 2007.

[25] J.-P. Caliste and C. Bourret, "Contribution to a Typological Analysis of Processes : From Conformity to Agility / *Contribution à une analyse typologique des processus : de la conformité à l'agilité,*" UTC Quality Notebooks / *Les Cahiers de la Qualité de l'UTC*, Vol 2, G. Farges and al.., Lexitis éditions, pp. 113-116, 2015.

[26] F. Martin-Juchat, The body and the media. The flesh experienced by the media and social spaces / *Le corps et les*

médias. La chair éprouvée par les médias et les espaces sociaux, Bruxelles: De Boeck, 2008.

[27] E. Morin, Introduction to Complex Thought / *Introduction à la pensée complexe,* Paris : ESF, 1990, rééd., Points-Seuil, 2005.

[28] J.-L. Le Moigne, Formalisms of Systemic Modelling / Les formalismes de la modélisation systémique, 2005, Available on :www.intelligence-complexite.org/fileadmin/docs/0505formalismesvfr.pdf, Retrieved May 2017, 1st.

[29] A. Mucchielli, Systemic and Communicationnal Approach of Organizations / *Approche systémique et communicationnelle des organisations,* Paris : Armand Colin, 2002.

[30] L. L. Putnam, A.M. Nicotera, Building Theories of Organization. The Constitutive Role of Communication, New York / London : Routledge, 2009.

[31] K. Mossakowski and J. Mandziuk, "Learning without human expertise. A case study of the Double Dummy Bridge Problem," Transactions on Neural Networks, IEEE, vol. 20, Issue 2, pp. 1-23, Available on : ieeexplore.ieee.org/iel5/72/4776562/04749256.pdf – Retrieved May 2017, 1st.

[32] O. Zara, Management of Collective Intelligence / *Le Management de l'intelligence collective*, Paris : M21 Editions, 2008.

[33] D. Goleman, Working with Emotional Intelligence, Bloomsbury: London, 1998.

[34] M. Callon, " Sociology of the Network Actor / *Sociologie de l'Acteur Réseau,*" in M. Akrich, M. Callon and B. Latour., Sociology of the Translation : Founding Texts / *Sociologie de la Traduction : Textes fondateurs*, Presses de l'Ecole des Mines de Paris, pp. 267-276, 2006.

[35] A. Dumas and F. Martin-Juchat, "Communication approach to emotions in organizations: questions and methodological implications / *Approche communicationnelle des émotions dans les organisations : questionnements et implications méthodologiques* ," French Review of Information and Communication Sciences / *Revue française des sciences de l'information et de la communication*, 9/ 2016, Available on: http://rfsic.revues.org/2103 ; DOI : 10.4000/rfsic.2103 . Retrieved 2017, February 5th.

[36] Y. Algan, B. Crépon, E. Huillery and W. Parienté, "Impact of Creators' groups: teaching a controlled experiment / *Impact des Groupements de Créateurs : enseignement d'une expérience contrôlée*", J-PAL et CREST Laboratories, Paris, 2016. Available on: http://www.lesechos.fr/economie-france/social/0211576808894-jeunes-le-dispositif-groupement-de-createurs-a-fait-ses-preuves-2049670.php. Retrieved 2017, February 5th.

[37] L. Ferry, Destructive Innovation / *L'innovation destructrice*, Paris: Plon, 2014.

[38] S. Hessel and E. Morin, The Way of Hope / *Le Chemin de l'Espérance*, Paris :Fayard, 2011.

[39] C. Bourret, "Elements for an Approach of Territorial Intelligence as a Synergy of Local Projects to Develop a Collective Identity / *Eléments pour une approche de l'intelligence territoriale comme synergie de projets locaux pour développer une identité collective,*" International Journal of Projectics, n° 1, Bruxelles: De Boeck, pp. 79-92, 2008.

[40] M. Godet, P. Durance and M. Mousli, Unleashing innovation in the territories / *Libérer l'innovation dans les territoires,* Paris : Conseil d'Analyse Economique - La documentation Française, 2010.

[41] B. Carayon, Economic Intelligence, Competitiveness and Social Cohesion, / *Intelligence économique, compétitivité et cohésion sociale*, Paris : La Documentation française, 2003. Available on : http://www.ladocumentationfrancaise.fr/rapports-publics/034000484/index.shtml. Retrieved 2017, May 1st.

[42] N. D'Almeida, The Promises of Communication / *Les promesses de la communication,* Paris : PUF, 2001.

Hierarchical Cooperative Tracking of Vehicles and People Using Laser Scanners Mounted on Multiple Mobile Robots

Yuto Tamura, Ryohei Murabayashi
Graduate School of Science and Engineering
Doshisha Unversity
Kyotanabe, Kyoto 610-0394 Japan
e-mail: {ytamura915, ryo040978}@gmail.com

Masafumi Hashimoto, Kazuhiko Takahashi
Faculty of Science and Engineering
Doshisha Unversity
Kyotanabe, Kyoto 610-0394 Japan
e-mail: {mhashimo, katakaha}@mail.doshisha.ac.jp

Abstract—**This paper presents a tracking (estimation of the pose and size) of moving objects such as pedestrians, cars, motorcycles, and bicycles, using multiple mobile robots as sensor nodes. In this cooperative-tracking method, nearby sensor nodes share their tracking information, enabling the tracking of objects that are invisible or partially visible to an individual sensor node. The cooperative-tacking method can then make the tracking system more reliable than the conventional individual tracking method by a single robot. We previously presented a centralized architecture of cooperative tracking. Each sensor node detected moving objects in its own laser-scanned images captured by a single-layer laser scanner. It then sent measurement information related to the moving objects to a central server. The central server estimated the objects' poses (positions and velocities) and sizes from the measurement information using Bayesian filter. However, such a centralized method might have poor dependability and impose a computational burden upon the central server. To address this problem, this paper presents hierarchical architecture of cooperative tracking. Each sensor node locally estimates the poses and sizes of moving objects and then sends these estimates to the central server, which then merges the pose and size estimates. Experimental results using two sensor nodes in outdoor environments show that the proposed hierarchical cooperative-tracking method provides slightly inferior tracking accuracy and has a smaller computational cost in the central server than a previous centralized method.**

Keywords—moving-object tracking; cooperative tracking; centralized and hierarchical methods; laser scanner; mobile robot.

I. INTRODUCTION

This paper is an extended version of an earlier paper presented at the IARIA Conference on Intelligent Systems and Applications (INTELLI 2016) [1] in Barcelona. Throughout this paper, the term 'tracking' means the estimation of the pose (position and velocity) and size of a moving object.

The tracking of multiple moving objects (such as people, cars, and bicycles) in environments is an important issue in the safe navigation of mobile robots and vehicles. The use of vision, radar or laser scanner (Lidar) in mobile robotics and vehicle automation has attracted considerable interest [2]–[8]. When compared with vision-based tracking, laser-based tracking is insensitive to lighting conditions and requires less data processing time. Furthermore, due to its directionality, laser-based tracking provides better tracking accuracy than radar-based tracking. Therefore, in this paper, we focus on a tracking method for moving objects using laser scanners mounted on mobile robots and vehicles.

Many studies have been conducted on multi-robot coordination and cooperation [9][10]. When multiple robots are located in the same vicinity, they can share their sensing data through a communication network system. Thus, the multi-robot team can be considered to be a multi-sensor system. Even if moving objects are located outside the sensing area of a robot or are occluded in crowded environments, they can be recognized using tracking data from other nearby robots. Hence, multi-robot system can improve the accuracy and reliability with which moving objects are tracked.

Figure 1. Application of cooperative tracking to a vehicle automation field.

Such cooperative tracking using multiple robots and vehicles can also be applied to vehicle automation, including intelligent transportation systems (ITS) and systems for personal mobility devices, as shown in Fig. 1. Cooperative tracking enables the detection of moving objects in the blind-spot of each vehicle and can be used to detect sudden changes in a crowded urban environment such as people appearing on roads or vehicles making unsafe lane changes. It can therefore prevent traffic accidents.

In this paper, we present a hierarchical cooperative-tracking method for moving objects using multiple mobile robots as sensor nodes. The sensor nodes locally track moving objects and transmit the tracking information to a central server, which then merges the tracking information.

For simplicity, in this paper, moving-object tracking using multiple mobile sensor nodes is referred to as 'cooperative tracking,' whereas that by an individual robot in a team is referred to as 'individual tracking.'

The rest of the paper is organized as follows. Section II presents an overview of related work. Section III gives our experimental system. In Sections IV to VII, cooperative tracking method is discussed. In Section VIII, we describe experiments of moving-object tracking using two sensor nodes in outdoor environments. We will present our conclusions in Section IX.

II. Related Work

We previously presented a cooperative people-tracking method in which multiple mobile robots and vehicles were used as mobile sensor nodes and equipped with laser scanners [11][12]. The covariance intersection method [13] was applied to operate the tracking system effectively in a decentralized manner without a central server. In cooperative people tracking, each person could be assumed to be a point due to their small size, and mass-point tracking (only pose estimation) was then performed.

However, in the real world, several types of moving objects exist, such as people, cars, bicycles, and motorcycles. Therefore, we should design a cooperative-tracking system for these moving objects. In vehicle (car, motorcycle, and bicycle) tracking, we have to consider moving objects as rigid bodies and estimate both the poses and sizes to avoid collisions in a crowded environment. Tracking of a rigid body is known as extended-object tracking, and many related studies have been conducted [14]–[18]. However, to the best of our knowledge, cooperative tracking using multiple mobile sensor nodes covers only mass-point tracking under the assumption that the tracked object is small. It estimates only the object's pose but does not estimate its size [19]–[25].

Therefore, we presented a laser-based cooperative-tracking method for rigid bodies that estimates both poses and sizes of people and vehicles using multiple mobile sensor nodes [26]. In a crowded environment, a vehicle can be occluded or only rendered partially visible to each sensor node. To correctly estimate the size of the vehicle, the laser measurements captured by sensor nodes in the team have to be merged. Our previous cooperative-tracking method for rigid bodies applied a centralized architecture. Each sensor node detected laser measurements related to the moving objects in its sensing area and transmitted the measurement information to a central server, which then estimated the poses and sizes of the objects. Such a centralized architecture imposes a computational burden upon the central server. Furthermore, the architecture has a weakness against fault in the communication system between sensor nodes and the central server.

To address this problem, in this paper, we present a hierarchical method for cooperative tracking through which the poses and sizes of moving objects are locally estimated by the sensor nodes. Furthermore, these estimates are then merged by a central server. We will treat both vehicles and people as rigid bodies.

Figure 2. Overview of the mobile sensor nodes.

III. Experimental System

Fig. 2 shows the mobile-sensor node system used in our experiments. Each of the two sensor nodes has two independently driven wheels. A wheel encoder is attached to each drive wheel to measure its velocity. A yaw-rate gyro is attached to the chassis of each robot to sense the turning velocity. These internal sensors calculate the robot's pose using dead reckoning.

Each sensor node is equipped with a forward-looking laser scanner (SICK LMS100) to capture laser-scanned images that are represented by a sequence of distance samples in a horizontal plane with a field of view of 270°. The angular resolution of the laser scanner is 0.5°, and each scan image comprises 541 distance samples. Each sensor node is also equipped with RTK-GPS (Novatel ProPak-V3 GPS). The sampling frequency of all sensors is 10 Hz.

We use broadcast communication over a wireless local area network to exchange information between the central server and the sensor nodes. The model of the computers used in the sensor nodes and the central server is Iiyama 15X7100-i7-VGB with a 2.8 GHz Intel core i7-4810MQ processor, and the operating system is Microsoft Windows 7 Professional.

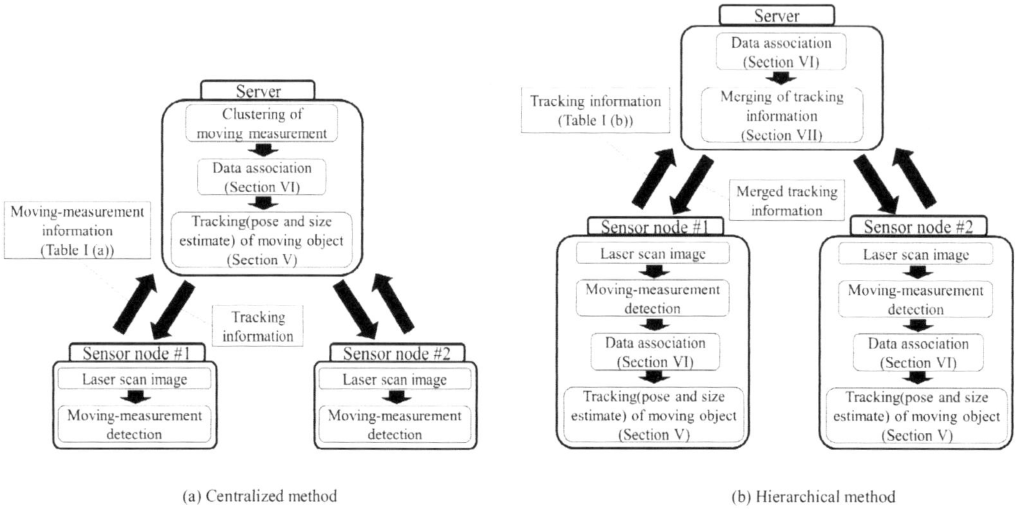

Figure 3. System overview of cooperative tracking.

IV. OVERVIEW OF COOPERATIVE-TRACKING SYSTEM

In Section VIII, we will evaluate our hierarchical cooperative-tracking method through experiments by comparing it with our previous centralized method. To allow readers to better understand our cooperative-tracking method, we detail both the centralized and hierarchical methods of cooperative tracking. Figs. 3 (a) and (b) show a sequence of centralized and hierarchical cooperative-tracking, respectively, using two sensor nodes and a central server.

A. Centralized Method [26]

Each sensor node independently finds moving objects in its own laser-scanned image using an occupancy-grid method [27]. Laser measurements (positions) are mapped onto the grid map represented in the world coordinate frame Σ_w. The mapped measurements are classified into moving and static measurements using the occupancy-grid method. The moving measurements are considered to originate from moving objects, whereas the static measurements are considered to be from static objects. The sensor node uploads moving-measurement information to a central server. This information is detailed in Table I (a).

Moving measurements coming from the same moving object have similar positions, whereas those from different moving objects are significantly different. Thus, the central server clusters moving measurements sent from two sensor nodes by checking the gap between two adjacent measurements. Subsequently, the server estimates the poses and sizes of the moving objects using the methods to be presented in Sections V and VI. The estimated information is then fed back to the sensor nodes.

The cell size of the grid map is set at 0.3×0.3 m in our experiments. To map the laser-scanned images onto the grid map, each sensor node accurately identifies its own position and orientation in Σ_w based on dead reckoning and GPS information via an extended Kalman filter. Our moving measurement detection using the occupancy-grid method and self-localization using an extended Kalman filter are detailed in references [27] and [12], respectively.

B. Hierarchical Method

In the hierarchical method, each sensor node classifies the mapped laser measurements into moving and static

TABLE I. INFORMATION AND DATA VOLUME SENT FROM EACH SENSOR NODE TO CENTRAL SERVER

(a) CENTRALIZED METHOD

Information	Data volume [bit]
Time stamp	2×32
Pose of sensor node (x, y, θ)	3×32
The number of moving objects (n)	32
The number of moving measurements comprising each moving object (m)	$n \times 32$
Coordinates of each moving measurement (x, y)	$n \times m \times 2 \times 32$
Total	$(6 + n + 2nm) \times 32$

(b) HIERARCHICAL METHOD

Information	Data volume [bit]
Time stamp	2×32
The number of tracked objects (n)	32
Position and velocity estimate of each tracked object $(x, \dot{x}, y, \dot{y})$	$n \times 4 \times 32$
Heading of each tracked object (θ)	32
Size (width and lenglth) of each tracked object (W, L)	$n \times 2 \times 32$
Total	$(4 + 6n) \times 32$

measurements using the occupancy-grid method and clusters moving measurements by checking the gap between two adjacent measurements. Subsequently, the sensor node locally estimates the poses and sizes of moving objects using the methods shown in Sections V and VI. This means individual tracking. The tracking information of the moving objects, which is detailed in Table I (b), is then uploaded to the central server.

After receiving the information regarding the tracked objects from two sensor nodes, the central server merges the information using the method in Section VII to improve the tracking accuracy. The merged poses and sizes of the moving objects are then fed back to the sensor nodes.

V. POSE AND SIZE ESTIMATION

In the hierarchical cooperative-tracking method, the pose and size are locally estimated by sensor nodes, whereas, in the centralized method, they are estimated by a central server.

We represent the shape of a moving object using a rectangle with width, W and length, L. We detail the size-estimation method in Fig. 4, where red circles indicate laser measurements of the moving object (hereafter referred to as moving measurements), and green lines are the feature lines extracted from these measurements. The green dashed rectangle is the estimated rectangle, and the green star is the centroid of that rectangle. As shown in Fig. 4, an $x_v y_v$-coordinate frame is defined, on which the y_v-axis aligns with the heading (orange arrow) of a tracked object. From clustered moving measurements, we extract the width, W_{meas} and length, L_{meas}.

When a moving object is perfectly visible, its size can be estimated from these moving measurements. In contrast, when it is partially occluded by other objects, its size cannot be accurately estimated. Therefore, the size of a partially visible object is estimated using the following equation [14]:

$$\begin{cases} W_{(t)} = W_{(t-1)} + G_W (W_{meas} - W_{(t-1)}) \\ L_{(t)} = L_{(t-1)} + G_L (L_{meas} - L_{(t-1)}) \end{cases} \tag{1}$$

where W and L are estimates of the width and length, respectively, and t and t-1 are time steps. G is the filter gain, given by $G = 1 - \sqrt[t]{(1-p)}$ [14], and p is a parameter. As the value of p increases, the reliabilities of the current measurements of W_{meas} and L_{meas} increase. We assume that a vehicle passes at 60 km/h in front of the sensor node. After the vehicle enters the surveillance area of the sensor node, we aim to estimate 99% of the size (p = 0.99) within 10 scans (1 s) of the laser scanner. We can then determine G as follows:

$$G = \begin{cases} 1 - \sqrt[t]{(1-0.99)} & \text{for } t \le 10 \\ 1 - \sqrt[10]{(1-0.99)} = 0.369 & \text{for } t > 10 \end{cases} \tag{2}$$

For a perfectly visible object, we set the gain G_w (G_L) as follows: if $W_{(t-1)}$ ($L_{(t-1)}$) < W_{meas} (L_{meas}), then G_w (G_L) =1, else G_w (G_L) = 0.

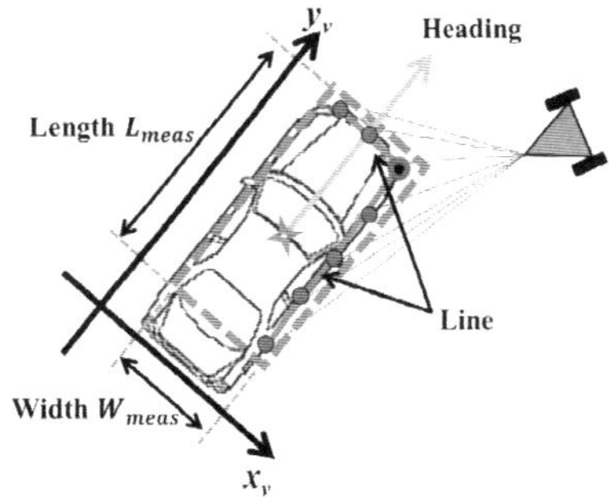

Figure 4. Size estimation of a vehicle.

The estimated size of the tracked object is used to classify the object as a person or a vehicle (i.e., car, motorcycle, and bicycle). If the estimated length or width is larger than 0.8 m, the object is determined to be a vehicle. If the size is less than 0.8 m, it is determined to be a person.

We then define the centroid position (green star in Fig. 4) of the rectangle estimated from (1) by (x, y) in Σ_w. From the centroid position, the pose of the tracked object in Σ_w is estimated using the Kalman filter [28] under the assumption that the object is moving at an almost constant velocity. The rate kinematics is given by:

$$\begin{aligned} \boldsymbol{x}_{(t)} &= \boldsymbol{F}\boldsymbol{x}_{(t-1)} + \boldsymbol{G}\Delta\boldsymbol{x}_{(t-1)} \\ &= \begin{pmatrix} 1 & \tau & 0 & 0 \\ 0 & 1 & 0 & 0 \\ 0 & 0 & 1 & \tau \\ 0 & 0 & 0 & 1 \end{pmatrix} \boldsymbol{x}_{(t-1)} + \begin{pmatrix} \tau^2/2 & 0 \\ \tau & 0 \\ 0 & \tau^2/2 \\ 0 & \tau \end{pmatrix} \Delta\boldsymbol{x}_{(t-1)} \end{aligned} \tag{3}$$

where $\boldsymbol{x} = (x, \dot{x}, y, \dot{y})^T$. $\Delta\boldsymbol{x} = (\Delta\ddot{x}, \Delta\ddot{y})^T$ is an unknown acceleration (plant noise). τ (=0.1 s) is the sampling period of the laser scanner.

The measurement model related to the moving object is then:

$$\begin{aligned} \boldsymbol{z}_{(t)} &= \boldsymbol{H}\boldsymbol{x}_{(t)} + \Delta\boldsymbol{z}_{(t)} \\ &= \begin{pmatrix} 1 & 0 & 0 & 0 \\ 0 & 0 & 1 & 0 \end{pmatrix} \boldsymbol{x}_{(t)} + \Delta\boldsymbol{z}_{(t)} \end{aligned} \tag{4}$$

where $z = (z_x, z_y)^T$ is the centroid position represented in Σ_w. Δz is the measurement noise.

From (3), the pose $\hat{x}$ of the object and its associated error covariance $\boldsymbol{P}$ can be predicted using the Kalman filter:

$$\begin{cases} \hat{\boldsymbol{x}}_{(t/t-1)} = \boldsymbol{F}\hat{\boldsymbol{x}}_{(t-1)} \\ \boldsymbol{P}_{(t/t-1)} = \boldsymbol{F}\boldsymbol{P}_{(t-1)}\boldsymbol{F}^T + \boldsymbol{G}\boldsymbol{Q}_{(t-1)}\boldsymbol{G}^T \end{cases} \tag{5}$$

where $\boldsymbol{Q}$ is the covariance of the plant noise Δx .

When the measurement z is obtained from the tracked object, the pose of the tracked object and its associated error covariance are updated using:

$$\begin{cases}\hat{\boldsymbol{x}}_{(t)} = \hat{\boldsymbol{x}}_{(t/t-1)} + \boldsymbol{K}_{(t)}(z_{(t)} - \boldsymbol{H}_{(t)}\hat{\boldsymbol{x}}_{(t/t-1)}) \\ \boldsymbol{P}_{(t)} = \boldsymbol{P}_{(t/t-1)} + \boldsymbol{K}_{(t)}\boldsymbol{H}_{(t)}\boldsymbol{P}_{(t/t-1)}\end{cases} \qquad (6)$$

where $\boldsymbol{K}_{(t)} = \boldsymbol{P}_{(t/t-1)}\boldsymbol{H}_{(t)}^{T}\boldsymbol{S}_{(t/t-1)}^{-1}$, and $\boldsymbol{S}_{(t/t-1)} = \boldsymbol{H}_{(t)}\boldsymbol{P}_{(t/t-1)}\boldsymbol{H}_{(t)}^{T} + \boldsymbol{R}_{(t)}$. $\boldsymbol{R}$ is the covariance of the measurement noise Δz.

In our experiment, the covariances of the plant and measurement noises in (3) and (4) are set at $\boldsymbol{Q}$ = diag (1.0 m^2/s^4, 1.0 m^2/s^4) and $\boldsymbol{R}$ = diag (0.01 m^2, 0.01 m^2), respectively, through trial and error.

In this paper, a moving object is assumed to move at an almost constant velocity, and it is tracked using the usual Kalman filter. If it moves with various different motions, such as moving at a constant speed, going or stopping suddenly, or turning suddenly, the use of multi-model-based tracking, such as an interacting-multiple-model estimator, can improve the tracking performance [29] [30].

To extract W_{meas} and L_{meas} from the moving measurements, the heading information of the tracked object is needed. As shown in Fig. 4, we extract two feature lines (green lines) from the moving measurements using the split-and-merge method [31] and RANSAC [32] and determine the heading of the tracked object from the orientation of the feature lines. When the two feature lines cannot be extracted, we determine the heading from the velocity estimate of the object using arctan ($\dot{y}/\dot{x}$).

VI. Data Association

To track objects in crowded environments, we apply data association (i.e., one-to-one or one-to-many matching of tracked objects and moving measurements). In the hierarchical cooperative-tracking method, data association is performed by sensor nodes, whereas in the centralized method, it is performed by a central server.

As shown in Fig. 5, a validation region (black rectangle) is set around the predicted position (black circle) of a tracked object. The validation region is rectangular, and its length and width are 0.5 m longer than those of the object estimated at the previous time step (green dashed rectangle).

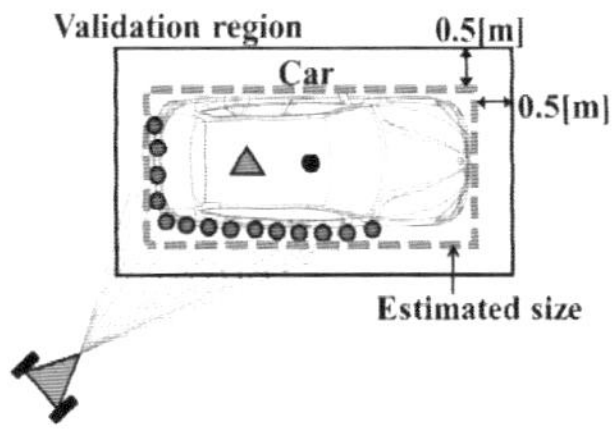

Figure 5. Moving measurements and data association.

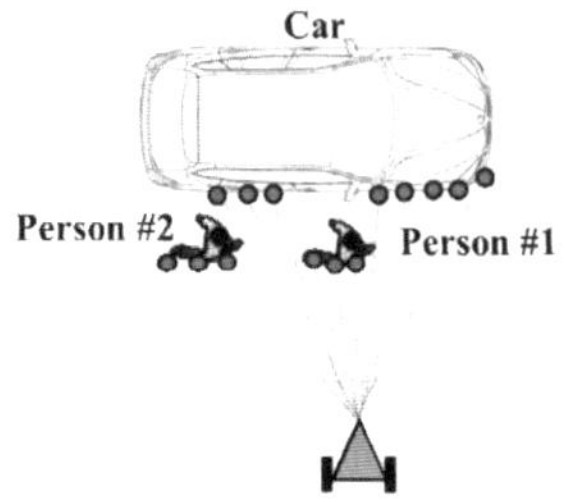

Figure 6. Moving measurements, in which two people move near a car.

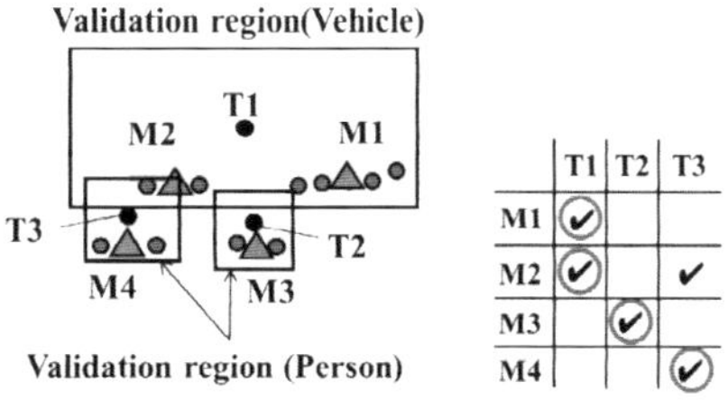

Figure 7. Data association for Fig. 6.

We refer to the representative point of clustered moving measurements (red circles) as the representative measurement (light blue triangle). The position of the representative measurement is the mean position of clustered moving measurements. Representative measurements inside the validation region are assumed to originate from the tracked object and are used to update the pose of the tracked object using (6), whereas those outside the validation region are identified as false alarms and discarded.

Figs. 6 and 7 illustrate an example of data association, in which two people move close to a car. In these figures, red circles indicate moving measurements, light blue triangles indicate representative measurements, and black circles indicate predicted positions of tracked objects. The right table in Fig. 7 shows the correspondence between tracked objects and representative measurements.

As shown in Fig. 7, multiple representative measurements are often obtained inside a validation region, and multiple validation regions also overlap. To achieve reliable data association (i.e., matching of tracked objects and representative measurements), we introduce the following rules:

1) Person: Because a person is small, he/she usually results in a representative measurement. Therefore, if a tracked object is assumed to be a person, one-to-one matching of a tracked person and a representative measurement is performed.

2) Vehicle (car, motorcycle, and bicycle): Because a vehicle is large, as shown in Fig. 6, it often results in several representative measurements. Thus, if a tracked object is assumed to be a vehicle, one-to-many matching of a tracked vehicle and representative measurements is performed.

As shown in Fig. 6, on urban streets, people often move close to vehicles, whereas vehicles move far away from each other. Thus, when representative measurements of people exist in the validation region of a tracked vehicle, they might be matched to the tracked vehicle. To avoid this situation, we begin data association with people.

We now detail our data association method from Fig. 7, in which the validation regions of a person (T3) and a car (T1) overlap. If tracked objects T2 and T3 are determined to be people from their estimated sizes (less than 0.8 m), the representative measurement M3 is matched with T2 and the representative measurement M4 nearest to T3 is matched with T3, both through one-to-one matching. Subsequently, if a tracked object T1 is determined to be a vehicle from the estimated size (larger than 0.8 m), the two representative measurements M1 and M2 in the validation region are matched with T1 through one-to-many matching. If validation regions of several people overlap, one-to-one matching is performed using the global nearest neighbor (GNN) method [12] [33].

Moving objects appear in and disappear from the sensing area of the sensor node. They are also occluded by each other and other objects in an environment. To maintain reliable tracking under such conditions, we implement following tracking rules.

1) Tracking initiation: If a representative measurement that is not matched with any tracked objects exists, it is assumed to either originate from a new object or to be an outlier. Therefore, we tentatively initiate tracking of the measurement with the Kalman filter. If the representative measurement remains visible in more than N_1 scans, it is assumed to originate from a new object and tracking is continued. If the representative measurements disappear within N_1 scans, it is assumed to be an outlier, and tentative tracking is terminated.

Because the size of the new tracked object is unknown at the initial time (scan), a rectangular validation region cannot be used for data association. Instead, we use a circular validation region with a constant radius of 2 m at the initial scan, and when the tracked object is matched with a representative measurement at the next scan, we estimate the size and decide whether the object is a vehicle or a person.

2) Tracking termination: When the tracked objects leave the sensing area of the sensor node or they meet occlusion, no representative measurements exist within their validation regions. If no measurements arise from the temporal occlusion, the measurements appear again. We thus predict the positions of the tracked objects using (5). If the representative measurements appear again within N_2 scans, we proceed with the tracking. Otherwise, we terminate the tracking.

In our experiments described in Section VIII, we set N_1 = 9 scans (0.9 s) and N_2 = 30 scans (3 s) through trial and error.

VII. Merging of Pose and Size Estimates by a Central Server

In the hierarchical cooperative-tracking method, each sensor node transmits the information of the tracked objects, which is shown in Table I (b), to the central server. When the central server receives this information from sensor nodes, it combines all the information together. It also merges the size, position and velocity of the moving objects locally estimated by the sensor nodes.

To combine the information, we apply data association (matching of tracking information). We present an example of our data association procedure in Figs. 8 and 9, in which two sensor nodes are tracking a car. In Fig. 8, red and blue rectangles indicate the sizes of the tracked objects #A (TA) and #B (TB), estimated by sensor nodes #1 and #2, respectively. Orange arrows indicate the headings of the objects.

If two tracked objects originate from the same object, the position, velocity and heading estimated by both sensor nodes will have similar values. Furthermore, if the tracked object is a vehicle, the size estimated by both sensor nodes will be large. If it is a person, the estimated size will be small. Therefore, we set a validation region with a constant radius of 3 m around the TA position (red star in Fig. 8) and match TB with TA by applying the following rules:

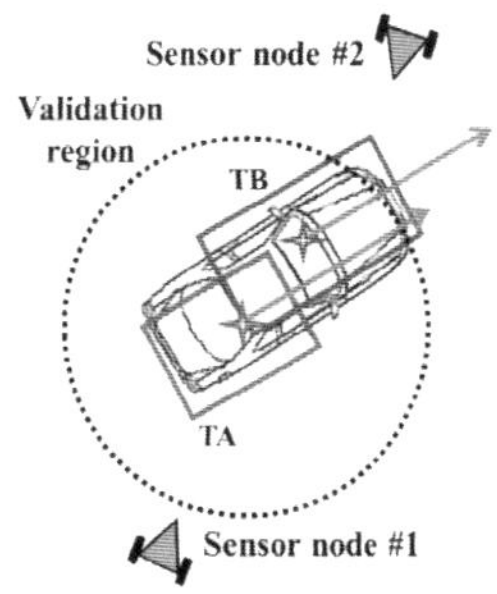

Figure 8. Data association of tracking information related to tracked objects TA and TB.

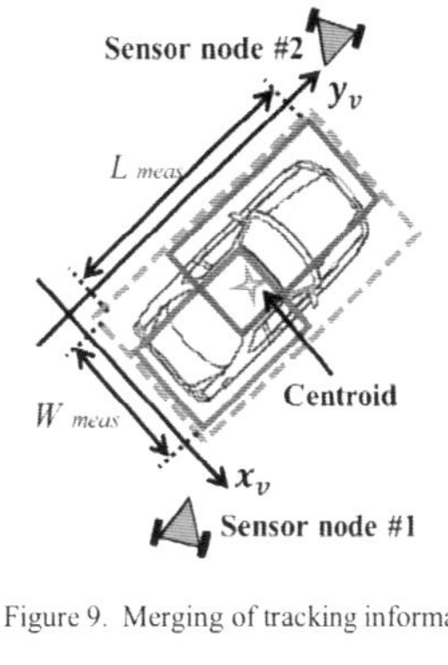

Figure 9. Merging of tracking information.

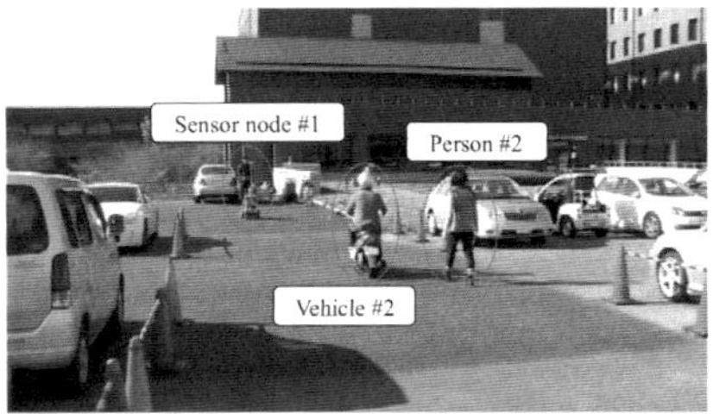

(a) Photo by camera #A

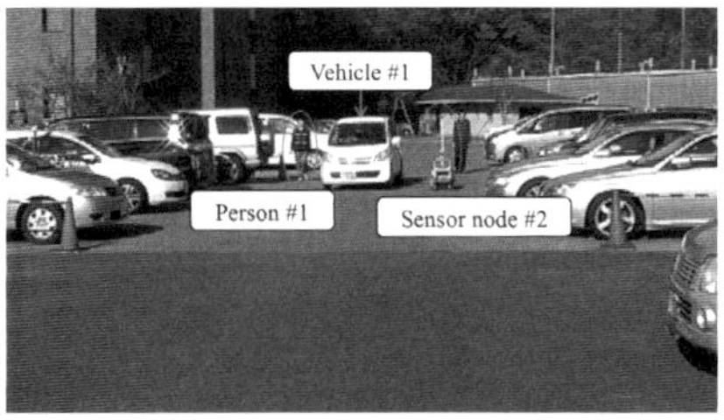

(b) Photo by camera #B

Figure 10. Photo of the experimental environment.

1) Same or different object: When the estimated position of TB (blue star) is located within the validation gate, and the differences in the velocity and heading estimates of TA and TB are less than D_1 m/s, and D_2°, respectively, the objects TA and TB are determined to originate from the same object. Otherwise, the objects TA and TB are determined to be different objects.

2) Vehicle or person: When the width and/or length estimates of the matched objects TA and TB are larger than 0.8 m, their objects are determined to originate from the same vehicle. When their width and length estimates are less than 0.8 m, the objects TA and TB are determined to originate from the same person.

When more than two tracked objects (e.g., TB and TC) are present in the validation region of TA, similar data association rules are applied. In our experiments described in Section VIII, we set D_1 = 0.8 m/s and D_2 = 15° through trial and error.

After the two tracked objects TA and TB have been matched, the tracking information is merged. As shown in Fig. 9, we select the tracked object TB, which has a larger rectangle (blue rectangle) than TA (red rectangle), and define an $x_v y_v$-coordinate frame on which the y_v-axis aligns with the heading of TB. Subsequently, a rectangle (the green dashed rectangle in Fig. 9) is then generated that encloses two rectangles of TA and TB using the position information of their vertices. We then estimate the size of the integrated object using (1) from the width and length of the new rectangle.

From the centroid position (green star) of the new rectangle, the position and velocity of the integrated object is estimated using the Kalman filter ((5) and (6)) under the assumption that the object is moving at an almost constant velocity.

VIII. Experimental Results and Discussion

A. Tracking by Two Mobile Sensor Nodes

We evaluated our cooperative-tracking method by conducting an experiment in a parking environment, as shown in Fig. 10. Two mobile sensor nodes tracked a car (vehicle #1), a motorcycle (vehicle #2), and two pedestrians (persons #1 and #2). Fig. 11 shows the movement paths of the sensor nodes (black dashed lines), vehicles #1 and #2 (blue and green lines), and persons #1 and #2 (red and black lines). The moving speeds of the sensor nodes, car, motorcycle, and persons were approximately 1.5, 15, 20, and 6 km/h, respectively.

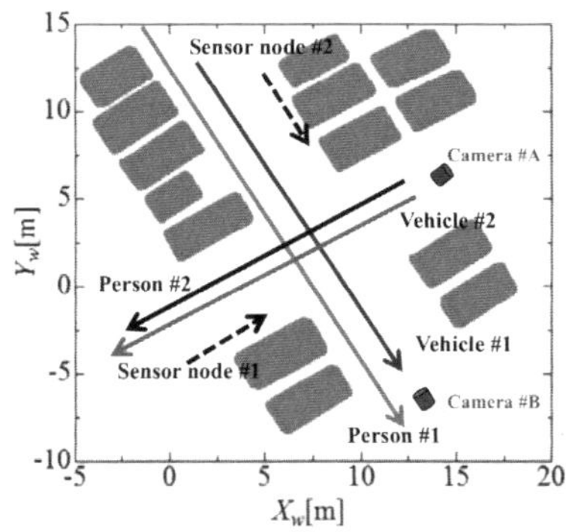

Figure 11. Movement paths of sensor nodes and moving objects.

Fig. 12 (a) shows the results of the position and size estimated using hierarchical cooperative tracking. We plot the estimated rectangles every 1 s (10 scans). Fig. 12 (b) shows the results of our previous centralized cooperative-tracking method. For comparison, individual tracking by each sensor node was also conducted. The tracking results for sensor nodes #1 and #2 are shown in Figs. 13 (a) and (b), respectively.

The estimated sizes of the car (vehicle #1) using cooperative and individual tracking are shown in Figs. 14 and 15, respectively. In these figures, red and blue lines indicate the estimated length and width, respectively. Two dashed lines indicate the true length and width of the car.

In individual tracking (Figs. 13 and 15), each sensor node partially tracks moving objects because the objects leave the sensing area of the sensor nodes and are blocked by parked cars. In contrast, in cooperative tracking, they always track their moving objects (Figs. 12 and 14) because the two sensor nodes share tracking data. It is clear from these figures that cooperative tracking provides better tracking accuracy than individual tracking.

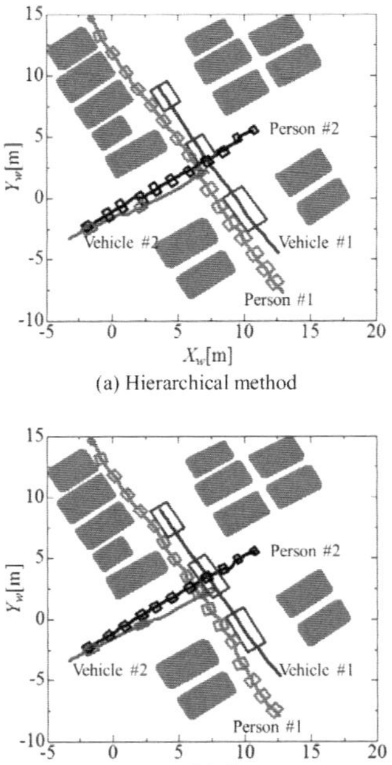

(a) Hierarchical method

(b) Centralized method

Figure 12. Estimated track and size of moving objects using cooperative tracking.

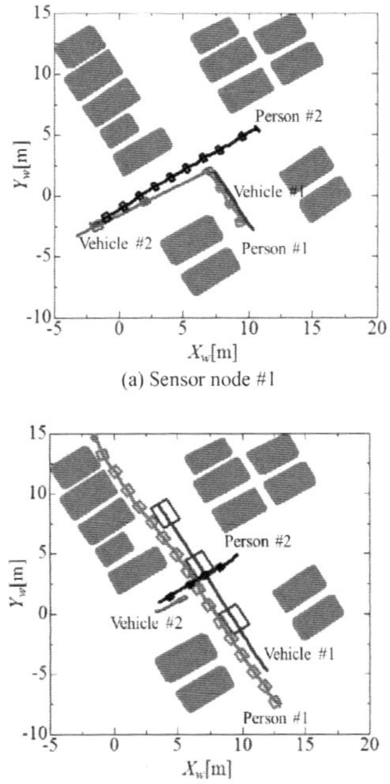

(a) Sensor node #1

(b) Sensor node #2

Figure 13. Estimated track and size of moving objects using individual tracking.

As described in Section VI, when new moving objects appear in the sensing area of the sensor node, our tracker uses 9 scans (0.9 s) for the track initiation and begins to track the new objects from the 10th scan (1 s). In the 9 scans for the track initiation, vehicles #1 and #2 (car and motorcycle) have already moved over a long distance. This is the reason why the estimated tracks of vehicles #1 and #2 in Figs. 12 and 13 are shorter than their true movement paths shown in Fig. 11.

As shown in Fig. 14, the car (vehicle #1) size estimated using hierarchical and centralized cooperative-tracking methods are different. In the experiment, sensor node #2 detected vehicle #1 after 3 scans and began to track it from the 13th scan, whereas sensor node #1 detected vehicle #1 after 20 scans and began to track it from the 30th scan. In hierarchical cooperative tracking, each sensor node locally tracks the vehicle. The track initiation for vehicle #1 was executed in 3–13 scans by sensor node #2 and in 20–30 scans by sensor node #1. Therefore, the server received tracking information from sensor node #1 at the 30th scan and merged the information together.

On the other hand, with centralized cooperative tracking, the central server estimates the size based on the moving measurements sent from the sensor nodes. Therefore, the track initiation for vehicle #1 was executed in only 3–13 scans by sensor node #2. When the server received the moving measurements from sensor node #1 at the 20th scan,

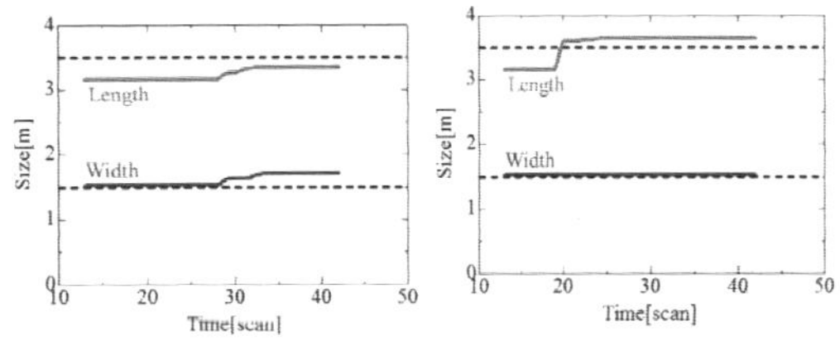

(a) Hierarchical method

(b) Centralized method

Figure 14. Estimated size of car (vehicle #1) using cooperative tracking.

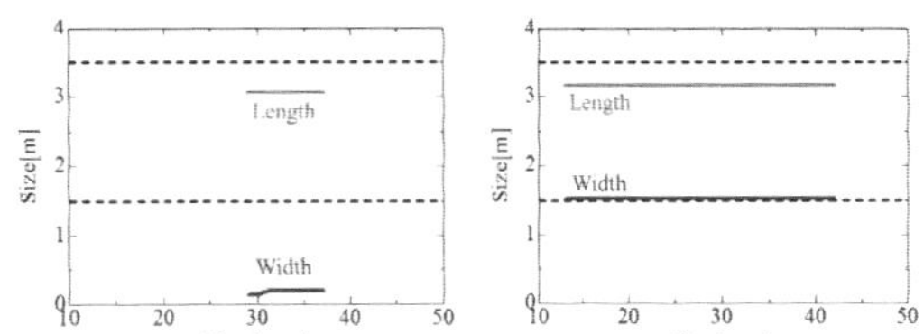

(a) Sensor node #1

(b) Sensor node #2

Figure 15. Estimated size of car (vehicle #1) using individual tracking.

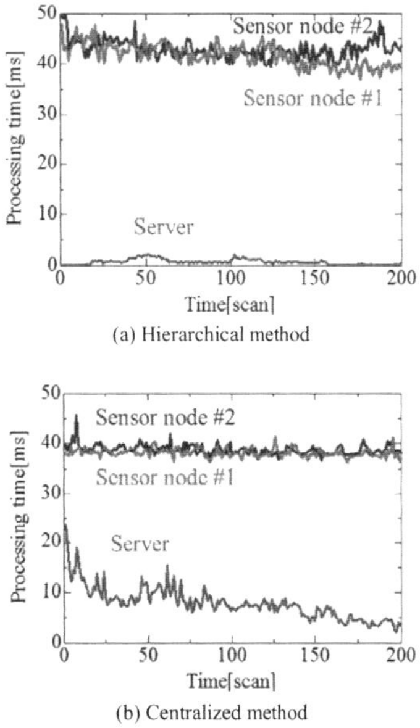

(a) Hierarchical method

(b) Centralized method

Figure 16. Processing time of sensor nodes and central server.

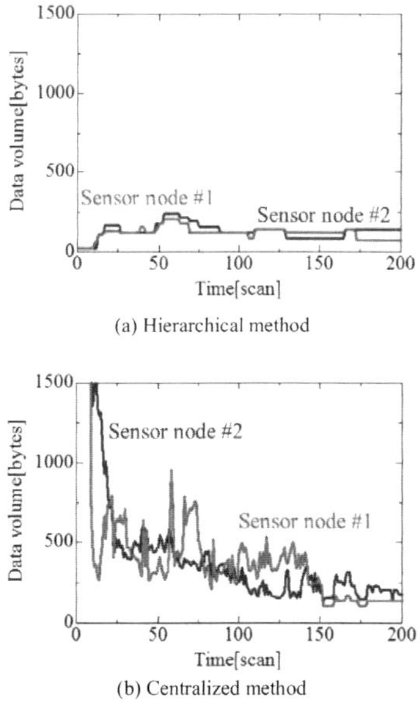

(a) Hierarchical method

(b) Centralized method

Figure 17. Data volume sent to central server from sensor nodes.

TABLE II. PROCESSING TIME OF SENSOR NODES AND CENTRAL SERVER

(a) HIERARCHICAL METHOD

	Max. [ms]	Min. [ms]	Mean [ms]
Central server	2.3	0.1	0.8
Sensor node #1	47.9	36.8	41.7
Sensor node #2	49.8	39.3	43.0

(b) CENTRALIZED METHOD

	Max. [ms]	Min. [ms]	Mean [ms]
Central server	23.8	2.2	7.9
Sensor node #1	41.5	36.1	38.2
Sensor node #2	45.7	36.5	38.8

TABLE III. DATA VOLUME SENT TO CENTRAL SERVER FROM SENSOR NODES

(a) HIERARCHICAL METHOD

	Max. [byte]	Min. [byte]	Mean [byte]
Sensor node #1	204	24	30
Sensor node #2	240	24	28

(b) CENTRALIZED METHOD

	Max. [byte]	Min. [byte]	Mean [byte]
Sensor node #1	3628	104	477
Sensor node #2	4952	136	540

it quickly merged the measurements with those from sensor node #2 and estimated the car size. As a result, compared to centralized cooperative tracking, hierarchical cooperative tracking causes a slight time lag when merging the information from both sensor nodes. This is why the car (vehicle #1) sizes estimated using hierarchical and centralized cooperative tracking are different.

In our experimental system, the model of the computers used in the sensor nodes and central server is Iiyama 15X7100-i7-VGB with a 2.8 GHz Intel core i7-4810MQ processor, and the operating system used is Microsoft Windows 7 Professional. We examined the processing time of the sensor nodes and the central server in the experiment.

The results for hierarchical and centralized cooperative tracking are shown in Fig.16 and Table II. In centralized cooperative tracking, the central server estimates the poses and sizes of moving objects based on the moving-object measurements sent from the sensor nodes. On the contrary, in hierarchical cooperative tracking, the sensor nodes estimate the poses and sizes of moving objects, and the central server merges their estimates. Therefore, compared with centralized cooperative tracking, hierarchical cooperative tracking reduces the computational burden on the central server.

Fig. 17 and Table III show the data volume sent to the central server from the sensor nodes in the experiment. Fig. 18 and Table IV also show the communication time required from the sensor nodes to the central server. In centralized cooperative tracking, sensor nodes upload the information shown in Table I (a), whereas in hierarchical cooperative tracking, sensor nodes upload the information shown in Table I (b), to the central server. It is clear from these figures and tables that the data volume and communication time for hierarchical cooperative tracking is less than that for centralized cooperative tracking.

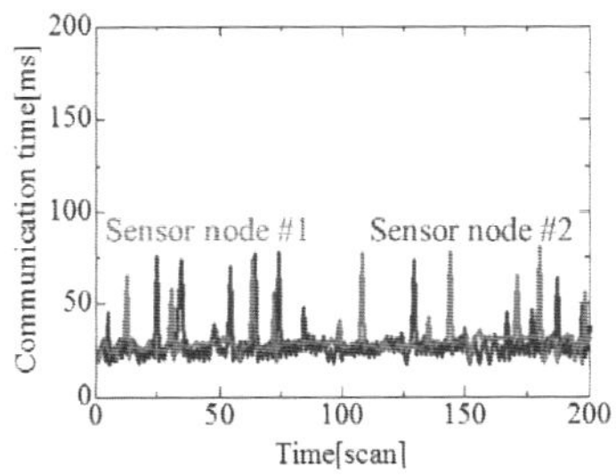

(a) Hierarchical method

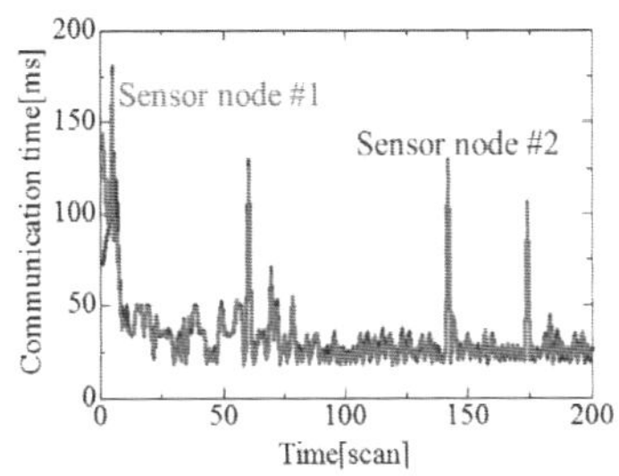

(b) Centralized method

Figure 18. Communication time required from sensor nodes to central server.

TABLE IV. COMMUNICATION TIME FROM SENSOR NODES TO CENTRAL SERVER

(a) HIERARCHICAL METHOD

	Max. [ms]	Min. [ms]	Mean [ms]
Sensor node #1	81.2	17.5	30.1
Sensor node #2	77.9	17.2	28.1

(b) CENTRALIZED METHOD

	Max. [ms]	Min. [ms]	Mean [ms]
Sensor node #1	175.9	17.7	33.8
Sensor node #2	180.3	18.0	34.0

B. Tracking by Two Static Sensor Nodes

We evaluated the accuracy of the pose and size estimates when using our cooperative-tracking method. For this purpose, we used Zhao's data set [34]. As shown in Fig. 19 (a), two laser scanners (SICK LMS200) were set at the height of 0.4 m in an intersection environment, and laser measurements were captured every 26 ms. We assumed that their measurements were captured by two sensor nodes and evaluated the tracking performance. The experimental duration was 108 s (4154 scans). Fig. 19 (b) shows the tracking result at 770 scans, where the green rectangles indicate the estimated size, and the light blue lines indicate the estimated heading. Red and blue dots indicate the laser measurements captured by sensors #1 and #2, respectively.

We examined the tracking performance for objects moving in the central area of the intersection (blue area in Fig. 20) where the sensing areas of the two sensor nodes overlapped.

Tables V and VI show the performance of the pose and size estimates when using cooperative and individual tracking, respectively. 'Actual objects' in tables were identified from camera images. 'Correct estimate of pose' means that the tracking method could always maintain a correct pose estimate of objects moving in the central area of the intersection, whereas 'incorrect estimate of pose' means that they failed in estimating the position. As described in Section V, the estimated size of the tracked object is used to classify the object as a person or a vehicle (i.e., car, motorcycle, and bicycle). If the estimated size in length or width is larger than 0.8 m, the object is determined to be a vehicle. If it is less than 0.8 m, the object is determined to be a person. In Tables V and VI, 'Correct

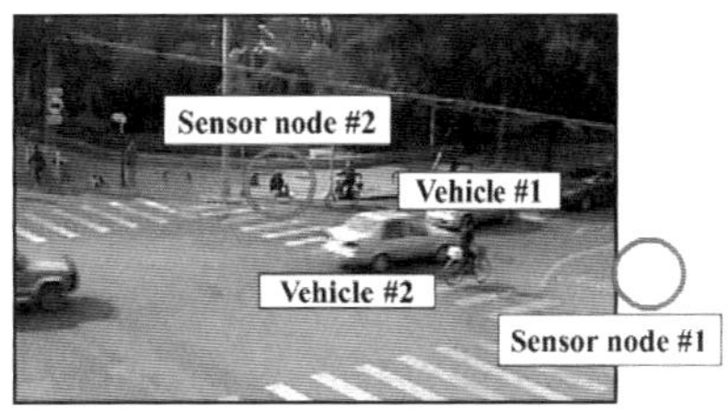

(a) Experimental environment

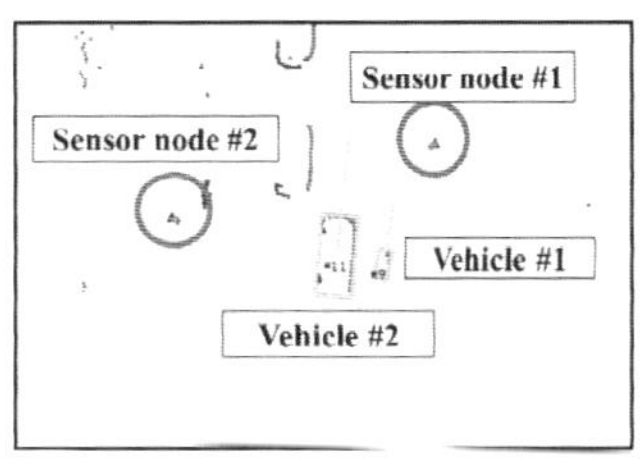

(b) Tracking result

Figure 19. Photo of the experimental environment and tracking result after 770 scans.

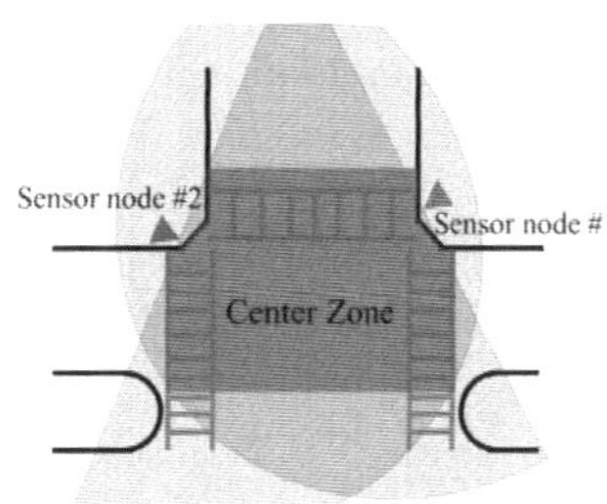

Figure 20. Overlapping sensing areas of two sensor nodes.

TABLE V. THE NUMBER OF OBJECTS WHOSE POSE (OR SIZE) ARE ESTIMATED CORRECTLY AND INCORRECTLY USING COOPERATIVE TRACKING

(a) HIERARCHICAL METHOD

		Correct estimate of pose (size)	Incorrect estimate of pose (size)
Actual object	Person	2 (2)	2 (0)
	Bicycle	20 (20)	3 (0)
	Car	30 (30)	7 (0)

(b) CENTRALIZED METHOD

		Correct estimate of pose (size)	Incorrect estimate of pose (size)
Actual object	Person	2 (2)	2 (0)
	Bicycle	23 (21)	0 (2)
	Car	31 (31)	6 (0)

TABLE VI. THE NUMBER OF OBJECTS WHOSE POSE (OR SIZE) ARE ESTIMATED CORRECTLY AND INCORRECTLY USING INDIVIDUAL TRACKING

(a) SENSOR NODE #1

		Correct estimate of pose (size)	Incorrect estimate of pose (size)
Actual object	Person	2 (2)	2 (0)
	Bicycle	18 (14)	5 (4)
	Car	26 (26)	11 (0)

(b) SENSOR NODE #2

		Correct estimate of pose (size)	Incorrect estimate of pose (size)
Actual object	Person	2 (2)	2 (0)
	Bicycle	18 (17)	5 (1)
	Car	22 (22)	15 (0)

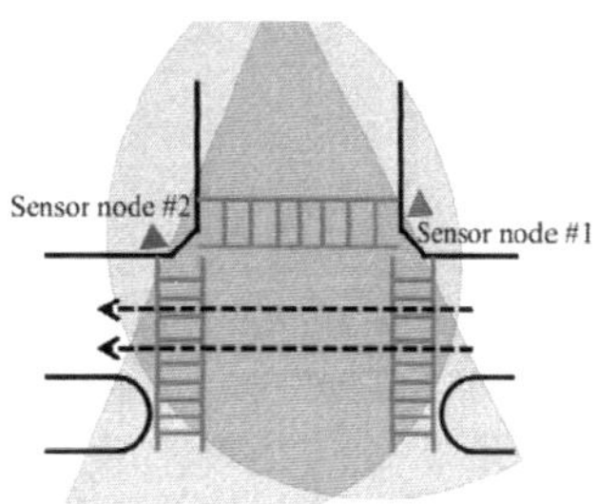

Figure 21. Movement paths of cars.

estimate of size' means that the tracking method could always maintain a correct classification of objects moving in the central area of the intersection, whereas 'Incorrect estimate of size' means that they failed in the classification.

It is clear from these tables that cooperative tracking provides better tracking accuracy than individual tracking. The performance of the pose and size estimates when using hierarchical cooperative tracking is slightly inferior to that of the centralized method. The pose estimation of cars using cooperative and individual tracking deteriorates when compared with people and bicycles. When cars moved along the paths shown by the dashed lines in Fig. 21, sensor nodes captured laser measurements related only to the right side of each car. In addition, they only partially captured laser measurements of cars due to occlusions. These cause incorrect pose estimation of cars.

IX. CONCLUSION AND FUTURE WORK

This paper presented a laser-based cooperative-tracking method for moving objects (vehicles and people) using multiple mobile sensor nodes located in the vicinity of the objects. In cooperative tracking, nearby sensor nodes share the tracking information. Hence, they enable the constant tracking of objects that may be invisible or partially visible to an individual sensor node.

We treated people and vehicles as rigid bodies and estimated both the poses and sizes of the objects. In a crowded environment, a vehicle can be occluded or rendered partially visible to each sensor node. To correctly estimate the vehicle's size, the laser measurements captured by sensor nodes have to be merged well. Therefore, we presented hierarchical cooperative-tracking method. Each sensor node obtained measurements related to the moving objects (moving measurements) and locally estimated the poses and sizes of the moving objects from the moving measurements using a Bayesian filter. It then sent these estimates to the central server, which then merged the pose and size estimates.

The performance of the hierarchical cooperative-tracking method was evaluated from two experimental results in outdoor environments by comparing it with a previous centralized method. The hierarchical method provided slightly inferior tracking accuracy than the centralized method. However, it had a smaller data volume sent to the central server from sensor nodes and a smaller computational cost in the central server than the centralized method. Therefore, the hierarchical method makes the tracking system scalable and robust.

In this paper, single-layer laser scanners were applied to sense the surrounding environment using mobile sensor nodes. Multilayer laser scanners can also capture height information from objects, and thus enable more accurate recognition of the surrounding environment than single-layer laser scanners. Current research is directed to the design of cooperative tracking by multiple sensor nodes equipped with multilayer laser scanners. To achieve cooperative tracking, the sensor nodes should always identify their own poses with a high degree of accuracy in a world coordinate frame. In this paper, we applied localization methods using dead reckoning and RTK-GPS. However, in city-canyon environments, the performance of localization using GPS deteriorates due to GPS multipath errors, diffraction problems and so on. To address this problem, we will embed a cooperative-localization method into our tracking system.

ACKNOWLEDGMENT

This study was partially supported by the Scientific Grants #26420213, the Japan Society for the Promotion of Science (JSPS) and the MEXT-Supported Program for the

Strategic Research Foundation at Private Universities, 2014–2018, Ministry of Education, Culture, Sports, Science and Technology, Japan.

We would also like to thank Professor Huijing Zhao of Peking University for providing the laser-scanning and vision data set for experiments in Section VII-B.

REFERENCES

[1] Y. Tamura, R Murabayashi, M. Hashimoto, and K. Takahashi, "Laser-based Cooperative Estimation of Pose and Size of Moving Objects using Multiple Mobile Robots," Proc. of the Fifth Conf. on Intelligent Systems and Applications (INTELLI 2016), pp. 13–19, 2016.

[2] K. O. Arra and O. M. Mozos, Special issue on: People Detection and Tracking, Int. J. of Social Robotics, vol.2, no.1, pp. 1–107, 2010.

[3] C. Mertz, et al., "Moving Object Detection with Laser Scanners," J. of Field Robotics, vol.30, pp. 17–43, 2013.

[4] T. Ogawa, H. Sakai, Y. Suzuki, K. Takagi, and K. Morikawa, "Pedestrian Detection and Tracking using In-vehicle Lidar for Automotive Application," Proc. of IEEE Intelligent Vehicles Symp. (IV2011), pp. 734–739, 2011.

[5] A. Mukhtar, L. Xia, and T.B. Tang, "Vehicle Detection Techniques for Collision Avoidance Systems: A Review," IEEE Trans. on Intelligent Transportation Systems, vol. 16, pp. 2318–2338, 2015.

[6] H. Cho, Y. W. Seo, B.V.K. V. Kumar, and R. R. Rajkumar, "A Multi-sensor Fusion System for Moving Object Detection and Tracking in Urban Driving Environments," Proc. of Int. Conf. on IEEE Robotics and Automation (ICRA2014), pp. 1836–1843, 2014.

[7] D. Z. Wang, I. Posner, and P. Newman, "Model-free Detection and Tracking of Dynamic Objects with 2D Lidar," Int. J. of Robotics Research, vol.34, pp. 1039–1063, 2015.

[8] D. Z. Wang, I. Posner, P. Newman, "What could move? Finding cars, pedestrians and bicyclists in 3D laser data," Proc. of IEEE Int. Conf. on Robotics and Automation (ICRA2012), pp. 4038–4044, 2012.

[9] Z. Yan, N. Jouandeau, and A. A. Cherif, "A Survey and Analysis of Multi-Robot Coordination," Int. J. of Advanced Robotic Systems, vol. 10, pp. 1–18, 2013.

[10] S. Nadarajah and K. Sundaraj, "A Survey on Team Strategies in Robot Soccer: Team Strategies and Role Description," Artificial Intelligence Review, vol. 40, pp. 271–304, 2013.

[11] K. Kakinuma, M. Hashimoto, and K. Takahashi, "Outdoor Pedestrian Tracking by Multiple Mobile Robots based on SLAM and GPS Fusion," Proc. of IEEE/SICE Int. Symp. on System Integration (SII2012), pp. 422–427, 2012.

[12] M. Ozaki, K. Kakinuma, M. Hashimoto, and K. Takahashi, "Laser-based Pedestrian Tracking in Outdoor Environments by Multiple Mobile Robots," Sensors, vol. 12, pp. 14489–14507, 2012.

[13] S.J. Julier and J.K. Uhlmann, "A Non-divergent Estimation Algorithm in the Presence of Unknown Correlations," Proc. of the IEEE American Control Conf., pp. 2369–2373, 1997.

[14] F. Fayad and V. Cherfaoui, "Tracking Objects using a Laser Scanner in Driving Situation based on Modeling Target Shape," Proc. of the 2007 IEEE Int. Vehicles Symp. (IV2007), pp. 44–49, 2007.

[15] T. Miyata, Y. Ohama, and Y. Ninomiya, "Ego-Motion Estimation and Moving Object Tracking using Multi-layer LIDAR," Proc. of IEEE Intelligent Vehicles Symp. (IV2009), pp. 151–156, 2009.

[16] K. Granstrom, C. Lundquist, F. Gustafsson, and U. Orguner, "Radom Set Methods, Estimation of Multiple Extended Objects," IEEE Robotics & Automation Magazine, pp. 73–82, June 2014.

[17] L. Mihaylova, et al., "Overview of Bayesian Sequential Monte Carlo Methods for Group and Extended Object Tracking," Digital Signal Processing, vol. 25, pp.1–16, 2014.

[18] J. Lan and X. R. Li, "Tracking of Extended Object or Target Group using Random Matrix Part I: New Model and Approach," Proc. of 15th Int. Conf. on Information Fusion (FUSION2012), pp.2177–2184, 2012.

[19] Z.Wang and D. Gu, "Cooperative Target Tracking Control of Multiple Robots," IEEE Trans. on Industrial Electronics, vol. 59, pp. 3232–3240, 2012.

[20] K. Zhou and S. I. Roumeliotis, "Multirobot Active Target Tracking with Combinations of Relative Observations," IEEE Trans. on Robotics, vol. 27, pp. 678–695, 2011.

[21] A. Ahmad and P. Lima, "Multi-robot Cooperative Spherical-Object Tracking in 3D Space based on Particle Filters," Robotics and Autonomous Systems, vol. 61, pp. 1084–1093, 2013.

[22] P. U. Limaa, et al., "Formation Control Driven by Cooperative Object Tracking," Robotics and Autonomous Systems, vol. 63, Part 1, pp. 68–79, 2015.

[23] C. Robin and S. Lacroix, "Multi-robot Target Detection and Tracking: Taxonomy and Survey," Autonomous Robots, vol. 40, pp. 729–760, 2016.

[24] C. T. Chou, J. Y. Li, M. F. Chang, and L. C. Fu, "Multi-Robot Cooperation Based Human Tracking System Using Laser Range Finder," Proc. of IEEE Int. Conf. on Robotics and Automation (ICRA2011), pp. 532–537, 2011.

[25] N. A. Tsokas and K. J. Kyriakopoulos, "Multi-robot Multiple Hypothesis Tracking for Pedestrian Tracking," Autonomous Robot, vol. 32, pp. 63–79, 2012.

[26] M. Hashimoto, R. Izumi, Y. Tamura, and K. Takahashi, "Laser-based Tracking of People and Vehicles by Multiple Mobile Robots," Proc. of the 11th Int. Conf. on Informatics in Control, Automation and Robotics (ICIT2014), pp. 522–527, 2014.

[27] M. Hashimoto, S. Ogata, F. Oba, and T. Murayama, "A Laser-based Multi-Target Tracking for Mobile Robot," Intelligent Autonomous Systems 9, pp. 135–144, 2006.

[28] Y. Bar-Shalom and T. E. Fortmann, "Tracking and Data Association," Academic Press,Inc., 1988.

[29] H.A.P.Blom and Y.Bar-Shalom, "The Interacting Multiple Model Algorithm for Systems with Markovian Switching Coefficient," IEEE Trans. on Automatic Control, vol.33, pp.780–783, 1988.

[30] E. Mazor, A. Averbuch, Y. Bar-Shalom, and J. Dayan, "Interacting Multiple Model Methods in Target Tracking: A Survey," IEEE Trans. on Aerospace and Electronic Systems, vol.34, pp.103–123, 1998.

[31] V. Nguyen, A. Martinelli, N. Tomatis, and R. Siegwart, "A Comparison of Line Extraction Algorithms using 2D Laser Rangefinder for Indoor Mobile Robotics," Proc. of 2005 IEEE/RSJ Int. Conf. on Intelligent Robots and Systems (IROS2009), pp. 1929–1934, 2009.

[32] M. Fischler and R. Bolles, "Random Sample Consensus: A Paradigm for Model Fitting Applications to Image Analysis and Automated Cartography," Proc. of Image Understanding workshop, pp. 71–88, 1980.

[33] P. Konstantinova, A. Udvarev, and T. Semerdjiev, "A Study of a Target Tracking Algorithm Using Global Nearest Neighbor Approach," Proc. of Int. Conf. on Systems and Technologies, 2003.

[34] H. Zhao, "Open Resource, Networked horizontal laser scan data at intersection (20071012)," available from <http://www.poss.pku.edu.cn/download.html>, (accessed on 12 December 2014).

A Life-cycle Equipment Labeling System for Machine Classification in Smart Factories

Susana Aguiar, Rui Pinto, João Reis, Gil Gonçalves

Institute for Systems and Robotics
Faculty of Engineering of University of Porto
Rua Dr. Roberto Frias, s/n 4200-465, Porto, Portugal
Email: {saguiar, rpinto, jpcreis, gil}@fe.up.pt

Abstract—**Nowadays, due to ever decreasing product life cycles and high external pressure to cut costs, the ramp-up of production lines must be significantly shortened and simplified. This is only possible if a forecast of the impact of modification within an existing production environment is available, helping during decision making of production methods. This type of predictions will have a direct impact on the cost-effective production process, maintaining concerns regarding the environmental and social impacts. These are the ideas behind the project Innovative Reuse of modular knowledge Based devices and technologies for Old, Renewed and New factories (ReBorn). The present paper describes the System Assessment Tool, a software application developed in ReBorn, which is used for assessing the sustainability of highly adaptive production systems through the use of Reliability, Life Cycle Cost and Life Cycle Assessment metrics, in the form of a equipment labeling scheme. This labeling scheme consists on classifying the dependability of industrial equipment, based on the collected metrics. To that intent, several simulation processes were performed, in order to assess the suitability of the labeling system, in comparison to the Quality metric that is highly preferable among the industrial partners. The simulation results show that a two-layer equipment labeling system is the most suitable approach to be used for classification.**

Keywords–Smart factories; Equipment label; Life-cycle assessment; Re-use; Production systems.

I. INTRODUCTION

ReBorn was a European Project funded by the Seventh Framework Programme of the European Commission. The vision of ReBorn was to demonstrate strategies and technologies that support a new paradigm for the re-use of production equipment in factories. This re-use will give new life to decommissioned production systems and equipment, helping them to be "reborn" in new production lines. Such new strategies will contribute to sustainable, resource-friendly and green manufacturing and, at the same time, deliver economic and competitive advantages for the manufacturing sector.

The developments made in ReBorn allow production equipment to extend its life cycle, contributing to economic and environmental sustainability of production systems [1]. This concept of modular production equipment may also be re-used between different production systems, after servicing and upgrading. This new business paradigm will move from an equipment-based business to a value added business, where equipment servicing and equipment knowledge are main business drivers.

The proposed paradigm is built on self-aware and knowledge-based equipment, which requires capabilities to collect and manage information, regarding its functionalities, evolution over time due to its use and wear, and maintenance operations, upgrade and refurbishment over lifetime. For this to be possible, versatile and modular task-driven plug&produce devices, with built-in capabilities for self-assessment and optimal re-use were implemented, along with strategies for their re-use and models for factory layout design and adaptive configuration.

The ReBorn [2] developments demonstrated to be successful for intelligent machine repair, upgrade and re-use of equipment, and (re-)design of factory layouts [3]. Most of these developments were demonstrated within several industrial demonstration scenarios at 2016 AUTOMATICA fair (21-24 June) in Munich, Germany [4].

During its life-cycle, industrial equipment goes through three main stages, namely 1) the initial incorporation into the production line, 2) the operation and maintenance/upgrade, and 3) the end-of-use and disassemble. Throughout these stages failures or malfunctions can potentially cause costly machine downtime or even downtime in the entire production system. Downtime of equipment operation is usually avoided based on engineers and shop-floor operators decision making, which are most of the times based on the experience of these individuals. Sometimes the individual's know-how and gained knowledge by experience is hard to be transferred to other individuals and may be lost [5]. This problem was tackled in ReBorn by developing a software tool named Workbench.

The Workbench is a decision making support tool, which combines simulations with the historical process data gathered at equipment level. It provides methods and algorithms for assessing the various potential possibilities of industrial equipment, regarding change, upgrade, reuse, dismantle and disposal. These possibilities are evaluated based on the corresponding reconfiguration effect on the overall system cost, performance and status throughout the life-cycle(s) of the manufacturing system. The analysis and comparison of industrial equipment is achieved using a System Assessment Tool (SAT), which performs Life Cycle Cost (LCC) and Life Cycle Assessment (LCA) analysis, based on reliability metrics.

In order to have a more generic and simple way of comparing industrial equipment, the SAT has a functionality, which main goal is to calculate an equipment Label. This Label measures a dependability factor, as for example the appliances energy consumption label, grades equipments from A to F, being A very dependable and F less dependable. This paper presents three simulations that were defined and executed, in order to test the usability and correctness of the Label. The basic idea behind all the three simulations is to use as much information as possible, from the information available in the SAT, that is, all the metrics that the SAT can calculate. Each metric has a weight associated to it, which was defined based on a questionnaire that was sent to the industrial partners of the ReBorn project. The equipment Label simulations indicate that using all the metrics available in a straight way might not give the best results, because this allows the possibility of having equipments with a Label grade that is higher or lower, with a difference of two or more grades, than the quality grade, which is, for the industrial ReBorn partners, the most important metric. This lead to a two layer Label scheme that provides grading results closer to the values of the most important metrics.

This paper is organized in five more sections. Section II defines the concepts of LCC and LCA and overviews the current state of the art, regarding tools and metrics used to perform this type of equipment analysis. In section III, an overview of the Workbench tool is presented, along with a description of its different modules, including the SAT. In Section IV, a detailed analysis and description of the SAT is presented. Section V explains one of the SAT functionalities, the equipment Label, where several simulations are defined and its results presented and discussed. Finally, Section VI concludes the paper by exposing some final remarks about the work developed.

II. Related Work

Several models, tools, and standards have been developed to analyze equipment reliability [6], [7], LCC [8]–[12], and LCA [13]–[18]. Although these techniques have usually been treated as separate analysis tools, defined by their own metrics and standards, some authors attempted to bring them closer [19]–[22] by presenting the relation between different sustainability assessment tools, focusing on the life cycle assessment as central concept for sustainability [23]. For the interested reader, several surveys of existing methodologies and tools regarding equipment analysis have been performed over the years [11], [21], [23]–[25].

A. Life Cycle Assessment

LCA is an approach for assessing industrial systems from creation to disposal [26]–[30]. This approach begins with the gathering of raw materials of the mother nature to create the product, ending when the product is dismantle and the disposal of all materials to the environment [14], [15].

According to Currant [13], LCA had its beginnings in the 1960's due to concerns over the limitations of raw materials and energy resources. The work published by Harold Smith [31] is considered as one of the firsts in this field. In that work he reported his calculations of cumulative energy requirements for the production of chemical intermediates and products.

In 1969, researchers initiated an internal study for The Coca-Cola Company (that was not officially published but it is mentioned in most of the LCA works [13], [32], [33]), which laid the foundation for the current methods of life cycle inventory analysis in the United States. In this study, the used raw materials and fuels, as well as the environmental loadings from the manufacturing processes for each container, were quantified. The comparison between the different beverage containers allowed to determine which container had the lowest releases to the environment and which least affected the supply of natural resources. The process of quantifying the resource use and environmental releases of products became known as a Resource and Environmental Profile Analysis (REPA) in the United States, and as Ecobalance in Europe.

From 1975 through the early 1980's, as influence of the oil crisis faded, environmental concerns shifted to issues of hazardous and household waste management. However, throughout this time, life cycle inventory analysis continued to be conducted and the methodology improved through a slow stream of about two studies per year, most of which focused on energy requirements. During this time, European interest grew with the establishment of an Environment Directorate (DG X1) by the European Commission [34]. European LCA practitioners developed approaches parallel to those being used in the USA. Besides working to standardize pollution regulations throughout Europe, DG X1 issued the Liquid Food Container Directive in 1985, which charged member companies with monitoring the energy and raw materials consumption and solid waste generation of liquid food containers. When solid waste became a worldwide issue in 1988, LCA emerged again as a tool for environmental problems analysis.

In 1991, concerns over the inappropriate use of LCA to make broad marketing claims made by product manufacturers resulted in a statement issued by eleven State Attorneys General in the USA, denouncing the use of LCA results to promote products. Such assessments should be conducted by uniform methods, by reaching a consensus on how this type of environmental comparison can be advertised non-deceptively. This action, along with pressure from other environmental organizations to standardize LCA methodology, led to the development of the LCA standards in the International Standards Organization (ISO) 14000 series (1997 through 2002) [35].

In 2002, the United Nations Environment Program (UNEP) joined forces with the Society of Environmental Toxicology and Chemistry (SETAC) to launch the Life Cycle Initiative, an international partnership. This Initiative has characterized by three programs: (1) the Life Cycle Management (LCM) program creates awareness and improves skills of decision-makers by producing information materials, establishing forums for sharing best practice, and carrying out training programs in all parts of the world; (2) the Life Cycle Inventory (LCI) program improves global access to transparent, high quality life cycle data, by hosting and facilitating expert groups work results in web-based information systems; (3) the Life Cycle Impact Assessment (LCIA) program increases the quality and global reach of life cycle indicators, by promoting the exchange of views among experts, whose work results in a set of widely accepted recommendations.

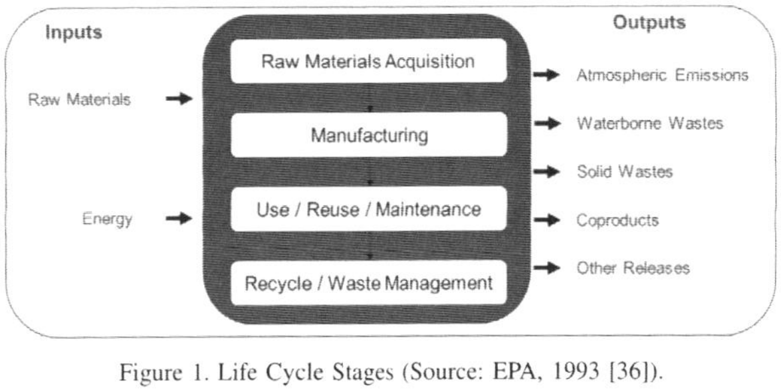

Figure 1. Life Cycle Stages (Source: EPA, 1993 [36]).

LCA evaluates all stages of a product's life cycle, from the perspective that they are interdependent, meaning that one operation leads to the next. Figure 1 presents the possible life cycle stages that can be considered in a LCA as well as the typical inputs and outputs measured. LCA enables the estimation of cumulative environmental impacts that resulted from all stages in the product life cycle, often including impacts not considered in more traditional analyses (e.g., raw material extraction, material transportation, ultimate product disposal, etc.). By including these impacts throughout the product life cycle, LCA provides a comprehensive view of the environmental aspects of the product or process and a more accurate picture of the true environmental trade-offs in product and process selection.

The LCA process is a systematic, phased approach and consists of four components as illustrated in Figure 2: 1) Goal Definition and Scope - Define and describe the product, process or activity, by establishing the context in which the assessment is to be made and identify the boundaries and environmental effects to be reviewed for the assessment; 2) Inventory Analysis - Identify and quantify energy, water and materials usage and environmental releases, such as air emissions, solid waste disposal and waste water discharges; 3) Impact Assessment - Assess the potential human and ecological effects of energy, water, material usage and the environmental releases identified in the inventory analysis. Inputs and outputs are categorized in different impact categories midpoints, such as climate change and land use, and endpoints, such as human health and resource depletion; 4) Interpretation - Evaluate the results of the inventory analysis and impact assessment, in order to select the preferred product, process or service with a clear understanding of the uncertainty and the assumptions used to generate the results.

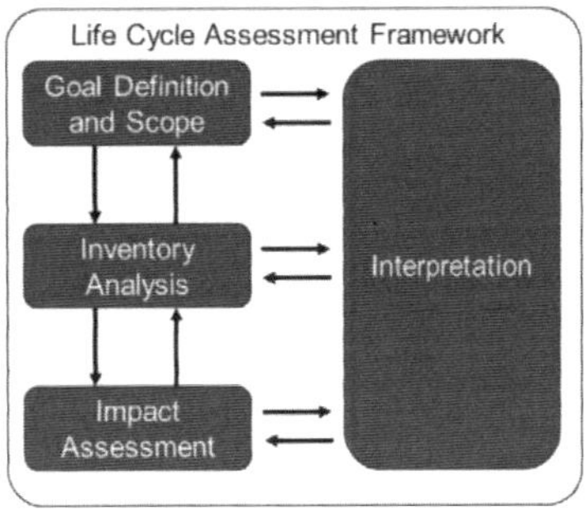

Figure 2. Phases of a LCA Process.

Conducting a LCA study have the main benefit of developing a systematic evaluation of the environmental consequences associated with the creation of a given product. This evaluation provides means to analyze the environmental trade-offs associated with one or more specific products/processes, in order to help the stakeholder gain acceptance for the planned action. Moreover, the evaluation allows to quantify environmental releases to air, water and land, in relation to each life cycle stage and/or major contributing process, assisting in the identification of significant shifts in environmental impacts between life cycle stages and environmental media. Also, the assessment of the human and ecological effects of material consumption and environmental releases to the local community, region, and world allows to identify impacts to one or more specific environmental areas of concern and compare the health and ecological impacts between specific products/processes.

However, LCA studies may present some limitations, such as very high resource and time consuming processes. Data gathering can be problematic, due to availability issues, resulting in inaccuracy of the final results. Also, a LCA study will not determine which product or process is the most cost effective or works the best. The information provided by a LCA study is used as a small component of a more comprehensive decision process, such as Life Cycle Managements.

B. LCC - Life Cycle Costing

LCC is a process used to determine the sum of all the costs associated with an asset or with part of an asset. These costs include acquisition, installation, operation, maintenance, refurbishment, and disposal. LCC can be carried out during any or all phases of an asset's life cycle. LCC processes usually include steps such as [8], [10]–[12], [19]: 1) Life Cost Planning, which concerns the assessment and comparison of options/alternatives during the design/ acquisition phase; 2) Selection and development of the LCC model, namely designing cost breakdown structure, identifying data sources and uncertainties; 3) Application of LCC model; and 4) Documentation and review of LCC results.

The main goal for carrying out LCC calculations is to aid decision making regarding assessment and control of costs, by identifying cost significant items, selection of work and expenditure of planning profiles. Early identification of acquisition and ownership costs enables the decision-maker to balance performance, reliability, maintenance support and other goals against life cycle costs. Decisions made early in an asset's life cycle have a greater influence on the Life Cycle Costing than those made late, leading to the development of the concept of discounted costs. The LCC process can be divided into several steps, which are represented in Figure 3. As it can be seen in this figure, the LCC process has 6 stages, that are divided into two groups. The first step is to develop a plan that addresses the purpose, and scope of the analysis. The second step is the selection or development of the LCC model that will conform with the objectives of the analysis. Step three is the application of the model defined in step two. In Step four all the results gathered in the analysis are documented, and the Life Cost Planning phase is finished. In Step five, the model defined in step two is applied using nominal costs, initiating the Life Cost Analysis. Finally, step six involves the continuous monitoring in order to identify areas in which cost savings may be made and to provide feedback for future life cost planning activities. This step finishes the Life Cost Analysis phase. All these steps may be performed iteratively as needed. Assumptions made at each step should be rigorously documented to facilitate iterations and to help in the interpretation of the results of the analysis.

The method used to estimate the cost elements in LCC calculations will depend on the amount of information needed to establish the usage patterns and operational characteristics, in order to infer the expected remaining life, along with the information needed to understand the technology employed. In [12] several methods are presented. The Engineering Cost Method is used when there is detailed and accurate capital and

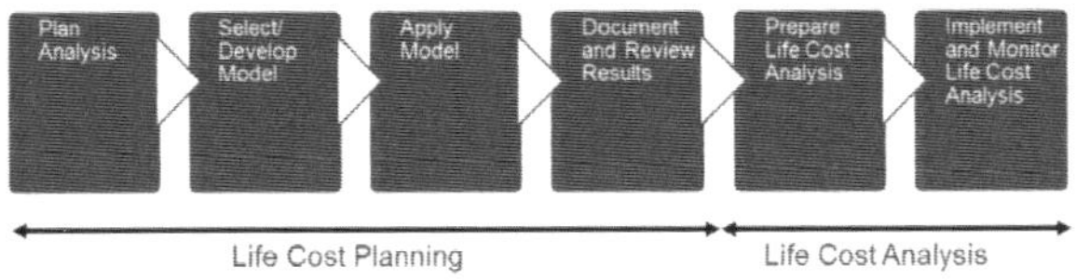

Figure 3. LCC Process.

operational cost data for the study. It involves the direct estimation of a particular cost element by examining component-by-component. It uses standard established cost factors, such as firm engineering and/or manufacturing estimates, in order to develop the cost of each element and its relationship to other elements (known as Cost Element Relationships - CER). The Analogous Cost Method provides the same level of detail as the Engineering Cost Method, but draws on historical data from similar components that have analogous size, technology, use patterns and operational characteristics. Finally, the Parametric Cost Method is employed when actual or historical detailed component data is limited to known parameters. These available data from existing cost analyses is used to develop a mathematical regression or progression formula, which can be solved for the cost estimate required.

The basic deterministic methods are underlying virtually all LCC investigations. The process begins with the customer needs and ultimately ends with the customer selecting a preferred option. In this context, the LCC procedure employed is used to support a decision-making process focused on customer satisfaction. The deterministic approach assigns each LCC input variable a fixed discrete value. The analyst determines the most likely input parameters values that occur, usually based on historical evidence or professional judgment. Collectively, these input values are used to compute a single LCC estimation. Traditionally, applications of LCC have been deterministic ones. A deterministic LCC computation is straightforward and can be conducted manually using a calculator or automatically with a spreadsheet. However, it fails to convey the degree of uncertainty associated with the Present Value (PV) estimate.

The deterministic method of the LCC investigations allows to have a logical ordering of analytical activities and a means of ranking [11]. This ranking includes feasible options for the construction, refurbishment, and on-going management and support of infrastructures. However, this straightforward deterministic approach provides little guidance to the engineer or designer, which attempts to adequately represent the complexity and uncertainty inherent to LCC investigations. For this reason, the basic method is usually extended. A common extension to the basic method of LCC involves the use of sensitivity analysis and risk analysis [37]. Sensitivity analysis involves the behavior of model variables over predetermined bounds to determine their relative effect on model outcome. Through this process, analysts can identify some subset of model variables that exert significant influence on model results and/or determine break-even points that alter the ranking of considered options.

Following an initial deterministic ranking of feasible design options, sensitivity analysis is employed to establish the sensitivity of model results and rankings across model variables of particular concern to analysts and decision makers. While sensitivity analysis provides decision-makers insights regarding the flexibility of model results across a range of variable estimates and corresponding bounds, it has some shortcomings. First, it may fail to identify a dominant alternative among considered design options. This is certainly the case where perturbations in model variables disturb the ranking of feasible design options. Second, since sensitivity analysis typically involves the independent perturbation of each model variable, engineers and, therefore, customers do not gain a sense of the combined and simultaneous influence of several "perturbed" model variables on LCC results and rankings. Finally, in the absence of defined probability distributions, the likelihood that particular values occur is unexplored.

The purpose of risk analysis is to address these shortcomings through probabilistic comparison of considered options. Used properly, risk analysis addresses the bulk of limitations associated with sensitivity analysis.

C. *Tools*

Currently, there are several tools that can perform LCA and/or LCC calculations. In this subsection, some of the most commonly used tool will be briefly described.

The Economic Input-Output Life Cycle Assessment (EIO-LCA) [38] method estimates the materials and energy resources required for activities in the economy, and the environmental emissions resulting from those activities. Researchers at the Green Design Institute of Carnegie Mellon University operationalized the Leontief's method in the mid-1990s, since sufficient computing power was widely available to perform the large-scale matrix manipulations required in real-time. Their work consisted on developing a user-friendly on-line tool that implemented the EIO-LCA method. The website performed fast and easy evaluations to a commodity or service, as well as its supply chain. The EIO-LCA method, models, and results represent the inventory stage of the LCA. The results are used to estimate the environmental emissions or resource consumption associated with the life cycle of an industrial sector. However, it fails to estimate the actual environmental or human health impacts that the emissions or consumption patterns cause. The results of the EIO-LCA analysis represent the impacts from a change in demand on an industrial sector. As a LCA tool, the EIO-LCA models applied are incomplete, since the included environmental effects are limited.

EconomyMap [39] is another tool, which uses CEDA 3.0 LCA Economic Input/Output (EIO) database [40], to provide visualization of the same economic activity and indirect environmental impacts. It provides an easy way to dynamically explore and understand the sources and flow of goods, services, and environmental impacts among major industrial sectors. EconomyMap is intended to be a free resource for public interest lawyers and policymakers, to help them identify and prioritize opportunities to reduce environmental impacts. It also serves as an educational resource for broader audiences.

openLCA [41] is a professional LCA tool and footprint software created by GreenDelta in 2006, with a broad range of features and many available databases. It is an open source software and is publicly available to be modified, offering resources such as professional life cycle modeling, up-to-date usability, a broad choice of life cycle databases and a collaboration environment for teams. Gabi6 [42] is a sustainability solution with a powerful LCA engine to support several applications, namely Life Cycle Assessment, Life Cycle Costing, Life Cycle Reporting and Life Cycle Working Environment.

Gabi6 - GaBi [42] is a product sustainability solution with a powerful LCA engine to support the following applications: (1) LCA, characterized by the design for environment, eco-efficiency, eco-design and efficient value chains. Products should meet environmental regulations, by reducing material, energy and resource use, as well as smaller environmental footprints such as fewer GHG emissions, reduced water consumption and waste. Also, the efficiency of value chains should be enhanced; (2) LCC, characterized by the designing and optimization of products and processes for cost reduction; (3) Life Cycle Reporting, characterized by the product sustainable marketing, sustainability reporting and LCA knowledge sharing. Environmental communication, product sustainability and analysis for internal departments, management and supply chain should be reported, using product sustainability claims and Environmental Product Declarations (EPDs); (4) Life Cycle Working Environment, characterized by a responsible manufacturing, where manufacturing process should address social responsibilities.

III. WORKBENCH

The Workbench is a web based on-line tool developed in the scope of the ReBorn project, used to demonstrate novel factory layout design techniques. This tool will help manufacturers to keep their production at an optimal level of efficiency and, therefore, at the most optimal point of operation in terms of time, costs and quality. The Workbench integrates five different models to support the system design phase, namely the Requirements Configurator, the Marketplace, the Solution Generator, the System Assessment Tool, and the Layout Planner. The Workbench user interface is represented in Figure 4.

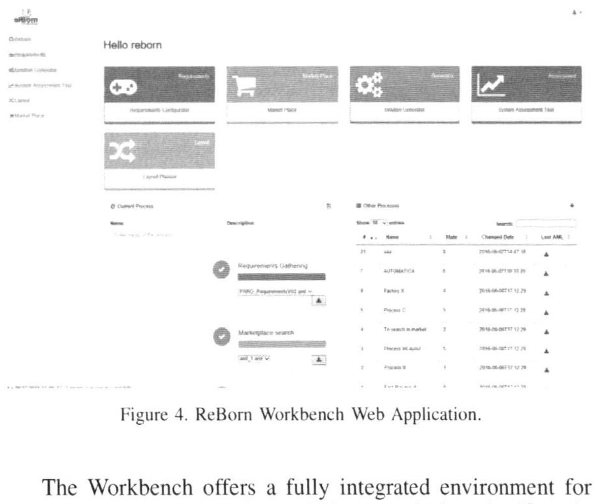

Figure 4. ReBorn Workbench Web Application.

The Workbench offers a fully integrated environment for generating multiple solutions, aiming at reducing significantly the time of the overall design process. It also provides the ability to explore the different solutions generated by the different tools, which opens the scope for considering options within a reduced time frame. It has the capability to ask and receive component's data, needed for a dedicated simulation task. With the help of real data, based on discrete event simulations, the Workbench helps to ensure shorter ramp-up and change-over times and, therefore, reduce costs. The different modules can run independently or they can work together, through the modification and sharing of Automation Markup Language (AML) files [43]. The Workbench modules will be described in the next sections.

A. *Requirements Configurator Module*

The Requirements Configurator is a tool for gathering all key requirements of a production line and provide the captured data in a formalized way. This process achieved by a web application, which guides the user through several forms, in order to collect its inputs. Each user is asked to input information regarding the company (name and country), the factory, such as available space and the layout, Key Performance Indicators (KPIs), components that are required for the production (dimensions and required feeder), and assembly processes, which specifies how an assembly is built together. The requirements information is stored and available to be re-used later, when different scenarios or corrections are considered. As soon as the requirements specifications are stored, they are formalized in the ReBorn enhanced AutomationML format and exported in AML file, which will be used by other modules in the Workbench for further processing. Figure 5 represents the Requirements Configurator web application.

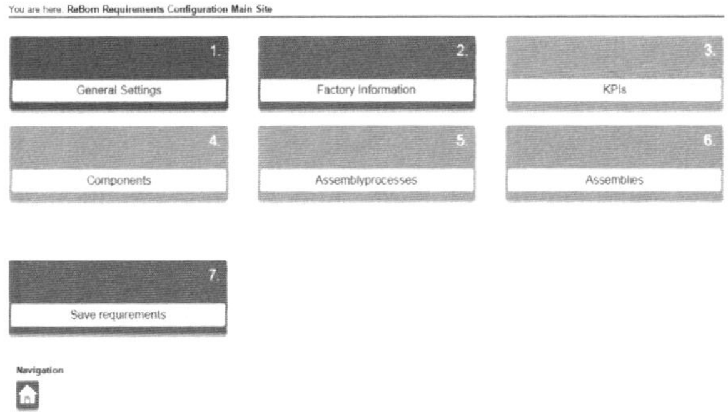

Figure 5. Requirements Configurator Web Application.

B. *Marketplace Module*

The ReBorn Marketplace (RBM) [44] is an on-line platform that allows industrial equipment owners and buyers to have a common ground to communicate, offering services like Platform as a System (PaaS). The RBM enables a multi-sided environment that allows connection between market actors, regarding industrial equipment re-selling. Figure 6 represents the Marketplace web application.

The RBM is a n-sided market, with service providers on one end and service consumers on the other. This market is attractive to service suppliers, since they are able to quickly respond to demand. This demand side is comprised of any potential end-user to the services being provided in the platform. Service Consumers comprise the marketplace participants, which mainly relate to the RBM service offerings. The Marketplace Service Suppliers can normally be instantiated by any entity capable of offering its services to the platform

Figure 6. Marketplace Web Application.

while altogether adding value to the platform's base proposition. Service Suppliers are industrial equipment builders who provide equipment, as well as equipment information, functionalities (software), and operations. Entities capable of providing complementing services to the platform, in order to co-create value, are labeled as Complementors. These can be, for instance, independent software developers that provide additional equipment functionalities.

C. Solution Generator Module

The Solution Generator provides configuration solutions, based on the established requirements gathered by the Requirements Configurator and the existing equipment modules (both old and new). This module requires the use of IBM ILOG CPLEX [45], which is a software optimization package. The Solution Generator uses the information in the AML file to significantly reduce the solution space. Then, it generates an AML file for each of the optimized solutions generated. Figure 7 represents the Solution Generator module.

Figure 7. Solution Generator Application.

D. Layout Planner Module

The Layout Planner is the component of the Workbench responsible for finding the optimized layout for the factory shop floor. It delivers an equipment layout solution, taking into consideration several constraints like space restrictions, equipment to be included and restrictions on material flow. The Layout Planner provides several optimization methods in order to find a solution that minimizes the total cost of material handling associated with the equipment layout considered. This cost is calculated by the the sum of the costs of having specific equipment located in a given area of the shop floor layout and the costs of material handling between equipment. Material handling costs are represented by the relationship between flow of material and distance between equipments. Pinto *et al.* [3] developed an approach based on Genetic Algorithms (GA), which was implemented in the Layout Planner and proved to be more efficient that other genetic algorithm approaches to tackle Facility Layout Problems (FLP). Figure 8 represents the Layout Planner module.

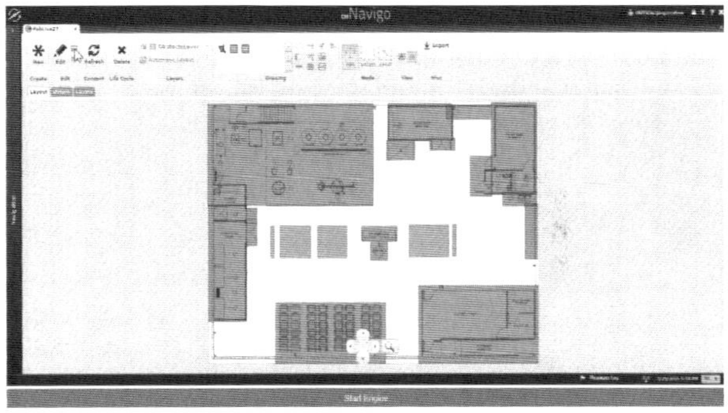

Figure 8. Layout Planner Web Application.

E. System Assessment Tool Module

The SAT integrates reliability and life cycle status information during early design and costing of assembly automation projects. The life-long cost assessment of the system is accomplished through the data collection of the system performance throughout its life cycle. Based on this performance data, the SAT performs the life cycle cost assessment and analysis of the effect on the overall reconfigured system. Figure 9 represents the SAT module.

The SAT is able to compare machines and production lines in terms of: 1) Reliability metrics, such as failure rate, Mean Time Between Failure (MTBF), Mean Time To Repair (MTTR), reliability, availability, performance, quality and Overall Equipment Effectiveness (OEE); 2) LCC metrics, such as Future Value (FV), PV, Net Present Cost (NPC) and Net Present Value (NPV) with initial costs; and 3) LCA metrics, such as life cycle emissions and impact categories, like Global Warming Potential or Ozone Depleting Potential. A detailed overview of the SAT is presented in the next section.

IV. System Assessment Tool

The SAT has two main objectives, namely providing an easy and intuitive way for a user to compare machines or production lines and providing a web API service, capable of receiving requests and share the results with the other modules

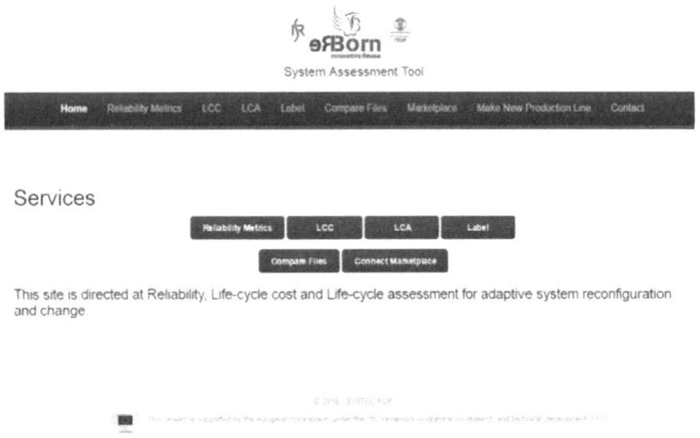

Figure 9. System Assessment Tool Web Application.

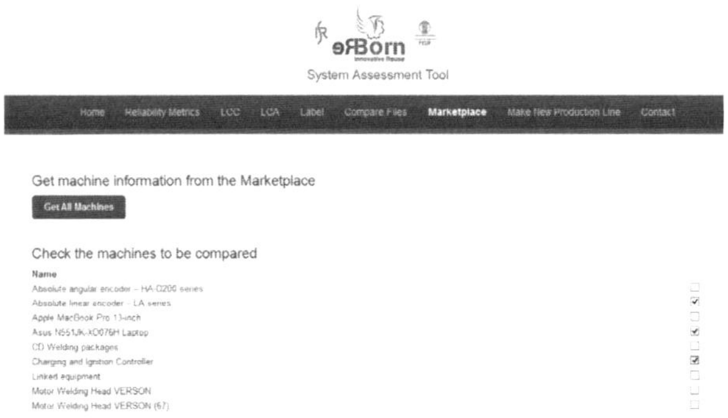

Figure 11. SAT - Marketplace Connection.

in the Workbench or other future applications. As mentioned before, the SAT provides an easy and intuitive way for a user to compare machines or production lines, in terms of reliability, LCC, LCA, classifying each machine with a label, based on a grading system. Figure 10 represents an overall architecture of the SAT, which consists on four main groups of metric parameters: 1) Reliability; 2) LCC; 3) LCA and 4) Equipment Label. These groups will be further detailed in the next sections.

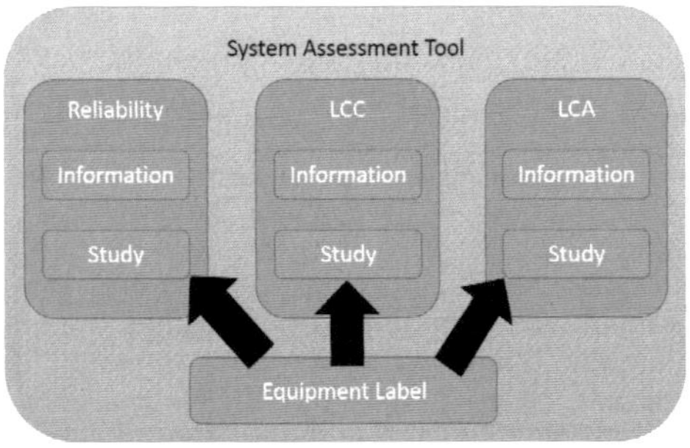

Figure 10. System Assessment Tool Overall Architecture.

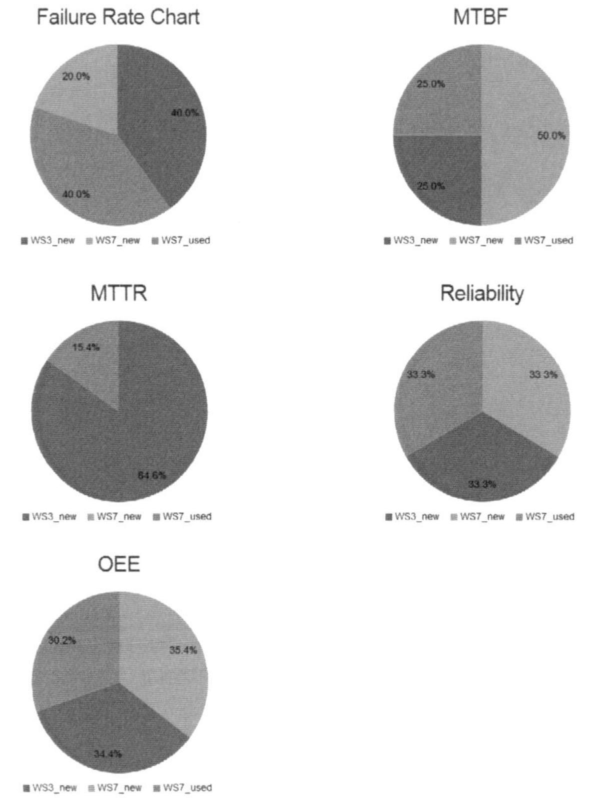

Figure 12. Machine comparison - Reliability metrics.

Regarding communication interfaces, the SAT can interact directly with the Marketplace, as represented in Figure 11, or it can interact with other applications, using a web API or the available web interface. The SAT is prepared to receive requests for performing analysis of equipment, using the available metrics, where both equipment information and the analysis results are imported/exported to an AML file or stored locally into a database.

Available machines in the Marketplace can be compared with machines available in the SAT scope. The user can select from a list the machines to be compared and perform the analysis. Figure 12 represents and example of the results provided by a comparison analysis between two industrial machines. In this case reliability metrics are shown. Each graph shows the percentage of each equipment for each metric.

A. *Reliability Metrics Functionality*

Regarding reliability metrics of equipment operation, the SAT [1] can calculate several parameters, namely the failure rate, MTBF, MTTR, reliability, availability, performance, quality and OEE.

1) Failure rate: Failure rate, represented by Fr, can be defined as the frequency that an engineered system or component fails. Fr is calculated by the ratio between the number of failures F that occur and the operating time O_t of the equipment, as shown in Equation (1).

$$Fr = \frac{F}{O_t} \tag{1}$$

2) Mean Time Between Failure: MTBF, represented by $MTBF$, is defined as the predicted elapsed time between inherent failures of a system during operation. It is the inverse of the Failure Rate and is thus calculated from the same parameters, namely the number of failures F that occur during the operating time O_t, as shown in Equation (2).

$$MTBF = \frac{O_t}{F} \tag{2}$$

3) Mean Time To Repair: MTTR, represented by $MTTR$, is a basic measurement of the maintainability of repairable items, which reflects both the severity of breakdowns and the efficacy of repair activities. It represents the average time required to repair a failed component or device and depends on the number of expected breakdown times D_t and the number of failures F in a given period of time, as shown in Equation (3).

$$MTTR = \frac{\sum_{n=1}^{N} D_{t_n}}{F} \tag{3}$$

4) Reliability: Reliability, represented by R, is the probability that the equipment will finish successfully a task of duration t without failures, as shown in Equation (4).

$$R = e^{-(Fr \times t)} \tag{4}$$

5) Availability: Availability A represents the percentage of scheduled time that the operation is available to operate. It is defined as the ratio between the actual operating time O_t and the scheduled production time of an equipment P_t, as shown in Equation (5).

$$A = \frac{O_t}{P_t} \tag{5}$$

The scheduled production time of an equipment P_t can be calculated as the sum of the operating time O_t with the expected down time D_t, as shown in Equation (6).

$$P_t = O_t + D_t \tag{6}$$

6) Performance: Performance P represents the speed at which the equipment runs as a percentage of its designed speed. It is the ratio between the actual number of units produced Pt and the number of units that theoretically can be produced, considering the rate of operation that the equipment is designed for, represented by the ideal cycle time C_t, as shown in Equation (7).

$$P = \frac{Pt \times C_t}{O_t} \tag{7}$$

7) Quality: Quality Q represents the good units produced as a percentage of the total units produced. It is the ratio between the number of good units Pg and the total number of units Pt that were produced, as shown in Equation (8).

$$Q = \frac{Pg}{Pt} \tag{8}$$

8) Overall Equipment Effectiveness: OEE, represented as OEE, quantifies how well a manufacturing unit performs relative to its designed capacity, during the periods when it is scheduled to run, which can be determined by the the ratio between the theoretical maximum good output during the production time and the actual good output. Equation (9) represents a practical form to calculate the OEE, which depends on the availability A, the performance P and the quality Q.

$$OEE = A \times P \times Q \tag{9}$$

B. LCC Metrics Functionality

Regarding LCC metrics, the SAT performs calculations regarding the Capital Cost Unit Over Service Life, the Capital Annualized Cost Unit, the future and present values, Net Present Cost and Net Present Value.

1) Capital Cost Unit Over Service Life: Capital Cost Unit Over Service Life CC represents the cost of producing a unit over the equipment expected service life. As shown in Equation (10), this cost is calculated by the sum of all costs associated with the equipment, namely: 1) acquisition and installation T_{Ci}; 2) operation and maintenance T_{Cm}, considering also the energy consumption (where c_e is the default annual energy consumption, r_e is electricity rate and E_{sl} is the equipment expected service life); and 3) disposal T_{Ce}.

$$CC = T_{Ci} + T_{Cm} + E_{sl} \times (c_e \times r_e) + T_{Ce} \tag{10}$$

Acquisitions and installation costs include hardware and software acquisitions, service contracts, administrative, set up installation and other initial costs. Operation and maintenance costs include training maintenance support, material costs, equipment upgrade and other maintenance operation. Operation and maintenance costs include the equipment energy consumption, where the default annual energy consumption c_e can be calculated using the power consumption in active Pw_a and sleep mode Pw_s, and the time that the equipment is turned off T_{off} and in standby T_{sleep} during workdays, as shown in Equation (11).

$$c_e = 365 \times (Pw_a + Pw_s) \times 24 \times (1 - (T_{off} + T_{sleep})) \tag{11}$$

2) Capital Annualized Cost Unit: Capital Annualized Cost Unit CA is the cost of the equipment producing a unit per year, which depends on the Capital Cost Unit Over Service Life CC and the machine expected service life E_{sl}, as shown in Equation (12).

$$CA = \frac{CC}{E_{sl}} \tag{12}$$

3) Future Value: FV, represented as FV in Equation (13), is the economical value of an asset at a specified date in the future, which is equivalent to the economical value of a specific sum today. Based on the time value of money, the value of an equipment today is not equal to the value of the same equipment in a future time. In this case, FV grows linearly, since it's a linear function of the initial investment Ci. Ci is based on the initial acquisitions and installation costs, such as hardware and software acquisitions, service contracts, administrative, set up installation and other initial costs. FV also depends on the interest rate r and the time for the equipment to be analyzed T.

$$FV = \sum_{n=1}^{N} Ci_n \times (1 + r \times T) \tag{13}$$

4) Present Value: PV, represented as PV in Equation (14), is the economical value in the current day of an equipment that will be received in a future date. Costs that occur at different points in the equipment life cycle cannot be compared directly because of the varying time value of money. They must be discounted back to their present value through, e.g., Equation (14), where PV depends on the value in the future FV, the interest (discount) rate r and the time (number of years) for the equipment to be analyzed T.

$$PV = \frac{FV}{(1+r)^T} \tag{14}$$

5) Net Present Cost: NPC, represented as NPC in Equation (15), is the sum of all costs, such as capital investment, non-fuel operation and maintenance costs, replacement costs, energy costs, such as fuel costs and any other costs, such as legal fees, etc, after taking into account the interest rate. If a number of options are being considered, then the option with the lowest NPC associated will be the most favorable financial option. NPC depends on the present value PV, the discount rate r and the total cash flow T_{Cf} over the reviewed period.

$$NPC = PV + r \times T_{Cf} \tag{15}$$

6) Net Present Value: NPV is used to determine the profitability of an investment that is calculated by subtracting the present values of cash outflows from the present values of cash inflows over a given period of time. The NPV may consider or not the initial costs, which are represented as the Net Present Value without Initial Costs NPV_{wo} and Net Present Value with Initial Costs NPV_{wi}, shown in Equations (16) and (17) respectively. They depend on the cash flows Cf during the reviewed period T, the discount rate r and, in the case of NPV_{wi}, it is considered the initial costs Ci.

$$NPV_{wo} = \sum_{t=1}^{T} \frac{Cf_t}{(1+r)^t} \tag{16}$$

$$NPV_{wi} = \sum_{t=1}^{T} \frac{Cf_t}{(1+r)^t} - Ci \tag{17}$$

C. LCA Metrics Functionality

The LCA is a "cradle-to-grave" approach for assessing industrial systems. The realization of an LCA study is a complex process that needs large amounts of different data, which usually is not commonly available. For that reason, most of the times, only simpler metrics related to the environmental impacts and their characterization are considered, such as global warming, stratospheric ozone depletion and human health.

1) Global Warming: Global Warming Potential, represented as GWP in Equation (18), is calculated over a specific time interval, commonly 20, 100 or 500 years, and is expressed as a factor of carbon dioxide [15]. To calculate this impact, several types of flows must be taken into account, such as Carbon Dioxide CO_2, Nitrogen Dioxide NO_2, Methane CH_4, Chlorofluorocarbons (CFCs) like Sulfur Hexafluoride SF_6, Hydrochlorofluorocarbons (HCFCs) like Nitrogen trifluoride NF_3 and Methyl Bromide CH_3Br.

$$\begin{aligned} GWP = CO_2 + 25 \times CH_4 + 5 \times CH_3Br + 298 \times NO_2 \\ + 22800 \times SF_6 + 17200 \times NF_3 \end{aligned} \tag{18}$$

2) Stratospheric Ozone Depletion: Stratospheric Ozone Depletion, represented as ODP in Equation (19), is characterized by the Ozone Depleting Potential [15]. ODP of a chemical compound is the relative amount of degradation to the ozone layer it can cause. To calculate this impact, several types of flows must be taking into account, such as CFCs, HCFCs and Halons. CFCs include Dichlorodifluoromethane CCl_2F, Trichlorofluoromethane CCl_3F, Trichlorotrifluoroethane $C_2Cl_3F_3$, Dichlorotetrafluoroethane C_2F_4Cl and Chloropentafluoroethane C_2ClF_5. HCFCs include Chlorodifluoromethane $CHClF_2$ and Trichloroethane CH_3CCl_3. Halons include Bromotrifluoromethane CF_3Br, Bromochlorodifluoromethane CF_2BrCl and Tetrachloromethane CCl_4.

$$\begin{aligned} ODP = CCl_2F + CCl_3F + 1.07 \times C_2Cl_3F_3 \\ + 0.8 \times C_2F_4Cl + 0.5 \times C_2ClF_5 \\ + 0.055 \times CHClF_2 + 0.12 \times CH_3CCl_3 \\ + 16 \times CF_3Br + 4 \times CF_2BrCl + 1.08 \times CCl_4 \end{aligned} \tag{19}$$

3) Human Health: Human Health, represented as HH in Equation (20), is characterized by the median lethal concentration (LC50) and calculates the amount of toxic material released [15]. To calculate this impact, several types of flows must be taking into account, such as Carbon Monoxide CO, Nitrogen Oxide NOx and Sulfur Dioxide SO_2.

$$HH = 0.012 \times CO + 0.78 \times NOx + 1.2 \times SO_2 \tag{20}$$

Grade	Range (%)
A	100-90
B	89-70
C	69-50
D	49-30
E	29-10
F	10-0

Figure 13. Equipment Label Scale.

TABLE I. Metrics Weights Used in Simulations 1 and 2.

Metric Type	Metric	Use / Willing (%)	Import.	W_{V1}	W_{V2}	W_{V3}
Reliability	Fr	75%	55%	0.05	0.04	0.04
	$MTBF$	100%	91%	0.09	0.09	0.09
	$MTTR$	100%	91%	0.09	0.09	0.09
	R	75%	48%	0.04	0.03	0.03
	A	100%	90%	0.09	0.09	0.09
	P	75%	93%	0.09	0.09	0.09
	Q	100%	98%	0.10	0.20	0.23
	OEE	100%	80%	0.08	0.07	0.07
LCC	CC	100%	83%	0.08	0.07	0.07
	CA	75%	45%	0.04	0.03	0.03
	NPV_{wo}	25%	33%	0.03	0.02	0.01
	NPV_{wi}	25%	28%	0.02	0.01	0.01
	NPC	50%	43%	0.04	0.03	0.03
	FV	25%	18%	0.01	0.01	0.00
	PV	25%	18%	0.01	0.01	0.00
LCA	Ec	100%	75%	0.08	0.07	0.07
	Rm	75%	40%	0.04	0.03	0.03
	Ic	50%	34%	0.02	0.02	0.02

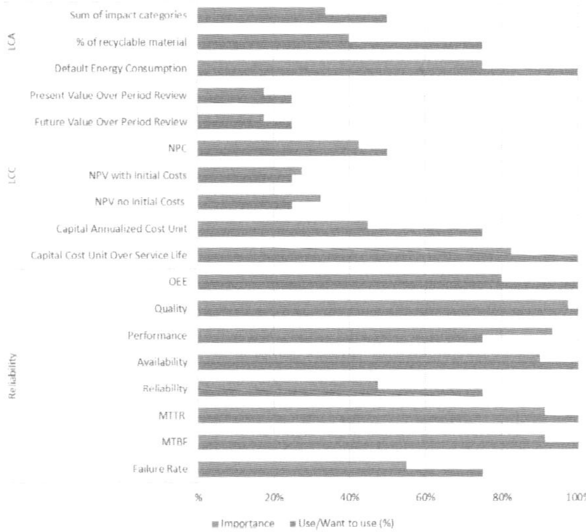

Figure 14. Metrics Questionnaire Results Resume.

D. Equipment Label

The equipment Label is a form of equipment classification, based on the results of the metrics calculated in the SAT, described in sections IV-A, IV-B and IV-C. The classification consists on assigning a grade from A to F to the considered equipment, being A very dependable and F less dependable, as represented in Figure 13, similar to the labeling of the European Union energy [46]. Grades are determined by the sum of the analysis metrics (Reliability, LCC, and LCA), after attributing weights to each of the metrics.

Aguiar *et al.* [1] presented a simple grading system that is represented in 21 to calculate the label L. This first approach used a few of the possible metrics (along with the corresponding weights), such as reliability R, Overall Equipment Effectiveness OEE, initial Ci, operational Cm and disposal Ce costs, energy consumption Ec and percentage reusable Pr.

$$L = W_R \times R + W_{OEE} \times OEE + \frac{Cm}{W \times (Ci + Ce)} + W_{Ec} \times Ec + W_{Pr} \times Pr \tag{21}$$

V. TESTS AND RESULTS

Although Aguiar *et al.* [1] presented good labeling results based on the most commonly used metrics calculated by the SAT, some industrial companies may have different priorities regarding the metrics used for the analysis. For this reason, in order to identify the importance of the metrics used, a survey was carried out among the industrial partners of the ReBorn Consortium. This survey consisted on a questionnaire, where industrial partners specify the metrics that they usually use and the importance of each metric. Figure 14 represents a resume of the results gathered from the survey.

After inspection of the survey results, it is clear that some metrics are more relevant that others. The most important metric is Quality Q, with an importance of 98%, followed by MTTR $MTTR$, MTBF $MTBF$ and Availability A, which all have an importance above the 90%.

Based on the information that resulted from the survey, a new labeling system was devised, as shown in Equation (22). In this case, Label L depends on several metrics and the corresponding weights, namely the Failure Rate Fr, Mean Time Between Failures $MTBF$, Mean Time To Repair $MTTR$, Reliability R, Availability A, Performance P, Quality Q, Overall Equipment Effectiveness OEE, Capital Cost Unit Over Service Life CC, Capital Annualized Cost Unit CA, Net Present Value without Initial Costs NPV_{wo}, Net Present Value with Initial Costs NPV_{wi}, Net Present Cost NPC, Default Energy Consumption c_e, percentage of recyclable material Rm and the sum of the impact categories values Ic.

$$\begin{aligned} L = {} & W_{Fr} \times Fr + W_{MTBF} \times MTBF + W_{MTTR} \times MTTR \\ & + W_R \times R + W_A \times A + W_P \times P + W_Q \times Q \\ & + W_{OEE} \times OEE + W_{CC} \times CC + W_{CA} \times CA \\ & + W_{NPV_{wo}} \times NPV_{wo} + W_{NPV_{wi}} \times NPV_{wi} \\ & + W_{NPC} \times NPC + W_{c_e} \times c_e + W_{Rm} \times Rm \\ & + W_{Ic} \times Ic \end{aligned} \tag{22}$$

In order to be widely accepted, the labeling system must be simple, clear and generic enough to be used by different industrial users, with different metric priorities. To validate the effectiveness of the labeling system, represented in Equation (22), three different simulations were performed in a Matlab environment and are presented in the next sections.

All three simulations have the same principles. It was assumed that the values for the metrics were normalized and are expressed in percentage. The metrics values were assigned based on a 1000 uniformly distributed random generated numbers. For Simulation 1 and 2 the corresponding metrics weights were generated in three different versions (W_{V1}, W_{V2} andW_{V3}), which are presented in Table I. W_{V1} was defined based on the importance given by each industrial partner of the ReBorn Consortium. The other weight versions were defined by increasing the Quality value, because it is the metric with higher importance, and decreasing the value of the metrics with lower importance, keeping in mind that the sum of all weights is equal to 1. For Simulation 3, the same philosophy is applied, in terms of the weight calculation. The difference between Simulation 3 and Simulation 1 and 2, is that the weight calculation for the first layer in Simulation 3 is done in blocks (Reliability, LCC, and LCA).

To be able to compare all the simulations, the mean and standard deviation are calculated for four different values: 1) number of quality values lower than the Label; 2) number of quality values lower than the Label by two or more grades; 3) number of quality values higher than the Label; 4) number of quality values higher than the Label by two or more grades. Ideally, all the four values, as well as it's mean and standard deviation values, should be as small as possible. Having small values for mean and standard deviation means that the difference between the metrics used (e.g., Quality) and the equipment Label is short, and the influence of such metrics is very high regarding the Label being calculated.

A. *Simulations 1 and 2*

Regarding the simulations 1 and 2, the simulations consist on calculating the equipment Label, based on the metrics and the corresponding weights, as shown in Equation (22). For Simulation 1, Figure 15 presents the relationship of the Quality values and the equipment Label calculated for the three versions of metrics weights. From the figure and after observing the results, several equipment labels were identified, where the most important metrics refereed previously had values much lower or higher than the equipment label, that is, with a difference of two or more grades between the equipment Label and the most important metrics.

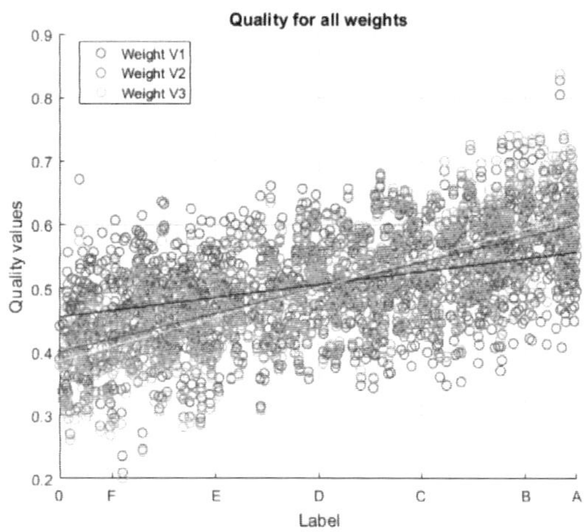

Figure 15. Simulation 1 - Quality values for the three metrics weights versions.

In order to have a meaningful labeling system that is truthfully usable by the industry, the label classification must reflect the most important metrics that are relevant for the users. Based on the survey performed, Simulation 2 consisted on calculating the equipment Label, considering the most important metrics that resulted from the survey, namely Quality, MTBF, MTTR, and Availability.

In Simulation 2, the equipment Label was calculated using Equation (22), the same way as used in Simulation 1. The difference lays in the importance given for specific metrics. For all the equipment Labels that differ from the Quality value, the Label is recalculated using only the top four metrics, as shown in Equation (23).

$$L = W_{MTBF} \times MTBF + W_{MTTR} \times MTTR + W_A \times A + W_Q \times Q \tag{23}$$

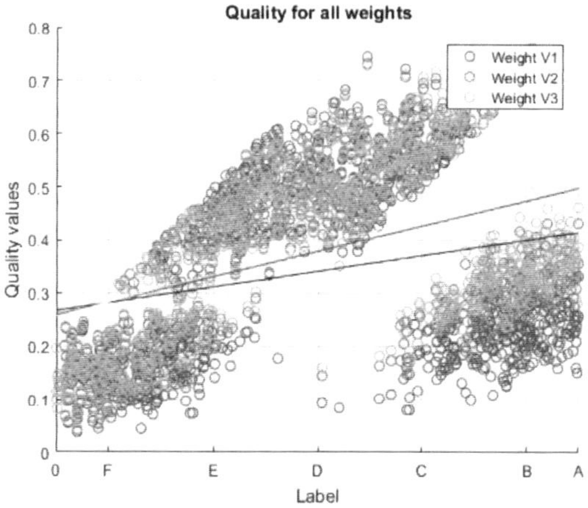

Figure 16. Simulation 2 - Quality values for the three metrics weights versions.

The results of Simulation 2 are presented in Figure 16, which consists on the relationship of the Quality values and the equipment Label calculated for the three versions of metrics weights.

The mean μ and standard deviation σ of the number of equipments that have a Quality value higher or lower then the Label, were calculated and are presented in Table II. This allows for a better understanding and comparison of the simulations results, and to evaluate if the equipment Label calculated is more or less accurate when compared with the Quality value of the equipment. The equipments considered were those who present a Quality different from the calculated equipment Label, and that the difference is higher than one grade from the labeling system.

B. *Simulation 3*

Taking into account the results from the previous Simulations 1 and 2, and based on the fact that the most important metrics chosen from the industrial partners belong to the Reliability metrics group, a different approach was taken in Simulation 3, where the equipment Label calculation is performed at two levels, as represented in Figure 17. First, the equipment Label is calculated three times, one from each metric group, namely Reliability, LCC and LCA metric groups. These Label results will be used to calculate an overall equipment Label. For each group, the equipment label only considers the parameters that belong to that group of metrics.

Equation (24) is used to calculate the equipment label regarding the Reliability group L_{Rel}, considering only the

TABLE II. Equipments with Quality different from the Label - Simulation 1.

		Simulation 1			Simulation 2		
		W_{V1}	W_{V2}	W_{V3}	W_{V1}	W_{V2}	W_{V3}
$Q < L$	μ	390.50	375.50	372.00	370.5	351.50	347.50
	σ	127.71	145.83	150.90	240.92	228.59	230.65
$Q < L$ (2 or more grades)	μ	386.50	372.75	367.00	379.50	357.00	354.75
	σ	131.50	148.33	153.26	246.21	236.02	235.75
$Q > L$	μ	378.50	368.00	362.75	368.75	345.00	343.75
	σ	142.65	153.83	158.66	256.05	242.73	241.96
$Q > L$ (2 or more grades)	μ	392.50	378.75	373.25	369.75	340.50	337.50
	σ	126.75	142.41	148.66	256.92	244.63	245.94

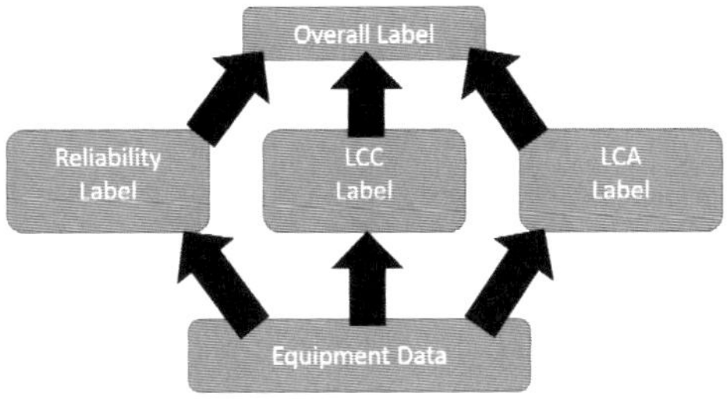

Figure 17. Overall Label - two layer label calculation.

Failure Rate Fr, Mean Time Between Failure $MTBF$, Mean Time to Repair $MTTR$, Reliability R, Availability A, Performance P, Quality Q, and Overall Equipment Effectiveness OEE, with the corresponding weights.

$$L_{Rel} = W_{Fr} \times Fr + W_{MTBF} \times MTBF + W_{MTTR} \times MTTR + W_R \times R + W_A \times A + W_P \times P + W_Q \times Q + W_{OEE} \times OEE \quad (24)$$

Equation (25) is used to calculate the equipment label regarding the LCC group L_{LCC}, considering only the Capital Cost Unit Over Service Life CC, Capital Annualized Cost Unit CA, Net Present Value Without Initial Costs NPV_{wo}, Net Present Value With Initial Costs NPV_{wi}, Net Present Cost NPC, Future Value FV, and Present Value PV, with the corresponding weights.

$$L_{LCC} = W_{CC} \times CC + W_{CA} \times CA + W_{NPV_{wo}} \times NPV_{wo} + W_{NPV_{wi}} \times NPV_{wi} + W_{NPC} \times NPC \quad (25)$$

Equation (26) is used to calculate the equipment label regarding the LCA group L_{LCA}, considering only the Default Energy Consumption c_e, percentage of recyclable material Rm, and the sum of the impact categories values Ic, with the corresponding weights.

$$L_{LCA} = W_{c_e} \times c_e + W_{Rm} \times Rm + W_{Ic} \times Ic \quad (26)$$

Based on the three equipment Label that were determined for each metric group, namely the Reliability Label L_{Rel}, LCC Label L_{LCC}, and LCA Label L_{LCA}, the equipment overall Label can be calculated, as shown in Equation (27).

$$L_{Overall} = W_{L_{Rel}} \times L_{Rel} + W_{L_{LCC}} \times L_{LCC} + W_{L_{LCA}} \times L_{LCA} \quad (27)$$

In this case, Step 1 consists on equipment Label calculation for each metric group, using the same weights assigned in Simulation 1 and 2 (W_{V1}, W_{V2} ND W_{V3}). Step 2 consists on the overall equipment Label calculation, considering the Labels determined in Step 1 and assigning the corresponding weights, namely $W_{L_{Rel}}$, $W_{L_{LCC}}$ and $W_{L_{LCA}}$. The weight generation on Step 2 is defined based on the importance of each metric type and keeping the sum of all weights is equal to 1. Table III resumes the weights used for the two layer approach in Simulation 3.

The results of Simulation 3 are presented in Figure 18, which presents on the relationship of the Quality values and the equipment Label calculated for the three metrics weights $W_{L_{Rel}}$, $W_{L_{LCC}}$ and $W_{L_{LCA}}$.

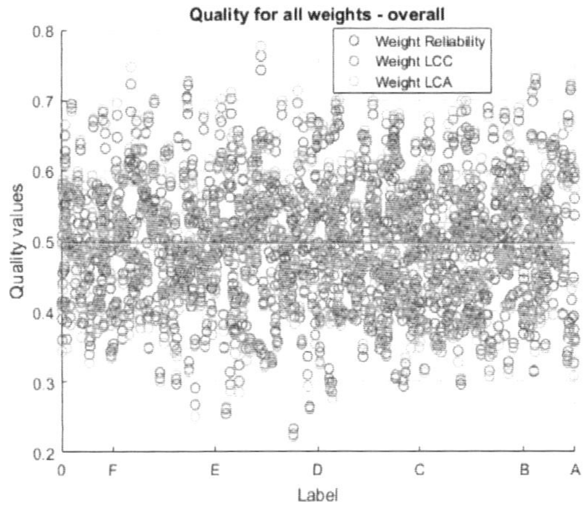

Figure 18. Quality values with the 3 different weight versions - Simulation 3.

As performed in Simulation 1 and 2, the mean μ and standard deviation σ of the number of equipments that have a Quality value higher or lower then the Label, were calculated and are presented in Table IV.

C. Summary

As previously described, the equipment Label aims at providing a simple and straightforward way of classifying and comparing industrial equipments. The idea is to attribute a grade to each equipment, A-F, where A is the best grade and F the worst, based on several metrics than can be collected from the equipment. Three simulations where executed in order to gain a better understanding of how the grade should be calculated and its usability. From the survey carried out among the industrial partners in the ReBorn project, the metric Quality is the most important metric, but there are others that are also considered very important, such as MTTR, MTBF, and Availability. Since Quality was the metric with the highest importance value, it was used as a baseline for comparing the grade calculated by the system.

TABLE III. Weights Used in Simulation 3.

Metric Type	Metric	Step 1 - Single Label			Step 2 - Overall Label		
		W_{V1}	W_{V2}	W_{V3}	$W_{L_{Rel}}$	$W_{L_{LCC}}$	$W_{L_{LCA}}$
Reliability	Fr	0.09	0.07	0.06	0.61	0.70	0.75
	$MTBF$	0.14	0.13	0.13			
	$MTTR$	0.14	0.13	0.13			
	R	0.07	0.05	0.04			
	A	0.14	0.13	0.13			
	P	0.14	0.13	0.13			
	Q	0.15	0.25	0.28			
	OEE	0.12	0.11	0.10			
LCC	CC	0.31	0.35	0.38	0.25	0.20	0.18
	CA	0.17	0.17	0.17			
	PV_{woCi}	0.12	0.11	0.11			
	PV_{wCi}	0.10	0.09	0.09			
	NPC	0.16	0.16	0.15			
	FV	0.07	0.06	0.05			
	PV	0.07	0.06	0.05			
LCA	Ec	0.50	0.60	0.65	0.14	0.10	0.07
	Rm	0.27	0.22	0.20			
	Ic	0.23	0.18	0.15			

TABLE IV. Equipments with Quality different from the Label - Simulation 3.

		$W_{L_{Rel}}$			$W_{L_{LCC}}$			$W_{L_{LCA}}$		
		W_{V1}	W_{V2}	W_{V3}	W_{V1}	W_{V2}	W_{V3}	W_{V1}	W_{V2}	W_{V3}
$Q < L$	μ	501.30	504.33	504.44	500.52	504.09	504.16	499.94	503.97	504.21
	σ	14.55	14.49	14.31	14.80	14.29	14.33	14.72	14.53	14.49
$Q < L$ (2 or more grades)	μ	301.85	305.51	305.69	301.79	305.22	305.34	301.34	305.08	305.37
	σ	13.16	13.16	13.03	12.93	13.01	12.91	12.92	12.89	12.97
$Q > L$	μ	498.70	495.67	495.57	499.49	495.91	495.85	499.49	496.04	495.80
	σ	14.55	14.49	14.31	14.80	14.29	14.33	14.80	14.53	14.49
$Q > L$ (2 or more grades)	μ	299.78	296.61	296.77	300.85	296.52	296.61	301.25	296.66	297.03
	σ	13.04	12.83	12.69	12.89	12.96	13.11	12.92	13.00	13.00

In Simulation 1, a high number of equipments where identified where the grade calculated was two or more grades higher or lower than the Quality value. In order to try to reduce the number of equipments that have two or more grades of difference to the Quality value, Simulation 2 was devised. In this second simulation some values were improved, but the results where not significantly better. These results lead to the design of Simulation 3, where a different approach was taken. Simulation 3 uses a two step approach, as show in Figure 17. With this approach there was a significant improvement in the results, as it can be seen in the Table V.

TABLE V. Resume of the Results of Simulation 1,2 and 3.

		Simulation 1	Simulation 2	Simulation 3	
				Reliability	Overall
$Q < L$	μ	373.00	347.00	496.65	497.08
	σ	147.20	239.79	15.37	15.95
$Q < L$ (2 or more grades)	μ	372.00	339.25	299.79	298.09
	σ	147.81	243.48	14.76	15.16
$Q > L$	μ	376.50	344.50	503.36	502.92
	σ	143.34	232.56	15.37	15.95
$Q > L$ (2 or more grades)	μ	374.00	337.50	306.12	303.25
	σ	146.16	239.81	15.35	14.66

VI. Conclusion and Future Work

In the last ten years, there has been a growing desire of industrial companies and equipment integrators, in several domains, to achieve higher levels of equipment flexibility to be re-usable later in different environments. In order to infer if a given equipment is suitable to be re-use in a different layout to perform different tasks, the state of the equipment must be evaluated first. This evaluation usually consists on comparing the considered equipment with others of the same family, using Quality metrics.

This paper proposes a new approach to classify industrial equipment called labeling system and compares it to the Quality metric, in order to conclude which one performs better at classifying equipment. This approach was implemented in the System Assessment Tool, which is a module of the Workbench, for decision support and production planning, developed within the ReBorn project.

As previously mentioned, the Workbench was developed within the ReBorn project. This tool is composed of several modules that can work together or independently. One of these modules is the System Assessment Tool, which aims at integrating reliability and life cycle status information in one single tool and assigning a label to each equipment. This labeling system is an dependability classification system for industrial equipment, which aims to be similar to the energy efficiency system for appliances.

The labeling system allows the easy comparison of industrial equipment, taking into account several metrics, such as Reliability, LCC and LCA. The assigned grade for each equipment may vary from A to F. A first approach of the labeling system was presented by Aguiar *et al.* [1], which is the work that originated this paper, after further research. This first approach by Aguiar was redefined, based on the results of a survey that was filled by the industrial partners in the ReBorn Consortium, which stated the most important metrics used by the partners.

Three different simulations were performed, in order to experiment different approaches to calculate the equipment Label and explore different results. In Simulation 1 and 2, different weights were assigned to each metric, according to the importance stated in the survey. Using this metric weights resulted in an improvement in the metrics collected and in the equipment Label calculation. However, this improvement was not meaningful, since there were a large number of equipments that were classified with a Label that was must lower or higher than the Quality. Quality is the metric used for comparison and evaluation of the labeling system, because it is the main metric used in industry.

Simulation 3 was based on a different approach, in order to improve the labeling system in comparison to the Quality metric. This approach consisted on a two step labeling classification: 1) Calculate the equipment Label according to the group of metrics considered, namely Reliability, LCC and LCA Labels; 2) An overall equipment Label is calculated based on the previously group labels.

Table V is a resume of the simulations results obtained in the previous section, which presents the mean and standard deviation of the equipments that had the Quality metric different form the calculated Label. There is a improvement from the Simulation 1 to the Simulation 2, in a general way in terms of the mean values. However the standard deviation values are lower in the Simulation 1. In Simulation 3, two parameters are presented, namely the Reliability calculated in the first step and the overall Label calculated in step.

When comparing Simulation 1 and 2 to Simulation 3, there are two results that are very clear. The first one is that the standard deviation values are smaller in the Simulation 3, which indicates that the quality values are closer to the equipment Label calculated. The second result is that although there are more equipments with a Quality value lower or higher than the Label, the number of these values that have more than one grade of difference are smaller, in comparison to the results in Simulation 1 and 2. This second result is obviously supported by the standard deviation values. These results validate the decision to use Equation (27), as tested in Simulation 3, as the most suitable for industrial purposes, in comparison to the highly important Quality metric.

As future work, the proposed labeling scheme must be validated with real industrial scenarios, instead of simulated data. Also, further interaction with industrial partners outside the ReBorn Consortium must be taken, in order to validate the usability and significance of the labeling system.

ACKNOWLEDGMENT

This research was partially supported by the ReBorn project (FoF.NMP.2013-2) - Innovative Reuse of modular knowledge Based devices and technologies for Old, Renewed and New factories - funded by the European Commission under the Seventh Framework Program for Research and Technological Development. We would like to thank all partners for their support and discussions that contributed to these results.

REFERENCES

[1] S. Aguiar, R. Pinto, J. Reis, and G. Gonçalves, "Life-cycle approach to extend equipment re-use in flexible manufacturing," in INTELLI 2016, The Fifth International Conference on Intelligent Systems and Applications. IARIA, 2016, pp. 148–153.

[2] "ReBorn Project web site," URL: http://www.reborn-eu-project.org/ [accessed: 2015-01-01].

[3] R. Pinto, J. Gonçalves, H. L. Cardoso, E. Oliveira, G. Gonçalves, and B. Carvalho, "A facility layout planner tool based on genetic algorithms," in 2016 IEEE Symposium Series on Computational Intelligence (SSCI), Dec 2016, pp. 1–8.

[4] "Automatica Fair," URL: http://automatica-munich.com/ [accessed: 2016-07-01].

[5] M. Oppelt, M. Barth, and L. Urbas, "The Role of Simulation within the Life-Cycle of a Process Plant. Results of a global online survey," 2014, URL: https://www.researchgate.net/ [accessed: 2016-06-01].

[6] V. Cesarotti, A. Giuiusa, and V. Introna, Using Overall Equipment Effectiveness for Manufacturing System Design. INTECH Open Access Publisher, 2013.

[7] K. Muthiah and S. Huang, "Overall throughput effectiveness (ote) metric for factory-level performance monitoring and bottleneck detection," International Journal of Production Research, vol. 45, no. 20, 2007, pp. 4753–4769.

[8] "Standard practice for measuring life-cycle costs of buildings and building systems," 2002, URL: https://www.astm.org/Standards/E917.htm [accessed: 2016-06-01].

[9] F. Bromilow and M. Pawsey, "Life cycle cost of university buildings," Construction Management and Economics, vol. 5, no. 4, 1987, pp. S3–S22.

[10] D. Elmakis and A. Lisnianski, "Life cycle cost analysis: actual problem in industrial management," Journal of Business Economics and Management, vol. 7, no. 1, 2006, pp. 5–8.

[11] D. Langdon, "Literature review of life cycle costing (lcc) and life cycle assessment (lca)," 2006, URL: http://www.tmb.org.tr/arastirma_yayinlar/LCC_Literature_Review_Report.pdf [accessed: 2016-06-01].

[12] "Life cycle costing guideline," 2004, URL: https://www.astm.org/Standards/E917.htm [accessed: 2016-06-01].

[13] M. A. Curran, "Life cycle assessment: Principles and practice," 2006, URL: http://19-659-fall-2011.wiki.uml.edu/ [accessed: 2016-06-01].

[14] G. Rebitzer, T. Ekvall, R. Frischknecht, D. Hunkeler, G. Norris, T. Rydberg, W.-P. Schmidt, S. Suh, B. P. Weidema, and D. W. Pennington, "Life cycle assessment: Part 1: Framework, goal and scope definition, inventory analysis, and applications," Environment international, vol. 30, no. 5, 2004, pp. 701–720.

[15] D. Pennington, J. Potting, G. Finnveden, E. Lindeijer, O. Jolliet, T. Rydberg, and G. Rebitzer, "Life cycle assessment part 2: Current impact assessment practice," Environment international, vol. 30, no. 5, 2004, pp. 721–739.

[16] R. A. Filleti, D. A. Silva, E. J. Silva, and A. R. Ometto, "Dynamic system for life cycle inventory and impact assessment of manufacturing processes," Procedia CIRP, vol. 15, 2014, pp. 531–536.

[17] J. Tao, Z. Chen, S. Yu, and Z. Liu, "Integration of life cycle assessment with computer-aided product development by a feature-based approach," Journal of Cleaner Production, vol. 143, 2017, pp. 1144–1164.

[18] J.-P. Schöggl, R. J. Baumgartner, and D. Hofer, "Improving sustainability performance in early phases of product design: A checklist for sustainable product development tested in the automotive industry," Journal of Cleaner Production, vol.

140, Part 3, 2017, pp. 1602 – 1617. [Online]. Available: http://www.sciencedirect.com/science/article/pii/S0959652616315360

[19] R. Hoogmartens, S. Van Passel, K. Van Acker, and M. Dubois, "Bridging the gap between lca, lcc and cba as sustainability assessment tools," Environmental Impact Assessment Review, vol. 48, 2014, pp. 27–33.

[20] R. Heijungs, G. Huppes, and J. B. Guinée, "Life cycle assessment and sustainability analysis of products, materials and technologies. toward a scientific framework for sustainability life cycle analysis," Polymer degradation and stability, vol. 95, no. 3, 2010, pp. 422–428.

[21] B. Ness, E. Urbel-Piirsalu, S. Anderberg, and L. Olsson, "Categorising tools for sustainability assessment," Ecological economics, vol. 60, no. 3, 2007, pp. 498–508.

[22] D. Cerri, M. Taisch, and S. Terzi, "Proposal of a model for life cycle optimization of industrial equipment," Procedia CIRP, vol. 15, 2014, pp. 479–483.

[23] R. K. Singh, H. R. Murty, S. K. Gupta, and A. K. Dikshit, "An overview of sustainability assessment methodologies," Ecological indicators, vol. 9, no. 2, 2009, pp. 189–212.

[24] C. Böhringer and P. E. Jochem, "Measuring the immeasurable—a survey of sustainability indices," Ecological economics, vol. 63, no. 1, 2007, pp. 1–8.

[25] I. T. Cameron and G. Ingram, "A survey of industrial process modelling across the product and process lifecycle," Computers & Chemical Engineering, vol. 32, no. 3, 2008, pp. 420–438.

[26] F. Cucinotta, E. Guglielmino, and F. Sfravara, "Life cycle assessment in yacht industry: A case study of comparison between hand lay-up and vacuum infusion," Journal of Cleaner Production, vol. 142, 2017, pp. 3822–3833.

[27] F. Iraldo, C. Facheris, and B. Nucci, "Is product durability better for environment and for economic efficiency? a comparative assessment applying lca and lcc to two energy-intensive products," Journal of Cleaner Production, vol. 140, 2017, pp. 1353–1364.

[28] J. Auer, N. Bey, and J.-M. Schäfer, "Combined life cycle assessment and life cycle costing in the eco-care-matrix: A case study on the performance of a modernized manufacturing system for glass containers," Journal of Cleaner Production, vol. 141, 2017, pp. 99–109.

[29] S. H. Mousavi-Avval, S. Rafiee, M. Sharifi, S. Hosseinpour, B. Notarnicola, G. Tassielli, and P. A. Renzulli, "Application of multi-objective genetic algorithms for optimization of energy, economics and environmental life cycle assessment in oilseed production," Journal of Cleaner Production, vol. 140, 2017, pp. 804–815.

[30] J. I. Martínez-Corona, T. Gibon, E. G. Hertwich, and R. Parra-Saldívar, "Hybrid life cycle assessment of a geothermal plant: From physical to monetary inventory accounting," Journal of Cleaner Production, vol. 142, 2017, pp. 2509–2523.

[31] H. Smith, "Cumulative energy requirements for the production of chemical intermediates and products," in World Energy Conference, 1963.

[32] J. Guinée and R. Heijungs, Introduction to life cycle assessment. Springer, 2017.

[33] R. G. Hunt, W. E. Franklin, and R. Hunt, "Lca—how it came about," The international journal of life cycle assessment, vol. 1, no. 1, 1996, pp. 4–7.

[34] "EU DG," URL: http://ec.europa.eu/dgs/environment/ [accessed: 2016-07-01].

[35] "ISO 14000," URL: http://www.iso.org/iso/iso14000 [accessed: 2016-07-01].

[36] B. W. Vigon, B. Vigon, and C. Harrison, "Life-cycle assessment: inventory guidelines and principles," 1993.

[37] M. A. Ehlen, "Life-cycle costs of new construction materials," Journal of Infrastructure systems, vol. 3, no. 4, 1997, pp. 129–133.

[38] "Economic Input-Output Life Cycle Assessment (EIO-LCA)," URL: http://www.eiolca.net [accessed: 2016-06-01].

[39] "EconomyMap," URL: http://www.economymap.org/ [accessed: 2016-06-01].

[40] "CEDA Comprehensive Environmental Data Archive," URL: http://iersweb.com/services/ceda/ [accessed: 2015-01-01].

[41] "openLCA," URL: http://www.openlca.org/ [accessed: 2016-06-01].

[42] "Gabi6," URL: http://www.gabi-software.com/index/ [accessed: 2016-06-01].

[43] "AutomationML," URL: https://www.automationml.org/o.red.c/home.html [accessed: 2016-06-01].

[44] R. Fonseca, S. Aguiar, M. Peschl, and G. Gonçalves, "The reborn marketplace: an application store for industrial smart components," in INTELLI 2016, The Fifth International Conference on Intelligent Systems and Applications. IARIA, 2016, pp. 136–141.

[45] "CPLEX," URL: http://www-03.ibm.com/software/products/en/ibmilogcpleoptistud [accessed: 2016-06-01].

[46] "Energy Efficient," URL: http://ec.europa.eu/energy/en/topics/energy-efficiency/energy-efficient-products [accessed: 2016-06-01].

International Journal on Advances in Intelligent Systems, vol 10 no 1 & 2, year 2017, http://www.iariajournals.org/intelligent_systems/

Design Pattern-based Modeling of Collaborative Service Chains

Maik Herfurth
Hilti Befestigungstechnik AG
Buchs SG, Switzerland
e-mail: maik.herfurth@hilti.com

Thomas Schuster
Pforzheim University of Applied Sciences
Pforzheim, Germany
e-mail: thomas.schuster@hs-pforzheim.de

***Abstract*—Increased market competition between service providers has promoted differentiation, currently often based on offerings of so-called hybrid services. Hybrid services are complex since service providers and service consumers collaborate and interact in network structures – also called service chains. Service chains also include collaborative, cross-company service processes amongst different participants. The effectiveness of these processes constitutes a major competitive factor since they possess potential to increase efficiency and reduce cost. Along with hybrid services, e-procurement becomes strategically important. While basic service processes are typically company internal, service chains include cross-company administration, especially for service e-procurement. If enough domain specific data is available, information systems can support service operations and e-procurement in an integrated mode. Hence, a precise description, modeling and analysis of service processes is required for the implementation of process-oriented information systems is required to unlock these potentials and optimize network collaboration. To improve the transition from planning to implementation of collaborative service chains with incorporated e-procurement, we suggest an integrated and formalized modeling approach. Our modeling approach is based on Petri nets and includes a pattern-based tactic to develop business process models. To improve this collaboration systematically we distinguish hierarchically between service phase patterns and service module patterns. Finally, our approach will be demonstrated by case studies taken from the domain of industrial service procurement.**

Keywords*—*service processes; service objects; service e-procurement; hybrid services; integrated modeling approach; modeling language; design patterns; service phase pattern; service module pattern

I. INTRODUCTION

This article is an extended version of the recently published paper "*Integrated Modeling Approach iServMod for Modeling, Analysis and Execution of Collaborative Service Processes in Service Chains*" [1]. The service sector is a fast-growing sector in all industrial nations and therefore, it has gained significant importance for all national economies [2]. Today, the strategic impact of services outruns products. With shifting the towards services and moving away from a product centric view, a new paradigm known as *service dominant logic* is postulated [3]. Current surveys highlight that services increasingly create value offerings to customers and thus constitute an integral element of many products [4].

This includes industrial services as one example of hybrid services. Industrial services contribute a significant share of companies total spending and ensure required operational levels and availability of systems and facilities. Therefore, industrial service e-procurement is gaining importance and an integrated perspective of goods and services is required [5],[6]. New business models are arising with cross-company network structures where service providers and service consumers act in service networks. These cross-company value chains with incorporated flows of goods, cash and information are called *service chains* [7]-[9]. Progressively companies outsource different areas and reduce the degree of company-internal value-add. An important example of service chains are industrial maintenance services. They are typically delivered through third-party service providers which guarantee availability and reliability of industrial facilities and infrastructures.

With more services sourced externally, the meaning of service procurement is increasing exponentially. For the procurement of industrial services, several service providers and service consumers must interact in multilateral service chains. Capital goods producers, goods and service consumers, as well as specialized service providers interact to produce, operate and administrate these hybrid services. Hence, the ability to integrate and share product and service offerings of external business partners turns out to be a major competitive factor. In consequence, service providers take focus on supporting consumer processes or even on offering to provide larger parts of value creation processes. Since service consumers request different service types from different service providers, new types of flexible collaborations are emerging.

In this case, service e-procurement constitutes an important segment of e-business activities. It compasses extensive use of *Information and Communication Technology* (*ICT*) to improve productivity and business processes. Electronic processes support business interactions reducing interfaces, process and throughput times and enhance coordination of activities, procedures and integration of resources.

Additionally, e-business standards can help to support a shared process understanding and increase process transparency amongst business partners by harmonization and structuring of exchanged business data. As follows, e-business standards facilitate enhanced interoperability.

Electronic business processes of service chains are in focus throughout planning (modeling level) and operation (execution level). A business process, which defines the control flows of service procurement, is called *service process*. A process object, which represents flow of business data is called *service object*. Within the network structures of service chains, the complexity of service processes is raising. New requirements on service-oriented procurement result from the service definition. Characteristics that add further requirements are *immateriality* and *integrality*. Both determine the specific characteristics of transactions between service providers and service consumers. The use of modern information architectures such as service-oriented architecture (SOA) for the electronic service processes and service e-procurement is promising improvements. Nevertheless, there is still a lack of a precise modeling, analysis and benchmarking approach for these service processes. The efficiency and performance of service processes still has to be improved and cost has to be reduced. Due to the increasing competition and cost pressure in the domain of service procurement, service processes leverage the improvement potential and come to the fore of companies.

This article is focusing on the development of a systematic and structured approach for an integrated analysis and modeling of service processes in service chains. The approach is based on patterns leading to a harmonization and integration of service processes. In consequence, this leverages transparency and structure of service chains. We suggest a formalized modeling method for collaborative service processes in service chains for further improvement. We developed two new patterns, namely, *Service Phase Patterns* and *Service Module Patterns*. Their application is presented based on examples and their advantages are outlined. Our concentration within that is on service e-procurement. The overall research approach is based and evaluated on case studies of a research and standardization project [10].

The remainder of this article is structured as follows: in Section II, the current challenges of service procurement are outlined and the pattern-based modeling approach of *integrated Service Modeling* (*iServMod*) is motivated. An overview of the state of the art in service modeling is shown in Section III. In Section IV, the modeling approach of *iServMod* is presented. Design patterns are proposed and we introduce Petri nets as a formal modeling language. In Section V, the modeling of service objects is demonstrated and Section VI introduces two different design pattern types for service processes. In Section VII, we present the *Service Phase Pattern* (*SPP*) and continue with the pattern of *Service Module Pattern* (*SMP*) in Section VIII. The modeling of Service nets *eSN* is shown in Section IX, and in Section X, the modeling of high-level Service nets *hSN* is described in detail. Based on the modeling of *eSN* and *hSN*, Section XI introduces the *Evolutionary Procedure Model* (*EPM*) for the pattern-based integrated modeling approach. Finally, the use case driven application of *iServMod* in Section XII and final remarks, findings and an outlook on future work in Section XIII conclude this article.

II. Challenges and Motivation

Service chain collaborations achieve economies of scale, economies of scope and lower transaction costs. These collaborations are confronted with several challenges: missing harmonization, integration and standardization of cross-company service processes. Therefore, the creation of new collaborations often suffers from low quality of business interactions caused by integration and transaction costs, manual exception handling, offline communication (media breaks) and long lead times resulting in less transparency and low quality of processes and data. Today's service procurement processes of small and medium-sized companies are mostly defined by heterogeneous and product-oriented business processes [11]. Also, a high amount of manual process tasks and therefore, missing automation can be observed [12].

In contrast to products, services typically require personal interaction and are more difficult to describe and to measure. Therefore, the procurement of services turns out to be particularly complex due to (1) process descriptions, (2) data descriptions, (3) process iterations, (4) unknown result of a service after a service request, and (5) individuality of services. Cross-company process structures are heterogeneous and the process and data flow design are influencing each other: an information asymmetry results out of different proprietary data formats and inconsistent data. Thus, the electronic procurement of services has still not reached a high level of maturity [13]. Inefficiencies result from internal and especially cross-company handling und coordination of transactions and non-harmonized and non-integrated electronic service processes. Service processes must support procedural rules and service logic of required interactions as well as communication between service providers and service consumers [5].

In turn industrial service e-procurement is still a source of high costs because underlying service processes are error prone. Errors and failures occur foremost through the absence of coherent e-business standards and reference frameworks. Together, both could offer meta-models for processes, standardized data objects and interaction patterns for the service logic. Summarized, we observe the following challenges:

- complex collaborative internal and cross-company service process models lead to high opacity, iterations and adjustment costs

- heterogeneous service processes, long running processes and use of different media lead to error-prone process execution
- heterogeneous data structures, different data formats and descriptions lead to non-integration and non-harmonization of data
- heterogeneous *Information Technology* (*IT*) landscapes with different interfaces lead to missing integration
- low maturity level of service process automation lead to long throughput times, redundancy of tasks and source of errors

As stated above, the aforementioned shortcomings result from missing standards in document exchange and lack of information harmonization. In addition, service processes for administrative order processing in service chains did not draw much attention in the past. However, especially these processes require many resources and incorporate long process and throughput times. Existing business process modeling methods for modeling, analysis and implementation of service processes aren`t mature enough and only cover partly the domain-specific needs for service e-procurement. Thus, new methods for the harmonization, integration and standardization have to be established and need to include:

- best practice based definition for improved understanding of service processes and data
- harmonization and integration of service processes and service data
- integration of information systems with support of these service processes and service data

These challenges can be addressed by a formal modeling approach based on domain-oriented design patterns. In this article, we present a new domain-oriented analysis and modeling approach based on the formal modeling language Petri nets. This Petri net based modeling language incorporates design patterns that build upon best practice knowledge as well as an integrated modeling approach for process and data structures. Design patterns provide an immediate benefit (1) by reducing design and integration efforts, (2) by encouraging best practices, (3) by assisting in analysis, (4) by exposing inefficiencies, (5) by removing redundancies, (6) by consolidating interfaces and (7) by encouraging modularity and transparent substitution [14].

A. *Research objectives*

Within this article, we follow paradigms defined in design science. Thus, knowledge can be gained by creation and evaluation of artifacts in the form of models, methods and systems. In contrast to empirical research, the goal is not necessarily to evaluate the validity of research results with respect to their truth, but rather the usefulness of the built artifacts as a tool to solve certain problems [15]. In this spirit, we will impose requirements driven by analysis of service and service e-procurement literature, interviews with domain experts as wells as hypotheses. The requirements analysis will disclose the decisions for the design concept of our planning approach. In contrast to an approach driven by theory, the basis for the design has not necessarily to be formulated as hypothesis. Hence, the planning method will be constructed, implemented and tested in a real environment.

In this article, we propose a model-based approach for the following reasons: information and knowledge must be captured before it can be part of sound analysis and utilization. Informal, semi-formal as well as formal models offer an abstract possibility to represent information and knowledge. Furthermore, graphical representations such as class diagrams, data-flow diagrams, state-transition diagrams or Petri nets ease understanding and exchange between stakeholders, both for the expert and the non-expert. Overall, this facilitates the communication between persons of different domains. In addition, formal languages allow description of certain phenomenon uniquely and precisely, but with a high level of abstraction. In addition, they can be evaluated and verified or be used to automate certain tasks. The goal of this article is the definition of a modeling method, which improves the quality of service chains by a domain-specific modeling approach, linked collaborative, cross-company service processes, hierarchical modeling structures, and precise modeling of processes and data.

B. *Planning and modeling requirements*

Due to these challenges, the modeling of service processes seeks for an adequate and precise integrated modeling approach as well as a precise system design for information systems. So far, no adequate modeling approach based on a modeling language that focusses the domain-specific context of service e-procurement is existing. Furthermore, a modeling approach for system design should be based on a formal modeling language to enable the following advantages [16]:

- adequate concept for the representation of domain-specific description of data and control flow,
- formal semantics of electronic business processes due to a formalized syntax,
- uniqueness of syntax and graphical descriptions for an easy understanding,
- expressiveness for a precise system modeling,
- mathematical foundation for the evaluation and sound proof of system design,
- analysis of information systems for properties like deadlocks, performance or the correctness of information systems,
- interoperability and vendor independence of the modeling language to support different modeling and analysis tools, and consideration of
- static and dynamic elements in service processes to describe the control flow and data flow.

III. State of the Art

Scientific literature reveals several approaches for service procurement with different emphasis and granularity. *FlexNet Architect* [17] offers reusable modules for the scenario-based modeling of hybrid value creation. For planning and modeling of hybrid value creation networks, the cooperation definition, actors, areas and information flows can be modeled. The *HyproDesign* [18] modeling language was developed for modeling customer-specific configurations and calculations of hybrid bundles of services and is based on a meta-model to describe variants and configurations. Single modules are described as semantic models via *Entity Relationship diagrams* [19]. Winkelmann and Luczak [20] propose a Petri net-based approach for the cooperative supply of industrial services by using *colored Petri nets* (*CPN*) [21]. Becker and Neumann [22] define central components like processes and activities, technical objects, contacts and service offers based on data models for the order transaction of technical services. Che et al. [23] are using *XML nets* [24] for modeling, execution and monitoring of cross-company business processes. Mevius and Pibernik [25] propose XML nets for the support of business processes for the *Supply Chain Process Management* (*SCPM*). Each of these approaches considers certain aspects of the description of services and service processes. However, none of them represents a comprehensive model for the description of service objects and service processes for industrial services based on a formalized approach. For the modeling of collaborative service processes and service objects in service transactions of service e-procurement, none of these approaches takes domain-specific characteristics of service processes for service e-procurement into account.

IV. Integrated Modeling Approach for Service Modeling *iServMod*

To meet the challenges and requirements described before, an integrated modeling approach based on a formal modeling language considering the domain-specific context of service procurement will be presented in this article. The integrated modeling approach *integrated Service Modeling* (*iServMod*) is based on Petri nets [26]. We use domain-specific extensions to Petri nets which will serve as a basis for a detailed and precise modeling of service processes (design time) to integrate service processes on the execution level (run time). In a first step, the modeling of *service objects* as static components of data schemas is presented. *Service nets* as dynamic components of business processes are developed: *Service nets* (*eSN*) are defined on basis of place/transition nets. In a second step, *high-level service nets* (*hSN*) based on XML nets are developed. This formal modeling approach will promote the following advantages:

- *increased transparency in service chains*: service processes lack transparency due to individual internal service processes of service providers and service providers.
- *precise modeling of collaborative service processes and data flow*: the precise modeling of service processes and service objects serves as a basis for high quality documentation and analysis. With an adequate modeling approach, internal service processes can be modeled separately and put together in service process models.
- *analysis of service processes*: application of analysis methods for the quantitative and qualitative evaluation of service process models serve as a basis for benchmarking.
- *integration of domain-specific context*: integration of service e-procurement context for its integration into information systems.
- *support of modeling and execution layers*: the modeling and the execution of service processes rounds up the comprehensive analysis of service process models.

Such a modeling approach results in improved efficiency (performance) and productivity of the service processes due to (1) the reduction of process costs, (2) reduction of process times, (3) reduction of process throughput time, (4) the improvement of process quantity, (5) improvement of process transparency, and (6) the increase of process flexibility.

A. Modeling concepts

Based on modeling concepts, service processes and corresponding service objects can gradually be modeled in a top-down approach – thus in detail and on a higher level of abstraction. This allows stepwise transformation of service processes into different formalization stages and enables hierarchical scaling and modularization. For the modeling of different formalized service processes, the *screen model* [27] serves as a modeling concept for Petri nets (see Figure 1).

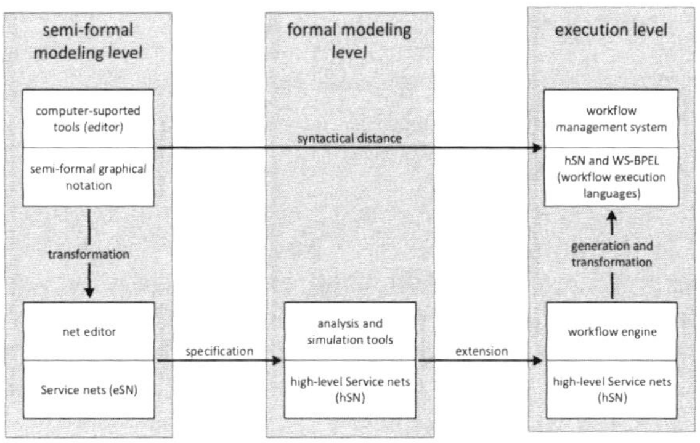

Figure 1. Screen model for gradual transformation of abstraction levels

This modeling concept supports four different modeling language types, beginning with informal modeling languages up to programming modeling language types for an automated execution (such as XML nets [24]). The screen model defines a gradual conversion of different formalization level of Petri net variants. Therefore, modeling languages used in our approach can be classified into four different groups:

- application-oriented, informal modeling languages support the documentation and visualization of business processes. Petri nets can be used to describe the implicit domain knowledge. The process models are described colloquially.
- application-neutral, semi-formal modeling languages provide more structure and a higher abstraction level due to a partial formalization of the business process models. Petri nets can be used to describe more detailed process models.
- formal, platform-independent modeling languages enable to model precise models by their power of description logic. Process models can be analyzed for the validation and plausibility checks. High-level Petri nets with individual tokens enable a precise and individual description of process and data concepts.
- machine-readable programming languages support the automated execution of business processes on the execution level. Service processes with integrated choreography and orchestration of web services can be automated. Web Service nets as extension of XML nets can be used and be transformed into executable code in WS-BPEL to call web services [28],[29].

The hierarchical and modular modeling of service processes is supported by the *layer model* [28]. The layer model supports the modeling of service processes on four different abstraction levels. In addition, modelers are guided from specific process phases to detailed service process descriptions within a top-down approach to describe a coordinated realization of service processes on the execution level. Thus, the overall structure of service processes will be improved by the hierarchical modeling layers. Software architectures based on the concept of service-oriented architectures may also be developed by means of such a hierarchical structure.

Service processes can be gradually refined. On a higher and abstract modeling level, a choreography is composed by several service process phases. The choreography resides on the highest level of abstraction and defines the logic of service processes. It is data driven and determines the order of lower level process phases. While the capsulated service processes are modeled by process phases on higher abstraction levels, distributed capsulated service processes are represented by process modules on a detailed level. Process modules incorporate complex electronic processes. These processes are implemented based on web service interfaces and thus can be orchestrated. Overall, from choreography to electronic processes on the lowest modeling layer, the logic consequence is the implementation of a service-oriented architecture. While process phases consist of process modules, they are linked by internal and cross-company process interfaces – which can be implemented by web services. Process modules encapsulate service processes and partial service processes.

Within service chains, a choreography of process phases serves as a link between distinct orchestrations of process modules and service processes. A combination of these coordination patterns process phases and process modules leads to (1) a choreography of process phases driven by the data exchange and (2) to the orchestration of their internal service processes. This results in a global, cross-company service process. In the domain of service e-procurement, service providers and service consumers collaborate for the execution of a procurement transaction. The choreography is being used to define the overall service process out of several orchestrated service processes with supervision of different process participants. Within our approach, the interaction of partners based on exchanged data can be pre-described and the order of is pre-defined. This results in valid orders of exchanged data. This approach defines the basis for agreements and contracts to define the necessary process interfaces in complex Business-to-Business (B2B) scenarios for the domain of service e-procurement.

B. Petri Net based modeling of service processes

Petri nets are a formal modeling language to describe, analyze, simulate and execute distributed, discrete systems. A Petri net is a based on a mathematical definition. Petri nets are bipartite graphs (consisting of the node types place and transition). They allow to capture static and dynamic characteristics of systems (by the concept of tokens). With different extensions to basic Petri nets, the modeling of different levels of formalization (precision) can also be accomplished. As a result, Petri nets may even be used for application-oriented, informal and semi-formal modeling. Besides the modeling of static and dynamic aspects, Petri nets offer to model limited capacities of places and anonymous tokens for modeling process objects.

With Petri nets allow to model typical process patterns such as sequence, iteration, alternative, concurrency, synchronization and further complex patterns as well as their combination. Dynamic properties like liveness, reachability, and soundness can be formally analyzed [30]. Petri nets are graphically represented by *tokens* (process objects), *places* (conditions), *transitions* (nodes for events) and *directed arcs* (arrows). Places are containers for tokens and pre- or post-conditions for transitions. Places represent local conditions and are static process components. Transitions are dynamic components and represent local state transitions [31]. For a formal, platform-independent and machine-readable modeling approach and an automated execution of business processes (execution level), *high-level Petri nets* allow a precise description of individualized tokens as well as the definition and formalization of further domain-specific process elements [32].

C. Design pattern

A *pattern* is a discernible regularity and the elements of a pattern repeat in a predictable manner. Patterns are an abstraction of a concrete form and define a static structure, which was recognized due to its identical re-appearing [33]. Thus, patterns represent best practice solutions to common problems and are a result of experiences and behavioral observation. They represent identical modes of thought, design fashions, behaviors or courses of action, which can be repeated and reproduced. Patterns can be observed in a lot of domains, maybe at first recognized in the domain of architecture. *Software design patterns* are introduced in the domain of software engineering. They are a general solution to solve a problem in programming. A design pattern provides a reusable architectural outline that may speed up the development of many computer programs [34]. It is considered as a recurrent solution template for software architecture and software development [35].

Design patterns [36] represent solutions to common design problems in a given context and improve software quality substantially. This can also help to reduce development costs. *Creational patterns* are used for the creation of objects independent of concrete implementation. *Structural patterns* support the design of software by providing templates for relations between classes. *Behavioral patterns* model the complex behavior of software and are used to increase flexibility. Nowadays, design patterns are widely used since they capture and promote best practices in software design like patterns for software engineering from Gamma et al. [34] and patterns for the enterprise integration scenarios of software applications from Hohpe and Woolf [37].

Business process design patterns describe business process models in a certain domain being harmonized with best practices. These patterns are also based on empirical knowledge how process activities should be executed. Business process design patterns are formalizing common structures of activities of process and data flows [38]. They are characterized by situations in courses of business and problems of the realization of modeling languages and implementation solutions [34]. Barros et al. [39] define bilateral and multilateral service interaction patterns, which allow emerging mechanisms such as choreography and orchestration to be benchmarked. Domain-oriented design patterns offer a flexible architecture with clear boundaries in terms of well-defined and highly encapsulated parts being aligned with the natural constraints of the considered domain [40].

D. Petri net based process patterns

As a well-established modeling language, Petri nets enable an integrated modeling of process and data structures. Additionally, analysis of software-based execution of business processes can easily be implemented with Petri nets. Van der Aalst and ter Hofstede [41] define fundamental *Workflow patterns* based on Petri nets to formalize requirements of workflow management and information systems. These patterns are further distinguished into *exception handling patterns*, *control flow patterns*, *data flow patterns* and *resource patterns*. Further existing examples for Petri net process patterns are *TimeNET* [42], a software tool to model, analyze and control manufacturing systems based on colored Petri nets, *EXSPECT* [43], a repository of tool for standardized business processes in logistics and production or *CIMOSA* [44], the modeling and analysis of cross-company value chains. To formally model supply chains as business processes with an integrated sense and respond capability, Liu et al. [45] are using Petri nets to define basic patterns of supply chains. Schuster [33] proposes resource assignment patterns and defines higher-level resource nets for improved support of these patterns.

V. Modeling of Service Objects

Service objects describe object-oriented components, which are being handled within service processes. Service objects literally are data objects, which describe central *service* master data and transaction data. These data either characterizes a service consumer or service provider, materials, business documents, a service specification, a service order, a service invoice or any other service-relevant document needed for service transactions of service e-procurement. Hence, service objects represent input, intermediate and output objects of service processes. They convey economically relevant data, which is transformed, created or simply needed as execution support in electronic service processes (also known as service workflows).

As graphical modeling representation, service objects can be modeled with the *XML schema model* (*XSM*) [24]. *XSM* can be utilized as modeling construct to describe object structures in XML nets. *XSM* serves as a formal object description method to describe complex object structures in conjunction with organizational processes. Data structures in XML nets are associated with places to integrate them in the process flow. In this fashion, places combine structured service objects with a common schema (typification of places). The modeling constructs of XML schema models are element types represented by type classes and dependencies represented by association types. As an example, the service object *industrial service description* is shown in Figure 2. The example reveals a complex data structure, which can be applied in XML nets to describe typical objects in industrial service processes.

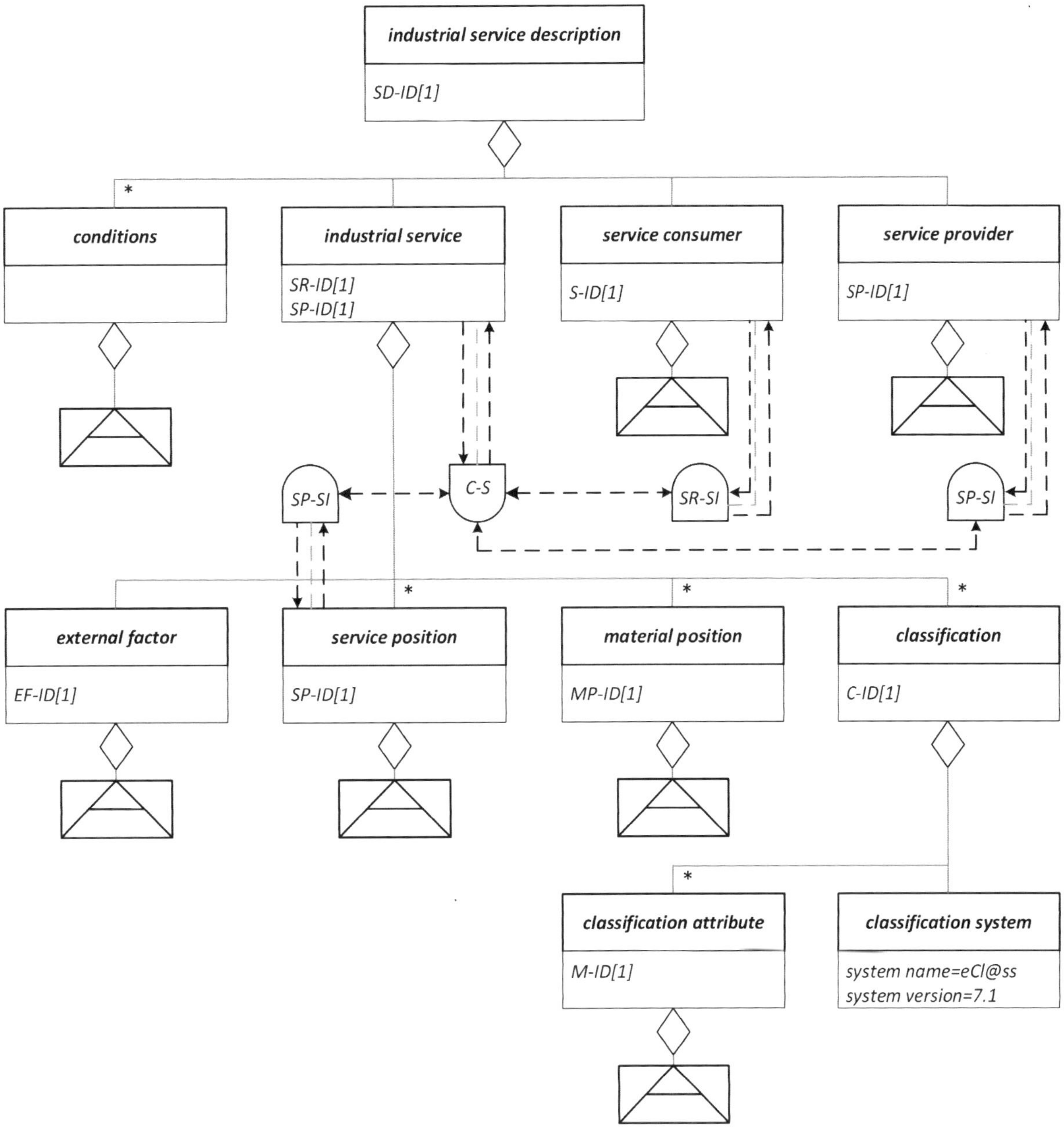

Figure 2. Service object industrial *service description*

VI. Service Process Design Patterns

In the domain of service procurement, service providers and service consumers collaborate in a concrete instance of a service procurement process model. An instance of a service process model again is defined as choreography of specific service phases and comprises internal and cross-company service processes and service modules. The order of exchanged messages is predefined. Choreography is used to define a cross-company service process out of several independently orchestrated service processes (see Figure 3). The interaction between several partners for the procurement of services based on the exchanged data is described [46]. Only valid orders of data between partners may be defined.

Based on our review of scientific literature [47] and empirical case studies [49], we derive new patterns for service e-procurement, which represent best practice of service procurement processes. We introduce the design patterns *Service Phase Patterns* (*SPP*) and *Service Module Patterns* (*SMP*) which support the development of software architectures based on service-oriented architecture. These patterns define hierarchic structures and provide a structured concept for the modeling and implementation phase of service procurement process models. *SPP* and *SMP* ensure and precisely describe the order of message exchange and interaction in bilateral and multilateral service chains and constitute required process interfaces.

Service processes between service providers and service consumers are characterized by highly collaborative service processes. The collaboration is defined by specific process and data flows based on specific process interfaces. It can be observed that typical recurrent service procurement process models are characterized by a specific order of data flow and by specific service procurement types. These recurrent orders of process and data flow defining service procurement types can be described by patterns.

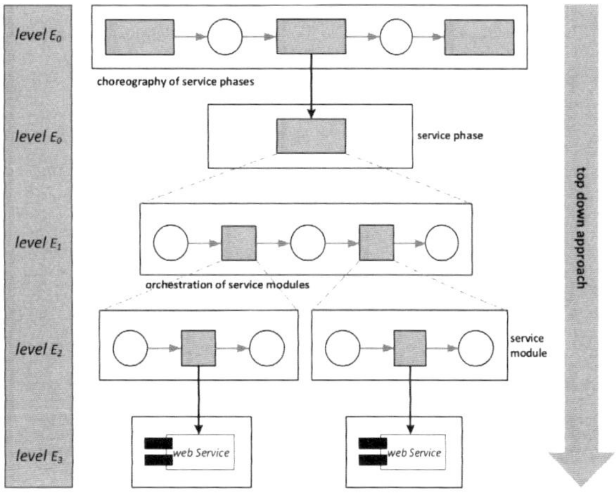

Figure 3. Choreography of service phases and orchestration of service modules on different abstraction levels

A sequence of *SPP* includes data flow, complex service processes and web services. *SPP* consist of *SMP* and are linked by internal and cross-company process interfaces. The choreography of *SPP* serves as a connector between orchestrations of *SMP* and their internal service processes. A concrete sequence of *SMP* is pre-defined. The combination of *SPP* and *SMP* results into global, cross-company service processes, which define the interaction of internal service processes accordantly. The pattern-based application using *SPP* and *SMP* leads to a top-down approach from specific process phases down to detailed service process descriptions, executed by web services. The pattern-based approach enables a coordinated realization of service processes in information systems at the execution level. In a first modeling and description approach of service e-procurement process descriptions, we use Petri nets as modeling language to describe domain-specific service phase patterns and service module patterns. Based on this definition, we further develop these patterns based on XML nets [49], a high-level Petri net variant.

VII. Service Phase Pattern (SPP) for the Choreography of Process Flow and Data Flow

The best practice for procurement of services is based on service procurement types. Service procurement types are characterized by a specific order of service process phases and a specific data flow to represent and manage cross-company interaction. A service procurement type pre-defines a service process model, which represents a specific process flow occurrence for service procurement. The following service procurement types can be defined:

- A planned need of a service is required and a frame contract doesn't exist.
- A non-planned need of service is required and a frame contract doesn't exist.
- A planned need of a service is required and a frame contract exists.
- A non-planned need of service is required and a frame contract exists.

Based on the identified procurement types, we define a new pattern. *Service Phase Pattern* (*SPP*) are further introduced and described, the modeling support is presented, a definition is given and the composition and syntactical compatibility definition and as well as an example provided.

A. Pattern description

A standard pattern-based formal modeling approach based on best practice for service procurement has not been provided yet. Recurring service process phases as well as the validation of the correct order of service processes and service data for service process phases are not supported. The pattern offers the description of service procurement types by a choreography of service phases based on data flow. The valid composition of service process phases is ensured by the syntactical compatibility. The logic of process flow instances is determined as well. *SPP* are characterized by capsulated service procurement processes on a higher abstraction level.

B. Modeling support

This pattern can be modeled by Petri nets and high-level Petri nets and can be integrated into Petri net-based and high-level Petri net-based service processes. To support the pattern-based modeling approach, a domain-specific modeling extension for service process phases is necessary to support modelers in the design phase.

C. Service Phase Pattern definition

SPP are transition-bounded service processes and are represented in a Petri net as a single transition, which can be extended to sub nets. *Service places* are defined by a set of service object-specific places, which are classified into *service object places SO, static and dynamic service interface places SI* and *service document places SD* (see Figure 4).

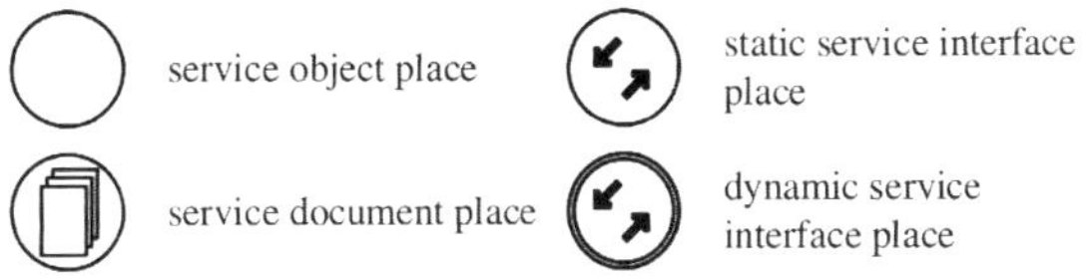

Figure 4. Service object specified places *SO*, *SD* and *SI*

SPP represent a self-contained set of cross-company collaborative service processes. *SPP* are connected by cross company interfaces defined by service object-specific interface places *SI* and *SD*. *SPP* are represented graphically by a rectangle, which includes the service phase name (see Figure 5).

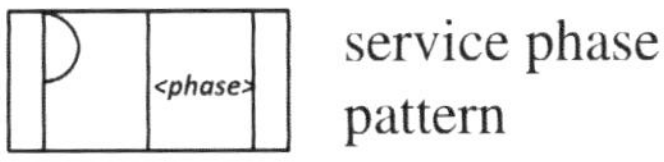

Figure 5. SPP modeled as Petri net

Domain-specific concepts for a formal modeling approach of service processes in the context of service e-procurement are also formalized based on high-level Petri nets. The transfer of the presented formalized concepts further enables communication and information context. *SPP* are further developed into formalized patterns based on high-level Petri nets with individualized and distinguishable tokens representing the service e-procurement-specific data transfer in information systems. Specific interfaces in collaborative and cross-company service processes represented by service process phases are identified, formalized and defined as patterns based on high-level Petri nets. The set of service object-specific places *SPS* are typified as object containers for service processes and defined as a coarsened XML net. *SPS* represent the complex data flow based on XML service objects to define the data and document exchange in collaborative cross-company service processes. The set of typified service object-specific places *SPS* is further distinguished into the set of service object places *SSO*, service interface places *SSI* and service document places *SSD*. The domain specific stereo types of *SPP* are proposed. *SPP* based on XML nets represent coarsened structures of capsulated service processes and *SMP*. *SPP* are defined based on specific, typified input and output places and also represent process patterns. *SPP* are defined based on the process and data flow of collaborative service e-procurement processes and consider the specific phases.

D. Composition and syntactical compatibility

In case of a composition of two service phases $t^i_{sp_a}$ and $t^i_{sp_b}$, input and output places are melted. The set of *TSP* is defined as single transitions of transition bounded sub XML nets $XN'=(S',T',F')$ and service process modules $t^i_{SM} \in TSM$. The syntactical compatibility is a requirement for the composition of *SPP*. The syntactical compatibility postulates that each interface of *SPP* is an output place S^{OUT}_{SP} of a *SPP* $t^i_{sp_i}$ and an input place S^{IN}_{SP} of a *SPP* $t^i_{sp_j}$. Syntactically compatible *SPP* do not necessary have completely overlapped interfaces. While the interfaces of two *SMP* during a composition are melted, the common non-empty subset of interfaces is modeled. A mandatory condition for the syntactical compatibility is the partly overlapping of interfaces. The partly overlapping of interfaces is also a sufficient condition for *SPP*.

E. Example

Based on a specific service procurement type, *SPP* can be configured to choreograph the data flow and process flow (see Figure 6).

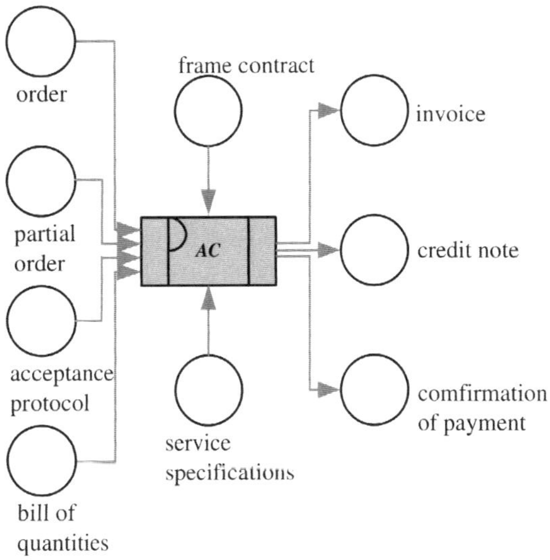

Figure 6. *SPP* example Accounting *AC* modeled as an XML net

Figure 7 shows the example of the pattern of the service phase *Accounting AC*. *SPP* are formally defined as the set *TSP* based on single transitions with dedicated service object-specific places. The sets of input places S^{IN}_{SO} and output places S^{OUT}_{SO} are assigned and consist of the sets of service object places *SSO*, service interface places *SSI* and service document places *SSD*. Each service phase $t^i_{sp_j}$ is defined by its internal structure, which enables the composition of service phases.

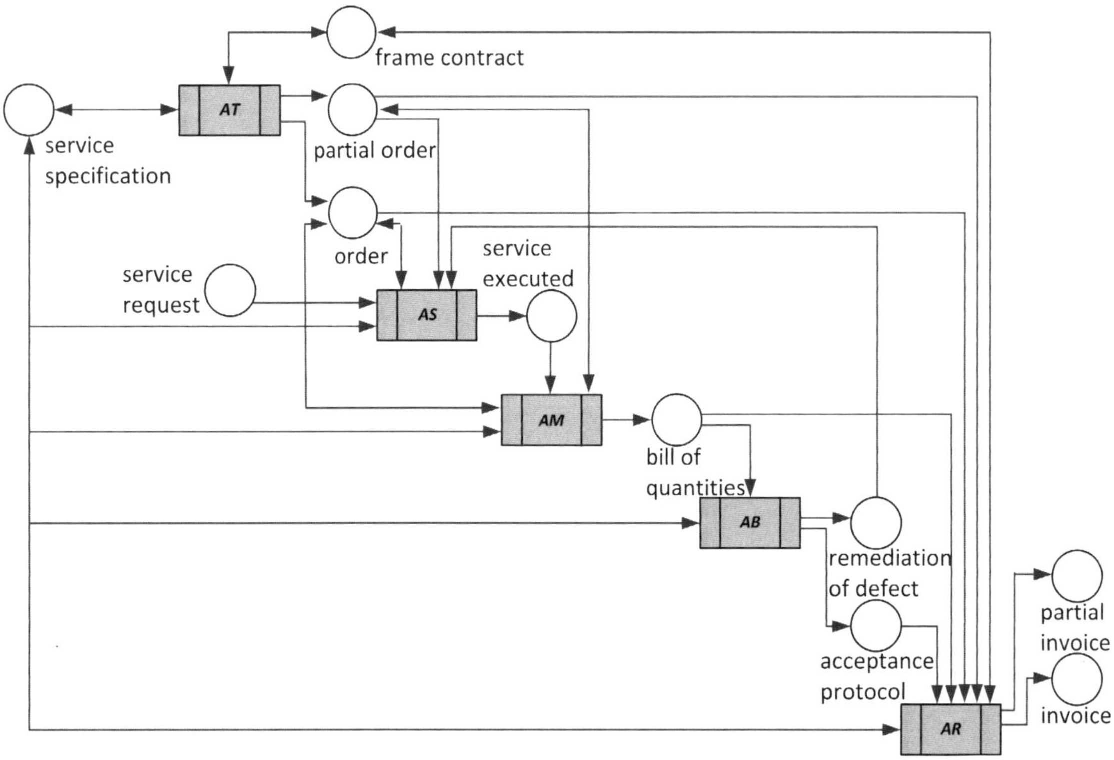

Figure 7. Service procurement type as choreography of *SPP* modeled as Petri net

F. *Advantages of SPP*

SPP enable a pre-defined data flow. The order of exchanged data is prescribed for the definition of domain-specific standard for the interaction and data exchange for partners [50]. The definition of specific data and process sequences provides the basis for required process interfaces in complex B2B scenarios. Hence, *SPP* for service processes of service procurement process models enable the following advantages:

- *SPP* choreograph service procurement phases and data flow and therefore, they define recurring process flow and data flow orders based on best practice in service procurement.
- *SPP* are defined patterns for the service procurement phases specification, request, quotation, order, execution, measurement, acceptance and accounting.
- *SPP* configure best practice service procurement types.
- *SPP* enable a pre-defined data flow. The order of exchanged data is prescribed for the definition of domain-specific standard for the interaction and data exchange for partners [50]. The definition of specific data and process sequences provides the basis for required process interfaces in complex B2B scenarios.

VIII. Service Module Pattern (SMP) for the Orchestration of Process Flow and Data Flow

Service procurement transactions and service processes are developed in a collaborative way: service providers and service consumers interact closely. Service processes and single service sub processes are characterized by a service provider or a service consumer. Based on service process phases, we define a new pattern. *Service Module Pattern* (*SMP*) are further introduced and described, the modeling support is presented, a definition is given and the composition and syntactical compatibility definition and as well as an example provided.

A. *Pattern description*

A standard pattern-based formal modeling approach based on best practice collaborative service processes in the domain of service procurement has not been provided yet. Recurring service processes as well as a collaborative and modularized modeling approach based on the process participants for service processes are not supported. The pattern offers the description of collaborative service processes and service sub processes by the orchestration of service modules based on data flow. The valid composition of service process modules is ensured by the syntactical compatibility. The predefined order of recurring service phases can be further structured into detailed service modules.

These patterns of detailed service modules describe a recurring process and data flow characterized by specific process interfaces. *SMP* are characterized by capsulated electronic service processes. *SMP* define orchestrations of their internal capsulated service processes. The process and data flow is orchestrated. The activities of these service processes are executed by web services for the horizontal and vertical integration of different information systems. One of the main characteristics of *SMP* is collaboration: the collaborative service process of a process participant is further capsulated into service modules.

B. *Modeling support*

This pattern can be modeled by Petri nets and high-level Petri nets and can be integrated into Petri net-based and high-level Petri net-based service processes. To support the pattern-based modeling approach, a domain-specific modeling extension for service processes is necessary to support modelers in the design phase.

C. *Service Module Pattern definition*

Collaborative *SMP* are transition-bounded service processes and are represented in a Petri net as a single transition, which can be extended to sub nets. *SMP* are defined as self-contained collaborative service processes of one collaboration participant (service provider or service consumer). *SMP* are represented graphically by a rectangle, which includes the specific service phase name as well as the participant of the service process (see Figure 8). The set of *SI* and *SD* are input and output places of *SMP*.

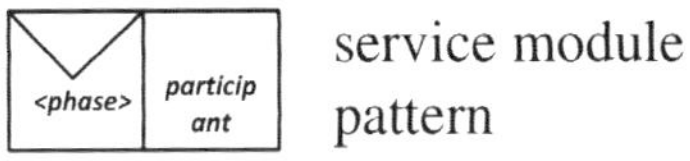

Figure 8. SMP modeled as Petri net

SMP are defined based on high level Petri nets. *SMP* represent coarsened collaborative service processes of one process participant. The collaborative service process consists out of several *SMP* representing all process participants and therefore, the entire service process of a *SPP*. *SMP* are connected via a set of input and output places *SPS* to model bidirectional interaction and communication patterns like *sending* and *receiving*. The internal structure of a *SMP* is built by a coarsened service net and consists out of a set of internal input and output places (S_{SM}^{IN}, S_{SM}^{OUT}) and internal transitions. The set of input and output places is defined as an internal *module interface* of a *SMP*. The internal structure of a *SMP* fulfills the requirements of a workflow net [51] and soundness criteria [52]. A *SMP* interface $S_{sm_1}^{IN/OUT}$ of one *SMP* t_{sm}^1 can be melted with the *SMP* interface $S_{sm_2}^{IN/OUT}$ of another *SMP* t_{sm}^2. The set of *SMP TSM* is defined as single transition of a transition-bounded sub XML net *XN'=(S',T',F')* as part of an XML net and dedicated to one *SPP* of the set of *SPP TSP*. The composition of *SMP* causes the melting of the common set of interface places.

D. *Composition and syntactical compatibility*

The syntactical compatibility of *SMP* enable the composition of *SMP*. Syntactically compatible *SMP* have completely overlapping process interfaces. The syntactical compatibility postulates that each module interface of *SPP* is an output place S_{SM}^{OUT} of a *SPP* $t_{sm_i}^1$ and an input place S_{SM}^{IN} of a *SPP* $t_{sm_j}^2$. For every output place, it exists a corresponding input place. Syntactically compatible *SMP* have completely overlapped interfaces. While the interfaces of two *SMP* are melted during a composition, the common non-empty subset of interfaces is modeled. A mandatory condition for the syntactical compatibility is the partly overlapping of interfaces. The completely overlapping of interfaces is also a sufficient condition for *SMP*.

E. *Example*

Based on a specific *SPP*, a capsulated service process can be further detailed into *SMP* to orchestrate the data flow and process flow (see Figure 9). The input place $S_{sm_1}^{IN_1}$ and the output place $S_{sm_1}^{OUT_1}$ of service process hSN'_{sm_1} and hSN'_{sm_2} of a *SMP* are melted and create a common internal place S_{sm_3}.

F. *Advantages of SMP*

SMP for service procurement processes enable the following advantages:

- *SMP* orchestrate the process flow and data flow and therefore, they define recurring collaborative service processes based on best practice in service procurement.
- *SMP* define patterns for the detailed service procurement processes *specification*, *request*, *quotation*, *order*, *execution*, *measurement*, *acceptance* and *accounting*.
- *SMP* enable a modularization concept for modeling and implementing collaborative service processes. The defined activities can be further modeled and implemented by web services.

IX. Service Nets eSN

For the modeling of *eSN*, we utilize *place/transition nets (P/T nets)* to support initial modeling phases. Places and tokens of these nets represent the current status of a service chain. In addition, we define domain-specific process interface place types and process transition types to standardize the modeling approach. Static interface places between service processes and dynamic interface places for capsulated interface processes are defined.

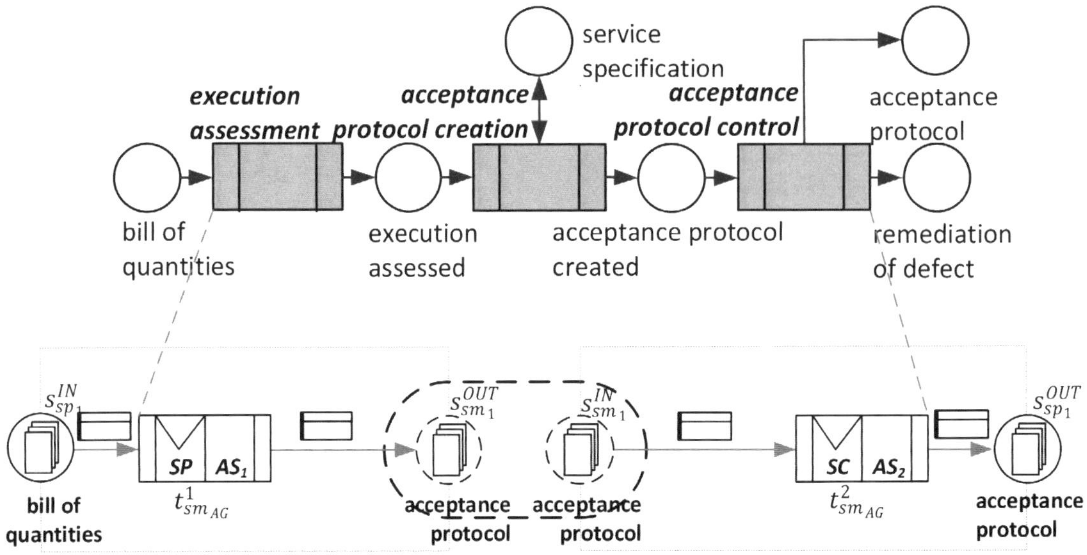

Figure 9. Composition of *SMP* modeled as an XML net

Therefore, we define the interface place types *service object places (SO)*, *service interface places (SS)* and *service document places (SD)*. *SO* places are containers for general service objects. *SS* places are internal and cross-company interfaces for the data flow. *SD* places serve as containers for service document types. For transition concepts, *Service Phase Patterns* are defined to reflect the specific process phases in service procurement.

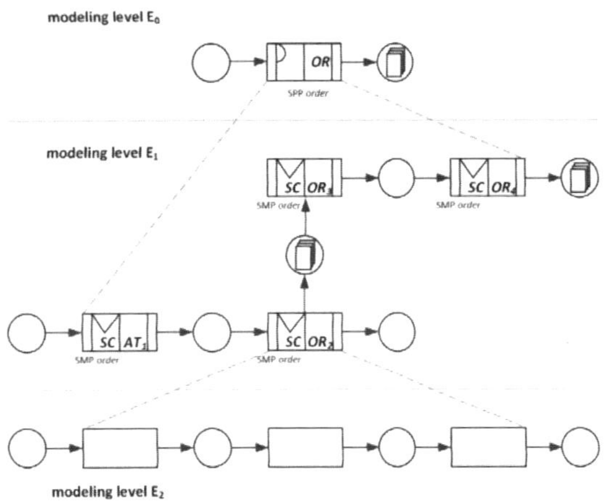

Figure 10. Hierarchic structuring of service processes

Service Module Patterns represent service processes of a collaboration participant (service provider or service consumer). *SPP* and *SMP* represent both a black box for sub-processes, which can be modeled separately in further detailed service processes. A *SPP* consists out of several *SMP*. *SPP* and *SMP* represent and apply hierarchical modeling concepts to support the layer model. In an early modeling stage, *SPP* and *SMP* act as a place holder for concrete service processes, which can be modeled at a later point of time. These internal (private) service processes are modeling by using pools. Specific *SMP* are assigned to *SPP* to structure service processes and organize them into a hierarchy (see Figure 10). As an example, a single collaborative service process between a service provider and a service consumer is shown in Figure 11.

X. High-Level Service Nets hSN

The use of P/T net concepts accompanies a couple of disadvantages: the semantic correctness cannot be checked, domain-specific modeling constructs are not supported, communication and information concepts are not designed, the structured hierarchical modeling is not supported and tokens cannot be specified individually. Thus, we introduce modeling extensions of *eSN* with transfer to high-level Service nets based on XML nets with individual tokens. High-level Service nets (*hSN*) are based on XML. Operational sequences and the data flow are based on XML, tokens are represented by complex structured XML objects. All activities correspond to operations on XML documents. *hSN* are characterized by domain-specific extensions, and individual tokens. Furthermore, within *hSN*, the phases of service chains are standardized.

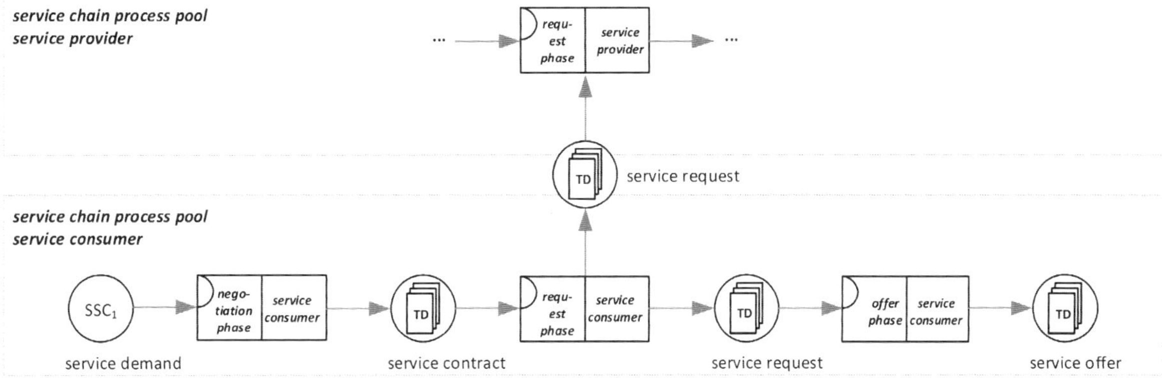

Figure 11. Single collaborative service process with pools of service provider and service consumer

A high-level Service net *hSN* is defined as follows:

A Service net is defined as a tuple $hSN = (S, SSO, SSI, SSD, T, TSP, TSM, F, \Phi, I_S, I_T, I_F, I_{SSO}, I_{SSI}, I_{SSD}, M_0)$, where

1. $XN = (S, T, F, \Phi, I_S, I_T, I_F, M_0)$ is an XML net.
2. $\Phi = (\mathrm{E}, \mathrm{FKT}, \mathrm{PRE})$ is a structure consisting of a non-empty and finite individual set E of Φ, a set of formula and term functions FKT defined on E, and a set of predicates PRE defined on E.
3. The set of places is structured in the sets process object places SPO and service object specific places SPS. The set of SPS is further structured in the sets of service object places SSO, service interface places SSI and service document places SSD.
4. The set of transitions is structured in the sets of process activities TPA and service process activities TPS. The set of TPS contains of *SPPs* TSP and *SMPs* TSM. The set of TPS is defined as a real set of transitions T: $TPS \subseteq T$.
5. I_{SSO} is the function that assigns a valid XML schema as a place typification to each place $s_{so} \in SSO$.
6. I_{SSI} is the function that assigns a valid XML schema as a place typification to each place $s_{si_s} \in SSI$.
7. I_{SSD} is the function that assigns a valid XML schema of a service documents type j as a place typification to each place $s_{sd_j} \in SSD$.
8. I_T is the function that assigns a predicate logical expression as inscription to each transition on a given structure Φ and the set of variables, which are contained on all adjacent arcs.
9. I_F is the function that assigns a valid XSLT expression to each arc, which is conform to the adjacent XML scheme.

Electronic service processes and their data flow can be precisely modeled, analyzed, simulated, executed and maintained. For the process interface place types, places are typified based on the domain-specific context. *SPP* are represented by coarsened transitions with capsulated service processes based on *SMP*. *SMP* are also coarsened transitions and contain capsulated service processes of one process participant (internal service process). A *SMP* is defined by an internal structure and communicates with other modules based on process interface places. *SPP* and *SMP* contains typified input and output places *SO*, *SS* and *SD*. *SPP* are defined with specific typified places. The *SPP offer* ($t_{sp_{AG}}$) is modularized by two *SMPs* (Figure 12).

The service process consists of the service process hSN'_{sm_1} of the *SMP* $t^1_{sm_{AG}}$ and hSN'_{sm_2} of the *SMP* $t^2_{sm_{AG}}$. hSN'_{sm_1} of the service provider is modeled as an XML net. The representation of XML filter schemes FS_i, transition inscriptions TI_i and place type definition ST_i are not modeled. The service process of the service requester is represented by the *SMP* $t^2_{sm_{AG}}$. The place $s^{IN_1}_{sp_1}$ and the place $s^{OUT_1}_{sp_1}$ are the in- and output of hSN. The input place $s^{IN_1}_{sm_1}$ ($s^{IN_1}_{sp_1}$) and the output place $s^{OUT_1}_{sm_1}$ as the input place $s^{IN_1}_{sm_2}$ and the output place $s^{OUT_1}_{sm_1}$ ($s^{OUT_1}_{sp_2}$) are module interface places of the *SMP*.

A. *Modeling of distributed service processes based on SOA*

Service processes can be modeled as dynamic interface processes and be executed by web services in *service-oriented architectures (SOA)*. *iServMod* supports the modeling and analysis of distributed service processes based on web services by *Web Service nets (WSN)* [53]. A web service is considered as an implementation of a local service process (interface process). A distributed service process can be realized by the composition of web services. Input and output messages represent the data flow in Web Service nets.

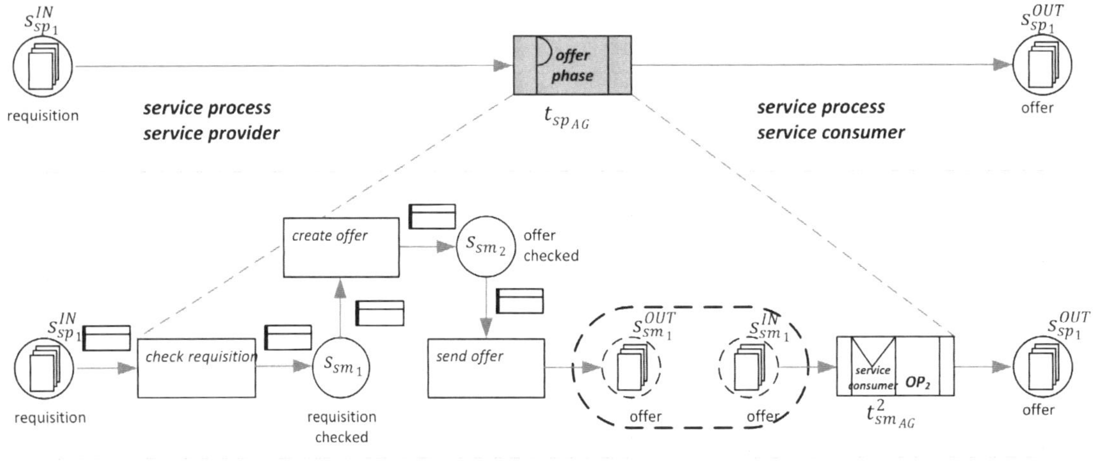

Figure 12. Modularization of a *SPP* by a *SMP*

Web Service nets also support the composition concepts like the orchestration and choreography. The example *service process validation of incorrect orders* is models as an abstract Web Service net with web service selection (Figure 13).

B. *Transformation and execution of Web Service Nets*

Based on the precise modeling of all aspects of service processes with Web Service nets, *Web Service Business Process Execution Language* (*WS-BPEL*) elements can be derived to use standardized web service technologies like interface description (*WSDL*), protocols (*SOAP*) and mechanisms for service discovery.

Web service process models [54] can be modeled and the transformation of Web Service nets into executable WS-BPEL code is based on control flow and data flow structures. An XML-based notation and semantics for the description of the behavior of service processes enrich Web Service nets based on web service calls. In this context, the WS-BPEL model is called *web service process model*. A web service or several web services describe the behavior and the interaction of process instances, process participants and resources using web service interface places of the Web Service net. Specific structures and elements can be identified and transformed into equivalent XML and WS-BPEL structures. A detailed transformation of Web Service net structures into WS-BPEL code with a transformation algorithm is defined in [29].

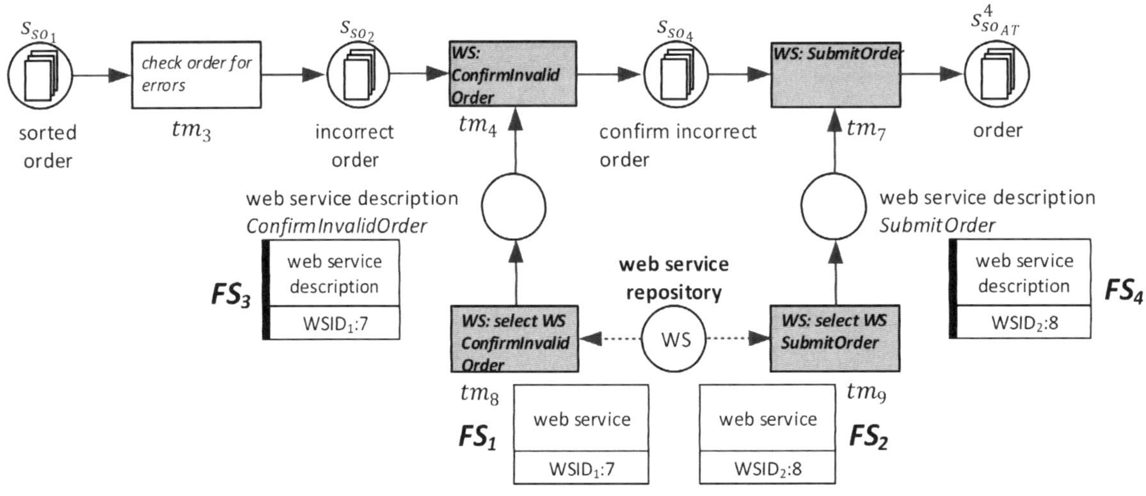

Figure 13. Web Service net with web service selection

XI. Evolutionary Procedure Model for the Integrated Modeling of Service Processes

We propose the *Evolutionary Procedure Model* (*EPM*) for the development of process-oriented information systems based on service processes. *EPM* is structuring the development and the application of the integrated modeling method *iServMod* for the domain service e-procurement. *EPM* incorporates the developed methods, models and modeling concepts of the integration service modeling approach. The evolutionary procedure model consists out of several phases, which can be aggregated to the main phases modeling, model analysis and implementation. The phases of the *EPM* are presented (Figure 14).

A. *Project initialization*

The phase project initialization defines and plans a project for the development of an information systems. The scope of the project is defined, the involved organization and teams are identified. The project parameters project budget, available resources, and temporal frame conditions are defined and a project plan is created. The project-specific targets are determined and are prioritized. As a first step, a process landscape is created, which represents the topmost hierarchical layer for a service process model for the gradual modeling of service processes.

Single service processes are graphically represented amongst their reciprocities. The modeling language group of application-oriented, informal modeling language is used. On an abstract level, relevant service processes are represented by single transitions and their relations based on places, which represent interfaces.

B. *Functional modeling design*

The existing service processes are modeled in a semi-formal way. For the adequate modeling of process instances, a detailed process structure of service process models is developed. Interfaces and data objects are identified and described. The description of service processes is based on an informal modeling level in a first modeling round. As applications-oriented, informal modeling language, Service nets can be used. The explicit interface description is a central modeling aspect. Interfaces are defined as input and output places, which represent input service objects and output service objects. Roles and resources are identified and assigned to transitions. For the functional modeling design, roles and resources are annotated and modeled by resource places. Resources are represented as anonymous, non-typified tokens in places.

C. *Detailed modeling design*

The service processes are modeled top-down on different abstraction layers based on detailed levels. The layer model [29] supports the hierarchical modeling. The modeling language group of application-neutral, semi-formal modeling language of Service nets is used. The definition of hierarchies and a modularized concept is based on process phase patterns and process module patterns. The target of the modularization of service processes is the reduction of complexity of service process modeling by a break down into small process units [55]. As soon as the process phases are identified, process modules are modeled successively as refinement. Process modules build up the corresponding collaborative service process of a service consumer or service provider. The input and output of a service process of an abstraction layer is derived from the descriptions of abstraction layer, which is dominated by it. The hierarchical modeling approach supports the collaborative modeling since service process models are modeled in a distributed way and can be integrated in a structured way. This decentral modeling approach incorporates several autonomous modelers, which can model partial service processes independently of each other. The procedure model supports the consistent, individualized model creation and the integration of partial service process models. Interfaces of service processes are illustrated on each modeling layer and data objects are identified.

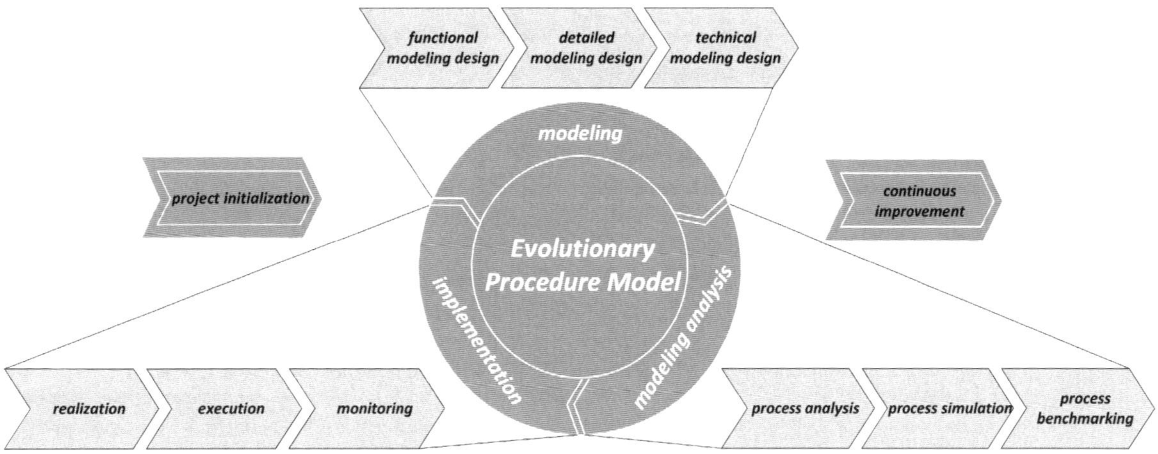

Figure 14. EPM for the development of process-oriented information systems

D. *Technical modeling design*

The technical modeling design is determined and incorporated. New requirements decide whether existing information systems are still used, or will be changed or replaced. Existing infrastructures of collaborating service providers and service consumers are analyzed in detail and relevant systems are being documented. The analysis data will be used for the technical modeling design. Modeled hierarchical service process models will be enriched by technical modeling details. Out of the group of formal, platform-independent modeling languages, high-level Service nets are used.

They support the modeling typified places for the detailed description of interfaces and data objects. Data objects are modeled based on XML schemata. Static and dynamic interfaces for coupling of collaborative service processes are differentiated. The modeling of *SPP* and *SMP* detail the typified places. The detailed service process of a *SMP* are modeled by (semi-)automated service processes.

E. *Process analysis*

For the process analysis, qualitative and quantitative analysis methods are used. Qualitative process analysis checks for the logical behavior of service process models to exclude modeling errors. Quantitative analysis methods define process targets to prevent exceptions.

F. *Process simulation*

The quantitative analysis method of simulation serves as an efficient method for the validation of potential behavior of service process models compared to the behavior of the intended service processes. The complex system of service process models is analyzed by process simulation.

G. *Process benchmarking*

The simulation-based process benchmarking can be used to discover the root causes and potentials of improvements by a systematic analysis of performance differences [4].

H. *Realization*

The modeled service process models are implemented into process-oriented information systems. The modeling language group of machine-readable programming language is used. Based on service-oriented architectures, web services can be modeled and can be related to corresponding WS-BPEL implementations of service processes. Web services are implemented and be called and executed with WS-BPEL after the implementation of service processes [28].

I. *Execution*

Electronic service processes are executed for the commence operations. Distributed, collaborative service processes of all involved parties are integrated to improve the execution of service processes.

J. *Monitoring*

The operative service processes must be monitored continuously. The monitoring serves as a base for a continuous improvement. As soon as potentials for improvement are identified, single phases of the procedure models are traced back and service process models are improved iteratively.

XII. APPLICATION OF ISERVMOD IN USE CASES

The integrated modeling approach *integrated Service Modeling (iServMod)* serves as an adequate method for a precise modeling and analysis of service processes. The advantages of *iServMod* increase the value of business process simulation and business process benchmarking. The simulation of service processes based on key performance indicators reveals gaps and weaknesses. The execution of a process benchmarking identifies differences of relevant factors like throughput times, resource assignments or cost items. The causes of performance gaps can be analyzed. For the modeling and simulation of service process models, the software tool *Horus* [56] was enhanced by the new modeling extensions of Service nets and used for a software based simulation. As business process simulation method, a discrete event driven business process oriented simulation was used [57]. The strengths of the independent simulative analysis are the possibility of a "*playground*" by simulating different process alternatives. Evaluation of simulation results can shed light on correlations of system parameters at build time and can be used to develop action strategies [4]. Unlike analytical procedures, the simulation can be used for the analysis of large systems. Based on benchmarks, performance gaps can be quantified. Redundant service processes and non-value creating activities as well as automation potentials for service processes can be identified and the error data is reduced. Also, the cost-effectiveness of service processes can be ensured.

The integrated modeling approach *iServMod* has been successfully applied in a research projects in the domain of service procurement [5]. The service process models of 18 use cases between six service suppliers and four service requesters were analyzed, modeled, simulated and benchmarked [4],[10],[58]. Service process models were modeled with high-level Service nets. The modeling of Service nets was based on a reference process model [5] to structure and align the individual service processes. *iServMod* supported the precise modeling of service processes and service objects in a syntactical correct and semantic formal way. The data flow could be modeled based on XML. Service processes could be modeled in a hierarchical modeling approach based on different abstraction levels to support modeling user groups with different modeling experiences.

Service processes could be modeled top down from high-level process description to detailed service processes as workflows using web services and representing and supporting a further implementation in information systems. *SPPs* and *SMPs* allow for reusability of pre-defined concepts by assuring the syntactical and semantic compatibility in service process models. The evaluated uses cases were compared pairwise for benchmarking by applying *EPM*.

XIII. Conclusion and Outlook

We presented the integrated modeling approach *iServMod*. *iServMod* supports integrated modeling of service processes and service objects based on formalized modeling techniques. Additionally, *iServMod* offers an adequate modeling approach for the precise analysis and implementation of service chains. *iServMod* is focusing on collaborative service processes, which are modeled independently by different companies and their domain experts (modelers). It furthermore supports the domain-specific requirements of service e-procurement in service chains.

The presented modeling concepts enact different formalization levels, starting from a semi-formal description of service process models up to formalized and executable service process models. This includes a hierarchical order of service processes typically modeled in a top down approach. The patterns *SPP* and *SMP* enable for both the choreography of service phases and the orchestration of service modules in collaborative cross-company service chains. These design patterns are intended to describe recurring service process sequences based on observed best practices. *SPP* and *SMP* support the modeling and implementation of electronic service processes. *SPP* and *SMP* are also defined within our Petri net based modeling approach for service e-procurement. While *eSN* serve as an initial modeling approach, further analysis is based on *hSN*, which enable an integrated modeling of service processes and service objects for the design of information systems.

Both the formal modeling language of Petri nets, as well as the service procurement domain-specific patterns lead to improved domain understanding, and support simulation-based analysis and process implementation. The definition of *SPP* and *SMP* enables

- an *integrated, formalized modeling approach* of service processes and service objects,
- the modeling of *hierarchic service processes and modularization* of collaborative service processes,
- the definition and modeling of *service process interfaces*,
- a step-wise transformation of modeling different *formalization levels*,
- the support of *distributed business processes* based on service-oriented architectures (SOA), and
- syntactic and semantic correctness to verify service process models.

The pattern-based modeling approach is concluded by integrated description of web service calls to implement sound information systems at execution level. The syntactic domain-specific extensions both of service object-specific process interface place types and process transition types enable a precise hierarchical modeling of process participants, modular service processes, e-procurement service phases, pre-defined process patterns, interfaces and service data objects.

Our pattern-based approach is derived from typical use cases of service e-procurement of industrial services. Hence, the integrated modeling and design approach was evaluated with real-life case studies [5]. The service process models have been modeled and analyzed. The developed extension of the software tool *Horus* supports the overall modeling of collaborative service chains.

As next steps, we intend to extend the verification of these patterns. We will evaluate our pattern-based approach by analysis of further service e-procurement use cases. Furthermore, the adoption and application of *iServMod* in different domains and hence different types of service chains are planned. E-procurement of other service domains will also be analyzed and validated. We also intend to formulate experiments in other service domains to ensure the general usability, the level of detail and completeness of the defined patterns. In addition, the pattern-based modeling approach can be transferred to further service process types besides procurement. Analog service process types are repair orders, return orders and warranty service orders. The pattern based modeling approach will also be used for simulation and benchmarking of collaborative service processes of different service provider and service consumer combinations. We also strive to further evaluate the performance, quality and efficiency of this approach together with several leading companies in the domain of industrial services. Thus, we foresee the evaluation of *iServMod* by a survey of domain specific users.

References

[1] M. Herfurth and T. Schuster, "Integrated Modeling Approach iServMod for Modeling, Analysis and Execution of Collaborative Service Processes in Service Chains," COLLA 2016, The Sixth International Conference on Advanced Collaborative Networks, Systems and Applications, Spain, pp. 70-77, 2016.

[2] A. Linhart, J. Manderscheid, and M. Roeglinger, "Roadmap to Flexible Service Processes - A Project Portfolio Selection and Scheduling Approach," ECIS 2015, paper 125, pp. 1-16, 2015.

[3] R. F. Lusch and R. Nambisan, "Service innovation: a service-dominant logic perspective," MIS Quarterly volume 39 (1), pp. 155-175, 2015.

[4] M. Herfurth, T. Schuster, and P. Weiß, "Simulation-based Service Process Benchmarking in Product-Service Ecosystems," Proceedings of Collaborative Systems for Reindustrialization: 14th IFIP WG 5.5 Working Conference on Virtual Enterprises, PRO-VE 2013, Germany, pp. 40-47, 2013.

[5] P. Weiß, M. Herfurth, and J. Schumacher, "Leverage Productivity Potentials in Service-oriented Procurement Transactions: E-Standards in Service Procurement," Proceedings of RESER 2011, pp. 1-20, 2011.

[6] A. Eggert, C. Thiesbrummel, and C. Deutscher, "Heading for new shores: Do service and hybrid innovations outperform

product innovations in industrial companies?," Industrial Marketing Management, volume 45, pp. 173-183, 2015.

[7] O. Kleine and R. Schneider (editors), "Service Chain Management in the industry – an approach for planning of cooperative industrial services," VDM Dr. Müller, 2010.

[8] J. Johanson and L. G. Mattsson, "Internationalisation in Industrial Systems — A Network Approach," in Knowledge, Networks and Power, pp. 111-132, 2015.

[9] T. Baltacioglu, E. Ada, M. Kaplan, O. Yurt, and C. Kaplan, "A New Framework for Service Supply Chains," Services Industry Journal, volume 27, No. 2, pp. 105-124, 2007.

[10] M. Herfurth, T. Schuster, and P. Weiß, "E-Business for Services: Simulation-based Analysis of E-Business Solution Concepts for Service Procurement Scenarios," eChallenges e-2012 Conference Proceedings, Paul Cunningham and Miriam Cunningham (editors), IIMC International Information Management Corporation, 2012.

[11] L. R. Smeltzer and J. A. Ogden, "Purchasing Professionals' Perceived Differences between Purchasing materials and Purchasing Services," Journal of Supply Chain Management, volume 38 (19), pp. 54-70, 2002.

[12] M. Herfurth and P. Weiß, "Conceptual Design of Service Procurement for collaborative Service Networks," Collaborative Networks for a Sustainable World: 11th IFIP WG 5.5 Working Conference on Virtual Enterprises, PRO-VE 2010, France, pp. 435-442, 2010.

[13] P. P. Maglio and J. Spohrer, "Fundamentals of Service Science," Journal of the Academy of Marketing Science, volume 36 (1), pp. 18-20, 2008.

[14] R. J. Glushko and T. McGrath, "Designing Business Processes With Patterns," The MIT Press Cambridge, Massachusetts, 2005.

[15] A. R. Hevner, S. T. March, J. Park, and S. Ram, "Design Science in Information Systems Research," MIS Quarterly, 28(1), pp. 75-105, 2004.

[16] W. M. P. van der Aalst, "The Application of Petri Nets to Workflow Management," The Journal of Circuits, Systems and Computers, volume 8(1), pp. 21-66, 1998.

[17] J. Becker, D. Beverungen, R. Knackstedt, M. Matzner, O. Müller, and J. Pöppelbuß, "Flexible information system architectures for hybrid value creation networks (FlexNet)," work report of the institute for business informatics no. 130, Westpahlian Wilhelms University Muenster, 2011.

[18] J. Becker, D. Beverungen, R. Knackstedt, and O. Müller, "Conception of a modeling language for the software supported modeling, configuration and evaluation of hybrid bundles of services," in: O. Thomas and M. Nüttgens (editors), "Service modeling," Physica, pp. 53-70, 2009.

[19] P. P.-S. Chen, "The entity-relationship model - towards a unified view of data," ACM Transactions on Database Systems 1 (1976) 1, pp. 9-36, 1976.

[20] K. Winkelmann, "Prospective evaluation of cooperative service delivery of industrial services in manufacturing systems engineering via simulation of Petri nets," Dissertation RWTH Aachen, 2007.

[21] K. Jensen, "Coloured Petri Nets: A high-level Language for System Design and Analysis," LNCS volume 483, Springer, 1990.

[22] J. Becker and S. Neumann, "Reference models for workflow applications of technical services," in: H.-J. Bullinger, and A.-W. Scheer, "Service Engineering", Springer, pp. 623-647, 2006.

[23] H. Che, M. Mevius, Y. Ju, W. Stucky, and R. Trunko, "A Method for Interorganizational Business Process Management," Proceedings of the IEEE International Conference on Automation and Logistics, China, 2007.

[24] K. Lenz and A. Oberweis, "Interorganizational Business Process Management with XML Nets," in: Petri Net Technology for Communication Based Systems, LNCS 2472, pp. 243-263, 2003.

[25] M. Mevius and R. Pibernik, "Process Management in Supply Chains - A New Petri-Net Based Approach," Proceeding of the 37th Hawaii International Conference on System Sciences (HICCS'04), IEEE Computer Society, 2004.

[26] W. Brauer, W. Reisig, and G. Rozenberg, "Petri Nets. Part I and Part II," Lecture Notes in Computer Science 254 and 255, Springer Verlag, 1987.

[27] J. Desel and A. Oberweis, "Petri nets in applied computer science: introduction, basics and perspectives," in: Business Informatics, volume 38(4), Vieweg Teubner, pp. 359-367, 1996.

[28] M. Herfurth, T. Karle, and F. Schönthaler, "Reference Model for service oriented Business Software based on Web Service Nets," Third AIS SIGSAND European Symposium on Analysis, Design, Use and Societal Impact of Information Systems SIGSAND-EUROPE, pp. 55-69, 2008.

[29] M. Herfurth, T. Karle, and R. Trunko, "Model Driven Implementation of Business Processes Based on Web Service Nets," Proceedings of the 2008 SIWN Congress 2nd International Conference on Adaptive Business Systems (ABS 2008), Glasgow, pp. 32-38, 2008.

[30] W.M.P. van der Aalst and K. van Hee, "Workflow Management: Models, Methods, and Systems," MIT Press, 2004.

[31] W. Reisig, "Petri nets – an Introduction," Springer, 1982.

[32] J. Desel and A. Oberweis, "Petri nets in applied informatics: introduction, basics and perspectives," Business Informatics, volume 38(4), pp. 359-367, Vieweg + Teubner, 1996.

[33] T. Schuster, "Modeling, integration and analysis of resources in business processes," KIT Scientific Publishing, 2012.

[34] E. Gamma, R. Helm, R. Johnson, and J. Vlissides, "Design Patterns: Elements of Reusable Object-Oriented Software," Addison–Wesley, 2001.

[35] J. Arlow and I. Neustadt, "Enterprise Patterns and MDA," Addison-Wesley, 2003.

[36] E. Gamma and K. Beck, "Eclipse to be extended. Principles, Patterns and Plug-Ins," Addison-Wesley, 2005.

[37] G. Hohpe and B. Woolf, "Enterprise Integration Patterns: Designing, Building, and Deploying Messaging Solutions," Addison-Wesley Longman Publishing Co. Inc., 2004.

[38] O. Barros, "Business process patterns and frameworks: Reusing knowledge in process innovation," Business Process Management Journal, volume 13 (1), pp. 47-69, 2007.

[39] A. Barros, M. Dumas, and A.H.M. ter Hofstede, "Service Interaction Patterns," Proceedings of the 3rd International Conference on Business Process Management, France, Springer, pp. 302-318, 2005.

[40] D. Port, "Derivation of domain specific desing patterns," USC-CSE Annual Reasearch and Technology Week Presentations and Binder Materials, 1998.

[41] N. Russell, A.H.M. ter Hofstede, W.M.P. van der Aalst, and N. Mulyar, "Workflow Control-Flow Patterns: A Revised View," BPM Center Report BPM-06-22, BPMcenter.org, 2006.

[42] A. Zimmermann, J. Freiheit, and A. Huck, "A Petri net based design engine for manufacturing systems," Journal International Journal of Production Research, volume 39 (2), pp. 225-253, 2001.

[43] W.M.P. van der Aalst and A.W. Waltmans, "Modeling logistic systems with EXPECT," in: H.G. Sol, K.M. van Hee, "Dynamic Modeling of Information Systems," pp. 269-288, 1991.

[44] M. Dong and F. F. Chen, "Process modeling and analysis of manufacturing supply chain networks using object oriented Petri nets," Robotics and Computer Integrated Manufacturing, volume 17, pp. 121-129, 2001.

[45] E. Liu, A. Kumar, and W.M.P. van der Aalst, "Managing Supply Chain Events to Build Sense-and-Response Capability," in: D. Straub and S. Klein (editors), Proceedings of International Conference on Information Systems (ICIS 2006), Milwaukee, Wisconsin, pp. 117-134, 2006.

[46] M. Weske, "Business Process Management: Concepts, Languages, Architectures," Springer, 2007.

[47] M. Herfurth, A. Meinhardt, J. Schumacher, and P. Weiß, "eProcurement for Industrial Maintenance Services," Proceedings of Leveraging Knowledge for Innovation in Collaborative Networks: 10th IFIP WG 5.5 Working Conference on Virtual Enterprises, Greece, pp. 363-370, 2009.

[48] P. Weiss, M. Herfurth, and J. Schumacher, "Leverage Productivity Potentials in Service-oriented Procurement Transactions: E-Standards in Service Procurement," RESER Conference, Germany, pp. 1-22, 2011.

[49] K. Lenz, "Modeling and execution of e-business processes with XML nets," Dissertation J.W. Goethe University Frankfurt am Main, 2003.

[50] A. Grosskopf, G. Decker, and M. Weske, "The Process. Business Process Modeling Using BPMN," Meghan-Kiffer Press, 2009.

[51] W.M.P. van der Aalst, "Modeling and Analyzing Interorganizational Workflows," in: L. Lavagno and W. Reisig (editors), Proceedings of the International Conference on Application of Concurrency to System Design (CSD'98), IEEE Computer Society Press, pp. 1-15, 1998.

[52] W.M.P. van der Aalst, "Interorganizational Workflows: An Approach based on Message Sequence Charts and Petri Nets, Systems Analysis - Modeling – Simulation," volume 34 (3), pp. 335-367, 1999.

[53] A. Koschmider and M. Mevius, "A Petri Net based Approach for Process Model Driven Deduction of BPEL Code," OTM Confederated International Conferences, Agia Napa, Cyprus, Springer, pp. 495-505, 2005.

[54] A. Martens, "Analyzing Web Service based Business Processes," Proceedings International Conference on Fundamental Approaches to Software Engineering (FASE), volume 3442 of LNCS, Scotland, pp. 19-33, 2005.

[55] W. Kersten, B. Koeppen, C. Meyer, and E.-M. Kern, "Reduction of process complexity through modularization," Industry Management, volume 21 (4), pp. 11-14, 2005.

[56] Y. Li and A. Oberweis, "A Petri Net-Based Software Process Model for Developing Process-Oriented Information Systems," Proceedings of the 18th International Conference on Information Systems Development (ISD2009), China, pp. 27-39, 2009.

[57] J. Banks, J. S. Carson, B. L. Nelson, and D. M. Nicol, "Discrete-Event System Simulation," Pearson Education, 2005.

[58] M. Herfurth, T. Schuster, and P. Weiß, "Decision Support Based on Simulation Analysis of Service Procurement Scenarios," eChallenges e-2013 Conference Proceedings, Paul Cunningham and Miriam Cunningham (editors), 2013.

From Rule Based Expert System to High-Performance Data Analysis for Reduction of Non-Technical Losses on Power Grids

Juan Ignacio Guerrero, Antonio Parejo, Enrique Personal, Íñigo Monedero, Félix Biscarri, Jesús Biscarri, and Carlos León

Department of Electronic Technology
EPS
University of Seville
C/ Virgen de África, 7
41011, Seville, Spain
e-mail: juaguealo@us.es, aparejo@us.es, epersonal@us.es, imonedero@us.es, fbiscarri@us.es, jbiscarri@us.es, cleon@us.es

***Abstract*—The Non-Technical Losses represent the non-billed energy due to faults or illegal manipulations in customer facilities. The objective of the Midas project is the detection of Non-Technical Losses through the application of computational intelligence over the information stored in utility company databases. This project has several research lines, e.g., pattern recognition, expert systems, big data and High Performance Computing. This paper proposes a module which uses statistical techniques to make patterns of correct consumption. The main contribution of this module is the detection of cases, which are usually classified as consumers with Non-Technical Loss increasing the false positives and decreasing the total success rate. This module is integrated with a rule based expert system made up of other modules, such a text mining module and a data warehousing module. The correct consumption patterns (consumers without Non-Technical Losses) are generated using rules, which will be used by a rule based expert system. Two implementations are proposed. Both of them provided an Intelligent Information System to reach unapproachable goals for inspectors. Additionally, some highlighted cases of detected patterns are described.**

Keywords - non-technical losses; pattern recognition; expert system; big data analytics; high performance computing; high-performance data analysis.

I. INTRODUCTION

Information systems have provided a new advantage: the capability to store, manage and analyze great quantities of information without human supervision. This paper proposes one solution to a very difficult problem: the Non-Technical Losses (NTLs) reduction in power utility. This paper is an extended version of a conference paper [1].

NTLs represent the non-billed energy due to the abnormalities or illegal manipulations in client power facilities. The objective of this work (called Midas project) is the detection of NTLs using computational intelligence and Knowledge Based Systems (KBS) over the information stored in Endesa databases. The Endesa company is the most biggest distribution utility in Spain with more than 12 million clients. Initially, this project was tested with information about low voltage customers. The system used consumer information with monthly or bimonthly billing. Although the system can analyze large volume of data, and which poses a very high cost in time when there are more than four million consumers. Notwithstanding, this volume of information would be unfathomable to analyze for an inspector. In order to reduce this cost, a hybrid architecture based on big data and high performance computing is currently applied to create a High-Performance Data Analysis (HPDA). This architecture has been successfully applied in biomedical topics [2], text data classification [3], and other scientific datasets [4].

Moreover, Smart Grids have provided a new scope of technologies, for example, Advanced Metering Infrastructure (AMI) with smart metering, Advanced Distribution Automation (ADA), etc. There are several references about the advantages of Smart Grids, and there are a lot of initiatives related to Smart Grids in the world (e.g., [5][6][7], etc.). Additionally, several studies about the utilization of AMI in Smart Grid (e.g., [8][9][10], etc.) to improve the power quality (e.g., [11][12], etc.) and demand management (e.g., [13][14], etc.) can be found in the current state of art. These new infrastructures increase the information about consumers, taking hourly or even quarterly measurements.

This paper proposes a model which uses statistical techniques to detect correct consumption patterns. These patterns are used to generate rules, which are applied in a Rule Based Expert System (RBES). The RBES is described in [15][16] and the module of text mining is described in [17]. In this paper, an improvement on the data mining module functionality is proposed.

The proposed solution is described as follows. Section II shows a review over the state of the art in NTLs detection. Following this review, the architecture and technical characteristics of a new proposed solution is described in Section III. Section IV provides a brief description of RBES, and whose text mining module and statistical pattern generator modules are described in Section V and Section VI respectively. In Section VII, the consumption characterization of consumers without NTLs is proposed. In Section VIII, the improvements of the proposed HPDA architecture are included. Section IX shows the new parameters for consumption characterization of consumers without NTLs in the proposed HPDA architecture. In Section X, a brief description of evaluation and experimental results are presented. After that, Section XI shows a description of several highlighted cases, which traditionally are wrongly classified as an NTL. Finally, Section XII poses the conclusions and future research lines.

II. Bibliographical Review

In terms of consumption in utilities, a great spectrum of techniques can be applied; data mining, time series analysis, etc. Basically, the use of any type of statistical technique is essential to detect anomalous patterns. This idea is not new. Several researchers usually apply statistical or similar techniques to detect or analyze anomalous consumption (e.g., [18][19][20][21][22]). Some of these techniques are based on studies of the historical customer consumptions; for example, Azadeh et al. [23] made a comparison between the use of time series, neural network and ANOVA, always with reference of the consumption of the same customer. However, these techniques have several problems, the main one being that it is necessary to have large historical data about customer consumptions. Other researchers use different studies to make good patterns of consumption, which compare the consumption of a customer with others who have similar characteristics. For example, Richardson [24] compared both neural networks and statistical techniques; in the performed tests, statistical techniques are 4% more efficient than neural networks. Hand and Blunt [25] proposed the identification of some characteristics, which make the identification of consumption patterns applying statistical techniques that use them as anomalous patterns possible. Other methods propose the use of advanced techniques to make other profiles or patterns of consumption. In this sense, Nagi et al. [26] used support vector machines and [27] applied rough sets, both of them in NTLs detection.

There are other examples, e.g., Aguero [28] proposed a method to improve the efficiency of the distribution systems for reducing technical and non-technical losses. They use the utility information system, which includes computational models of feeders and advanced modeling software systems and is based on the implementation smart grid approaches. In the same way, Paruchuri and Dubey [29] proposed the use of smart metering and advanced communication protocols to detect NTLs. Iglesias [30] proposed an analysis of energy losses for activity sectors (domestic, etc.) using a load balance, by means of consumer information, the distribution transformers and several measurement points. Alves et al. [31] suggested an upgrade of the measurement equipment by means of electronic devices such as alarm systems, connection systems, remote reconnection, and protections of drivers.

Nizar et al. [32] described a series of detection rules based on feature selection and clustering techniques, using the costumer consumption history. Depuru et al. [33] proposed the use of consumption patterns, which are generated starting

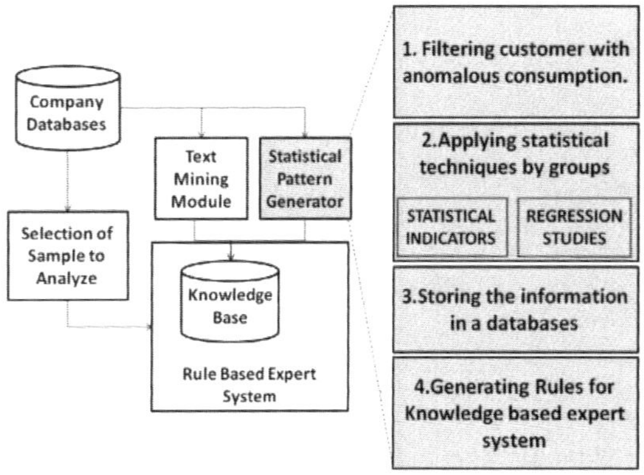

Figure 1. Local Expert System Architecture and Details of Statistical Pattern Generator Module.

from the consumer history, using a Support Vector Machine (SVM) and the gathered data from smart meters; the consumers are classified according to the pattern that they propose. Ramos et al. [34] proposed the use of an Optimum Path Forest (OPF) clustering technique based on supervised learning; so, a dataset with obtained frauds of a power distribution company is used. These references are based on the use of learning techniques using available information about the consumer consumption to model a pattern for anomalous consumption.

Other applications of advanced techniques, mainly Artificial Neural Network (ANN), which are not typically used for detection of NTLs, but could be used, are the applications for demand forecasting. In this sense, the forecasting can be done in short [35], medium [36], or long [37] term.

III. Architecture and Technical Characteristics

Initially, the architecture of original RBES is shown in Figure 1. This architecture is detailed for the Statistical Pattern Generator, showing the different stages of this process. The system was run in a single machine, and it has been successfully tested on four million clients. This volume of analysis forced the system to do partitions in order to analyze more than four million customers.

Currently, the new architecture applies big data and High Performance Computing (HPC). The big data architecture is based on Apache Spark with a database stored in HBase implemented in Apache Hadoop. The analytics are implemented in MLlib, GraphX, and library to send jobs to Graphics Processor Units (GPUs, based on Compute Unified Device Architecture or CUDA® cores). The architecture is shown in Figure 2.

The proposed system has still not been deployed over a real cluster of machines. However, a prototype was successfully implemented over a simple cluster of two nodes. The first node had an Intel® Core™ i7 (3GHz), 16GB RAM and an Nvidia® GeForce® GTX750 graphic adapter (2GB and

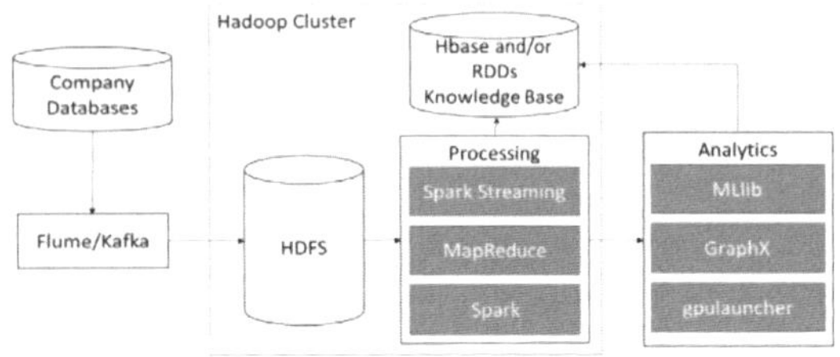

Figure 2. Architecture of Expert System in a High-Performance Data Analysis.

640 CUDA® cores). The second node had an Intel® Xeon® E5 (2GHz), 64GB RAM and an Nvidia® Quadro® K1200 graphic adapter (4GB and 512 CUDA® cores).

IV. RULE BASED EXPERT SYSTEM (RBES)

This RBES is described in [38]. This system uses the information extracted from the Endesa staff. The RBES has several additional modules, which provide dynamic knowledge using rules. The expert system has additional modules, which use different techniques: data warehousing (it is used as a preprocessing step), text mining, and statistical techniques.

The RBES can be used as additional methods to analyze the rest of information about the customer. The company databases store a lot of information, including: contract, customers' facilities, inspectors' commentaries, customers, etc. All of them are analyzed by RBES using the rules extracted from the Endesa staff and others obtained from the statistical techniques and text mining modules.

The system can be used alone or with other modules to provide additional methods to analyze the information. These modules are described in the following Sections.

V. TEXT MINING MODULE

The text mining module, which is described in [17], uses Natural Language Processing (NLP) and neural networks. This method is used to provide a tool to analyze the inspectors' commentaries. When an inspection is made in a customer's location, the inspector should register their observations and commentaries. This data is stored in company databases.

This information is not commonly analyzed because the traditional models are only based on consumption studies. The text mining module complete these studies using additional information because the inspectors' commentaries provide real information about the client facilities, which may be different from the stored in database.

This technique uses NLP and fuzzy algorithms to extract concepts from inspectors' commentaries. This process is implemented and performed in the SPSS Modeler. The NLP process consists of four engines (as described in Figure 3):

- String matching engine. This engine is based on fuzzy logic with synonym dictionaries. A fuzzy ratio is added to each word to identify similar words and mistakes. The mistake correction can be applied according to the length of words.
- Syntactic engine. This engine assigns a function to each word, according to its position and the previous and following words.
- Concept engine. This engine generates several concepts, the words with the same syntactic function and meaning in the same sentence are grouped in the same concept.
- Semantic engine. This engine assigns a semantic function to each concept. The different semantic categories are defined according to the inspectors' knowledge.

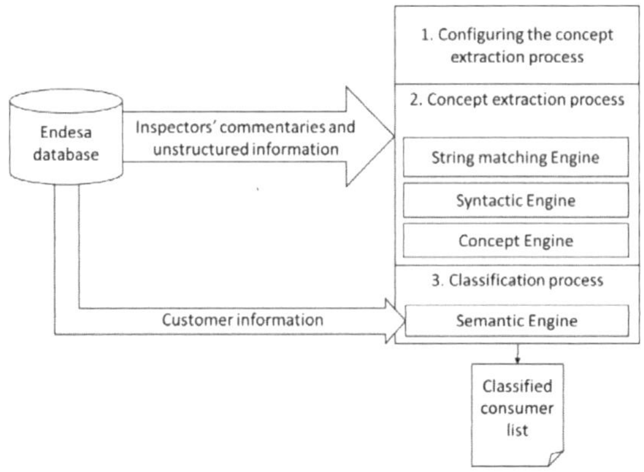

Figure 3. Diagram flow of Text Mining Module.

The different dialects were extracted by means of synonym dictionaries, these dictionaries allowed this module to include the different dialects in the extraction process. The extraction process involves the application of fuzzy techniques for string matching and correction of mistakes.

This set of categories was used in the second step as a training set:

- CLOSED. This category groups the concepts that represent consumers who are: closed, uninhabited, on holiday, demolished, and so on. These scenarios are usually confused with NTL by the detection of an algorithm because of the consumption pattern.
- CORRECT. This category identifies consumer installations that are correct or without NTLs. This category could prevent false positives.
- INCORRECT. This category identifies consumers whose consumer installation might have an NTL. This category represents concepts that usually identify a measurement problem in the consumer facilities.
- LOW CONSUMPTION. This category identifies consumers who usually have a low or very low consumption, due to their activity. The consumers classified in this category are filtered because the correct consumption is irregular or very low. For example, some consumers with agricultural activities

have water pumps, which have irregular and low consumption.

- UNUSEFUL. This category has 101 subcategories, which are not used in the filtering process. These subcategories include the UNKNOWN category, which contains the concepts that could not be classified. Additionally, there are several subcategories that contain information about names, numbers (currency, telephone numbers, address, etc.) and dates. These three subcategories represent 23% of the total number of concepts. This category is excluded from the set of the most frequent concepts.

These concepts are classified initially according to their frequency of appearance. The most frequent concepts are classified manually according to their meaning. Additionally, consumption indicators, date of commentary, number of measurements (estimated and real), number of proceedings, source of commentary, frequency of appearance, time discrimination band and some others are associated to each concept. Some of these indicators are generated by a Statistical Pattern Generator and applied in a Semantic Engine (Figures 4 and 5) This data is used in an ANN, which is trained with data of the most frequent concepts and is tested with the less frequent concepts. This ANN can be used to classify the new concepts, which could appear.

Additionally, the Statistical Pattern Generator is applied to whole samples when the system is in modelling time (Figure 4). Initially, this modelling process was applied to all the consumers in the Endesa database (around 12 million clients). In the analysis time, only limited size samples are usually analyzed. Thus, the Statistical Pattern Generator (Figure 5) is applied to generate some indicators, but is only applied in order to classify the consumer in a previously defined category. This classification can affect the final classification of consumer.

VI. Statistical Pattern Generator

The statistical pattern generator is based on basic statistical indicators such as: maximum, minimum, average and standard deviation. These indicators are used as patterns to detect correct consumption. Additionally, the slope of regression line is used to detect the regular consumption

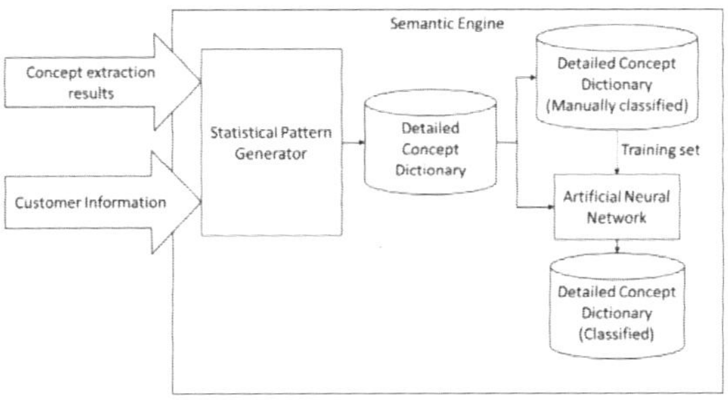

Figure 4. Role of Statistical Pattern Generator in Semantic Engine in modelling time

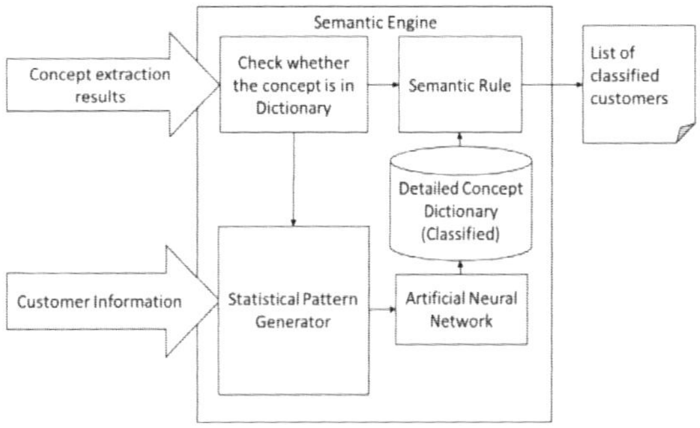

Figure 5. Role of Statistical Pattern Generator in Semantic Engine in analysis time.

trend. Each of these calculations is done for different sets of characteristics. These characteristics are: time, contracted power, measurement frequency, geographic location, postal code, economic activity and time discrimination band. Using these characteristics it is possible to determine the patterns of correct consumption of a customer with a certain contracted power, geographic location and economic activity.

The creation of these patterns needs to study a lot of customers. In this study, all customers are not used because the anomalous consumption of the customers with an NTL is filtered. This idea allows the system to eliminate the anomalous consumption getting better results.

Several tables of data are generated as a result of this study. This data is used to create rules, which implement the detected patterns. If a customer carries out the pattern, this means that the customer is correct. But if a customer does not carry out the pattern, this does not mean that the customer is not correct. These patterns are described in the next Section.

VII. Consumption Characterization

To find out what characteristics have more influence on consumption is a very difficult task because there is a lot of consumption information available. An in-depth analysis shows that some characteristics have more influence over the consumption: time, geographic location, postal code, contracted power, measurement frequency, economic activity and time discrimination band. The importance of these characteristics has also been analyzed in other utilities such as gas utility. Moreover, the results of these analysis have been compared with the knowledge provided by Endesa inspectors.

Each characteristic by itself is not efficient because the consumption depends on several characteristics at the same time. Thus, grouping characteristics can help find patterns of correct consumption, because these characteristics can determine the consumption with a low level of error rate providing, at least, one consumption pattern. These groups have a series of characteristics in common: geographic location, time, contracted power, and measurement frequency. These are named Basis Group because these are the main characteristics. The values for each of these

TABLE I. GROUPS OF CONSUMPTION CHARACTERISTICS

Consumption Characteristics	Description
Basis Group	This group provides consumption patterns by general geographic location: north, south, islands, etc.
Basis Group and Postal Code	This group provides patterns useful for cities with coastal and interior zones.
Basis Group and Economic activity.	The granularity of geographic location is decreased. In this way, the economic activity takes more importance. Nevertheless, the geographic location cannot be despised because, as for example, a bar has not the same consumption whether it is in interior location or coastline location.
Basis Group and time discrimination band.	There are several time discrimination bands. Each band registers the consumption at a different time range. This group provides consumption patterns in different time discrimination bands. These are useful because there exists customers who make their consumption in day or night time.

characteristics are wide; therefore, each of them shows great variations of consumption. A description of Basis Group and the other groups are shown in Table I.

Some characteristics have different granularity because they have continuous values or have a lot of possible values. The granularity is used because there are some problems related to the measurements. For example, the proposed framework performs a discretization of contracted power in 40 ranges. In the graph of Figure 6, the 14th range of contracted power is shown. This range groups the contracted power between 46,852 kW and 55,924 kW in the North of Spain. This Figure shows an abnormal level of consumption at 2002; this fact represents errors in measurements, which cannot be filtered.

In the graph of Figure 7, the average consumption in monthly periods for the 14th range is shown. In this case, the granularity of time is increased; therefore, it is possible to get another pattern, which is better than the one obtained from the graph of Figure 6. In this case, the consumption can be analyzed monthly.

Thus, several time ranges are used: absolute, monthly, yearly and seasonally. For example, the average consumption

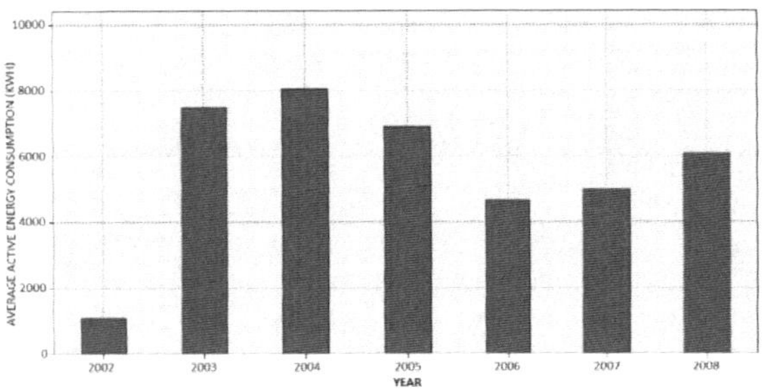

Figure 6. Average yearly consumption graph in power range 14th.

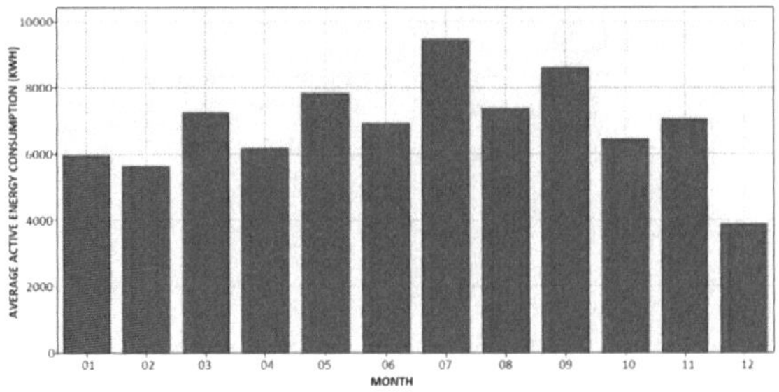

Figure 7. Average monthly consumption graph in power ranges 14th.

calculation provides different results: total average consumption (absolute), twelve/six average, monthly/bimonthly consumption, one average yearly consumption (when the measurements are available), and four average seasonal consumption. In the same way, the contracted power should be discretized in equal consumption ranges. In lower contracted power, the ranges are very narrow because there are a lot of consumers. When the contracted power is higher, the quantity of consumers is smaller, although the consumptions are very different. The reason for adding or aggregating the consumption (of supplies without NTLs) in different groups is because there are scenarios in which it is necessary to have other patterns.

These groups provided dynamic patterns, which can be updated according to the time granularity. Once the characteristics are identified, it is necessary to design a process, which finds patterns automatically. Initially, these studies were made bimonthly and were applied as a part of an integrated expert system to model correct consumption patterns (Figure 1). Currently, the process can be performed hourly through the architecture proposed in Figure 2. The system applies statistical techniques to get consumption patterns using the process detailed in Figure 1.

When the rules are created, they are used to analyze the customers in order to determine if there exist any NTLs. There are defined series of rules in RBES, which use the information generated by the proposed module. The antecedents of the rules are generated dynamically using the patterns generated in the described process and according to the characteristics of the customer who will be analyzed. In this way, the use of memory resources is minimized because only the necessary antecedents of the rules are generated.

When the consumption of a customer is analyzed, several rules can fit with the characteristics of that customer. Initially, the rules are applied in the most restrictive way; this means, the customer consumption will be correct if it fits in any correct consumption pattern. Moreover, the system notifies us if the pattern fails for each customer. For example, the correct consumption ranges of active energy for specific geographic zones, different contracted power ranges, and different measurement frequency (monthly or bimonthly) are shown in Figure 8. The proposed study includes a geographic study of consumption could replace the studies related to

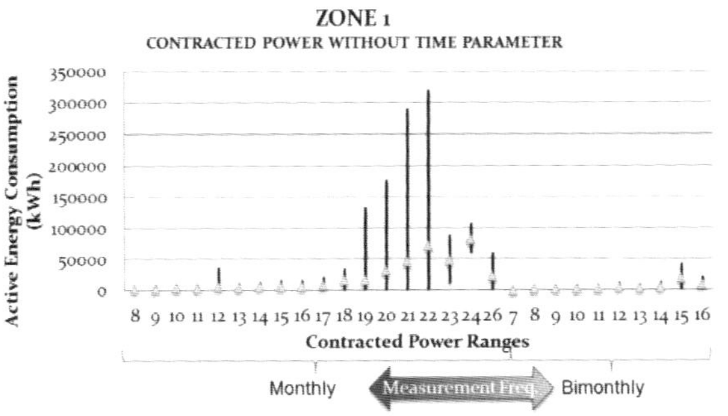

Figure 8. Graph of Active Energy Consumption Ranges vs. contracted power ranges without time parameter for a specific geographic zone.

weather conditions, because the consumers in the same zone have probably the same weather conditions. But, in this case, the contribution of adding information about weather probably does not explain the quantity of efforts and time consumption in analyzing it in front of the increment of success rate.

VIII. High Performance Data Analysis

The solution proposed in Figure 2 is a novel architecture. This solution is based on big data and HPC. The emergent technologies related to smart grids provide a great quantity of data with better temporal resolution. This solution is proposed to analyze a great quantity of information in an NRT period.

The main problem in the application of the proposed solution is the unavailability of data sources. Traditionally, this type of data sources has a very high security level and are used by other systems, which requires all resources. In these cases, it is very difficult to apply the solution, because it is necessary to load the data onto the proposed solution. Flume and Kafka are used to load the data from relational and non-relational databases. This load processes in the company databases are usually performed during the night. However, if the load of data were performed when a change in database is made, the system could operate in NRT. But, when the data is loaded in the proposed solution the operation is in real-time.

The architecture is based on Apache Hadoop and Spark, enhanced with a new daemon to take advantage of HPC architectures. This daemon, named gpulauncher, is invoked by processes in order to send jobs to GPUs. The processes can be part of a MapReduce or Analytics. Although the system implemented statistical and regression algorithms, the new algorithms will also apply multivariable inferences.

The gpulauncher daemon implemented several algorithms for analytics, functions for streaming the data to GPUs and functions for synchronization of nodes. These synchronization functions are in development. The main objective is the synchronization between GPUs of different nodes and working in near-real-time (NRT).

The loaded data is stored into HBase. The loading process includes several preprocessing steps in order to guarantee the data integrity, coherence, and anonymization. There are several processes to convert this data into a Resilient Distributed Dataset (RDD). In these processes, the data is preprocessed and transformed to the format, which is directly used by analytics algorithms.

The methods, techniques, and algorithms applied on the proposed solution (Figure 1) to fraud detection in monthly and bimonthly billing periods were adapted to the new smart grid scenario (Figure 2).

IX. Consumption Characterization in HPDA Solution

The consumption characterization in the proposed HPDA solution is increased with more temporal resolution in the data, adding additional time dimensions: hourly, daily, and weekly. A calendar is included and updated with working days and holidays in each geographic zone.

In the previous described solution, the generation of each pattern is updated monthly or bimonthly (according to the billing period). The solution based on HPDA makes it possible to update the pattern hourly. This scenario provides more accurate patterns. It is possible to establish the daily consumption pattern according to the type of day (working days or holiday) and the hours where the consumption is centered.

The solution based on HPDA increased the number of rules, which can be applied on a consumer. However, the criteria for applying the pattern is the same (like previously described solution). The consumer is initially selected as correct if the consumption carries out with any pattern. If the consumer does not fit any pattern if the consumer is selected as a possible NTL.

X. Evaluation and Experimental Results

The proposed module provides patterns of correct customer consumption. The analysis made by the mentioned expert system uses this module to create rules. The customer consumption analysis applies these rules according to the contract attributes: contracted power, economic activity, geographic location, postal code, and time discrimination band. Traditionally, the systems used to detect frauds or abnormalities in utilities make patterns for NTLs detection. However, in the proposed system, models of correct consumption ranges and trends are made. The use of these patterns increase the efficiency of the RBES. The Statistical Pattern Generator module is essential to analyze the customers. The RBES has been applied in real cases getting better results in zones with a lot of clients. The success of the RBES (Figure 1) is between 16,67% and 40,66% according to the quantity of clients and the quality of data, this success rate is related only to NTL detection. This fact is shown in Figure 9. But, the proposed solution classifies customers in NTL or CORRECT (without NTLs). Therefore, the success rate will be the sum of both cases.

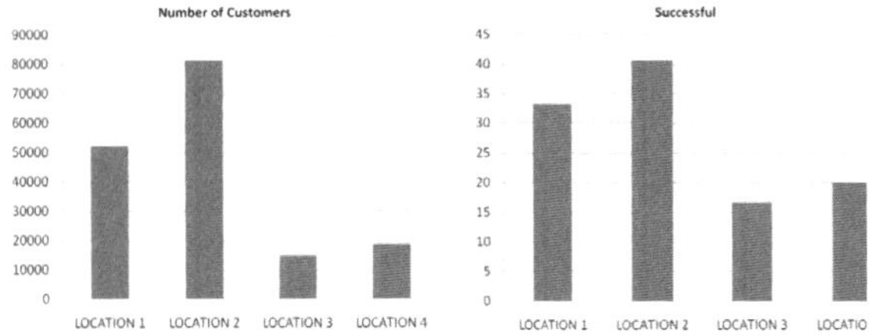

Figure 9. Number of customers vs. successful.

The evaluation of these processes is traditionally done using methods based on sensitivity and specificity measurements of the performance [39] or confusion matrix: true positive, true negative, false positive, and false negative. True and False are related to predicted and non-predicted values. Positive and Negative are related to correct and incorrect classifications. In this case, the correct classification is when the system successfully classifies the consumers (with and without NTLs). In this case, the consumers classified without NTLs are not usually inspected, and it is very difficult to get an exact value because it is not possible to know the results for all classified customers. Thus, this success rate is estimated because the consumers classified as CORRECT (without NTLs) are not inspected. Moreover, the authors check the information of results of other types of inspections made after the study (until three months) in order to verify the conclusion provided by RBES. In this case, the estimation provided a success rate between 82.3% and 91.2%, according to the quantity of clients of the corresponding location and quality of data.

The RBES was designed to deal with consumers with monthly or bimonthly billing periods. However, the new architecture based on HPDA makes the application of the expert system in NRT possible with hourly measurements. Thus, this system will be useful in the new Smart Grid infrastructures, based on AMI.

The solution proposed in Figure 1, has been successfully applied, as can be seen in previous published results [17] and [38]. The solution proposed in Figure 2, has not been tested with real inspections, it has been tested with real data provided by a retailer company but without inspections. The application of the proposed framework over the data provided several patterns for a determinate geographic location.

XI. Highlight Cases

The proposed framework in Figure 1 has been more efficient in analysis. There are some cases, which traditionally were very difficult to detect. Specifically, two cases are treated in this Section.

The first case is a client with an irrigation activity. The consumption of this type of client is strongly influenced by climate. The consumption of this client is very irregular, and difficult to analyze. These clients decrease their consumption when rainfalls increase. In this system, data about climate are not available, and only use the information about the client. Sometimes, variations of climate conditions make the data mining or regression analysis techniques select the client with irrigation activity. This client is analyzed by expert system, and normally it is dismissed according to the elapsed time since the last inspection.

The second case is a client with seasonal consumption. This type of client is very difficult to detect with traditional methods. The consumption of these clients shows one or two great peaks, which can be classified as a fraud. This type of clients can be hotels on the coast weather, which only has consumption on months with good climate or on holiday periods. The use of descriptive data mining and expert system allows the system to detect these cases.

The framework proposed in Figure 2 is useful in this case. Moreover, it is faster. However, this framework provided the identification or classification of another very difficult case: domestic clients. This case showed very high variability in the consumption, because it depended on a lot of factors: number of residents, age of each of them, housing area, etc. This information is usually unavailable for retailer and distribution companies. However, this framework has been applied over a sample of 20677 customers with a smart meter data. Thus, several patterns are identified in the groups previously described:

- High domestic consumption: These clients are characterized by periodic consumption. Inside this category there are several subcategories:
    - Full working day (only for working days). This type of clients only has high consumption between two high consumption peaks and the other periods are low consumption (Figure 10).
    - Part-time day (only for working days). The clients present low consumption several hours, between 4 to 10 hours. In these cases, there are three types centered in the morning (Figure 11), in the evening, or at night.
    - Holiday with consumption. This pattern usually models a day or a week consumption. This pattern is characterized by an irregular consumption, centering at lunch and dinner time (Figure 12).

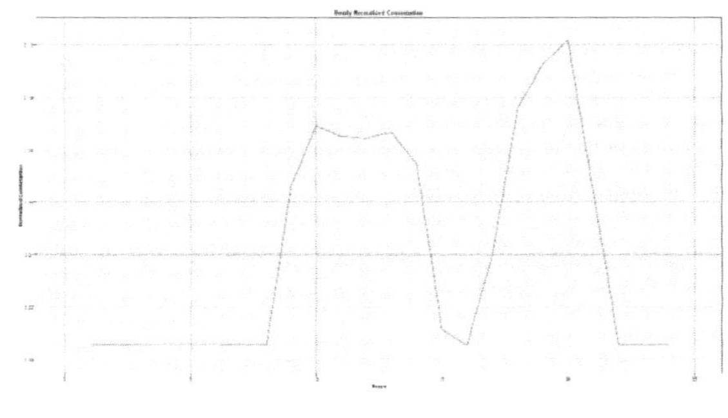

Figure 10. Graph of consumer who shows Full work day (only for working days) pattern.

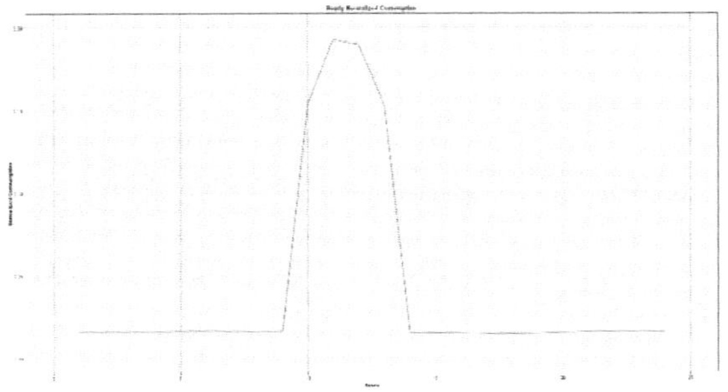

Figure 11. Graph of consumer who shows Part-time day (only for working days) centered in morning pattern.

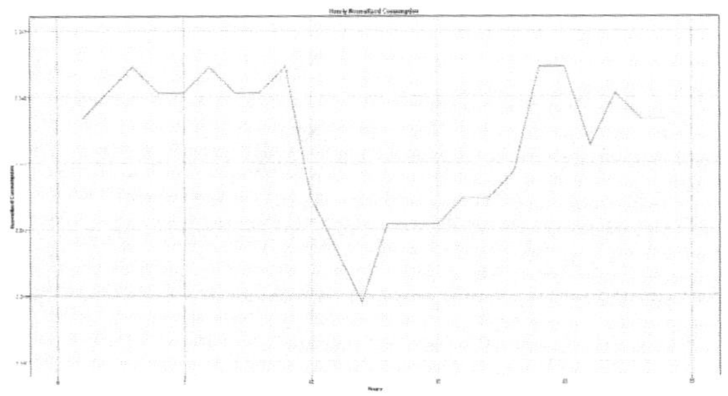

Figure 12. Graph of consumer who shows Holiday with consumption daily pattern.

- Holiday without consumption. This pattern usually models a day or a week consumption. This pattern is characterized by a constant consumption.
- Weekend with consumption. This pattern is equivalent to holiday with consumption, but in weekend.
- Weekend without consumption. This pattern is equivalent to holiday without consumption, but in weekend.

- Low domestic consumption. These clients are characterized by irregular consumption. Although, it is possible to identify the same subcategories like in high domestic consumption. In this case, two new subcategories could be described:
  - Irregular. This type of clients shows a very irregular consumption. Commonly, this pattern is overlap the other patterns. In this case, the analysis of consumption should be made for all time resolutions (weekly, monthly, and bimonthly).
  - Periodic. This type of clients shows periodic and low consumption.

Additionally, these patterns are mixed with some other patterns, which could make the interpretation or application of patterns very difficult. One of these patterns is the night shift consumption. This type of pattern modifies the pattern, increasing the consumption at night time (Figure 13).

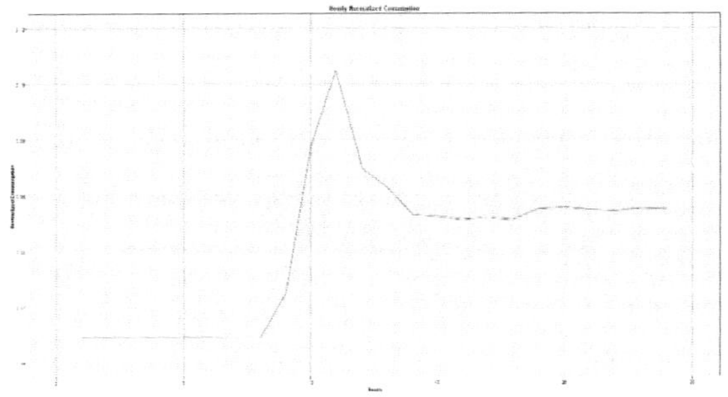

Figure 13. Graph of consumer who shows Part-time day (only for working days) with night shift.

Usually, this type of clients has contracted a time discrimination band.

The domestic consumers usually show a weekly pattern consumption. Usually, the consumption in domestic clients has three possible patterns: working days (Monday to Friday), weekend (Saturday and Sunday), and holidays. However, these different patterns fit in the previously proposed patterns. In this way, one consumer could carry out several patterns. Additionally, there are several problems that make it very useful the proposed solution:

- The domestic consumers are usually the largest sector in company databases.
- The domestic consumers are usually measured remotely (in Spain). The new smart meters, which support standards related to Meters&More, IEC 60870-5, IEC 61850, etc. are being installed in the power grid. This new technology has increased the quantity of information available about consumption.
- The consumption of domestic consumers has a very high variability, because it depends on several factors, which are not registered by distribution or retailer companies.
- The consumption of domestic consumers is very low if it is compared to other applications like service or industrial consumers.

XII. Conclusion and Future Work

The main contribution of the present paper is the definition of two frameworks for NTL reduction. Both frameworks are able to analyze great quantities of consumers. The first framework is applied in traditional power distribution grid with monthly and bimonthly measurements. The second framework is applied in Smart Grid scenario, with smart meter deployment. Both frameworks make detecting anomalous consumption and identifying consumers without NTLs possible.

The proposed framework in Figure 1 was implemented, tested and deployed in a real Power Distribution Company. This framework is part of a RBES. This model establishes a series of similarities with other utilities. For example, the utilization of frequency billing, geographic location, and time can be made in all utilities. However, the contracted power can be replaced by the contracted volume of flow in gas or water utilities.

The different modules of proposed solution, for example Statistical Pattern Generator or Text Mining module, can be added to other systems of NTLs detection to increase their efficiency by using rules or a translator of the knowledge generated by the module.

The solution based on HPDA was tested with real information from a Retailer Company with hourly consumption data. The test of this solution was focused in Statistical Pattern Generator module, which provides several consumption patterns, discovering some shifting of these patterns in clients. This module has not been tested for NTL detection based on inspections, but it was tested with results of other studies.

Usually, an inspector takes between 5 to 30 minutes to analyze the information about a customer in order to confirm whether an NTL exists. This period depends on the quantity of information to be analyzed; the average time of the analysis process takes 16.3 minutes. This means that the time to analyze four million customers (the maximum number of customers in case proposed in Figure 1) would be 1086666.6 hours of work. In the first case, the proposed system in Figure 1 takes 22 milliseconds per customer in the analysis process (24.4 hours in total). The HPDA provides the possibility of analyzing the information in NRT, without a limit in the number of customers. Notwithstanding, the analysis of the inspector will always be better than the machine analysis because inspectors usually work in the same zone and they have additional knowledge of facilities, which is not stored in the system. However, the analysis of the previously mentioned quantity of consumers is an unapproachable goal for inspectors. Additionally, the new AMI technologies provide information, which improves the efficiency of proposed methods.

The proposed RBES provides a double success rate because it is able to classify customers with and without NTLs. Therefore, the success rate is more difficult to evaluate and compare with because the traditional references deal with NTL detection. They do not deal with detection of customers without NTLs. In addition, there are some other problems:

- The total success rate is estimated according to the inspection results and the manual review of all customers classified without NTLs. Thus, the number of customers with informed inspections from other studies is very limited.
- This manual review takes a lot of time. When the proposed system analyzes great quantities of customers, the number of customers without NTLs is greater than the number of customers with NTL. The manual analysis of all cases classified without NTLs has a very big time period.
- Each zone has different cultural environment. This environment reduces the NTL in each of these zones and traditionally they have a low NTL level. Therefore, the number of customers and the success rate is low in these zones, due to the Statistical Pattern Generator establishes a very general pattern, which could provoke the increase of true negatives easily. Thus, the total success rate (consumers classified correctly with and without NTL) was estimated between 82.3% and 91.2% according to the location of sample and the quality of data. Notwithstanding, the success rate (only consumers with NTL) is not estimated, and it is calculated according to the results of study between 16.67% and 40.66%. Therefore, in case of the success rate of 82.3% (with and without NTLs), the success rate for customers with NTL is 16.67%. Therefore, in these cases, the proposed solution has more success rate identifying customers without NTLs.

Finally, several research lines for improving the efficiency of the proposed framework will be addressed:

- Application of techniques related to Information Retrieval, to increase the information about consumers.
- Test the new approach in a big scenario, based on AMI and with hourly measurements.
- Application of the proposed framework in other utilities.
- Enhance the analysis with application of multivariable inference.

ACKNOWLEDGMENT

The authors would also like to thank the backing of SIIAM project (Reference Number: TEC2013-40767-R), which is funded by the Ministry of Economy and Competitiveness of Spain.

REFERENCES

[1] J. I. Guerrero, A. Parejo, E. Personal, F. Biscarri, J. Biscarri, and C. Leon, "Intelligent Information System as a Tool to Reach Unaproachable Goals for Inspectors - High-Performance Data Analysis for Reduction of Non-Technical Losses on Smart Grids," *INTELLI 2016, The Fifth International Conference on Intelligent Systems and Applications*, 2016, pp. 83–87.

[2] E. Elsebakhi et al., "Large-scale machine learning based on functional networks for biomedical big data with high performance computing platforms," *J. Comput. Sci.*, vol. 11, pp. 69–81, Nov. 2015.

[3] A. Rauber, P. Tomsich, and D. Merkl, "parSOM: a parallel implementation of the self-organizing map exploiting cache effects: making the SOM fit for interactive high-performance data analysis," *IJCNN 2000, Proceedings of the IEEE-INNS-ENNS International Joint Conference on Neural Networks*, 2000, 2000, vol. 6, pp. 177–182 vol.6.

[4] J. Liu and Y. Chen, "Improving Data Analysis Performance for High-Performance Computing with Integrating Statistical Metadata in Scientific Datasets," *High Performance Computing*, Networking, Storage and Analysis (SCC), 2012 SC Companion:, 2012, pp. 1292–1295.

[5] V. Giordano et al., "Smart Grid projects in Europe: Lessons learned and current developments," *European Commission*, Luxembourg, EUR 25815 EN, 2013.

[6] "The Global Smart Grid Federation Report," 2012.

[7] P. Lewis, "Smart Grid 2013 Global Impact Report," Ventix, VaasaETT Global Energy Think Tank, 2013.

[8] M. P. McHenry, "Technical and governance considerations for advanced metering infrastructure/smart meters: Technology, security, uncertainty, costs, benefits, and risks," *Energy Policy*, vol. 59, pp. 834–842, Aug. 2013.

[9] C. Selvam, K. Srinivas, G. S. Ayyappan, and M. Venkatachala Sarma, "Advanced metering infrastructure for smart grid applications," 2012 *International Conference on Recent Trends In Information Technology (ICRTIT)*, 2012, pp. 145–150.

[10] L. Dan and H. Bo, "Advanced metering standard infrastructure for smart grid," *2012 China International Conference on Electricity Distribution (CICED)*, 2012, pp. 1–4.

[11] M. Naglic and A. Souvent, "Concept of SmartHome and SmartGrids integration," *2013 4th International Youth Conference on Energy (IYCE)*, 2013, pp. 1–5.

[12] Z. Luhua, Y. Zhonglin, W. Sitong, Y. Ruiming, Z. Hui, and Y. Qingduo, "Effects of Advanced Metering Infrastructure (AMI) on relations of Power Supply and Application in smart grid," *2010 China International Conference on Electricity Distribution (CICED)*, 2010, pp. 1–5.

[13] P. Siano, "Demand response and smart grids—A survey," *Renew. Sustain. Energy Rev.*, vol. 30, pp. 461–478, Feb. 2014.

[14] E. Valigi and E. Di Marino, "Networks optimization with advanced meter infrastructure and smart meters," *20th International Conference and Exhibition on Electricity Distribution - Part 1*, 2009. CIRED 2009, 2009, pp. 1–4.

[15] C. León, F. Biscarri, I. Monedero, J. I. Guerrero, J. Biscarri, and R. Millán, "Integrated expert system applied to the analysis of non-technical losses in power utilities," *Expert Syst. Appl.*, vol. 38, no. 8, pp. 10274–10285, Agosto 2011.

[16] J. I. G. Alonso, C. L. de Mora, F. B. Triviño, I. M. Goicoechea, J. B. Triviño, and R. Millán, "EIS for Consumers Classification and Support Decision Making in a Power Utility Database," *Enterp. Inf. Syst. Implement. IT Infrastruct. Chall. Issues Chall. Issues*, p. 103, 2010.

[17] J. I. Guerrero, C. León, F. Biscarri, I. Monedero, J. Biscarri, and R. Millán, "Increasing the efficiency in Non-Technical Losses detection in utility companies," *Melecon 2010 - 2010 15th IEEE Mediterranean Electrotechnical Conference*, 2010, pp. 136–141.

[18] I. Monedero, F. Biscarri, C. León, J. I. Guerrero, J. Biscarri, and R. Millán, "Using regression analysis to identify patterns of non-technical losses on power utilities," *Knowledge-Based and Intelligent Information and Engineering Systems*, Springer, 2010, pp. 410–419.

[19] C. C. . Ramos, A. N. de Sousa, J. P. Papa, and A. X. Falcão, "A New Approach for Nontechnical Losses Detection Based on Optimum-Path Forest," *IEEE Trans. Power Syst.*, vol. 26, no. 1, pp. 181–189, Feb. 2011.

[20] M. E. de Oliveira, D. F. . Boson, and A. Padilha-Feltrin, "A statistical analysis of loss factor to determine the energy losses," *Transmission and Distribution Conference and Exposition: Latin America*, 2008 IEEE/PES, 2008, pp. 1–6.

[21] M. Gemignani, C. Tahan, C. Oliveira, and F. Zamora, "Commercial losses estimations through consumers' behavior analysis," *20th International Conference and Exhibition on Electricity Distribution - Part 1*, 2009. CIRED 2009, 2009, pp. 1–4.

[22] A. H. Nizar and Z. Y. Dong, "Identification and detection of electricity customer behaviour irregularities," *Power Systems Conference and Exposition*, 2009. PSCE '09. IEEE/PES, 2009, pp. 1–10.

[23] A. Azadeh, S. F. Ghaderi, and S. Sohrabkhani, "Forecasting electrical consumption by integration of Neural Network, time series and ANOVA," *Appl. Math. Comput.*, vol. 186, no. 2, pp. 1753–1761, Mar. 2007.

[24] R. Richardson, "Neural networks compared to statistical techniques," *Computational Intelligence for Financial Engineering (CIFEr)*, 1997. Proceedings of the IEEE/IAFE 1997, 1997, pp. 89–95.

[25] D. J. Hand and G. Blunt, "Prospecting for gems in credit card data," *IMA J. Manag. Math.*, vol. 12, no. 2, pp. 173–200, Oct. 2001.

[26] J. Nagi, A. M. Mohammad, K. S. Yap, S. K. Tiong, and S. K. Ahmed, "Non-Technical Loss analysis for detection of electricity theft using support vector machines," *Power and Energy Conference*, 2008. PECon 2008. IEEE 2nd International, 2008, pp. 907–912.

[27] J. E. Cabral and E. M. Gontijo, "Fraud detection in electrical energy consumers using rough sets," *2004 IEEE International Conference on Systems, Man and Cybernetics*, 2004, vol. 4, pp. 3625–3629 vol.4.

[28] J. R. Aguero, "Improving the efficiency of power distribution systems through technical and non-technical losses reduction," *Transmission and*

Distribution Conference and Exposition (T D), 2012 IEEE PES, 2012, pp. 1–8.

[29] V. Paruchuri and S. Dubey, "An approach to determine non-technical energy losses in India," *2012 14th International Conference on Advanced Communication Technology (ICACT)*, 2012, pp. 111–115.

[30] J. M. R. Iglesias, "Follow-up and Preventive Control of Non-Technical Losses of Energy in C.A. Electricidad de Valencia," *Transmission Distribution Conference and Exposition: Latin America*, 2006. TDC '06. IEEE/PES, 2006, pp. 1–5.

[31] R. Alves, P. Casanova, E. Quirogas, O. Ravelo, and W. Gimenez, "Reduction of Non-Technical Losses by Modernization and Updating of Measurement Systems," *Transmission Distribution Conference and Exposition: Latin America, 2006*. TDC '06. IEEE/PES, 2006, pp. 1–5.

[32] A. H. Nizar, Z.-Y. Dong, and P. Zhang, "Detection rules for Non Technical Losses analysis in power utilities," *2008 IEEE Power and Energy Society General Meeting - Conversion and Delivery of Electrical Energy in the 21st Century*, 2008, pp. 1–8.

[33] S. S. S. R. Depuru, L. Wang, and V. Devabhaktuni, "Support vector machine based data classification for detection of electricity theft," *Power Systems Conference and Exposition (PSCE)*, 2011 IEEE/PES, 2011, pp. 1–8.

[34] C. C. O. Ramos, A. N. Souza, R. Y. M. Nakamura, and J. P. Papa, "Electrical consumers data clustering through Optimum-Path Forest," *2011 16th International Conference on Intelligent System Application to Power Systems (ISAP)*, 2011, pp. 1–4.

[35] B. F. Hobbs, U. Helman, S. Jitprapaikulsarn, S. Konda, and D. Maratukulam, "Artificial neural networks for short-term energy forecasting: Accuracy and economic value," *Neurocomputing*, vol. 23, no. 1–3, pp. 71–84, Dec. 1998.

[36] M. Gavrilas, I. Ciutea, and C. Tanasa, "Medium-term load forecasting with artificial neural network models," *Electricity Distribution, 2001. Part 1: Contributions. CIRED. 16th International Conference and Exhibition on (IEE Conf. Publ No. 482)*, 2001, vol. 6, p. 5 pp. vol.6-.

[37] K. Padmakumari, K. P. Mohandas, and S. Thiruvengadam, "Long term distribution demand forecasting using neuro fuzzy computations," *Int. J. Electr. Power Energy Syst.*, vol. 21, no. 5, pp. 315–322, Jun. 1999.

[38] J. I. Guerrero, C. León, I. Monedero, F. Biscarri, and J. Biscarri, "Improving Knowledge-Based Systems with statistical techniques, text mining, and neural networks for non-technical loss detection," *Knowl.-Based Syst.*, vol. 71, pp. 376–388, Nov. 2014.

[39] D. Powers, "Evaluation: From precision, recall and f-measure to roc., informedness, markedness & correlation," *J. Mach. Learn. Technol.*, vol. 2, no. 1, pp. 37–63, 2011.